Social Classes in Marxist Theory

Allin Cottrell

Social Classes in Marxist Theory

Routledge & Kegan Paul
London, Boston, Melbourne and Henley

First published in 1984
by Routledge & Kegan Paul plc

14 Leicester Square, London WC2H 7PH, England

9 Park Street, Boston, Mass. 02108, USA

464 St Kilda Road, Melbourne,
Victoria 3004, Australia and

Broadway House, Newtown Road,
Henley-on-Thames, Oxon RG9 1EN, England

Set in Baskerville by
Print Origination & Publicity Services Ltd, Aldershot
and printed in Great Britain by
T.J. Press (Padstow) Ltd
Padstow, Cornwall

Library of Congress Cataloging in Publication Data

Cottrell, Allin, 1953-

Social classes in Marxist theory.
Bibliography: p.
Includes index.
1. Social classes.   2. Marxian economics.   3. Social
classes   Great Britain   History   20th century.
I. Title.
HT609.C688   1984   305.5   83-19126

British Library CIP data available

ISBN 0-7100-9906-1

jeu
1-27-87

TO MY FATHER,
TIM COTTRELL

Contents

Acknowledgments

This book is based on a PhD thesis which I presented to the University of Edinburgh in 1981, and I should like to thank my supervisors at Edinburgh, Peter Vandome and John Holloway, for their guidance and for useful discussions of the evolving work. I also wish to thank Robin Murray for his detailed and constructive criticism of the completed thesis. If I have been too obstinate to heed all the objections received from these quarters, I am the only one to blame; the work is, nonetheless, the better for my heeding some of them.

Many of the ideas in the book have also been discussed extensively with Greg Michaelson, Robin Roslender and Paul Cockshott and I have greatly benefited thereby. My greatest intellectual debt is to Paul Cockshott, who has been an invaluable source of illumination, stimulation and pertinent questions. Naturally, none of the above is implicated in the conclusions I reach, or responsible for the blunders and problems which remain.

My thanks are also due to Marlyn Clark and Betty Shires for their rapid production of excellent typescript.

Lawrence & Wishart kindly gave permission to quote extensively from Marx and Engels, *Selected Works in One Volume* (1968).

Introduction

'Social classes in Marxist theory and in post-war Britain'. This book has a double object: first I wish to examine critically the conceptions of social class employed by Marx and by modern Marxist writers, to probe their problematic areas and to propose certain modifications to those conceptions; second I wish to 'test' the conclusions derived from this theoretical reflection against the task of analysing some aspects of the development of class relations in a particular social formation in a particular historical period: Britain over the post-war years and up to the present. In practice these two aims are not so discrete and distinct as this formulation might suggest. The emphasis in the first part of the book is placed upon the writings of Marx and Marxists but this does not exclude consideration of empirically-based arguments, and while the second part contains a greater empirical content relating to post-war Britain the dialogue with Marxist (and of course other) writers continues throughout. It is not a matter of deriving fully fledged concepts then merely 'applying' these to the particular case of post-war Britain.

It is appropriate, before giving an anticipatory summary of the particular arguments offered here, to outline the 'position' from which this book is written. If I say it is a Marxist work that does not in itself tell one very much — is perhaps even misleading — since it has become increasingly clear over the last two decades, if not over a longer historical period, that there is no unique Marxist orthodoxy to which one can refer with any confidence. Marx's work is open to a number of different interpretations and emphases and what we now see is not a unitary 'Marxism' but a variety of theoretical currents: the 'subjective' Marxism of the Frankfurt school; the 'structural' Marxism of Althusser and his collaborators; the 'form-determination' approach of German Marxist state theory; the 'historical' Marxism of Edward Thompson and others, and so on. And this theoretical diversity is of course paralleled by a political diversity: Leninism, Trotskyism, Maoism, Eurocommunism, and more amorphous political tendencies critical of all of these. Some of these theoretical and political tendencies

1

may claim to be the guardian of the true orthodoxy, but since the demise of Comintern hegemony over the international communist movement none has had the political means of enforcing its claim. There is, however, a theme which is common to all the Marxisms, and that is worth emphasising here: the work of theoretical analysis is fundamentally linked to the political project of the transformation of social relations in the direction of socialism (however 'socialism' is defined by the different tendencies). Marx's eleventh 'Thesis on Feuerbach' may be almost a cliche by now, but it still bears repetition: 'the philosophers have only *interpreted* the world in various ways; the point, however, is to *change* it' (Marx and Engels, 1968, p. 30). The questions posed in any theoretical discourse do not select themselves; they are always selected on the basis of some definite criterion of relevance, which one might call the *a priori* of the discourse. Marxism is quite explicit in arrowing its own *a priori*: fundamentally, questions are selected with a view to understanding the (social) world *in order to change it*, in order, in other words, to orient a political practice which aims at the abolition of the conditions of class antagonism. It need hardly be said, I hope, that this position does not have to collapse into a kind of theoretical opportunism, in which theories are selected or devised in order to justify a pre-given political line, although such deformations have occurred within Marxism.

So the 'interpretations of the world' offered in the following pages, and the questions which I have selected as most relevant, have been guided by a definite political interest, although the work has been 'open' in the sense that it has not been designed to 'discover' certain political conclusions which were already present at the outset. I leave it to the reader to judge whether the results fall within or outside of Marxism. Let me outline the main strands of argument pursued, showing the ways in which these have been shaped by this interest.

Chapter 1 considers Marx's conception of the two 'basic' classes of capitalism, bourgeoisie and proletariat, and then goes on to pose the problem of the connection, within Marx's writings, between these classes and the social and political forces active in particular capitalist social formations. This problem I regard as fundamental if class analysis is really to be of value in orienting politics. A word on the works by Marx which I have chosen to consider in this context: when one attempts to give an account of Marx's views on classes, and on the class/politics relationship, one immediately encounters a paradox. In one sense, almost everything which Marx wrote is concerned in one way or another with classes and class struggle, yet equally Marx nowhere gives a systematic definition of the concept of 'social class' or a systematic account of the relationships between class and political forces. There is only one place in his writings, so far as I am aware, where such a systematic presentation seems to be promised, and that is in the unfinished fragment 'on classes' found in Volume 3 of 'Capital' (Marx, 1972, pp. 885-6). But there Marx only gets as far as discounting the idea that classes are to be defined on the basis of the sources of their revenue before the manuscript breaks off. One has to work, therefore, from a variety of sources which show up different aspects of Marx's views. My account of Marx's definition of bourgeoisie and proletariat, on the basis of economic property relations, draws mainly upon that inescapable reference point for Marx's developed conception of capitalism, 'Capital'. On the class/politics relationship I have chosen to concentrate on two works of differing status: the 'Manifesto of the Communist Party' and the 'Eighteenth Brumaire of Louis Bonaparte' (Marx and Engels, 1968, pp. 36-63 and 96-179). These have been selected because they provide an interesting contrast, the former being concerned to sketch out the broad sweep of history, the necessary long-term relationship, as Marx sees it, between class structure and politics, while the latter gives a rich and detailed analysis of the class struggles of a particular, limited, period within a particular nation state. The principal thesis which I argue on the basis of my reading of these works is that the conception put forward in the Manifesto, and repeated *passim* in 'Capital' — a conception in which, in the 'last analysis', political forces coincide with the two basic economic classes in a necessary polarisation — is not sustainable, and is belied by the concrete analysis of the 'Eighteenth Brumaire'. In the latter work Marx deals with the relationship between classes and political forces under the sign of 'representation' (i.e. the latter are said to 'represent' the former) but I argue that the various contents given to the notion of representation overflow the boundaries of any unitary conception. In other words 'representation' is not a rigorous concept but a *word*, which marks the site of a problem. The word is applied to a range of disparate relationships between classes and political forces, and I argue that it is necessary to recognise the diversity of these relationships, and to abandon the idea of the reducibility of politics to a field in which pre-given 'interests' of economically-defined classes are merely 'represented' or 'expressed'.

Chapter 2 extends this line of argument through a consideration of various modern Marxist writings on social classes. I argue that the same problem emerges in these writings as in Marx, although it assumes a different form. Writers such as Poulantzas and Carchedi, unlike Marx, refuse to give an 'economic' definition of classes, and argue for a synthetic definition which encompasses economic, political and ideological criteria. This gives rise to two kinds of problems: on the one hand the introduction of political and ideological criteria into the definition of classes tends to undermine the avowedly 'primary' role of property relations in the determination of class relations, a role which these writers explicitly avow; but on the other hand, even when political and ideological criteria are brought in there is still a theoretical gulf between 'structurally' defined classes and the actual social and political forces active in any given historical situation. Poulantzas and others complicate the problem of the relationship between classes and politics, but do not resolve it. I argue in favour of a 'disaggregation' of the concept of class, a conception in which (a) the analysis of the economic class structure, in terms of the pattern of property relations, serves to identify what is 'at stake' in political struggles in the long run (i.e. the maintenance or transformation of the given pattern of possession of/separation from the means of production) but (b) it is not possible to 'read off', from one's analysis of the economic class structure, the definite political and social forces which will accomplish that maintenance or transformation; the political realm demands a specific analysis.

The following chapters then set out to justify this claim, and prove the value of this alternative conception of classes and the class/politics relationship. Chapters 3 and 4 develop the analysis of the economic class structure of modern capitalism, with special reference to Britain. It is not possible to deal with all aspects of this structure within the scope of this work, and my account concentrates on the forms of possession of the principal industrial means of production, and the conditions of financing of production.[1] I outline the development of the 'impersonal capital' as the dominant form of capitalist property, and explore some of the ramifications of the advanced separation of individuals from the means of production. Chapter 5 then presents certain implications for socialist politics, as I see them, of the forms of property characteristic of modern British capitalism, in terms of the constraints and opportunities connected with those forms of property. These implications are considered under the two headings of 'planning' and 'enterprise democracy'. My general contention is that the project of abolishing the separation of the producers from the means of production must be approached by means of a 'pincer action': gaining social control over investment funds, a project in which government must play a major role; and democratising the operations of enterprises 'from below', a project in which a left government can be helpful but the major part must be played by workers' own initiatives. These basic aims are elaborated with reference to the particular forms of property which are 'at stake' in modern Britain: I draw attention to the possible role of trade union pension funds in a struggle for social control over investment, and to the conditions for developing democratic control within large, and often diversified, multi-divisional enterprises.

In line with the general critical positions adopted in chapters 1 and 2, I do not consider that the analysis of property relations in chapters 3 and 4 provides a basis for 'reading off' the political forces which might accomplish the strategic transformations of property relations identified in chapter 5. In particular, in my discussion of property relations I employ a conception of the 'working class' which encompasses all workers separated from the means of production and obliged to sell their labour power for a wage or salary (i.e. including salaried managers and professionals), yet it is clear that this economic class is far from homogeneous politically and cannot act as a unified social force. Chapter 6 takes up this point and considers some of the relevant lines of division among the population of employees separated from the means of production. I discuss the role of the division of labour in this regard, and the pertinence of the 'working class'/'middle class' distinction within popular ideology, and then examine the patterns of party-political allegiance. The latter examination leads to an outline account of the development of politics in Britain over the post-war years — the ways in which the major political forces have defined their projects of social transformation/conservation, and have built, or failed to build, support blocs for those projects among the classes of society. Chapter 7 then focusses on the rise of 'Thatcherism', and the developing alignment of political forces and their support blocs in the period of Thatcherism 1979-82. In this context my aim is to draw together some of the conclusions derived in earlier chapters, by arguing that the 'core' economic programme of Thatcherism is rendered impossible by the dominant forms of capitalist property, and by examining the political capacity of the Labour Party, as it is currently developing, to achieve the kind of strategic socialist advances identified as important in chapter 5. Finally the conclusion attempts to tie together and assess the main theoretical and political points which emerge from this exercise as a whole, and to identify certain avenues of further investigation which I consider worth pursuing.

This is the outline of the main material of the book. It is

fundamentally shaped by the interest avowed at the outset, in that I attempt to identify (a) what is at stake in the transformation of economic class relations in a socialist direction, and (b) some of the opportunities and problems in building a support bloc for such changes under current conditions. But before proceeding to the substance of the arguments sketched above, it is necessary to give some preliminary indication of the meaning which I attached to certain general concepts of Marxism, concepts which are open to a variety of interpretations yet which must play an important role in any 'Marxist' analysis. I propose to devote the remainder of this introduction to a discussion of, first, certain 'concepts of structure' employed by Marx and Marxists (mode of production, relations of production, productive forces, base and superstructure) and second, the concept of socialism. It will not be possible to discuss these concepts in great detail here, and my remarks will necessarily be dogmatic in places, since the concepts of 'mode of production' or 'socialism' could well form the object of whole works in their own right, but nonetheless I feel it will be useful to give the reader some idea of which tradition, within the broad field of 'Marxism', my own arguments emanate from.

Some 'concepts of structure' in Marxism

According to Marx, the possibility of social class division arose as a consequence of the developing productivity of social labour. Once the productivity of labour had developed to a certain stage, it became possible to produce a social surplus product over and above that necessary to maintain the direct producers and their offspring. The appropriation of this social surplus product by a category of agents distinct from the 'direct producers' is seen as the origin and continuing foundation of the class division of society. The historic originality of Marx's theory, however, does not simply consist in the recognition of the existence of social classes and class antagonisms. One of the central propositions of his theory is that the form which class division and class struggle take on in particular epochs is fundamentally determined by the *mode of exploitation* or mode of extraction of the surplus product which characterises the successive *modes of production* which arise in the course of historical development. Now the concepts of 'mode of exploitation' and 'mode of production' are very much bound up with certain other original concepts of Marxism: relations of production, forces of production and the distinction between 'base' and 'superstructure'. In fact Marx wrote very little on their explicit definition, and on their place in the analysis of social classes and class struggle in particular social formations. I shall begin this survey by considering the few well-known quotations in which these questions are explicitly addressed, and then go on to examine some of the strands of recent debate over these questions.

First consider the position which Marx outlines as the 'guiding principle' of his studies, in his 'Preface to a Contribution to the Critique of Political Economy' of 1859:

'In the social production of their life, men enter into definite relations that are indispensable and independent of their will, relations of production which correspond to a definite stage of development of their material productive forces. The sum total of these relations of production constitutes the economic structure of society, the real foundation, on which rises a legal and political superstructure and to which correspond definite forms of social consciousness. The mode of production of material life conditions the social, political and intellectual process in general. It is not the consciousness of men that determines their being, but, on the contrary, their social being that determines their consciousness. At a certain stage of their development, the material productive forces of society come in conflict with the existing relations of production, or — what is but a legal expression for the same thing — with the property relations within which they have been at work hitherto. From forms of development of the productive forces these relations turn into their fetters. Then begins an epoch of social revolution.' (Marx and Engels, 1968, pp. 181-2).

In this passage Marx invokes certain objects: an 'economic foundation' of society (composed of the totality of the relations of production), 'material productive forces', a political/legal 'superstructure', and 'forms of social consciousness'. He also specifies certain relations between these objects: the superstructure 'rises upon' its foundation; forms of consciousness 'correspond to' the foundation. Also the relations of production can either be a 'form of development' of the productive forces or a 'fetter' upon them. In this text, however, neither the objects nor the relations between them are given a precise definition. This gives rise to a number of problems of interpretation, which one can place in two groups. First there are the problems relating to the concept of the economic foundation: what exactly is the content of the concepts of 'relations of production' and 'productive forces'?

What is the relationship between them? Is it true to say that the productive forces are conceived as the 'active element', and if so how does
one account for their development? Then there are the problems of
the base/superstructure relationship: in what sense is the economic
foundation 'basic'? How does it 'condition' the other levels of the social
formation?

As regards the first group of questions, concerning the nature of
the 'economic foundation', one can find some answers in 'Capital'.
Whereas the propositions put forward in the 'Preface' of 1859 are
sketchy in the extreme, Marx developed his concepts in a more precise
way when he was faced with the problem of analysing the particular
economic foundation of capitalist society in detail. Without quoting
particular passages, one can draw from 'Capital' as a whole a certain
conception of relations of production, productive forces, and of the
relations which hold between them. I offer the following as a first
approximation:

1. **Relations of production** : These are the relations of economic property which hold between the producers, the owners of the means
   of production, and the means of production. They permit the extraction of surplus labour from the producers, and their particular
   form determines the particular mode of exploitation. For instance,
   under capitalism the exclusive ownership of the means of production is in the hands of the capitalists, and the workers, who are
   separated from the means of production but who (unlike slaves)
   possess their own labour power as 'free' workers, are forced to sell
   their labour power to a capitalist. This results in the extraction of
   surplus labour in the particular form of surplus value.

2. **Productive forces** : The productive forces include all the elements
   of the production process: workers, means of production in a broad
   sense, and the objects which the workers transform through their
   labour. At any given stage of development these elements are combined in a definite *system* of productive forces — a particular
   technical organisation of the elements of production which makes
   possible an effective production process.

3. **Relations between relations of production and productive
   forces** : This point demands a rather more lengthy treatment. In
   the 1859 'Preface' these relations are presented in a rather one-sided
   way: the relations of production are conceived as a kind of 'shell'
   or envelope within which the productive forces develop. When the
   productive forces have exhausted the developmental possibilities
   afforded by given relations of production they break through this

'shell' and instigate an epoch of social revolution. The productive forces seem to have their own autonomous dynamic, and the relations of production are forced to 'keep in step' with this dynamic through the mechanism of social revolution. This conception is elsewhere aphoristically summed up in the remark that 'the water mill produces the feudal lord and the steam mill produces the capitalist' (Marx, 1963). That is, the character of economic property relations is determined by the level of productive technique. This view was taken up in the orthodoxy of the 3rd International (Comintern) after Lenin. In Stalin's 'Dialectical and Historical Materialism' one finds a philosophy of history in which the inexorable development of the productive forces secures the succession of modes of production from slavery through feudalism and capitalism to communism. There is a serious problem in this conception: what accounts for the timeless forward march of the 'productive forces'? It seems it can only be based on the philosophy of *homo faber* — the idea that humanity necessarily strives to develop the techniques of production, and that this tendency is prior to any particular historical form of social relations. But this surely contradicts Marx's strongly-expressed view that there are no such transhistorical human absolutes, and that 'human nature' itself is constructed and reconstructed in the process of historical development.[2]

There are some echoes of the conception described above, which one can label the theory of the 'primacy of the productive forces', in 'Capital', but in the detailed analysis of the transition from manufacture to modern industry (Marx, 1976, Chs. 14,15) a more complex conception is outlined. In this section of 'Capital' Marx argues that it is the dispossession of the direct producers, their forcible separation from their means of production, and the rise of the forms of wage labour and capital which 'determine' the specific form of development of the productive forces under capitalism. It is the compulsion for capital to extract increased surplus value through increasing the productivity of labour and driving down the time of 'necessary labour' which impels the development of the productive forces from the level of artisanal production to modern machine industry. The 'industrial revolution' took place not merely because certain key machines and sources of power were invented, but because the *social preconditions* for the large scale use of machinery and steam power had been developed by the gathering together of many dispossessed detail labourers in a system of cooperation under the roof of the employing capitalist, and because the *necessity* of creased productivity was posed by the exigencies of capitalist competition. In this argument a particular development of the productive forces is conceived as an *effect* of certain relations of production. To express my own view, however, it is not adequate simply to invert the theory of the primacy of the productive forces and proclaim the 'primacy of the relations of production'. Rather there is a complex interdependence between the two concepts. The dispossession of artisans and peasants was a necessary precondition for the development of capitalist manufacture (and this was not secured by the 'development of the productive forces' as such, but as a result of long and bitter social struggles). And the compulsion to extract increased profit and maintain a place in the developing competitive market system was the motive force in the development of machine industry. But in turn this development of the productive forces, and increase in the scale of production, was the precondition for subsequent changes in capitalist property relations such as the formation of joint stock companies.[3]

To conclude on the relationship between the relations of production and the productive forces, one can say the concept of 'mode of production' in Marxism refers to the *combination* of these two systems. Marx sometimes used the term 'mode of production' in a descriptive manner, to refer to the form of the direct labour process, but insofar as he uses it to denote a theoretical concept, this is the concept of the combination of a certain system of relations of production and a certain system of productive forces. Looking at the matter in terms of *process*, this can be rephrased as the combination of a particular mode of extraction of surplus labour and a particular mode of appropriation of nature. This notion of 'combination' should not, however, be taken to suggest an external linkage between two distinct entities: rather the social production process is simultaneously a process of appropriation of nature and a process of appropriation of surplus labour.

We now have a more developed conception of the 'economic base', and are in a position to consider the second set of problems raised by the passage from the 1859 'Preface' — those concerning the base/superstructure relations. The 'Preface' deals with this relation in rather loose metaphorical terms: the superstructure 'rises upon' the base. The classical Marxist development of this conception runs like this: the economic level is 'determinant in the last instance', but the various levels of the superstructure have a certain autonomy in that they can 'react back' and modify the base. But what is the mechanism of 'determination in the last instance'? And just how 'autonomous' is the superstructure?

Again, Marx himself had remarkably little to say explicitly on these questions, but I shall begin the enquiry by considering some of the passages where he does offer some hints at least. One is a footnote in Volume One of 'Capital' where Marx is replying to a critic who maintains that while the mode of production may condition the rest of social life under capitalism, this is not true of all societies. Marx writes:

'One thing is clear: the middle ages could not live on Catholicism, nor could the ancient world on politics. On the contrary, it is the manner in which they gained their livelihood which explains why in one case politics, in the other case Catholicism, played the chief part' (Marx, 1976, p. 176n).

The first point here — that people must eat before they can participate in politics or religion — is clearly true, but as Cutler et al. (1977) have noted, it does not in itself help to explain why the mode of production should determine the character of the superstructure. The second sentence presents a twofold conception. On the one hand the 'manner of gaining their livelihood', or 'economic foundation' in the words of the 1859 'Preface', is appealed to as the ultimate explanatory principle, but it is conceded that other 'levels' of the social formation such as politics or religious ideology may 'play the chief part'. The idea is that the character of the economic foundation determines which aspect of the social formation shall 'play the chief part'. But in this answer to his critic Marx only provides the merest hint as to how his own argument might be developed. In effect, by drawing a distinction between the ultimate explanatory principle (always the economic base) and the most prominent aspect of the social formation (variable) he only shows that his theory is *possible*, that it is not immediately contradicted by certain 'obvious facts' of history. He does not show the *necessity* of his theory — does not explain why the economic base is the ultimate explanatory principle, nor how it may come to promote other levels to the 'chief' role. A rather more substantial hint in this regard can be found in the following interesting passage from Volume Three of 'Capital':

'The specific economic form, in which unpaid surplus-labour is pumped out of the direct producers, determines the relationship of rulers and ruled, as it grows directly out of production itself and, in turn, reacts upon it as a determining element. Upon this, however, is founded the entire formation of the economic community which grows up out of the production relations themselves, thereby its specific political form. *It is always the direct relationship of the owners of the conditions of production to the direct producers* — a relation always naturally corresponding to a definite stage in the development of the methods of labour and thereby its social productivity — *which reveals the innermost secret, the hidden basis of the entire social structure, and with it the political form of the relation of sovereignty and dependence, in short, the corresponding specific form of the state'* (Marx, 1972, p. 791, emphasis added).

The context is a discussion of labour rent, and this passage is preceded by a more specific argument which relates the 'relationship of the owners of the conditions of production to the direct producers' under feudalism to its 'corresponding form of sovereignty and dependence'. Marx argues that under feudalism the direct producers were capable of producing on their own account, and that because of this the extraction of surplus labour demanded that the producers be bound to the ruling class in a relation of direct servitude:

'...it is evident that in all forms in which the direct labourer remains the "possessor" of the means of production and labour conditions necessary for the production of his own means of subsistence, the property relationship must simultaneously appear as a direct relationship of lordship and servitude, so that the direct producer is not free' (ibid., p. 790).

Poulantzas (1973) has developed and expanded this argument, and has used it to draw a contrast between feudalism and capitalism which is designed to elucidate the manner in which the economic base determines the character of the superstructure. Let us follow this development through. The first step is an elaboration of the concept of economic property relations. Poulantzas distinguishes between the codified juridical expression of property right, which belongs to the 'superstructure', and the 'real' property relations which exist in the economic base. Juridical property relations will generally serve to reinforce the real economic property relations but there is always the possibility of dislocation between the two. For instance in Russia after 1917, in the economic system which Lenin referred to as 'state capitalism', juridical ownership of the means of production was transferred to the state but in many cases real control was still in the hands of the capitalists. Then within the realm of economic property relations Poulantzas makes a distinction between 'economic owner-ship' and 'possession'. 'Economic ownership' means the power to assign the means of production to given uses and to dispose of the product obtained, whereas 'possession' means the power to put the means of production into operation. Poulantzas then analyses the difference between feudalism and capitalism in terms of these relations: in feudal society the feudal lords enjoyed 'economic ownership' of the means of production and appropriated the surplus labour of the peasant cultivators, but the producers themselves still had 'possession' of their instruments of labour. The individual peasant or peasant household *could* perform its own labour without the intervention of the feudal lord. This meant that the producers had to be bound to the lord by ties of personal dependence, supported by direct force and/or religious ideology, to ensure the extraction of surplus labour. The peasants worked on their own account, for their own subsistence, and the lord intervened to compel the producers either to surrender part of their product or to work the lord's fields for a certain proportion of the time.

In the capitalist mode of production, on the other hand, economic ownership and possession are united in the hands of the capitalists. The worker can no longer produce on his own account. Once capital has attained its developed form — fixed capital as a system of machinery in the capitalist factory — and the division of labour has been pushed to an extreme, the individual worker can no longer operate the means of production independently: the worker sells his 'bare labour-power' to a capitalist and then is incorporated into the 'collective labourer' on terms laid down by the capitalist. There is no longer, therefore, a 'visible' separation between necessary and surplus labour — rather, the latter is extracted through the wages system, whereby the workers exchange their labour-power against a wage and then work the capitalists' means of production to produce commodities, the difference between (a) the value they add to the commodities through their labour and (b) the value they receive in the form of means of subsistence in exchange for the wage (necessary labour) constituting (c) the surplus labour. Exploitation is 'concealed' by the appearance of equal exchange in the wage contract.

If this argument is accepted, it then becomes possible to trace the connection between the mode of exploitation and the form of the superstructure. Take for instance the form of the state under capitalism: first, the fact that economic ownership and possession of the means of production are united in the hands of capital, and that the workers have no option but to sell their labour-power, means that there is no need for the *direct* use of physical or ideological coercion in the extraction of surplus labour. Second, if the formally 'free and equal' exchange-relation between the owners of commodities (means of production and labour-power) is to be maintained, then the relations of force necessary in the last instance for the reproduction of any antagonistic relations of production must be abstracted from the sphere of production. There must be a locus of relations of force beyond the sphere of individual competing capitals, and apparently 'above classes': the bourgeois form of state.

I shall not consider all the questions which this kind of argument raises at this point, but note that it had led Poulantzas and other followers of Althusser to give the concept of 'mode of production' an extended definition. If the character and role of the superstructure is determined by the mode of exploitation — analysed as the configuration of economic property relations — then it becomes legitimate to conceive of the 'mode of production' in a broader sense as a structured totality, a totality in which the economic level plays the role of 'determinant in the last instance' in the sense that it fixes the overall 'matrix' of the mode of production and thereby can assign other levels of the mode to the position of 'dominance' (e.g. religious ideology in the feudal mode). Further, in the Althusserian conception the extended concept of 'mode of production' is conceived as the 'basic concept' of Marxist Historical Materialism, in the sense that real history is taken to be the effect of the structure of modes of production and their combinations.[4] Althusser uses the term 'structural causality' to denote this conception: the particular practices which appear in history are to be conceived as effects of the structure of the 'social formation', which is made up of one or more modes of production.

The concept of 'structural causality' has certain merits, or at least had certain merits in its polemical context. In the first place, it was designed to distance Marxism from the subjectivist conception of history as the product of the will and consciousness of historical actors ('subjects'), whether these be 'individuals' or classes. Althusser first developed his conception of structural causality in his attack on what he called theoretical humanism, i.e. the interpretation of all of Marx's work on the model of the concept of alienated human subjectivity contained in Marx's early works (in particular the Paris Manuscripts of 1844). Against what he argued was an over-emphasis on the role of human subjectivity, Althusser stressed the simultaneously theoretical and political 'break' between the humanism of the young Marx and the mature Marx's 'scientific' investigations into the objective laws governing the development of capitalism. The context of this polemic was the ideological crisis of Marxism which followed the first attempts at 'de-stalinization' in the Soviet Union: Althusser argued that while it was correct to attack the 'mechanical' version of Marxism which had become dominant in the Stalin period (in particular the primacy of the productive forces thesis referred to earlier) it was a grave mistake to reject along with this the idea of Historical Materialism as a scientific theory of historical development, and the corresponding conception of history as an objective process. The flowering of 'humanistic' interpretations of Marxism threatened to subvert its revolutionary materialist core and reinstate the old philosophies with which Marx had painstakingly 'settled accounts' in the 'German Ideology' [5]

'Structural causality' also contests the straightforward empiricist approach to history, in which particular practices, institutions and ideas are explained simply in terms of previous practices, institutions and ideas in a linear temporal sequence. In stressing this point Althusser could make reference to Marx's critique of Proudhon:

'How indeed could the simple logical formula of movement, of sequence, of time explain the body of society, in which all relations co-exist simultaneously and support one another' (Marx, 1963, pp. 110-111).

It was this 'simultaneous co-existence of relations' in the form of a complex structured totality which Althusser referred to as the structure of the social formation.

So, to summarise, the Althusserian doctrine of structural causality clarifies the conception of determination in the last instance by the economy. The 'last instance' is not a temporal limit: the matrix of the mode of production is always determined by the economic level, but within this matrix other levels may be promoted to 'dominance'. Also, in the Poulantzian version, the doctrine includes a more developed explanation than can be found in Marx of how the economic level comes to play the 'determinant' role.

Nonetheless, this general conception has been much criticised, on the grounds that it turns Marxist theory into a variant of 'structuralism' or more specifically that it sets up the mode of production as an eternally self-reproducing entity. Certainly the theory of structural causality runs into severe problems. If the development of a social formation is governed at all levels by the structure of a mode of production, or combination of modes, how does one explain the transition from the dominance of one mode of production to that of another? Althusser is concerned to avoid the Hegelian type of teleology in which each 'moment' of historical development contains the 'germ' of the succeeding higher moment, and therefore progress from each historical moment to the next is guaranteed by the inner logic of history. So he refuses to write into the concept of a mode of production the *necessity* of its eventual abolition, i.e. he refuses to conceive a mode of production as a *self-dissolving* contradiction.

How then to resolve the problem? In 'Reading Capital' it is left to Balibar to fill in this gap in the theory of structural causality, and he attempts to do so by invoking the concept of the 'transitional mode of production' (Balibar, 1970). The reproduction of a given mode of production proceeds up to a certain point, then in the period of transition between the dominance of that former mode and the establishment of a new mode, development is governed by a 'transitional mode of production'. For Balibar, in an established mode of production the relations of production and the productive forces 'correspond' to one another, whereas the 'transitional' mode is defined by a non-correspondence between relations of production and productive forces. He gives the example of 'manufacture' as a transitional mode between feudalism and capitalism: in 'manufacture' there is a non-correspondence between the newly-established capitalist relations of production and productive forces inherited from artisanal production.

This conception complicates the problem, but does not solve it, for how does one then explain the break between the dominance of the former mode of production and the emergence of the transitional mode? Either one gets involved in an infinite regression of 'transitional modes', or else the revolutionary break is inaccessible to the theory of structural causality. It seems therefore that while Althusserian Marxism has broken with the Hegelian teleology according to which the development of history towards its final goal is a predetermined necessity, it is in danger of substituting a static teleology in which the reproduction of a mode of production is an effect of the structure of that mode and in consequence there is no convincing way of theorising the revolutionary process in which the structure of an existing mode of production is broken and displaced.

It has been suggested (both by Balibar in later writings and by Hindess and Hirst, in rather different ways) that this theoretical impasse is the result of an exaggerated 'rationalistic' claim for the concept of mode of production. In 'Reading Capital' the mode of production was presented as the basic concept of Historical Materialism and this was understood to mean that for Marxism history must be grasped as the effects of a succession of modes of production. Balibar (1977) changes the emphasis by saying that 'mode of production' is not a 'basic concept' in this sense, rather it is 'basic' in that it serves to 'orient the problematic' of Marxism, i.e. it defines the nature of the major questions for Marxist analysis of particular social formations (e.g. what is the dominant mode of exploitation? What are the connections between this and the legal, political and ideological aspects of the social formation?). Hindess and Hirst (1977) also maintain that social formations cannot be grasped as the *effects* of modes of production or combinations of modes. Rather the concept of a social formation is the concept of a specific set of relations of production, along with the conditions of existence of those relations of production. Any set of relations of production has certain conditions of existence: political conditions, ideological conditions, technological conditions, and whether or not these conditions are met depends on the particular course of historical development, not on the 'structure of the mode of production' — a mode of production or set of relations of production cannot by itself secure its own conditions of existence. This conception displaces the idea of the mode of production as a totality 'determined in the last instance' by the economic level. By analysing the concept of a given set of relations of production one can arrive at an account of the general characteristics of the necessary conditions of existence of those relations of production (e.g. capitalist relations of production, dependent upon the existence of wage-labour, require some form of legal system adequate to define the wage contract) but one cannot deduce the specific form in which those conditions of existence are met. The political and ideological conditions required for the development or maintenance of a given set of relations of production are not simply tiers in the structure of the 'mode of production'.

This is the theoretical position which I find most acceptable. The relations of production — the forms of property relations and the conditions under which a social surplus product is produced and controlled — certainly form a central object of interest for Marxism, but the claim that they 'determine' the character of the 'superstructure' is not sustainable. If we now return to the argument which Poulantzas developed concerning the different modes of exploitation under feudalism and capitalism and the 'corresponding' forms of superstructure, we can assess it in these terms. If one accepts the Poulantzian account of the modes of exploitation in feudalism and capitalism (closely based on

Marx's views), it does not prove that the capitalist mode of exploitation generates a corresponding form of 'superstructure'.[6] Strictly, what it proves is that the mode of exploitation sets certain limits on the forms of political and ideological relations compatible with its development and continued reproduction. In certain social formations the forms of political and ideological relations may block the development of the capitalist mode; in certain instances the forms of politics and ideology may change over time and make the continued reproduction of capitalism difficult or impossible. And, of course, where the political and ideological forms are compatible with capitalist relations of production this leaves open a wide margin of variation in the particular characteristics of the former: this is surely the burden of Marx's comment in the 'Critique of the Gotha Programme' that the notion of the 'present-day state' is specious. Rather there are a number of states, showing certain common features yet differing in important respects in different nations.

In rejecting the concept of 'structural causality' in this way, one is not forced into accepting the positions which the Althusserians were originally concerned to attack: the 'theoretical humanism' which appeals to the essential creativity of humanity as its ultimate principle or the empiricism which is content to gather 'facts' and place them in chronological order. Instead one can reject all social-historical theories which appeal to an *essential* explanatory principle (be it human subjectivity, 'the facts', the structure of the mode of production, the spirit of the Age, the inexorable development of the productive forces or whatever). But at the same time one can take from Marx a focus, or an 'orientation', which prevents this resistance from collapsing into a more structureless eclecticism. One can insist that historical analysis[7] must take account of a whole range of agents (social movements, political parties, blocs of voters, bodies of armed men, prominent individuals, economic enterprises and so on) and that the activities of these agents are constrained and influenced in various ways by a wide range of factors (forms of political constitution, forms of property, the state of technology and so on), yet produce an order in one's analysis by focussing on the question of the maintenance/transformation of class relations (I shall argue that in effect this is precisely what Marx does in his 'Eighteenth Brumaire of Louis Bonaparte'). And this focus is not merely the result of an arbitrary choice, since it can be argued that the transformation of class relations (economic property relations and mode of appropriation of surplus labour) is a strategic necessity if many progressive social and economic changes are to be achieved.

Since the term 'social formation' will be employed quite often in the following analyses, it is appropriate to draw out further the meaning which is given to that term within the theoretical framework sketched above. We have seen that for the Althusserians a social formation is a *combination of modes of production*: this is conceived as a 'structure in dominance' in which one mode dominates the others and subordinates them to its expanded reproduction. For instance, Poulantzas (1973) says that the social formation of Bismarck's Germany presented a combination of the capitalist, feudal and patriarchal modes of production, with the capitalist mode emerging as dominant and tending to dissolve the others. But the critical comments concerning Althusserian 'structural causality' which have been noted above undermine this particular conception of 'social formation'. If the political, legal, technological and other conditions of existence of any given set of relations of production are not in any sense 'generated' by the relations of production themselves, and if these conditions can be met in a variety of different forms, then the concept of any definite social formation (Bismarck's Germany, post-war Britain) is not reducible to the concept of a combination of modes of production. One may well say that Bismarck's Germany sustained capitalist relations of production on an expanding scale and feudal relations on a diminishing scale, but just to say that is not to give the full concept of the German social formation of the time. Rather, the term 'social formation' refers to a specific set of relations of production, the conditions of existence of which are satisfied in certain specific forms. To give this schematic definition more substance I shall expand on what I mean by the 'social formation of post-war Britain' (or 'British social formation' for convenience). This concept presupposes the more general concept of capitalist relations of production, but it involves, or at least points towards, the specification of a particular form of those relations of production, and particular forms of politics, law, industrial structure and so on. For instance:

(i) Economic class relations are more closely specified in the concept of the British social formation than in the general concept of capitalist relations of production. The latter concept entails the two categories of 'capitalists' and 'workers'; the former entails an account of the particular form of organisation of 'capitalists' in Britain (as I shall argue, the 'capitalists' are largely impersonal enterprises) and also the particular forms of organisation of 'labour' (the patterns of division of labour, union organisation, cultural and geographical divisions and so on).

(ii) The general concept of capitalist relations of production pre-
      supposes certain 'productive forces' onto which the former are art-
      iculated; the concept of the British social formation points towards
      a specification of the form of these productive forces, in terms of
      industrial structure, patterns of technology and so on.

(iii) From the concept of capitalist relations of production in general
      one can deduce, as a necessary condition of existence of those rela-
      tions, a general form of state which presents a locus of relations
      of force outside of the immediate production process, and a form
      of law capable of defining labour contracts etc.; the concept of
      the British social formation points towards a specification of the
      particular forms of state and law in Britain: parliamentary
      democracy with universal suffrage; a particular electoral system;
      separation of judiciary and executive, and so on.

It should be stressed that these relationships of specification exist *within
theory*. In other words the 'British social formation' is a concept, albeit
of a different order from the 'capitalist mode of production', and not
some kind of 'raw reality' outside of theory, against which theory can
be measured. By the same token, specifying fully the concept of the
British social formation cannot be a matter of simply 'looking and seeing' the particular forms of relations of production, state, industrial
structure and so on, in Britain. Each of these specifications necessarily
involves the deployment of concepts. It is also important to stress
the distance between the concept of the British social formation and
the commonsense notion of 'British society': the latter carries the
suggestion of being a set of interpersonal relations, while the former
cannot be grasped in that way — relations of production are not just
interpersonal relations. Also the idea of 'British society' suggests a certain kind of ideological organic whole (the sense in which one can talk
of, say, unemployed blacks as not properly part of 'British society').
Further, 'British society', in general parlance, is something distinct
from the 'British economy', whereas the concept of the British social
formation involves both economic class relations and political and
cultural forms.

    Doubtless many questions are left unresolved, and many currents
of Marxism left unconsidered, in this brief discussion of Marxist 'concepts of structure'. These deficiencies will be made up to some extent
in the main body of the argument in the following chapters. But as
I indicated earlier it is not possible to question in depth all the concepts of Marxism at once. My aim in this section has been more
modest: merely to place my own analytical framework in relation to

certain of the currents of Marxism. I hope that the account given of the concepts of 'relations of production', 'productive forces' and 'mode of production' has met this aim. If it is not already apparent, I should say that my views on these concepts owe much to the work of Hindess and Hirst. The views of these writers have in turn been developed largely through a critical evaluation of 'Althusserian' Marxism: Althusser, despite all the critical comment which has been brought to bear on his work, had the great merit of posing the theoretical problems of Marxism in a clear and rigorous form, of, in a sense, bringing these problems to a head.

In the following, and final section of this introduction, I shall consider the concepts of socialism and communism within the Marxist tradition.

Socialism and communism

In the light of what I have already said concerning the political interest active in Marxist analysis, it is necessary to give some indication of how the term 'socialism' will be used in the following chapters. In the conventional usage of modern politics 'socialism' most often refers to a system of social economy characterised by state ownership of the means of production and economic planning, or to the political ideology concerned with the promotion of such a system. From the standpoint of Marxism (virtually any Marxism) such a definition is seriously inadequate. In this section I propose to give a brief account of the classical Marxist definition of socialism, and to indicate my own assessment of this definition (more detailed comments on what I take to be 'socialist objectives' under current circumstances will be given in later chapters).

To take Lenin's formulation first, the term 'socialism' refers to the *transition period between capitalism and communism*. Lenin maintained that

'Theoretically, there can be no doubt that between capitalism and communism there lies a definite transition period which must combine the features and properties of both these forms of social economy. This transition period has to be a period of struggle between dying capitalism and nascent communism' (quoted in Balibar, 1977, p. 139).

It is this period to which the name 'socialism' is given. Socialism, in other words, is not a coherent socio-economic system but a period of struggle 'on the road to' communism. Only the latter is a fully-achieved and distinctive social system. As Balibar (1977, p. 140) has put it, amplifying the Leninist view, 'there is no socialist mode of production in the sense that there is a capitalist mode of production or a communist mode of production'. The basic proposition here is that the socialist period is opened by a political revolution which establishes the 'state power of the working class', in distinction to the preceding political dominance of the bougeoisie, but that this change in the class character of the state power cannot at once revolutionise all aspects of economy and society. The bases of class division and antagonism remain — in the division of labour, in the form of commodity production — and the elimination of these demands a long period of struggle and social reconstruction. During this period political relations must take the form of the 'dictatorship of the proletariat', whereby the working class strengthens its dominance over opposed class forces working for the restoration of capitalism.[8] Only once the bases of class division are eliminated entirely will the socialist period come to an end and the period of communism begin. Communism will be a classless society, with no systematic social antagonisms (and therefore no need for a 'state' in the sense of a special body concerned with maintaining the conditions of class domination), with a fully planned and cooperative economy, and with distribution carried out entirely on the basis of 'need'.

The terminology here — 'socialism' as the period of transition and 'communism' as the end-point of transition — is Lenin's, but the substantive conception can be found in Marx, particularly in his 'Critique of the Gotha Programme'.[9] In that work Marx stressed that the society which emerges following a socialist revolution is

'a communist society, not as it has *developed* on its own foundations, but, on the contrary, just as it *emerges* from capitalist society, which is thus in every respect, economically, morally and intellectually, still stamped with the birthmarks of the old society from whose womb it emerges' (Marx and Engels, 1968, p. 319).

This form of society, which Marx refers to as the 'lower phase of communism', is the transitional form to which Lenin gives the name 'socialism'. Marx clearly distinguishes this from the 'higher phase of communist society', the system established

'after the enslaving subordination of the individual to the division of labour, and therewith also the antithesis between mental and physical labour, has vanished; after labour has become not only a means of life but life's prime want; after the productive forces have also increased with the all-round development of the individual, and all the springs of co-operative wealth flow more abundantly (ibid, pp. 320-321).

Marx also used the term 'dictatorship of the proletariat' to refer to the form of politics during the transition from capitalism to the ('higher stage' of) communism.

Later writers in the Leninist tradition have made the point forcefully that the socialist transition period should not be seen merely as a 'stage' of a steady and linear upward progress. If it is a period of acute struggles, there can be no guarantee that these struggles will progress in any automatic fashion towards the goal of communism. Hence, for instance, Mao Tse-Tung's insistence on the need for a series of 'cultural revolutions' to promote the communist tendencies in society, and his emphasis on the possibility of backsliding if the supposedly 'proletarian' state and party became distanced from the masses, authoritarian and unresponsive to popular criticism. As Althusser has stressed, socialism is a historical period in which the class struggle 'may — depending on the relation of forces and the "line" which is followed — either *regress* towards capitalism or *mark time* in frozen forms or again *progress* towards communism' (Althusser, 1977, p. 204). Sweezy and Bettelheim (1971) have argued the same point. This position is connected with the critique of the 'Stalinist' orthodoxy according to which the succession of modes of production is assured by the development of the productive forces, to which I have referred in the previous section of this Introduction.

In my view, the conception of socialism as a period of struggle and transition, the outcome of which is not pre-determined, as opposed to communism as the fully-developed classless society, has certain important merits, but I have certain reservations concerning the concept of 'communism' in Marxist theory. I shall develop these points in turn.

The fundamental value of the insistence that socialism is a contradictory period of transition is that it dispels the utopian illusion that any form of political revolution can 'at a stroke' transform economy and society. Whatever happens, we may be sure that fundamental changes in the relations of production will take a long period to accomplish, and will be fought over by opposed social forces regardless of the formal character of the state power. Neither commodity production nor the hierarchal division of labour can be simply 'abolished' by decree, and the development of planned, cooperative forms of social production will demand sustained constructive effort and will encounter definite forms of resistance. The socialism/communism distinction distances the Marxist view from any minimal conception of 'socialism' as, say, nationalisation of industry plus expansion of public service expenditure — from any programme which might be rapidly implemented following the election of an appropriate government, or even the storming of the barricades. It emphasises the point that communism as a political force sets its sights on a society so radically different from capitalism that it cannot possibly be achieved without a protracted historical period of struggle and transformation.

So far so good, but what of the Marxist concept of communism, the endpoint of socialist transition which governs the objectives of politics in the socialist period? What is immediately striking here is that the definition of communism (or the 'higher stage of communism' in Marx's terminology) is primarily *negative* in character: absence of classes; abolition of the subordination of the individual to the division of labour; absence of the state; absence of commodity relations. The 'positive' features of communism are merely gestured at: 'abundance', planning, and the 'all-round development of the individual'. The problem is that the definite social developments which could permit the various 'absences' that characterise communism (classes, state, commodities), as well as its positive features, are not really discussed.[10] Both Marx and Lenin were very much averse to the utopian practice of 'idle scheming' regarding the detailed character of the future society. In their view this would be determined in the course of the class struggle and could not be legislated in advance. But while the reluctance to engage in speculative scheming is quite defensible, the question arises: is there then any real basis for believing that 'communism', as defined schematically and mainly in the negative, is an attainable social order? If we cannot outline in advance the means of achieving communism, how can we know that it is indeed a real possibility? My view is that the Marx/Lenin conception of communism contains certain elements which are of great importance as objectives of socialist struggle, but there can be no guarantee that these objectives can ever be completely realised, that the 'transition', in other words, has a definite end-point. Indeed there are good grounds for believing that certain of the features of 'communism' are neither praticable nor desirable, if taken to the theoretical limit. I shall try to justify this view by reference to certain major 'themes' of communism: abolition of all subordination to the division of labour, of commodities and of the state, and 'abundance'.

1. **The division of labour** : As regards the abolition of subordination to the division of labour there are certain advances which clearly could be made, given appropriate political conditions: automation could be used to eliminate many of the tedious and oppressive positions within the present division of labour; a full programme of continuing education for all in both physical and intellectual skills, combined with other measures, could make people far more adaptable in moving between tasks during their working lives; workers' control over enterprises could break down the management/shopfloor division, and so on. But can these processes ever reach the stage of complete fluidity in the division of labour, a point at which (a) individuals are no longer constrained by the need to work at a definite, limited task for protracted periods, and (b) there are no longer any definite social groups with a focus of identification in their position within the division of labour, rather than with 'society' as a whole? This seems unlikely, and so long as distinct collectivities within the division of labour continue to exist, there will be a basis for conflicts of interest between them. Even if the *hierarchical* aspects of this division can be substantially broken down, there will still be room for conflict over the allocation of resources to different areas, branches of production, or enterprises.

2. **The abolition of commodity production**[11] : The development of social democracy, even, has shown that certain goods and services can be produced successfully on a non-commodity basis, and there is every reason to believe that the areas of non-commodity production could be greatly expanded, again given appropriate political conditions. But the same qualification arises: how can one prove that this process can be taken to the point of eliminating commodity production altogether, that all social production can be carried out according to a 'predetermined plan'? It requires an act of faith to believe that sufficiently flexible and decentralised models of planning can be evolved to displace the *a posteriori* adjustment of production to market demand in all sectors of the economy, while achieving maximum responsiveness to changing popular tastes (tastes and preferences will continue to change even if they are not orchestrated by high-pressure advertising!).

3. **The abolition of the state** : As regards this question, there is rather more to go on in the writings of Marx, Engels and Lenin.

This is because they recognised, in the Paris Commune, a concrete model for the abolition of the state. A word of explanation is needed here. The term 'state' is given two distinct meanings in Marxism, meanings which Lenin distinguished more clearly than his predecessors. On the more general of the two definitions the term simply refers to the political mechanism which functions to maintain the conditions of dominance of a given social class. Since in the Marxist conception the existence of class divisions necessarily implies class antagonism and the dominance of one class over others, the state in this general sense can disappear only once all class division has disappeared. Indeed this is a cardinal point of difference between Marxism and anarchism. But then the term 'state' is also given a more restricted definition: the state as a separate institution, standing (supposedly) 'above society' and 'above classes', immune to substantive popular control, incorporating a standing army isolated from the rest of the working population and a corps of privileged functionaries. What Marx saw in the Paris Commune was the abolition of the state in this second sense. Lenin took up Marx's view and expressed it by saying that the state of the Commune was no longer a state 'in the proper sense of the word'. The Commune, in other words, was a concrete model for the political mechanism maintaining the conditions of *working class* dominance — a mechanism which was necessarily fundamentally different from any state which functions to maintain the position of an exploiting class. The central features to which Marx, and later Lenin, drew attention in this regard were (a) abolition of the standing army and its replacement by the 'armed people', (b) all official posts made subject to election and all elected officials to be subject to recall by their constituents at any time, (c) delegates to be paid only workmen's wages, and (d) abolition of 'parliamentarism' and the fusion of legislative and executive functions. The tendency implicit in these measures was the abolition of the state as an institution standing 'above society' and its replacement by 'the proletariat organised as the ruling class' (Marx). So although the Commune was given very little chance to develop before it was suppressed, its organisation in an important sense 'prefigured' Communism. In an achieved communist society the military/repressive side of the state power would no longer be required — would in Engels' words 'wither away' — leaving only a system of administration. But if this administration were modelled on the lines of the Commune then there would be no distinct administrative apparatus as such — only a people organising itself.

This conception contains both vital insights and serious problems. The central insight is that socialism, if it is to produce more than a superficial transformation of society, must challenge the nature of the state. The projects of transferring the means of production to state ownership, or of expanding the range of services provided in non-commodity form by the state, will fail to produce a real emancipation of working people unless the state itself is subordinated to popular control — unless, in other words, the apparatuses of administration, policing, education, social welfare and so on are made open to popular participation and accountability, and the mystique of bureaucracy and the secrecy and material privileges of officialdom are broken down. But although certain features of the Paris Commune clearly show the way in which these objectives might be pursued, it seems to me (a) that some features of the Commune may be impractical as permanent characteristics of the organisation of a complex society, and (b) that Lenin's extrapolation of the tendencies of the Commune, to the point where the state apparatuses are ultimately dissolved into the self-regulation of society as a whole, is utopian.

On point (a), I would draw attention to the conception of elected representatives as mandated delegates, subject to recall at any time, and to the abolition of the legislative/executive distinction. Without offering a detailed argument here, I submit that although these measures may have been workable in the context of a relatively small and coherent political community exhibiting a high degree of solidarity in the face of a common enemy, it is by no means self-evident that they are practicable or desirable long term features of socialist organisation. If, as I believe, not all conflicts of interest in society are reducible to *class* conflict, then the political system will always have the task of reconciling and accommodating differing interests and points of view. And in this light, the principle of making all representatives into mandated delegates of their constituents threatens to paralyse the political process: no representative would be able to compromise the particular interests of his or her constituents for the greater good of society as a whole, or accept as a result of detailed argument among representatives a view different from that of the constituents, without running the risk of recall and replacement. Then take the legislative/executive problem. The progressive aim of the attack on 'parliamentarism' is to abolish the conditions under which the elected representatives of the people are involved merely in a 'talking shop', with the 'real' business of government being conducted elsewhere, behind closed doors. The representative institutions must be made more than just a 'dignified' element of the condition, to use Bagehot's term. But given the complexity of the business with which any modern government must deal (and *ipso facto* any socialist government on a national or international scale) it seems quite unrealistic to suppose that this aim can be achieved by the outright *abolition* of the division between legislative and executive functions. A more promising route seems to lie in the strengthening of the critical and supervisory role of parliament, involving increased access of representatives to information and specialist advice and enabling them to call senior executives to account.

Point (b) above concerned Lenin's extrapolation from the Commune to a fully 'stateless' society. My criticism here is closely related to my earlier remarks concerning the division of labour: I submit that there is no basis for arguing that the activities of administration, policing and so on can be eliminated as distinct branches of the division of labour, to be performed by the 'people as a whole'. Lenin suggests that the tasks of administration can be performed by 'any literate person' and that policing to cope with 'individual excesses' can be performed by the 'armed people', 'as simply and readily as any crowd of civilised people, even in modern society, interferes to put a stop to a scuffle or to prevent a woman from being assaulted' (Lenin, 1969, p. 83). On administration, it may be true that 'any literate person' could perform the tasks, but if the more routine and tedious clerical tasks can be progressively reduced, in view of the advances in information technology, then the remaining tasks will surely be more demanding. 'Any literate person' will require training and experience, and will need to build up a good working relationship with his or her colleagues, which is to say that total fluidity in the division of labour, or the parcelling out of administrative tasks among the whole working population on a rotating basis, is likely to prove impossible. On policing, I am again doubtful of Lenin's formulations. If one admits as Lenin does, that there will be a need for policing in any society, even if the aspect of class domination is eliminated, then one has to recognise the need for a disciplined and effective police force, and one that is better than arbitrary in its operations. Certainly, such a force in a socialist society would have to be very different from police forces as presently constituted, in terms of popular accountability in particular, and it would doubtless have a more restricted role, but the notion of policing being carried out in complete informality by the general citizenry raises an alarming prospect of both ineffectiveness in detecting the less visible forms of anti-social behaviour, and arbitrariness in discouraging and correcting such behaviour.

4. **'Abundance'** : This is the last aspect of communism on which I wish to comment here. 'Bourgeois' economics, and neoclassical economics in particular, lays great stress on the confrontation between limited resources and limitless wants, and elevates this confrontation to the status of the 'essential economic problem': resources will always be 'scarce' relative to their possible competing uses and there is therefore a need for 'choice', for a mechanism to allocate resources to the uses in which they will produce the greatest possible 'welfare'. The claim has often been made that the market, or at least an idealised market conforming to the canons of 'perfect competion' is the best possible mechanism for optimising this allocation of scarce resources. A common Marxist riposte to this whole conception is that 'scarcity' is not a universal constraint. The development of socialism towards communism will permit a vast increase in the productivity of labour on the one hand, and at the same time eliminate the excesses of 'consumerism' under capitalism (i.e. the stimulation of 'artificial' desires for the limitless acquisition of consumer goods by means of advertising and other pressures), and these changes will effectively eliminate the problem of scarcity.[12]

Again this position has both valuable features and problems. Clearly the productivity of labour could be greatly increased, given the technology already developed in capitalist economies let alone future development, if the question of productivity were to be approached in terms of broad social criteria rather than just in terms of the profitability and market position of individual enterprises. Here it is important to stress a point which Marx makes in the 'Grundrisse' concerning the possible 'virtuous circle' effect of the development of technologies which permit a reduction in the necessary labour-time. Marx argues that in a planned economy the reduction of the time of necessary labour would mean not unemployment but rather increased free time for the 'artistic and scientific' development of the people, and in turn this general raising of cultural standards would permit further great improvements in the development of productive techniques:

'The saving of labour time is equal to an increase of free time, i.e. time for the full development of the individual, which in turn reacts back upon the productive power of labour as itself the greatest productive power' (Marx, 1973a. p. 711).

Equally, it can be argued quite plausibly that the ethic of 'consumerism' can and should be undermined, and that insatiable avarice is not an intrinsic human characteristic. But here one must draw a line between the Marxist view and a certain kind of moralism which has become fashionable among elements of the middle classes in the advanced capitalist countries. A desire for the 'simple life' is no part of classical Marxism. Indeed Marx regarded the expansion of 'needs' under capitalism as a generally progressive development. In the 'Grundrisse' Marx notes that the capitalist, in his search for markets, 'searched for means to spur (the workers) on to consumption, to give his wares new charms, to inspire them with new needs by constant chatter etc.'. But far from leading up to a denunciation of all this, Marx goes on to say 'it is precisely this side of the relation of capital and labour which is an essential civilizing moment, and on which the historical justification, but also the contemporary power of capital rests' (Marx, 1973a, p. 287). In a similar vein, Aneurin Bevan once said that 'a society in which the people's wants do not exceed their possessions is not a socialist society. That sort of satisfaction is not socialism, it is senility' (quoted in Foot, 1973).

So on the one side the productivity of labour may well be greatly increased, while on the other, although certain kinds of frivolous and wasteful consumption stimulated under capitalism could usefully be discouraged, people's 'needs' and aspirations could be expected to develop further, rather than shrink into a 'senile' satisfaction, in a communist society. Can it honestly be maintained that the 'scarcity' problem then disappears? A further point must be brought into the reckoning: we have, since Marx's day, become much more conscious of the finitude of many natural resources, and although this does not justify the 'no-growth' ideology it does mean that the increased output of material goods will encounter definite constraints. In some cases alternative resources will be discovered or devised, but these too will have a definite cost. If one sets the natural resource constraints against the 'needs' of the majority of the world's population at present living close to, or below, subsistence conditions then it seems very rash to suppose that the problem of scarcity relative to the possible use of resources, and therefore also the need to order priorities and privilege certain uses of resources over others, will ever disappear. There is no need, of course, to accept the neoclassical contention that the competitive market is the best mechanism for carrying out this 'choice', or the idea that the scarcity/choice problem is *the* essential problem of economics, but there is a need to abandon the simplistic notion of 'abundance' insofar as it is conceived as dissolving the problem of allocating resources within definite constraints (although there may be 'abundance' relative to the present state of affairs). This also throws some doubt on the idea of a free distribution of the means of personal consumption: it will surely be possible to progress towards distribution according to 'need', but not necessarily to allow people freely to assess their own 'needs' in this respect and to take from the social consumption fund all they might aspire to.

In the discussion above I have made critical comments concerning the major defining features of 'communism'. If these comments are accepted then they put in question the idea of a definite end-point of socialist transition, with such-and-such clear cut features. My conclusion is that it is misleading to talk of 'communism' as if it had a platonic existence and merely awaits discovery. Balibar said 'there is no socialist mode of production in the sense that there is a capitalist mode of production or a communist mode of production': the point he was making about *socialism* has been taken, but can one really say that the communist mode of production 'exists'? It 'exists' only as a concept within Marxist theory, and a rather problematic and unelaborated concept at that.[13] I would rather say that the classical Marxist conception of communism contains certain important long term objectives of socialist advance, but that it is wrong to make the presumption that these can be taken to the limit-point envisaged by Marx, Engels and Lenin.

Let me summarise briefly the main long term socialist objectives which can be taken from the concept of communism. In my view these are: (a) to break down the subordination of individuals to the division of labour, and in particular to break down the hierarchical and authoritarian aspect of this division, so far as this is practicable; (b) to institute and develop planned and cooperative forms of production wherever practicable, while recognising that certain branches of production or sectors of the economy may be intrinsically difficult to plan; (c) to break down the 'separation' of the state from popular control, within the limits imposed by the need for a workable degree of autonomy for the political process of accommodating differing interests and viewpoints; (d) to pursue the objective of distribution according to 'need' (along with the democratic construction of what precisely 'needs' are), and the abolition of special privileges, while recognising that there may be a continuing requirement for definite social constraints on personal consumption.[14]

In the following chapters I shall refer to the pursuit of such objectives as 'the socialist project', and when I refer to a 'socialist' economy or society I shall mean a social system in which substantial progress has been made in the implementation of the socialist project.

1
Marx on classes and politics

In this chapter I shall first discuss Marx's definition of the basic classes of the capitalist mode of production — wage workers and capitalists — and then give an assessment of the relationship, in Marx's writings, between these 'basic classes' and the forces active in politics in capitalist societies. In the latter assessment I shall draw mainly on two works which show different faces of Marx: the 'Manifesto of the Communist Party' and the 'Eighteenth Brumaire of Louis Bonaparte'. I shall argue that while the 'Manifesto' affirms a clear and definite proposition concerning the necessary relationship between the basic classes and political forces — one in which the latter must eventually coincide with or correspond to the former — Marx does not actually sustain this proposition. Many of the 'necessary' developments which would tend to produce the correspondence affirmed in the 'Manifesto' turn out to be, in effect, *hypotheses* of greater or lesser plausibility. The 'Eighteenth Brumaire', by contrast, provides a useful account of the many complex forms of concrete relationship which may obtain between classes and political forces although Marx at times, misleadingly, attempts to condense all of these under the single concept of 'representation' of class interests. Through the critical reading of Marx on this question, I aim to develop a conception of class/politics relations which will be employed in my own analyses in later chapters.

First, Marx's definition of the basic classes of capitalism. This definition is bound up with the form of property relations in the capitalist mode of production. Some points have been made already concerning capitalist property relations (see Introduction) but it is necessary to specify these relations more fully. There are two main features of these relations:

1. **Separation between the units of production:** Under capitalism production is social, that is the products of each unit of production or enterprise are generally not intended for consumption within that unit of production (as opposed to the case of subsistence production in a peasant household). For instance few of the shoes produced in a shoe factory are going to be worn by the shoe workers.

Similarly the means of production employed within a given enterprise are generally produced elsewhere. The units of production are interdependent; each is a 'node' within a system of social production rather than a self-sufficient entity. But while production is social in this sense, appropriation is private. The units of production and their products are objects of private property and the owners will part with their products only on condition that they are exchanged for an equivalent[1] (so that 'property is conserved'). The product becomes a *commodity* and is exchanged for its 'equivalent' in money. Production becomes production for the market, for exchange.

This concept of the commodity form as the correlate of 'social production plus private appropriation' is one of the central elements of Marx's theory of value. In the case of private production by independent self-sufficient units of production there is no need for the exchange of products and therefore no commodity form. In the opposite case of a fully socialised economy, social production would be complemented by social appropriation of the product: there would be a need for *distribution* of products between units (e.g. distribution of producer goods from enterprise A to enterprises B and C where they would be employed to produce consumer goods for distribution to workers in A, B and C) but since the enterprises would not be objects of private property the need for *exchange of equivalents* would not arise. The commodity as 'product to be exchanged for its equivalent' would not exist. So it is only when products have to be distributed across the boundaries of independently controlled enterprises that products become commodities. This is the substance of Marx's answer to the question which classical political economy 'failed to pose': the problem of the specificity of the commodity, as opposed to the question of the determinants of the exchange ratios or prices of commodities.

2. **The separation of the direct producers from the means of production:** The basic historical presuppositions of capitalism are (i) the expropriation of the direct producers and the creation of a class of workers who cannot produce on their own account, and (ii) the concentration of exclusive possession of the means of production in the hands of a distinct class. Commodity production pre-dates capitalism, and the specifically capitalist mode of production develops only when the propertyless workers are constrained to sell their labour power to capital in return for wages. That is, the distinguishing feature of *capitalist* commodity production is that labour power becomes a commodity. Through the wage contract

the capitalist enterprise gains the right of disposition of the workers' labour power during the working day and the right of possession of the products thereof. The hiring of labour becomes a means of profit-making on the part of the capitalist enterprises.

As Marx argues in Volume One of 'Capital', the separation of the workers from the means of production is not only an historical presupposition of capitalism, it is also a result continually reproduced within capitalist relations of production. The worker starts out propertyless, sells his labour power in return for a wage which merely allows him to reproduce his labour power, produces surplus value for capital, and then finds himself back where he started: still propertyless, and constrained to sell his labour-power once again in order to live. Separation, in this sense, is not a once-and-for-all act, rather it is a double process. On the one hand 'separation' refers to the continuing dissolution of pre-capitalist forms of production, based on the artisanal unity of the producer and his means of production, with the expanded reproduction of capitalist relations. On the other hand it also refers to the condition whereby the means of production confront the worker as the property of another, which is constantly *reproduced* under capitalism.

It is worth emphasising that the economic definition of capitalism requires both these elements 1 and 2 above. I have pointed out that commodity production pre-dated capitalism — further, it may be impossible to abolish completely the commodity form in a socialist economy. The elimination of the need for commodity exchange depends not merely on the juridical re-definition of all means of production as 'public' or 'state' property and the abolition of personal and joint-stock forms of property, but rather on the elaboration of a planning mechanism which permits a completely socialised appropriation. To achieve a purely administrative 'transfer' of products as opposed to exchange, all enterprises in the economy would have to be under unified control in a manner analogous to the operating units of a multi-divisional capitalist enterprise (*within* which exchange relations are not necessary). And this latter state of affairs may be unattainable even given further development of the productive forces. It would probably require a quite prodigious centralisation, and it seems likely that in any socialist economy a (regulated) sphere of commodity exchange between (democratically accountable) enterprises will continue to exist. East European discussions of the role of the market in a socialist economy[2] cannot reasonably be dismissed as revisionist apologetics. What we can say is that where the workers remain separated from the means of production, and bound to commodity-producing enterprises through the wage contract in the absence of mechanisms of control over production by 'the associated producers', we are dealing with capitalist property relations. This discussion of the basic property relations of capitalism enables us to present the two fundamental categories of agents within capitalist production:

1. Wage workers: separated from the means of production and constrained to sell their labour power to capitalist enterprises.
2. Capitalists: owners of the means of production, and appropriators of the surplus product in the form of profits.

We can take these categories as a starting point and pose the problem of their adequacy for analysing the class forces present in capitalist societies, and therefore for orienting socialist politics. What, in other words, is the relationship between the 'economic' categories of wage labour and capital, and the actual socio-political groupings which are to be found fighting out the 'class struggle' at the point of production and in national (or international) politics? Are wage labour and capital not only economic categories but also historical actors? Should the active political groupings and parties be conceived as 'representing' (championing the interests of) the economically defined classes? Or is the relationship more complex than that?

In the following discussion I shall consider two strands of Marx's views on the matter, presented in the 'Communist Manifesto' and the 'Eighteenth Brumaire of Louis Bonaparte'. I say 'strands' because Marx's views on class do not form a unified essential whole: his positions changed over time in response to political and theoretical developments. The 'Manifesto', however, presents in particularly clear and striking form a broad interpretation which has been very influential and which is echoed later in certain passages of 'Capital' (especially Volume One, Chapter 32), while the 'Eighteenth Brumaire' presents a remarkably rich 'application' of Marx's theory to the class struggles of a definite historical period.

The Communist Manifesto

We should remember that the 'Manifesto' was a mobilising pamphlet, designed to crystallise and communicate the revolutionary ideology of the Communist League at a time of great political optimism, before the revolutions of 1848 had run into the sands. As such, it represents the polarisation of social forces around the wage labour/capital dichotomy as an inevitable tendency of capitalism. 'Wage labour' is a category within Marx's theory but the 'Manifesto' presents a scenario in which that category corresponds ever more closely to a real historical agency i.e. the gap between 'class' as economically defined entity and 'class' as social force is progressively eliminated, so that it becomes legitimate to use the one term to encompass both.

Let us examine this tendency as set out in the text. Marx begins by sketching the processes by which the bourgeoisie 'pushed into the background every class handed down from the middle ages' p. 37).[3] He argues that these processes have 'simplified' class antagonisms:

> 'society as a whole is splitting up into two great hostile camps, into two great classes directly facing each other: Bourgeoisie and Proletariat' (p. 36).

As regards the political sphere the state power is increasingly the naked materialisation of bourgeois power:

> '...the bourgeoisie has at last... conquered for itself, in the modern representative State, exclusive political sway. The executive of the modern state is but a committee for managing the common affairs of the whole bourgeoisie' (p. 37).

Further, all organic ideologies, such as religion, which could cut across class lines are drowned in the 'icy water of egotistical calculation' (p. 38). 'Free trade' becomes the supreme ideology. The 'professions' are converted into mere branches of wage labour. The family relation is reduced to a 'mere money relation' (p. 38). The exploitation of the world market has given rise to '..intercourse in every direction, universal inter-dependence of nations' which in turn makes 'national one-sidedness and narrow-mindedness more and more impossible' (p. 39). Therefore all the various social ties (religion, social status, family, nationality) which might obscure or override the formation of *class-based* social collectivities are progressively demolished.

The rise of bourgeois society from feudalism is summed up in the formula of the contradiction between productive forces and property relations — the formula of the 'Preface' of 1859. After a point, feudal property relations became a fetter on the already developed productive forces and they were therefore duly 'burst asunder'. It is made clear that bourgeois property is due for the same fate since the prodigious productive forces unleashed by capitalism are already...'too powerful for these conditions, by which they are fettered...' (p. 41).

The bourgeoisie was an historically progressive class so long as it represented the rising tendency of the productive forces but now the progressive class is the proletariat, the class which will revolutionise bourgeois property and liberate the productive forces for a new stage of development. Each class is 'tied' to a particular system of property relations, and as the development of the productive forces ensures the succession of forms of property (feudal — bourgeois — communist) it also ensures the successive dominance of different social classes (feudal lords — capitalists — proletariat). But what gives substance to this schematism? What of the actual mechanisms which turn the proletariat into the 'grave-diggers' of the bourgeoisie? Marx puts forward a number of arguments, many of which are effectively hypotheses concerning the social and political effects of economic development under capitalism although in the rhetoric of the 'Manifesto' they assume the form of already realised or inevitable tendencies. The following is a summary of Marx's arguments, to each strand of which I have appended a 'comment' noting certain relevant problems and debates. Many of these issues will be taken up in more detail in later chapters — in order to avoid disrupting the exposition of the logic of the 'Manifesto' they are only indicated briefly in this context.

1. **The effects of the application of machinery and the division of labour**: In the 'Manifesto' Marx clearly subscribed to the conception which would now be labelled 'de-skilling'. The work of the proletarians loses all its 'individual character' and 'charm'. So any grounds for identification with one's work are destroyed. Further, since the wage is merely the cost of production of labour power the simpler labour of machine-minding goes along with a reduction in wages while the 'burden of toil' increases. De-skilling also makes differences of age and sex less relevant on the labour market, to the extent that 'differences in age and sex no longer have any distinctive social validity for the working class.'

   Comment: The de-skilling notion has recently been argued and extended by Braverman (1974). Braverman's arguments have, however, been challenged by Cutler (1978) and Gershuny (1978) who conclude that, at a social level, there is no clear tendency towards simpler and more trivial work operating at present. Further, it may be argued that insofar as de-skilling does take place it can increase the competition among workers and undercut certain forms of craft-based union organisation. Depending on the context, resistance to de-skilling can appear as a divisive attempt to maintain privileged status for certain groups. On the tendency for wages to fall with the development of capitalist production, Rowthorn (1980) has shown that Marx's views were to change in later years. And on the 'social validity' of sex differences, it is clear that Marx was jumping the gun. The women's movement over recent years has made us more aware of the continuing effects of the sexual division of labour.

2. **Effects of large-scale factory organisation**: Labour becomes ever more regimented in the large-scale factory. More and more workers become concentrated under the despotic control of the 'overlookers' and the 'individual bourgeois manufacturer himself'. This concentration counteracts the isolating pressure of competition on the labour market and gives rise to 'revolutionary combination'. It goes hand in hand with an 'equalisation of the conditions of life' as distinct grades of labour are abolished and wages progressively reduced to the same low level.

Comment: The rise of large-scale factories certainly makes effective point-of-production organisation more likely, strengthening trade unionism. It does not follow, as Lenin emphasised, that the workers will necessarily subscribe to revolutionary politics. Even at the economic level, the concentration of the work force does not abolish differentiation of grades and wages. Concentration of industrial labour was an important point of emphasis for Marx, since in his day the dominant shift in the distribution of social labour was from agriculture and small-scale production to machine industry. Under present conditions socialists have to take into account the kind of 'deindustrialisation' investigated by Blackaby (1979) and face up to its implications for the possibilities of workplace organisation (Cutler *et al.,* 1978).

3. **Effects of commercial crises**: These occur on a larger and larger scale as the world market develops. They give rise to fluctuations in wages, and the threat of unemployment makes the workers' livelihood 'ever more precarious'.

Comment: Mass unemployment may make workers more bitter, but there is no guarantee that it increases their potential for combining as a political class. It may often weaken trade unionism and ironically sap the strength of the workers' movement just as it appears to strengthen the moral and economic case for socialism (although even the latter effect depends upon socialists putting forward a strong case showing that there is an alternative to unemployment).

4. **Effects of 'social mobility'**: In the course of capitalist development the proletariat is the expanding class, and it draws recruits

from all sections of the population. The lower strata of the middle class in particular 'sink gradually into the proletariat' either because, in the case of independent traders, their capital is too small to compete with the big bourgeoisie or, as in the case of artisans, their skills are rendered worthless by the development of machine industry. This 'downward mobility', to use the modern term, is presumed to furnish the working class with 'fresh elements of enlightenment and progress'. Enlightenment is also increased when progressive ideologists who have 'raised themselves to the level of comprehending theoretically the historical movement as a whole' defect from the bougeoisie and take up a proletarian standpoint. *Comment:* The only aspect of social mobility to be considered in the 'Manifesto' is the downward progress of the erstwhile middle classes into the proletariat. Two problems here. First, such downward movement does not necessarily help to cement the unity of the proletariat by supplying elements of 'enlightenment'. Indeed some writers have seen this kind of mobility as a source of 'infection' of the working classes by the individualistic ideology of the middle classes. Second, there is the problem of 'upward' social mobility and its effects on the solidarity of classes. This is an issue which Marx discussed in passing in other writings, and one which can hardly be ignored nowadays given the considerable expansion of the salaried strata.

5. **The effects of ruling class struggles**: In their struggle against the aristocracy or sections of the bourgeoisie whose interests are inimical to industrial development, the progressive bourgeoisie enlist the aid of the proletariat, hence 'dragging them into the political arena' and preparing them for the fight against the bourgeoisie.

   Comment: The working class may be 'drawn into politics' in this way, but this does not provide an unambiguous preparation for fighting the bourgeoisie. To the extent that the proletarians are influenced by the ideologies under the sign of which such 'ruling class battles' are fought, they may indeed be seriously deflected from open conflict with 'their' bourgeoisie. For instance, the case of national wars and the ideologies of patriotism, nationality and racism.

The general point to notice here is that the processes which Marx indicates seem far less determinate in their outcome, on closer inspection and with the benefit of historical perspective, than is claimed in the 'Manifesto'. The revolutionary political unity of the working class may be rendered more likely by certain developments within capitalism, but it is never guaranteed.

But let us return to the status of these tendencies within the argument of the 'Manifesto'. The combined effects of these processes (1 to 5) can be traced in the phases of development of the 'proletarian movement'. At first clashes between wage labour and capital are localised and often backward-looking: seeking to restore the 'vanished status of the workman of the middle ages'. At this stage competition still fragments the class. This is the era of Utopian Socialist system-building. The proleteriat offers the 'spectacle of a class without any historical initiative or any independent political movement' (p. 60), so the system-builders (Saint-Simon, Fourier, Owen *et al.*) seek to replace 'historical action' with 'their personal inventive action'. All the while, however, the proletariat is learning politics in the service of the bourgeoisie against the feudal classes.

Over time the processes indicated above (concentration, division of labour, recruitment) have the effect of progressively giving the 'collisions' between workers and capitalists 'the character of collisions between two classes' (p. 43). Trade union organisation proceeds apace, aided by the modern communications systems, giving rise to an 'ever expanding union of the workers'. Organised labour begins to have an impact on the legislative process, witness the 10 hours bill. This class-in-the-making is increasingly unencumbered by any ties of its own to 'secure and fortify', by any possible stake in bourgeois society. The proletarian has no property, no country — 'modern subjection to capital, the same in England as in France, in America as in Germany, has stripped him of every trace of national character' — and no illusions. Law, morality and religion are all seen through as 'so many bourgeois prejudices, behind which lurk in ambush just as many bourgeois interests' (p. 44).

The workers can find no route of individual advancement, and their situation within bourgeois society becomes increasingly intolerable:

> 'the modern labourer... instead of rising with the progress of industry, sinks deeper and deeper below the conditions of existence of his own class. He becomes a pauper, and pauperism develops more rapidly than population and wealth. And here it becomes evident that the bourgeoisie is unfit any longer to be the ruling class...' (p. 45).

Moreover there is no 'third way' which could provide a pole of political attraction distinct from the bourgeois/proletarian antagonism. The proletariat is the 'only really revolutionary class'. The lower middle classes may have antagonistic relations with the bourgeoisie proper but they can offer no viable historical project of their own:

> 'the lower middle classes; the small manufacturer, the shopkeeper, the artisan, the peasant, all these fight against the bourgeoisie, to save from extinction their existence as fractions of the middle class. They are therefore not revolutionary but conservative. Nay more, they are reactionary, for they try to roll back the wheel of history. If by chance they are revolutionary they are so only by virtue of their impending transfer into the proletariat, they thus desert their own standpoint to place themselves at that of the proletariat' (p. 44).

These classes either join the side of the proletariat, or they are condemned to historical marginality, fighting an ultimately useless battle against relegation to the proletarian ranks.

The proletariat therefore possesses the organisation (born of industrial concentration), the political education (from participation in bourgeois struggles), the theoretical vision (aided by progressive defectors from the bourgeoisie) and the motivation (alienated labour, pauperisation, precarious livelihood) to mount a full-scale assault on bourgeois power. Under these circumstances the proletarian movement becomes the 'self-conscious independent movement of the immense majority, in the interests of the immense majority'. Economic category (exploited wage-labourers) and socio-political force ('proletarian movement') become practically identical. Only once does Marx qualify this scenario, and even then the qualification is quickly turned into a re-affirmation of belief:

> 'This organisation of the proletarians into a class, and consequently into a political party, is continually being upset again by the competition between the workers themselves. But it ever rises up again, stronger, firmer, mightier' (p. 43).

The same conception as we have found in the Manifesto is reiterated in 'Capital' Volume One, Chapter 32 'The Historical Tendency of Capitalist Accumulation', in a famous passage:

> 'Along with the constant decrease in the number of capitalist magnates ... the mass of misery, oppression, slavery and degradation grows; but with this there also grows the revolt of the working

class, a class constantly increasing in numbers, and trained, united and organized by the very mechanism of the capitalist process of production. The monopoly of capital becomes a fetter upon the mode of production which has flourished alongside and under it. The centralization of the means of production and the socialization of labour reach a point at which they become incompatible with their capitalist integument. This integument is burst asunder. The knell of capitalist private property sounds. The expropriators are expropriated' (Marx, 1976, p. 929).

Appropriately, the chapter ends with a reference to the Manifesto.

Let us take stock of the implications of these arguments for the concept of class. The procedure will be to identify some important problems and themes from the 'Manifesto' and to develop these through a critical reading of the '18th Brumaire'. I shall then draw on this discussion to orient the investigation of more contemporary writings and the modern class structure. First, it is clear that the term 'class' is being used in two different senses. On the one hand we have class as economically-defined entity, as in 'the spectacle of a class without any historical initiative or any independent political movement'. Here the referent of the term must be the working class as the category of propertyless wage-labourers, at this historical stage having no broad organisation or political arm to define its common interests in opposition to the bourgeoisie. On the other hand, 'class' is sometimes used in a sense which ties it closely to the concept of an organised sociopolitical force:

'...This *organisation* of the proletarians into a class and *consequently into a political party*...' (Marx and Engels, 1968, p. 43, emphasis added).

Full 'classhood' here is achieved only when the occupants of a particular place within the structure of property relations form themselves into an organised body pursuing a political project in accordance with their 'historical mission' or 'class interest' as defined within Marx's theory.

Second, in this text Marx envisages a necessary convergence between these two referents of the term 'class': economic grouping and political agency. The owners of capital attain their political unity in the form of the modern representative state, presented as the typical or adequate form of state for capitalist society. The proletarians attain their political unity in the proletarian movement or party, and this 'self-conscious' organisation is only a matter of time, given the development of large-scale industry. In the long run economic class becomes historical actor. Or, in the language of the 'Poverty of Philosophy' (1847), 'class-in-itself' becomes 'class-for-itself'. I suggested, however, that despite the brilliance and passion of Marx's polemic the mechanisms whereby this convergence is to be secured remain sketchy and problematic.

Third, despite the pre-eminent position given to the opposition of Bourgeoisie and Proletariat, Marx recognises the existence of other classes in mid-19th century European society. He writes of the 'lower middle classes', small manufacturers and traders, artisans and peasants. But at the same time he denies them any real political importance. In contrast with the proletariat, that 'most characteristic product' of large-scale industry, the other classes are fated to 'decay and disappear' in the face of capitalist development. They are seen as a 'survival' from the pre-history of capitalism proper and are therefore only a transient complication in the splitting of society into 'two great hostile camps'. This view is very much in keeping with the 'productive forces' theory. Let us see how these ideas had developed by 1851.

The 'Eighteenth Brumaire of Louis Bonaparte'

This work presents an analysis of classes far more rich in historical detail than the 'Manifesto'. Obviously the text has a different status: it is an interpretation of specific historical events rather than a piece of virtuoso propaganda. Marx's political commitment and passion are equally evident, but by the winter of 1851/52 it was no longer possible to present such a 'triumphalist' vision of proletarian unity: the French working class had been defeated and one had the grotesque spectacle of Louis Bonaparte at the apex of French politics. In his 'Eighteenth Brumaire' Marx admits complexities and problems which were brushed aside in the enthusiasm of the 'Manifesto', so by drawing on the arguments of this text we can deepen and rectify some of the 'Manifesto's' propositions.

Engels saw this work as a 'test' for Marx's 'great law of motion of history':

'... the law according to which all historical struggles, whether they proceed in the political, religious, philosophical or some other ideological domain, are in fact only the more or less clear expression of struggles of social classes, and that the existence of and thereby the collisions, too, between these classes are in turn conditioned by the degree of development of their economic position...' (p. 95).[4]

And he claims that the law has 'stood the test brilliantly'. But what is of particular interest here is to see how the schematic 'law' of the 'Manifesto' and the 'Preface' was necessarily modified, and at points abandoned, in Marx's striving to understand the French politics of the time.

We noted in the 'Manifesto' the conception of 'economic' classes appearing as historical actors, constituting themselves into political forces in their own right (classes 'for themselves'). It is notable that this theme is largely absent from the 'Eighteenth Brumaire'. The nearest we get to a class appearing 'in person' on the political stage is the Paris proletariat in the June days of 1848, but even then it is precisely the *Paris* proletariat which arises, not the proletariat *tout court*, and the particular militancy and unity of the Parisian workers is a product of rather specific historical processes. Their position as wage-labourers was a necessary condition for bringing about that militancy and unity, but by no means a sufficient condition. After their defeat in June 1849 we find them submitting to political 'representation' by the Montagne, whose programme breaks the 'revolutionary point' off the 'social demands' of the proletariat, entraining them behind the petty bourgeoisie. In the boom year of 1850 we find the workers 'forgetting the revolutionary interests of their class for momentary ease and comfort'.

In general, the notion of classes appearing 'in person' in political struggles appears to be inapplicable to the period and it is replaced by the concept of representation: the political forces (parties, movements, even individuals) active at the time are often analysed as more or less adequate 'representatives' of definite class interests. Surveying the various uses made of the concept of representation in this context, it is evident that this concept in turn is problematic. The notion of 'representation' covers a highly heterogeneous set of relations between social classes and political or literary groupings. We have seen that the concept was used in the Manifesto, in the case of the bourgeoisie; there was a certain asymmetry in that the proletariat would achieve its political unity as a mass movement or Party while the bourgeoisie achieves its unity in the representative state — the 'executive committee' for managing its common affairs. In that context 'representation' was presented as a relatively straightforward affair: the representative state simply serves to pass off the interests of the bourgeoisie as the will of the 'people as a whole'. In form the government 'represents' the will of the electors, but in substance it represents the exclusive political sway of the bourgeoisie. But in the particular struggle in France, 'representation' becomes more ambiguous.

First there is no one-to-one mapping between classes and their political representatives: contrary to Engels' version of the 'general law', it is admitted that representation of class interest does not exhaust the field of political forces. For instance the political grouping which formed the official republican opposition under Louis Philippe and which found itself elevated to power in the latter half of 1848, draws this comment from Marx:

> 'it was not a faction of the bourgeoisie held together by great common interests and marked off by specific conditions of production. It was a clique of republican minded bourgeois, writers, lawyers, officers and officials that owed its influence to the personal antipathies of the country against Louis Philippe, to memories of the old republic, to the republican faith of a number of enthusiasts, above all, however, to *French Nationalism...*' (p. 104).

Marx accepts that it is not possible to analyse the political coherence of this grouping by reference to the conditions of production. It was a 'faction of the bourgeoisie' but one whose distinctiveness derived from common views on the desirable form of state, and nationalist sentiment, rather than from common 'economic' interests.

The cases of the army and the National Guard also illustrate this point. As the different factions within the state apparatus fight it out over the years, the affiliation of the armed forces is not given in advance. Certainly the soldiers have a definite class origin and the generals have at any one time definite political views, but their affiliation to one side or the other is partly open to determination by the skills of political calculation and timing of the contending groups. The Montagne, for instance, attempted to impeach Bonaparte and his ministers in June 1849 on the grounds that the bombardment of Rome which Bonaparte had ordered was unconstitutional. The National Assembly rejected the bill of impeachment and so the Montagne attempted a revolt.

'Since a section of the army had voted for it, the Montagne was now convinced that the army would revolt for it. And on what occasion? On an occasion which, from the standpoint of the troops had no other meaning than that the revolutionists took the side of the Roman soldiers against the French soldiers' (p. 122).

Thus Marx argues that a gross miscalculation by the Montagne ensured that it lost the support of the military. This can be contrasted with Bonaparte's sedulous cultivation of the troops through free picnics — the 'sausage of Satory' — which eventually paid off so well. So the armed forces, the decisive element in any showdown between political forces, were not linked to a particular class party by ties of 'representation'.

Second, even where Marx argues that a given political force does 'represent' a social class the relations between the two are by no means straightforward. Let us examine three examples: 'representation' of the petty bourgeoise by the Montagne; 'representation' of the bourgeoisie by the Party of Order; and 'representation' of the peasantry by Bonaparte himself.

The petty bourgeoisie and the Montagne

This is an interesting case in that Marx takes it as a basis for generalising about the representation relation. According to Marx the political demands of the Social-Democrats of the Montagne had as their content 'the transformation of society in a democratic way, but a transformation within the bounds of the petty bourgeoisie' (p. 119). Their programme remained within these bounds because insofar as democratic republican institutions were demanded, this was 'as a means, not of doing away with two extremes, capital and wage labour, but of weakening their antagonism and transforming it into harmony' (ibid.). This is taken as the characteristic politics of the petty bourgeoisie, by virtue of its place as a 'transition class' in which the interests of bourgeoisie and proletariat are 'simultaneously mutually blunted'. But all the same one must not imagine that the democratic representatives:

'... are indeed all shopkeepers or enthusiastic champions of shopkeepers. According to their education and their individual position they may be as far apart as Heaven from earth. What makes them representatives of the petty bourgeoisie is the fact that in their minds they do not get beyond the limits which the latter do not get beyond in life, that they are consequently driven, theoretically, to the same problems and solutions to which material interest and social position drive the latter practically. This is, in general, the relationship between the *political* and *literary representatives* of a class and the class they represent' (p. 120).

The concept of 'representation' is then a means for indicating a correlation between the political ideology of a party or group and the practical ideology of a social class. Not only may the 'representatives' remain blind to this correlation believing their political ideology to have a universal validity, but there is no guarantee that the bulk of the class will follow its representatives and faithfully support the latter's strategy. The miscalculation and political naivete of the Montagne in the crisis of summer 1849 led to a situation in which the petty bourgeoisie 'betrayed their representatives' by refusing to subscribe to their rebellious proclamation.

The point here is not to deny that we can usefully identify relationships between political ideologies and forms of 'practical thinking' bred in definite class positions. I shall be making use of this conception in the analysis of the class forces in modern Britain. Rather it is to question whether the concept of representation is an adequate means for grasping such linkages. The term 'representation' suggests the view in Engels' preface of political struggles as the 'more or less clear expression' of struggles between social classes, which, if taken literally, would seem to foreclose on the importance of the specific *political* uses to which 'class' ideologies are put, the specific forms of political calculation employed by the forces active in politics, and the complex and problematic relations between political forces and social classes in the course of actual struggles.

The bourgeoisie and the Party of Order

Marx takes the Party of Order to be the proper representative of the French bourgeoisie in the political struggles of the period. This party, which gained political dominance with the overthrow of the 'pure republicans' in December 1848, was a coalition of the rival royalist factions of Legitimists and Orleanists. The analysis of this coalition and the tension between its two factions is a classic source for the interpretation of Marx on classes. He claims that the ostensible reason for the rivalry between the factions — allegiance to competing Royal Houses — was a mere 'superstructure of sentiment' overlying the division between landed property and capital ('high finance, large-scale industry, large-scale trade').

'The Legitimate Monarchy was merely the political expression of the hereditary rule of the lords of the soil, as the July Monarchy was only the political expression of the usurped rule of the bourgeois *parvenus*. What kept the two factions apart, therefore, was not any so-called principles, it was their material conditions of existence, two different kinds of property... the rivalry between capital and landed property. That at the same time old memories, personal enmities, fears and hopes, prejudices and illusions, sympathies and anticipations, convictions, articles of faith and principles bound them to one or the other royal house, who is there that denies this? Upon the different forms of property, upon the social conditions of existence, rises an entire superstructure of distinct and peculiarly formed sentiments, illusions, modes of thought and views of life. The entire class creates them out of its material foundations and out of the corresponding social relations' (p. 117).

So although Legitimists and Orleanists came to believe that it was the question of succession which divided them, 'facts later proved that it was rather their divided interests which forbade the uniting of the two royal houses' (ibid.). Here we have a particularly clear statement of the principle of representation/expression of class interest. Specifically political and ideological factors are given an entirely subsidiary position, and in an interesting twist to the conception of 'class as historical actor' we find the 'entire class' itself creating its own superstructure of 'sentiments, illusions' etc. out of its 'material foundations' — a theme which is taken up by Lukács (1971) in his theory of classes as historical subjects.

But compare this account of the Legitimist and Orleanist factions with the account noted above of the 'pure republicans' — a faction which was not 'marked off by specific conditions of production'. In a recent discussion, Cutler *et al.* argued that there is a contradiction between the two.

'If political forces are not reducible to effects of the structure of the economy then "two different kinds of property" cannot account for what kept the two Royalist factions apart. Alternatively, if political forces are reducible to the effects of different forms of property then Marx has no business treating the republican faction as a distinct and real political force' (Cutler *et al.* 1977, p. 184).

There is no doubt that the 'republican faction' is treated as a real political force in Marx's analysis. Its dominant position within parliament did not last long but the constitution which it established had important effects on the subsequent struggles between Louis Bonaparte and the Party of Order. The point then is that if particular political and cultural conditions, not reducible to effects of property relations, were required to constitute the republican faction as a political force then surely it will not do to regard forms of property as a sufficient condition to explain the political distinctiveness of the Royalist factions, all the rest being mere superstructure. Again, although there are *definite links* between the royal houses and different forms of property a literal application of the principle of representation/expression threatens to establish a thorough-going reductionism which is contradicted elsewhere in Marx's analysis.

We can take this point further by considering the historical development and final breakdown of the Party of Order as a political force. Marx argues that as *Royalists* the two factions of the party are at loggerheads, yet they are able to rule conjointly within the form of the parliamentary republic.

'They do their real business as the *party of order*, that is, under a *social*, not under a *political* title; as representatives of the bourgeois world-order, not as knights of errant princesses' (Marx, *op. cit.*, p. 118).

So long as the parliamentary republic provides a reasonably stable form of rule the old loyalties are reduced to 'mere obeisances' and the restoration of the monarchy postponed 'ad infinitum'. And in the struggle against the executive power (Bonaparte) the Orleanists and Legitimists even appear willy nilly as defenders of republicanism. But a dilemma arises because the parliamentary regime does *not* prove stable. In order to preserve their dominant position in face of popular opposition the Party of Order 'royalists' are forced to restrict the suffrage and carry out violent repression. Their 'class rule' becomes increasingly transparent as such, and increasingly dangerous. They find themselves obliged to carry out measures which have the effect of reducing the apparent legitimacy of parliament and conversely giving credence to Bonaparte's claims to represent the 'popular will' as against parliament. Bonaparte, whose political acumen was seriously underestimated by the royalists, is eventually able to brand the Party of Order as — ultimate stigma — the *threat* to order. The party is so afraid of losing its position as defender of order in the eyes of the bourgeoisie outside parliament that it finally succumbs to political paralysis. Unable to challenge Bonaparte on substantive issues for fear of rocking the boat, it gets involved in inconsequential wrangles over trivial, formal questions. This leads to a crisis in which the bourgeoisie outside formal politics loses all trust in, and comprehension of, its 'representatives'. The 'aristocracy of finance', with much of its wealth tied up in state debts 'condemned the parliamentary struggle of the Party of Order with the executive power as a *disturbance of* order, and celebrated every victory of the President over its ostensible represen-tatives as a *victory of order*' (ibid., p. 157). The industrial bourgeoisie, likewise, 'proved that the struggle to maintain its *public* interests, its own *class interests*, its *political* power, only troubled and upset it, as it was a disturbance of private business' (ibid.). Again we find the possi-bility of radical dislocation between a class, carrying out its day-to-day business and its 'representatives', enmeshed in specifically political struggles and following a logic of their own.

Let us return to the two royal houses. It is only when the parliamen-tary republic has reached this paralytic crisis that the question of suc-cession is again seriously pursued. Now the statesmen of the Party of Order desperately attempt to stave off imperial usurpation by Bonaparte, by arranging a merger of the two contending houses. But the pretenders will have nothing to do with this; the 'diplomats' on either side are regarded as mere renegades. The Party of Order disintegrates and Bonaparte carries out his coup d'etat.

This in outline is the account which Marx gives of the fall of the political representatives of the bourgeoisie and the rise of Bonaparte. I am not concerned with the historical accuracy of the account and am not equipped to judge it on those grounds; the point is to examine how well it fits with the concept of political representation of class in-terest given in the initial discussion of the Legitimist and Orleanist factions. My claim is this: the historical account given does not square with the earlier statement that it was the divided interests of landed property and capital which 'forbade the uniting of the two royal houses'. The 'representatives' of landed property and capital had ruled quite effectively together for as long as the parliamentary regime was a feasible form of state. Indeed they were well on the way to forget-ting the rivalry of the royal houses or at least confining it to 'after-hours' activity, by Marx's admission. And Marx offers no argument to the effect that the parliamentary regime broke down due to antag-onism between landed property and capital. It is clear that in his analysis the principal factor was opposition on the part of the popular classes in France (working class, petty bourgeoisie, peasantry) which made it impossible for the Party of Order to gain a stable 'legitimate' majority and which threatened to turn liberal democracy into a means of realising revolutionary aspirations. And the last-ditch attempt at reconciliation of the houses surely failed because of the flatly incompatible claims and religious predilections of Bourbon and Orleans. The interests of landed property and capital may clash on certain issues, but there is the possibility of compromise and mutual accommodation in the face of a common challenge. The rival claims of the royal houses were, however, intrinsically mutually exclusive: there could be only one Monarch and only one dominant religion.

The contrast with the English case reinforces the point. In England the interests of landed property and capital clashed over the corn laws. Land-owners had a vested interest in restricting trade in order to preserve a high price for corn and therefore high agricultural rents, while manufacturers had an interest in free trade and reduction of the price of corn to reduce the cost of subsistence of industrial workers and permit a reduction in wages. There were political forces active on either side of the argument and the matter was not resolved without struggle. But this did not seriously disrupt the long-term process of interpenetration and accommodation between land-owners and capitalists in Britain. In the English case the fortunes of the two factions were not tied to competing pretenders and the parliamentary regime proved much more stable. It is not, therefore, possible to sustain the rigorous conception of representation/expression of class interest by political forces — the conception in which political forces are a mere reflex of class interests defined at the level of property-holding. The Bourbon and Orleans Houses did not merely 'express' an opposition of class interest, they *defined* that opposition in a particular way which made it highly inflexible. Political forces have specific effects, and although Marx clearly sets out the 'expression' principle at one point in the 'Eighteenth Brumaire' it is evident that the rest of the text is not 'bound' by that declaration. If it were, then much of its rich observation would be impossible.

The peasantry and Louis Bonaparte

The principle of representation undergoes further contortions in the case of the relationship between the French peasantry and Bonaparte. Remember that in his analysis of the New Montagne, Marx argued that the 'general relationship' between a class and its political representatives was one in which the 'representatives' took up, for whatever ostensible reasons, positions which were traceable as appropriate to the practical situation of the class. On this criterion, Bonaparte may be regarded as a representative of the lumpenproletariat, with his politics of criminal subterfuge, obsession with his debts and constant attempts to buy support. Marx indeed often casts him in this role

'This Bonaparte, who constitutes himself *chief of the lumpenproletariat*, who here alone discovers in mass form the interests which he personally pursues, who recognises in this scum, offal, refuse of all classes the only class upon which he can base himself unconditionally...' (p. 137).

But the lumpenproletariat in itself cannot provide a stable basis of social support for a regime. Accordingly, Bonaparte the successful usurper is forced to create alongside the 'actual classes of society' an artificial caste for which the maintenance of his regime becomes a bread-and-butter question' i.e. an enormous state bureaucracy. Here is a 'representative' who constructs his own constituency ex nihilo! Marx recognises that this will not do as a complete account of Bonaparte's basis of support. After noting the apparent 'complete independence' of the Bonapartist state machine from the civil society of France, he observes:

'And yet the state power is not suspended in mid-air. Bonaparte represents a class, and the most numerous class of French society at that, the *small-holding peasants*' (p. 170).

The discussion which follows this observation returns us to the dual conception of class which we noted in the 'Manifesto' (economic category/socio-political force). Marx first argues that the material conditions of life of the peasantry preclude their active combination as a social force in their own right:

'The small-holding peasants form a vast mass, the members of which live in similar conditions but without entering into manifold relations with one another... Each individual peasant family is almost self-sufficient... In this way, the great mass of the French nation is formed by simple addition of homologous magnitudes, much as potatoes in a sack form a sack of potatoes. Insofar as millions of families live under economic conditions of existence that separate their mode of life, their interests and their culture from those of other classes, and put them in hostile opposition to the latter, they form a class. Insofar as there is merely a local interconnection among these small-holding peasants, and the identity of their interests begets no community, no national bond and no political organisation among them, they do not form a class' (pp. 170-171).

If the peasantry are incapable of achieving full 'classhood', of combining as a social force, then their political 'representation' can only take the form of a governmental power which appears as an authority over and above them. 'The political influence of the small-holding peasants, therefore, finds its final expression in the executive power subordinating society to itself' (p. 171). Almost immediately, however, this 'expression' must be qualified. The peasantry is not a politically homogeneous category. There are peasant risings against Bonaparte; the army is obliged to raid and repress sections of the peasantry. It turns out that Bonaparte represents 'not the revolutionary, but the conservative peasant... not the enlightenment, but the superstition of the peasant...' (ibid.), and in turn the balance between 'enlightenment' and 'superstition' among the peasantry is in part the result of other cultural and political struggles — between the schoolmasters and the priests; between the *maires* and the prefects — struggles within which the Party of Order and its predecessors intervened on the side of reaction to quell any revolutionary yearnings in the countryside.

Again, the unitary concept of 'representation' seems inappropriate to grasp the complex relations involved. If Marx is saying that the existence of a large mass of conservative peasants with imperial yearnings was a necessary condition for the accession of Bonaparte to power then he is on strong grounds, but any suggestion that Bonapartism is reducible to the 'expression' of the 'mode of production' of the peasantry must be rejected.

It may be argued further that although Marx was not bound by his own declarations of principle on the matter of representation, and was able to produce analyses which go beyond reductionism, nonetheless he was in the end misled in his estimation of Bonaparte's regime by his theory of the necessary relations between classes and political forces. In discussing the future prospects for the regime, Marx reckoned that it was riven by impossible contradictions. Bonaparte wished to preserve 'bourgeois order'.

'But the strength of this bourgeois order lies in the middle class. He looks on himself, therefore, as the representative of the middle class and issues decrees in this sense. Nevertheless he is somebody solely due to the fact that he has broken the political power of this middle class and daily breaks it anew' (p. 176).

Marx seemed to find it incredible that Bonaparte, the representative of the peasantry, who had displaced the natural representatives of the bourgeoisie, could consolidate a regime under which capital accumulation could proceed and the social power of the bourgeoisie develop: 'Bonaparte throws the entire bourgeois economy into confusion... and produces actual anarchy in the name of order' (p. 178). As it happened, his domination was not the mere transitional anarchic interlude which Marx envisaged. Bonaparte may not have seemed a natural representative of the bourgeoisie, yet his *political* rule did provide adequate conditions for the continuing *economic* dominance of the bourgeoisie. Bonaparte's 'parasitic' state machine was thoroughly dependent on capitalist production to provide the surplus off which it lived, and therefore this state was not in a position to destroy the basic juridical framework that protects the free exchange of commodities. On the contrary, it can be argued that the Bonapartist regime was able to take more far-reaching measures to further the development of French capitalism than would have been possible under a 'bourgeois-democratic' regime.[5] The conclusion here is that political forces should be judged by their *effects* and not by the presumed tie of representation which binds them to one or other class.

Let us now organise and summarise the results we have reached through the reading of the 'Manifesto' and the 'Eighteenth Brumaire'. We began with the concept of the basic property relations of capitalism and the two classes which can be defined at that level and then posed the problem of the adequacy of these concepts in analysing the 'class forces' and political movements active in capitalist societies. We saw that the 'Manifesto' presents a ready general answer to this problem: the line-up of class forces and political movements in capitalist society at large will progressively approach the pure reflection of the antagonism of bourgeoisie and proletariat. Society will become organised into 'two great hostile camps' as (a) all intermediate classes decay and disappear and (b) bourgeoisie and proletariat attain their adequate forms of political organisation, impelled by the dynamic of large-scale industrial development. We also noted that this proposition rested on a theory which was present but not proven, the theory which would later be formalised in the 1859 'Preface'. Marx indicated some mechanisms by which the proletariat would attain the status of political class, but these remained sketchy. We then saw that the 'Eighteenth Brumaire' was written 'under the sign' of the same theoretical proposition: that political forces are the expression or representation of the interests of classes. Only this time two kinds of complication were implicitly admitted. First, the plurality of class interests: in place of the simple collision between bourgeoisie and proletariat we found intrusions of the interests of rival bourgeois factions, petty bourgeoisie, peasantry, and even state machine. It was revealed that there are fissures within the bourgeoisie which under certain conditions can be politically paralysing and that the intermediate classes, despite their precarious fate, can have important effects. These aspects of class were analysed in the context of the capital/wage labour antagonism but they were not reducible to epiphenomena on the latter. Second, although a unitary relationship between classes and political forces was affirmed by the repeated use of the terms 'representation' and 'expression', we found this unity effectively denied in the specifics of Marx's analysis. Political forces and classes were linked in various ways but there was no straightforward 'correspondence', and the former had their own effectivity. Marx recognised the existence of a realm of political forces pursuing more or less definite strategies which were by no means generated by the forms of property alone, and operating within definite political conditions (form of constitution; electoral system; allegiance of army and national guard) which affected their popular support and constrained their calculations in specific ways, and which were not themselves reducible to reflections of property relations.

I have argued that the 'Eighteenth Brumaire' reaffirmed the propositions of the 'Manifesto' in principle, but substantially qualified or modified them in practice. Marx himself did not see a radical discrepancy between the two texts. The 'Eighteenth Brumaire' deals with a few years of history, the 'Manifesto' with a whole epoch, and Marx held to the view that the tendency he had identified in the 'Manifesto' — 'the old Mole' — would in time grub its way through the complicating historical circumstances. Bonaparte was only perfecting the repressive state machine so that the proletariat, risen again, could smash it. Nonetheless, it is the analysis of the 'Eighteenth Brumaire' which provides the useful model for class analysis. Over a century later the 'complicating circumstances' are as effective as ever and what socialists need is a means of analysing that complexity so as to make the most effective use of their resources, rather than a promise of victory some day. Insofar as propositions of the kind found in the Manifesto serve to short-circuit the analysis of particular political forces and institutional forms they are positively harmful.

I have claimed that the 'Eighteenth Brumaire' provides the useful model for analysis. I shall now try to sharpen the sense of that proposition, as a prelude to considering contemporary Marxist analyses of class. First it means that we have to take seriously the range of 'class interests' active in particular social formations, other than the 'pure' interests of bourgeoisie and proletariat. We have to consider the ways in which the presence of other classes can either sharpen the political polarisation of society (e.g. the case of the Russian revolution) or, under other circumstances, blunt the antagonism of labour and capital (e.g. the case of the new Montagne). This refers us to the problem of the continued existence and effects of the classes which Marx recognised perforce in the 'Eighteenth Brumaire', yet saw as destined to disappear in the course of capitalist development: the European peasantry is still an important force in the 1980s (witness the struggles over the Common Agricultural Policy and its implications for the E.E.C.); 'petty bourgeois' modes of thought have a renewed significance in the economic policies of the Thatcher government in Britain. It also refers us to the problem of the 'new middle classes', however conceived, that is 'the constantly growing number of the middle classes, those who stand between the workman on the one hand and the capitalist and landlord on the other...' which Marx recognised in his later writings[6] in an observation which sits rather uneasily with the projections of the 'Manifesto', and which we can hardly ignore today. Finally under this head of the plurality of interests we have to consider the effects of differentiation within the 'basic' classes, discarding the myth of a necessary political homogeneity.

The second, related, lesson which can be derived from this reading of Marx is that when one is analysing the politics of a given period from a 'class' standpoint one always has to look for *particular* links between political parties or movements and the classes of society. One cannot assume 'correspondence' as the *a priori* norm. Depending on the context, it may be useful to ask the following kinds of questions of political forces: To what extent is their membership or active support drawn from certain classes? To what extent is their electoral support concentrated in certain classes? Do their strategies indicate an intention to better the position of certain classes? Do their policies or actions have the effect of bettering/unifying/dividing certain classes? Can their conceptions of society and social change be related to the mode of 'practical thinking' appropriate to a definite position in the class structure? The kinds of linkage which may be revealed in answering these questions should not be bound by any Procrustean conceptions of representation/expression.

The fulfilment of these tasks requires the rejection of one dominant strand within classical Marxism: when it is said that the antagonism between Labour and Capital is 'basic' this must not be taken to mean that it is the unique causal motor and that other antagonisms are marginal, or that it is the 'essence' and that specific struggles are merely 'forms of appearance'. It means rather that for socialists drawing upon Marx's analyses, the concept of the labour/capital antagonism serves to organise and orient theory and politics. This antagonism is taken as a 'basic' object of interest if one believes that far-reaching popular democracy and social planning of production can be achieved only with the supersession of bourgeois forms of property and with the active participation of a substantial fraction of the working class. This is not a licence for unbridled empiricism — the unstructured amassing of descriptive detail. The intention is to preserve the fundamental *interests* active in Marx's writing, but unsentimentally reject any concepts which constrict the pursuit of those interests by blocking off important avenues of investigation.

2
Modern Marxists on social classes

In the previous chapter I have begun to outline a conception which I trust will be useful in carrying out a class analysis of contemporary capitalist formations — a conception which emphasises the need for two movements: the identification of 'economic' classes with respect to the system of property relations, and the tracing of the complex connections between these classes and the political forces which operate on and define the dominant 'conflicts of interest' in society. In attempting to analyse classes in contemporary capitalism one is not, however, writing in a vacuum. The past two decades in particular have seen a considerable volume of Marxist writing on social classes and it is appropriate at this stage to offer a critical consideration of this work. My general contention will be that a good deal of this writing is marked by severe theoretical problems traceable to a reluctance to accept the kind of analytical dichotomy indicated above (economic classes/social and political forces). This chapter, then, will be concerned with substantiating that general criticism and with drawing out further certain themes and problems which will be of importance in the following analysis. I begin with Nicos Poulantzas, since his arguments concerning the definition of a 'new petty bourgeoisie' within the ranks of wage and salary-earning employees have had a formative influence on the subsequent debates. In effect, Poulantzas faced head-on the problem which Marx merely hinted at[1]: has capitalist development given rise to a 'third class', a new middle grouping between the bourgeoisie and the working class? If so, how should this class be conceptualised, and what are the implications for socialist strategy?

I then consider the critical development of Poulantzas' position by Erik Olin Wright. The latter's stress on property relations in the definition of classes leads me to a further discussion of property relations, in which I argue (in agreement with Cutler *et al.*, 1977) that they cannot really perform the particular analytical role which Olin Wright assigns them, i.e. separating out certain 'contradictory locations' between the bourgeoisie and the working class. I then consider the alternative analytical strategy proposed by Carchedi, which relies on the 'function

of labour'/'function of capital' dichotomy, and argue that it too
is problematic. In the reprise which follows I argue that the search
for the structural criterion which will 'correctly' locate the 'lines of
class division' within the category of wage and salary-earning
employees, is ultimately a false search, resulting from a question inade-
quately posed.

So, Poulantzas first. Poulantzas' concern was to apply and develop
the concepts of 'Althusserian' Marxism in relation to the problem of
social classes, and in particular the problem of the so-called 'new middle
class' of contemporary capitalism, with the ultimate aim of providing
a guide to socialist strategy and a means for criticising the strategies
of existing socialist political forces (in particular the French Communist
Party or PCF). This concern led him from a general theoretical treatment of 'Political Power and Social Classes' (1968), to the analysis
of particular kinds of capitalist social formation, notably in 'Fascism
and Dictatorship' (1970), to a synthesising account of 'Classes in
Contemporary Capitalism' (1974).[2] I shall devote most attention to
the latter work, but refer to earlier works where they can shed light
on his later positions.

Poulantzas employs two basic dichotomies in his development of
the theory of social classes in contemporary capitalism: the distinction between productive and unproductive labour, and the distinction
between mental and manual labour. His position is that social classes
are determined by the global structure of social relations, and that
within this determination economic relations play a primary role but
political and ideological relations also have a relatively autonomous
effectivity. The distinction between productive and unproductive
labour is used to specify the economic position of agents, then the
distinction between mental and manual is introduced to grasp the determinations at the level of ideology (and politics). Given the importance
which Poulantzas assigns to the criterion of productive labour it will
be necessary to preface the discussion of Poulantzas' own views with
a critical discussion of Marx's concepts of productive and unproductive labour, and their position within his theory of capitalist
reproduction.

Productive and unproductive labour

The distinction between productive and unproductive labour was first
formulated in classical political economy (notably by Adam Smith)
in the period during which the bourgeoisie in Britain was attempting

to cast off the fetters of feudal social relations. At this point it was an explicitly critical distinction, used to attack the feudal ruling classes and their retainers as 'unproductive' in relation to the 'productive' producers of commodities, as a drag on the process of capital accumulation. Only labour which was materialised in a 'vendible commodity' was to count as productive. But *pari passu* with the interpenetration and mutual accommodation between the bourgeoisie and the ex-feudal classes in nineteenth century Britain, the concepts of productive and unproductive labour effectively went underground. The development of subjective theories of value (the theories denounced by Marx as 'vulgar economy' and mere apologetics) undermined Smith's emphasis on the creation of value by means of the working-up of labour in tangible, enduing 'vendible commodities', and Smith's distinction was attacked as arbitrary. Meanwhile these concepts which had been expurgated from bourgeois economic theory were taken up and transformed by Marx in the context of his theory of capitalist production as a mode of extraction of surplus labour in the form of surplus value. Marx constructed his own definition of the labour which is 'productive' for capital — which contributes to the accumulation of capital.[3]

Insofar as Marx gives a definition of productive labour *in general*, this is simply labour considered from the standpoint of the product, that is, the process of combination of labourer, means of labour and object of labour viewed as leading to a result: a determinate product. But this definition was only a starting point. For Marx the distinction between productive and unproductive labour does not serve a moral purpose and it is not based on general ahistorical principles. Rather it must be specified in relation to each mode of production. Productive labour within the capitalist mode of production is specified by a specification of the product: the specific product of labour subordinated to capital is surplus value. So in the capitalist mode productive labour is that labour which produces surplus value, which serves as the means of the self-expansion of capital value. 'From the standpoint of capitalist production we may add the qualification that labour is productive if it directly valorizes capital, or creates surplus values' (Marx, 1976, pp. 1038-9). In order to fulfil this condition labour must clearly (a) produce value (b) produce more value than that which serves as the equivalent for the means of subsistence and reproduction of the worker. The creation of value is analysed by Marx as the expenditure of social labour in the production of use values. Marx argues that the commodity, the form of the product of social labour in capitalism, has two aspects: in terms of exchange value a commodity may be seen as the crystallisation of so much social labour time, while in terms of use value the commodity is considered as an object which satisfies some determinate need. In the same way productive labour has two aspects: it is at once abstract labour and concrete labour. That is, as regards the production of value labour counts only as a quantitative proportion of total social labour: this is its abstract aspect. But as regards the production of the particular use values in which that value is embodied each labour is specific and concrete.

The fact that productive labour, which creates surplus value, must be embodied in some kind of use value does not, however, mean that it must have any particular material content. We can clarify this point by considering Marx's first distinction between productive and unproductive labour. In this distinction Marx follows Adam Smith in defining unproductive labour at the level of exchange: if productive labour is labour subsumed by capital, i.e. is a function of labour power exchanged against variable capital for the purpose of the expansion of that capital through the extraction of surplus value, then unproductive labour is labour which exchanges against 'revenue' or 'simple money'. Unproductive labour is labour which is bought with a view only to the enjoyment of the particular useful quality of that labour. Now as Marx points out the same material labour may fall into either of these categories. I can buy the services of a tailor in order to make up a coat which I then wear. Here my money functions as simple money and the tailor's labour counts as unproductive labour. On the other hand I may own a tailoring establishment and buy the labour power of the tailor in order to get him to make coats which I then sell at a profit. In this case my money functions as capital and the tailor's labour counts as productive. Thus the same material labour may be either productive or unproductive. Here is Marx on the subject:

> 'It follows from what has been said that the designation of labour as *productive labour* has nothing to do with the *determinate content* of the labour, its special utility, or the particular use value in which it manifests itself. The *same* kind of labour may be *productive or unproductive* ... A singer who sells her song for her own account is an *unproductive labourer*. But the same singer commissioned by an entrepreneur to sing in order to make money for him is a *productive worker;* for she produces capital' (Marx, 1969, part one, p. 401).

He adds the examples of the hack writer and the teacher in a private, profit-making school — both 'productive' — to reinforce the point. The distinction rests upon the social relations within which the labour is carried out, and not its particular material characteristics. So far, the distinction is quite clear. Marx is drawing a line between those employed by capitalist enterprises with a view to making profit, and those employed in situations where the hiring of labour is not tied in any direct way to the expansion of capital values (e.g. the domestic servant or the civil servant).

Marx, however, regarded this first distinction as inadequate to grasp the process of production and realisation of surplus value. It had to be supplemented by a second distinction between labour of production and labour of circulation. By 'production' Marx means that activity in which humans enter into relations with nature in order to produce some determinate useful product or 'use value'. Where the social structure is such that these use values assume the form of commodities, that is the form of private property destined for exchange, there must also be an activity of 'circulation'. In any society there must be a *distribution* of the products of social labour to the sites at which they are to be used and for Marx the labour involved in the spatial distribution of products is productive. 'Circulation' on the other hand, is that purely social movement, the transfer of property titles, which is necessitated only by the fact that products assume the form of commodities. Thus Marx's distinction does not correspond to an *institutional* separation of production and circulation. Just as transport represents productive labour carried over into the 'sphere of circulation', so the productive industrial enterprise may employ some of its own circulation workers (unproductive labour in the 'sphere of production').

On the basis of this distinction between production and circulation Marx further specifies his theory of productive and unproductive labour in capitalism. The argument may be summarised as follows:

1. Labour in production creates surplus value, whereas labour in circulation, which produces no 'use values', serves only to realise the value materialised in the products, through sale and purchase.
2. For this reason the character of the consumption of labour power by capital is different in the two spheres. In production labour figures as the contradictory opposite of capital. Capital can expand only by setting labour power to produce use values, thereby calling upon a force which contradicts its own authority. In circulation, on the other hand, capital could hypothetically do without labour.[4] Commercial profit derives not from surplus value created in the

circulation process, for there is none. Rather it derives from the fact that productive capital sells its products to commercial capital below their values, or prices of production, so that commercial capital may then resell the products at their values. Productive capital realises a certain portion of the unpaid labour materialised in the product, then commercial capital realises the remainder.

3 . If commercial profit does not derive from surplus labour performed in the sphere of circulation, this raises the question of whether the workers employed by commercial capital are 'exploited'. Marx does not talk of 'surplus labour' in the sphere of circulation but he does talk of 'unpaid labour'. This points to the notion that while commercial workers are not exploited in the same way as productive workers (direct extraction of surplus value) none the less they are compelled to perform a greater number of hours of labour than they receive in the form of a wage.

This second distinction, between workers employed in production and those employed in circulation functions, is considerably more problematic than the first. Berthoud (1974) argues that it represents the dialectical completion of Marx's theory: the first distinction is inadequate on its own, while the second complements and refines it. But there is a tension between the two criteria which cannot be argued away. According to the first version, the actual tasks performed by the workers are irrelevant to the determination of their labours as productive or unproductive. All that matters is whether or not they are employed in order to expand capital. Yet in the second version the tasks do matter: operating a lathe or driving a truck in the pay of a capitalist enterprise is productive, while keeping accounts, arranging finance, advertising or selling the product, is not. The criterion to which Marx appeals in the second case is the production of 'use value'. Driving a truck to take a commodity to the point of sale is a contribution to the use value of the product (altering its spatial location) but selling it, or keeping account of its sale, is not. It doesn't matter what particular task the 'productive' worker performs, *so long as he is producing a use value* — the precondition for creating value. Now the principle of this exclusion is not that the circulation work fails to be 'really useful'. Marx is quite clear that the concept of 'use value' is not to be used as a moral category, defined in relation to a theory of 'true human needs'. Even the most frippery luxury destined for capitalist consumption is a 'use value' provided someone is willing to buy it. Rather, the labour of circulation is excluded from the sphere of 'use value' because it is supposedly necessitated solely by the fact that products take the form of private property·in a capitalist economy. It is this conception which is problematic. True, buying and selling, payment of money incomes, borrowing and lending money, keeping monetary accounts are all activities specific to a monetary economy, but on the other hand they represent certain functions in relation to the distribution process which would have to be performed in any developed economy. The *form* is specific to generalised commodity production but certain of the 'content' is not. Take for instance the labour involved in the payment of money incomes and in the sale of consumer goods to workers. As I mentioned in the Introduction, in criticism of Marx's idea of 'abundance' in communist society, it seems very likely that in any forseeable form of economy the output of many consumer goods will be less than the volume which people would like to consume if they could do so at no cost. Unless one envisages a system of universal rationing (which would itself require considerable labour to administer), a socialist economy would need some system of consumption allowances. These need not take the form of wages — they could be distributed on the basis of 'need' (however defined) rather than on work/bargaining-power/cost of development of labour power — but all the same there would be a need to calculate and distribute the allowances, and to 'cancel' acquisitions of consumer goods against the allowance. This is effectively what a part of commercial work accomplishes at present, through the form of money. Of course, it may be possible to reduce considerably the routine labour this activity currently involves, with the development of information technology, as well as the reorganisation of social relations, but then the same goes for a lot of routinised labour in eminently 'productive' manufacturing industry. I am not suggesting here that *all* the commercial and financial work in the sphere of circulation performs a necessary social function, irrespective of the form of property relations. The point is merely that 'keeping accounts' in the broad sense is not a specifically capitalist requirement. Indeed it may be argued that certain of the functions performed by accounting within the capitalist circulation process, while they would be transformed in a planned economy, would actually be expanded upon. 'Socialist accounting' in the context of planning would have to be more elaborate than capitalist, in that it would not deal in only the single dimension of monetary magnitudes but would have to construct indices of social costs and benefits.

If there is truth in this contention, that the labour involved in 'circulation' is at least in part a specifically 'monetarised' form of activities necessary in any developed economy, then Marx's second distinction between productive and unproductive labour must be problematic. Marx took Smith to task for taking an overly 'Scottish'' or arbitrarily literal view of what labour was to count as productive (Smith reckoned it had to be worked up in a solid, enduring 'vendible commodity'), and we have seen that Marx would include drivers, singers and teachers as productive provided they are employed in order to make profits, yet he seems to draw an equally arbitrary distinction himself in labelling the 'circulation' workers employed by capitalist enterprises as unproductive. Marx's second distinction between productive and unproductive labour is a shaky foundation for class analysis. Nonetheless, let us proceed to see what use Poulantzas makes of the criterion. I shall concentrate on his arguments concerning the middle classes of capitalism, for in his view 'the definition of the petty bourgeoisie is the focal point of the Marxist theory of social classes', in that it reveals very clearly the problem of the criteria to be used in defining the boundaries of class.

Poulantzas on social classes

In the third section of 'Classes in Contemporary Capitalism', Poulantzas deals with the complex of problems associated with the 'middle classes' of capitalism: how is the working class to be delimited? What is the class determination of those agents who are strictly speaking neither bourgeois nor proletarian? Among these latter what are the significant lines of division into strata and fractions? He sums these problems up as the 'question of the new petty bourgeoisie'. Here is the skeleton of his argument in attacking this question:

1. Productive labour is a necessary condition for membership of the working class, since for Marxism 'productive labour' in the capitalist mode designates the place of exploited labour within capitalist relations of production. Only workers who produce surplus value are exploited in the strict sense and thus they are the only candidates for membership of the proletariat proper.

2. On the other hand productive labour is not a *sufficient* condition for membership of the working class. The category of productive labour becomes extended, with the development of the 'collective labourer' in industry, to include those supervisors, low-level managers, engineers, technicians, draughtsmen, etc., whose labour forms a necessary part of the total 'productive organism' within capitalist machine industry. But not all of these agents are members of the working class. This is because the structure of the collective

labourer is not a 'neutral' outgrowth of the development of production, based on a technical division of labour alone. Rather it carries within it the specifically capitalist *social division of labour* — a double division between mental and manual labour and between supervisors and supervised, which forms the basis of a class division. The division of mental and manual labour cannot be understood in terms of general descriptive criteria ('handwork' vs. 'brainwork') but should be grasped as 'the form taken by the political and ideological conditions of the (production) process within the process itself'. Basing his arguments on Marx's treatment of the collective labourer in Volume One of 'Capital', Poulantzas maintains:

'(a) that the supports of mental labour tend to become part of the productive collective worker, but that (b) at the same time, and even for the same reasons (capitalist socialisation), mental labour separates off from manual labour in an "antagonistic contradiction" ' (Poulantzas, 1975, p. 235).

Thus he argues that the 'supports of mental labour' within the collective worker do not form part of the working class. The agents who perform mental labour occupy a place in the social division of labour which is antagonistic to the proletariat, since the whole apparatus of 'mental labour' functions to exclude the workers from 'knowledge', such as it is, and to give them the impression that they are fit for no more than donkey work.

For Poulantzas, the division between mental and manual labour is primarily an ideological structure, and an 'ideological' criterion of class membership, but it also has a political aspect. Poulantzas maintains that some of the 'supports of mental labour' are at the same time agents of a directly political domination over the working class: the foreman and supervisors. That is, he proposes that the relations of domination and subordination between supervisors and foremen and rank-and-file workers be understood as the reproduction in miniature of the global domination of the bourgeoisie over the proletariat. These relations of power at the place of production become a 'political' criterion of class differentiation.

3 . Poulantzas therefore defines the working class by the intersection of the criteria of productive labour and manual labour. In his argument this is a particularly restrictive definition, since he gives a rather narrow definition of both productive labour and manual

labour.

a)   *Productive labour:* Poulantzas starts off with the traditional Marxist definition of productive labour, i.e. labour which produces surplus value. But then he makes an addition to the definition:

'We shall say that productive labour, in the capitalist mode of production is that labour which produces surplus value *while directly reproducing the material elements that serve as the substratum of the relation of exploitation labour that is directly involved in material production by producing use values that increase material wealth'* (ibid., p. 216).

b)   *Manual Labour:* Poulantzas does not define mental and manual labour by reference to the content of labour, but rather by reference to the structure of ideological social relations within which labour is carried out.

'We could thus say that every form of work which takes the form of a knowledge from which the direct producers are excluded, falls on the mental labour side of the capitalist production process, irrespective of its empirical/natural content, and that this is so whether the direct producers actually do know how to perform this work but do not do so (again not by chance), or whether they in fact do not know how to perform it (since they are systematically kept away from it) or whether again there is quite simply nothing that needs to be known' (ibid., p. 238).

By the use of this criterion Poulantzas consigns to the realm of mental labour all the work involved in 'accounting, banking, insurance, "services" of various kinds, "office work", and the greater part of the civil service' (ibid., p. 258). 'Manual labour' then becomes restricted to the labour of the productive industrial proletarians.

4 . Having defined the working class, Poulantzas then has the problem of analysing the class determination of the substantial category of wage and salary earners who are excluded from the proletariat on his definition — all but the manual industrial workers. He delimits the bourgeoisie proper by reference to 'real economic ownership', that is, the power to assign the means of production to given uses and to dispose of the products obtained, and argues that all wage labour which does not fall into the categories of proletariat or bourgeoisie should be considered as forming a 'new petty bour-

geoisie'. Clearly the economic position of wage-workers engaged in 'mental labour' as employees of capitalist enterprises or the state is very different from the economic position of the traditional petty bourgeoisie of Marxist theory, since the latter class depends upon independent artisanal production and small scale trading. But Poulantzas argues that the 'structural determination' of social classes involves political and ideological, as well as economic, determinants, so that if seemingly disparate economic positions in fact produce similar effects at the political and ideological levels, the agents occupying those positions must be considered as members of the same social class. Broadly speaking, Poulantzas' contention is that the atomised bureaucratic organisation of 'mental labour' in capitalism and the possibilities for 'career advancement' in the sphere of 'mental labour', provide the material basis for 'petty bourgeois' politics and ideology. So the 'mental' wage workers should be considered as a petty bourgeois class fraction.

This, then, is the bare skeleton of Poulantzas' position: the working class is defined by the intersection of productive labour (economic determination) and manual labour (political and ideological determination), and the non-proletarian wage workers are to be grasped as a 'new petty bourgeoisie' by virtue of the effects of their intermediate position with respect to the antagonism of bourgeoisie and proletariat.

Of course Poulantzas' argument for this position is not as bare as is suggested in the summary above. In fact his argument is complex but clear, and is supported by a wide variety of suggestive observations. So it is not surprising that the critique of Poulantzas should have formed the starting point for two of the most serious recent attempts to develop the Marxist theory of classes, those of Olin Wright, and Cutler *et al*. Having exposed the skeleton of his argument, let us consider the ways in which it can be criticised. I shall first examine some problems in Poulantzas' use of the concepts of productive labour and manual labour, then move to Olin Wright's criticism, which centres on the conceptualisation of capitalist property relations. I said earlier that Poulantzas adopts a restrictive definition of both productive labour and manual labour. In fact, even if one accepts his definition of the proletariat by the intersection of productive labour and manual labour there is room for argument over the precise application of these criteria.

1. **Productive labour:** Poulantzas defines this as labour producing surplus value in *'material production'*. He presents this qualification of the definition of productive labour by reference to the production of surplus value alone, as a mere explication of what is implicit

in Marx, but it is clear that Marx did not hold this position. He held firmly to the determination of productive labour by the production of surplus value, regardless of the material form of the product. In order to be productive, a labour must produce use values which contain a surplus value, but these 'use values' need not be durable physical objects. Surplus value may just as well be materialised in the performance of a song, or the reading of a lecture, or the serving of a meal, as in nuts and bolts, if the workers performing these services are being employed by a capitalist in order to expand his capital. We have seen that Marx himself undermines the principle of the irrelevance of the 'determinate content' of the labour in the case of 'circulation' workers, but the licence for this inconsistency was the supposition that circulation workers do not produce any use values. I argued that this licence was spurious, but even if that argument is not accepted, Marx's qualification cannot validate Poulantzas' 'explication'. His addition to Marx's definition of productive labour is reminiscent of the Physiocrats, who saw the production of surplus value as the piling up of physical surplus wealth, rather than as a social relation.

2 . **Manual Labour:** We have seen that Poulantzas detaches the definition of mental and manual labour from the nature of the tasks performed. From a Socialist perspective it is quite correct to emphasise that the present division between 'mental' and 'manual' labour is not reducible to a neutral 'technical' division of tasks, and that it has the effect of reinforcing social divisions but there are problems in the way Poulantzas applies this conception. He seems to imply that only productive workers can be real 'manual' workers, since all unproductive labour is invested with ideological 'know-how', however spurious, which makes it socially 'superior' to industrial labour and inaccessible to the industrial workers. This position is hardly tenable. There is a substantial category of 'unproductive' labour which surely falls on the 'manual' side of the socially-constructed division between mental and manual labour: for example, the work of state-employed hospital porters and auxiliaries, the work of caterers and cleaners in state institutions, the work of local authority roadmen and transport drivers. This work is 'unproductive', in the sense that such workers are employed by the state to provide social use values rather than to expand capital value, yet the conditions of work, and the social status with which the work is invested, do not differ significantly from the case of employment by private capital.

If one accepts that the concept of 'manual' labour must have a broader application than Poulantzas admits, this opens up an anomaly in his delimitation of the working class. Poulantzas notes that not all productive workers are manual workers, but I also argue that not all 'manual workers' are productive workers. If this is the case, what is the class determination of the unproductive manual workers? Poulantzas maintains that productive labour is a necessary condition for membership of the working class, so on his reckoning they must form a fraction of the new petty bourgeoisie. But how does this square with his mode of argument in defining the new petty bourgeoisie? In that argument he maintains that agents occupying different economic places will be considered as members of the same social class if the positions with respect to the structure of political and ideological domination and subordination, corresponding to those different economic places, are sufficiently similar. So surely the division between mental and manual labour, which according to Poulantzas expresses the capitalist social division of labour, should be decisive in delimiting the working class. The working class should be defined by manual labour, regardless of whether the workers in questions are productive or unproductive, since manual labour corresponds to 'the place of political and ideological subordination' in capitalism. Poulantzas avoids this inconsistency by sweeping the possibility of unproductive manual labour under the carpet, and thus he leaves himself open to the charge that he is deploying his criteria in an attempt to establish essentially 'proletarian' status for a pre-given social category, manual workers in industry, without following through the logic of his concepts.

This problem of the relative decisiveness of the 'economic' criterion of productive labour as against 'political and ideological' criteria in delimiting social classes, forms the starting point of Erik Olin Wright's critique of Poulantzas.[5] Olin Wright points out that while Poulantzas maintains that the economic determination of social classes is the primary determination, in practice he lays much more weight on the 'political and ideological' criteria, both in excluding 'mental' productive workers from the working class and in establishing the unity of his 'petty bourgeoisie'. Poulantzas sets up a topology of criteria of class determination which looks something like this:

Economic criterion: Productive labour/Unproductive labour.
Political criterion: Supervision and policing of the workforce.
Ideological criterion: Mental labour/Manual labour.

Apart from the anomaly of the unproductive manual workers noted above, he makes the political and ideological criteria bear the main weight in defining both the working class and the 'new petty bourgeoisie'. Olin Wright argues that the distinction between productive and unproductive labour is not the relevant 'economic criterion' in differentiating social classes. He gives two arguments in support of this position. First he maintains that the distinction between productive and unproductive labour does not isolate two distinct categories of workers, but rather two 'dimensions' of labour activity. That is, many workers perform both productive and unproductive labour in the course of their work. This does not appear to be a valid objection. On the basis of Marx's second distinction (production/circulation) *some* workers could be regarded as performing both productive and unproductive labour. Consider an assistant in a supermarket: insofar as he or she is engaged in *transporting* and *storing* products his/her labour would be 'productive', but when he or she is tending the till and supervising payment for products as commodities his/her labour would be part of the 'unproductive' work of circulation. I have noted above the problems in maintaining this distinction, but even if one does subscribe to it this case of overlap would be seen as exceptional. The greater number of manual industrial workers perform, on this criterion, productive labour alone and all the employees in banking and finance are unproductive. Further, Marx's first distinction (labour employed by capital/labour employed out of 'revenue') draws a definite line between two categories of workers.

Olin Wright's second argument on this point is more telling. He maintains that even if productive and unproductive labour are generally distinct there is no good reason to believe that unproductive workers will, by virtue of their 'unproductive' nature alone, have a class interest which is distinct from that of productive workers. Olin Wright supports this point by reference to the 'interest in socialism' on the part of the unproductive workers. Now this reference to 'interest' is untheorised in his paper, and it rather begs the question, but it is possible to sustain the point in another way. Colliot-Thélène (1975) attacks the use of productive labour as a criterion of class division, from a different angle. For Marx, 'unproductive labour' is an economic category which covers all labour, in capitalist social formations, which does not contribute directly to the production of surplus value. As such it includes labours located in a wide variety of social positions, from domestic service and the labour of independent petty producers, to state employment in all its forms (other than commodity-producing nationalised industries), to the commercial labour of circulation which forms a necessary stage in the cycle of capital reproduction. Colliot-Thélène concentrates on the question of the workers employed in the sphere of circulation, and argues that they are just as much proletarians as the productive workers. Of course if this point is carried it does not prove that all unproductive wage-earners are 'proletarians', but it does show that Marx's concept of productive labour is not in itself relevant to the question of class determination.

Colliot-Thélène supports her position by pointing out that the problem Marx is addressing when he develops the concepts of productive labour in the sphere of production and unproductive labour in the sphere of circulation, is the problem of the functioning of the different fractions of capital in the global process of capital accumulation, and not at all the question of the class membership of commercial employees. It is true historically that in the earlier stages of capitalist development commercial workers were paid higher wages and salaries than industrial workers, that they had greater access to the 'secrets' of management, and that their labour carried a higher 'social status'. But as Marx pointed out, even in his day these relative advantages were being eroded. Commercial employees were paid higher wages because of the relatively high level of qualification presupposed by office work. But with the advance of public education there is no longer a premium on the skills of reading, writing, and arithmetic, and also much office work has become greatly simplified and reduced in scope by the increasing division of labour in the spheres of commerce and finance, so the initial advantages of such employment have been largely eliminated. The privileged position of commercial workers was a feature of the historically uneven development of proletarianisation, and not a structural feature of the capitalist mode of production. Just as industrial capital on the one hand and commercial and financial capital on the other form fractions of one class so the industrial, commercial and financial workers they employ are all fractions of the proletariat. In short, there is no evidence that Marx intended the concepts of productive and unproductive labour as definitive of a class division (he even wrote of the 'commercial proletariat'), and although that does not prove the point either way Poulantzas has not produced any compelling reasons why we should take the concepts in that way.

A different criterion of 'economic class place': Olin Wright

If we reject Poulantzas' identification of productive labour as the relevant 'economic criterion' for defining the proletariat, we topple the keystone of his argument, and we have to re-think both the content of the idea of 'economic class place' and the relation between economic and other determinations of social class. Both Olin Wright and Colliot-Thélène attempt to do this in such a way as to establish *property relations* as the key element in the economic determination of classes, and to relate the effectivity of determinations at the level of mental labour/manual labour and supervisory powers to the position of agents within the property relations of capitalism. As I argued above the core property relations of capitalism can be summed up schematically in the formula of a two-fold separation: (i) the separation of the units of production from one another, as objects of private property, and (ii) the separation of the direct producers from the means of production, such that the producers can operate the means of production only on terms laid down by their owners (the wage contract). Olin Wright and Colliot-Thélène take this second separation, the separation of the producers from the means of production, as their point of departure, and analyse its forms and conditions.

We have seen how Poulantzas analyses the concept of property in the means of production, breaking it down into the levels of economic ownership and possession. Olin Wright takes this analysis a stage further, and examines the way in which the differentiation of the functions of capital has affected the class determination of the agents in the capitalist production process. That is, he argues in terms of various 'degrees' of ownership of, and separation from, the means of production. His central thesis is that 'ownership of the means of production' and 'separation from the means of production' are not just two poles. Rather they may be considered as the ends of a spectrum. At the one extreme, full economic ownership of the means of production defines an unambiguously bourgeois class place, and at the other extreme complete separation from control over production defines an unambiguously proletarian class place, but in between we find what Olin Wright describes as 'contradictory class locations'. Employees who fall within the category of contradictory locations cannot be defined as proletarian or bourgeois at the level of economic relations alone.

In terms of Poulantzas' categories of property relations, Olin Wright retains the concept of economic ownership, to refer to control over investment and resources, but argues that 'possession', the concept which Poulantzas used to denote 'ability to put the means of production into operation', must be further analysed. The differentiation of the functions of capital through the increasing division of labour means that 'possession' is not a unitary power, but is broken down into the levels of control over the means of production and control over labour power. Using these concepts of property Olin Wright defines the class place of the bourgeoisie by reference to the union of the power of economic ownership and the powers of possession over means of production and the labour power of others. In this category he places the 'traditional' capitalist entrepreneur, who enjoys both legal ownership and economic control over his enterprise, and the top executive of the modern capitalist concern, who may or may not have a substantial shareholding in the enterprise but who, it is argued, exercises full economic ownership. At the bottom of the hierarchy the proletariat is defined by complete exclusion from control over the means of production and labour power, or in other words by economic 'propertylessness'. Between these class places Olin Wright identifies a series of 'contradictory locations', from the top managers, who exercise powers of possession over the means of production and labour power but have only limited access to the powers of economic ownership, down to the foremen and supervisors who are separated from the proletariat only by their limited control over labour power.

Using the same categories he marks out the class place of the traditional petty bourgeoisie of independent production by reference to economic ownership and possession of small-scale means of production, without any control over labour power. The petty bourgeois has his own means of production, but he works this by himself, or with family help, and does not hire wage workers. Two other 'contradictory locations' close to the petty bourgeoisie are considered: the semi-autonomous employees, who differ from the proletariat proper by virtue of their limited control over their production process, and the small employers, whose control over the labour power of others is minimal. There are thus two kinds of 'contradictory locations' in Olin Wright's theory. There is a contradictory location within the capitalist mode of production itself between the two major classes of that mode (the location occupied by managers) and there are the contradictory locations between the classes of the capitalist mode and the petty bourgeoisie (occupied by semi-autonomous employees and small employers). The petty bourgeoisie, based on petty commodity production and exchange, is not itself taken to be a class of this mode.

How does Olin Wright analyse these 'contradictory locations'? His position is that when an agent has a contradictory location at the economic level, political and ideological relations enter into the determination of his class position:

'The extent to which political and ideological relations enter into the determination of class position is itself determined by the degree to which those positions occupy a contradictory location at the level of social relations of production' (1976, pp. 39-40).
Or again:
' ... it is the indeterminacy of class determination at the economic level which allows political and ideological relations to become effective determinants of class position' (ibid., p. 40).

This conception solves the problem which Wright identifies in Poulantzas' theory: if the economic determination of social class is supposedly primary, how can political and ideological criteria override the economic criterion? Wright argues that if we develop the correct economic criterion the other criteria fall into place. 'We need a criterion for use of political and ideological relations which is itself determined by economic relations', and property is the basis for that criterion.

So much for the schematic presentation. Let us pause on this conception and consider in more detail the adequacy of Olin Wright's development of the concept of property relations.

Property relations once more

I have already argued in favour of taking property relations as the basis for defining the pattern of economic class relations. In Chapter 1, I showed the link between the concepts of bourgeoisie and proletariat and the form of exclusive possession of the means of production in capitalism. But Olin Wright's arguments oblige us to consider this point in more detail: what precisely do we mean by 'ownership' or 'possession' of the means of production? Can we properly talk of 'degrees' of possession? Can we make a precise identification of the class of 'owners' in modern capitalism?

Let us recall the Poulantzian conception of property which Olin Wright is concerned to develop. This conception involves a double distinction: first between the formal legal right to ownership of the means of production ('juridical ownership') and the substantive powers of control; second, within the latter set of powers, Poulantzas distinguishes 'economic ownership' ('the power to assign the means of production to given uses and so to dispose of the products obtained') and 'possession' ('the capacity to put the means of production into operation'). According to this schema, during the phase of 'manufacture' there was a dissociation between 'economic ownership' and 'possession' — the former being held by the capitalists and the latter by the artisans whom they employed, who were still in the position of directing their own labour process. With the rise of capitalist production proper (the 'real subsumption of Labour under capital' in Marx's terminology) 'economic ownership' and 'possession' (and also juridical ownership) are united in the hands of the capitalist entrepreneur. Henceforth, within capitalist development, economic ownership and possession are said to correspond to the 'place of capital'. The rise of the joint stock company complicates the issue, since it introduces a dissociation between juridical owners (shareholders) and the agents who carry out the substantive functions of economic ownership and possession (i.e. managers at various levels), but it does not change the essentials. Poulantzas is critical of the Berle and Means/Burnham 'managerial revolution' arguments: there is not really a 'divorce of ownership and control' in the modern corporation, since on his definition economic ownership *is* control. The partial 'divorce' between *juridical* and *economic* ownership does not mark any fundamental discontinuity in the reproduction of capitalist production relations. Poulantzas, employing Marx's conception of the individual capitalist as merely the 'bearer' or 'support' *(Trager)* of the capitalist property relation, argues that if the 'supports' of private property in early capitalism (i.e. the owner-entrepreneurs) were members of the bourgeoisie, then the 'supports' of corporate private property (the managers) are equally bourgeois.

We have seen that Olin Wright takes over this conception, only he develops it at one point: he argues that economic ownership and possession have become differentiated into matters of degree. The managerial functions are carried out by a hierarchical bureaucracy within the corporation and depending on his position within the hierarchy an individual may be *more or less* in control of means of production and labour power. This gives rise to the 'contradictory location' of those individuals who have sufficient powers of control to be classed as participating in capitalist property (and are therefore not proletarians in economic terms), yet do not have sufficient autonomy and 'high-level' sway to count as outright 'economic owners' (and so are not economically bourgeois either).

Now the distinction between juridical or formal property rights and effective economic control is important, and clearly stated by Poulantzas. But I would argue that the twofold schema of economic ownership/possession is too vague to be very useful in analysing the form of property in the modern joint-stock company. Holesovsky (1977) provides a more adequate breakdown of the substantive powers of ownership in his fourfold schema, quoted below:

1. *Custody rights*, i.e., authority to make decisions associated with the actual utilization of the owned asset. This is what is meant by 'possession', real 'control', or 'management' of the asset.
2. *Usufruct rights*, i.e., authority to claim the appropriation of new assets resulting from the utilization of the object of ownership (such as value added in production), either directly in the form of real products or in the form of income (wages, interest, rent or profit).
3. *Alienation*, in the sense of transferring the ownership through sale or bequest to another subject.
4. *Destruction*, which needs no comments.

(Holesovsky, 1977, p. 41)

In the following discussion, I propose to use this categorisation in place of that of Poulantzas. A terminological point should be noticed: in the Holesovsky scheme (as also in Cutler *et al.,* 1977) the term 'possession' is used to refer to real exclusive control over an asset, and is not used in Poulantzas' narrower sense (carried over by Olin Wright). Let us put these concepts to work. In the case of personal ownership of the means of production by a capitalist entrepreneur, all the substantive ownership powers are centred in the individual capitalist, along with the juridical title to those powers, but in the case of the public joint stock company the property relations are much more complex. It may be useful to set out the formal juridical relations first, then discuss any discrepancies between these relations and the allocation of substantive powers. In formal terms the owners of a joint stock company are its shareholders. The rights attached to this position include the right to receive part of the usufruct of the firm's assets (i.e. the profit) in the form of dividend payments, and the right to elect the board of directors who in turn appoint the top managers. The managers are conceived as the salaried employees of the owners, and their function is to conduct the affairs of the company in the best interests of the owners. At the same time, however, the joint stock company is itself a legal 'personality', capable of entering into contracts and of owning assets. The powers of custody and alienation of the means of production employed by the firm will generally belong not to any individual person but to the joint stock company as such.

Now, it is a commonplace to point out that effective control over the policy of larger joint stock companies by shareholders is a rarity. Shareholders who are also directors or top managers may be party to major decisions, but shareholding as such is not sufficient to ensure effective possession. In the economic literature, the credit for this observation is generally given to Berle and Means (1932) but Marx had argued the same point in Volume Three of 'Capital'. He wrote that the development of stock companies meant

> 'Transformation of the actually functioning capitalist into a mere manager, administrator of other people's capital, and of the owner of capital into a mere owner, a mere money-capitalist... The total profit (for the salary of the manager is, or should be, simply the wage of a specific type of skilled labour, whose price is regulated in the labour-market like that of any other labour)... is henceforth... mere compensation for owning capital that now is entirely divorced from the function in the actual process of reproduction, just as this function in the person of the manager is divorced from ownership of capital' (Marx, 1972, pp. 436-7).

One could hardly wish for a clearer statement of the 'divorce of ownership and control' thesis. In the same pages Marx refers to the dividend payments received by the rentier shareholders as 'interest', emphasising the similarity of the position of shareholders and simple creditors of a company. Shareholders have a legal title to part ownership of the company while creditors do not, but according to Marx this legal title is an increasingly irrelevant fiction. The rentier shareholders are essentially functionless parasites ('mere money-capitalists') who take no part in the actual direction of the firm's activities. Now when Burnham (1944), following Berle and Means, argued the thesis of the divorce of ownership and control, he gave it a particular political inflection: history had played a trick on the Marxists, capitalism had indeed been superseded, not by socialism but by a 'managerial' system. Ironically, Marx's own reflections on the implications of the joint stock form appear consistent with this kind of equivocation. He saw the stock company as a 'transitional' form, representing a contradictory break with the essential features of capitalist property.

> '... the stock company is a transition toward the conversion of all functions in the reproduction process which still remain linked with capitalist property, into mere functions of associated producers, into

social functions' (Marx, 1972, p.437).

Or again:

'... This is the abolition of the capitalist mode of production within the capitalist mode of production itself, and hence a self-dissolving contradiction, which *prima facie* represents a mere phase of transition to a new form of production' (ibid.).

In Marx's view, then, the managers of the joint stock companies were hired employees, the price of whose labour power was determined on the market, and not a new property-owning class. Private property became an irrelevant vestige, ripe for outright abolition. But there has now existed for some considerable time an economic system in which the major branches of large-scale industry are dominated by public joint-stock companies. Either Marx really did 'overlook' the possibility of a post-capitalist 'managerial' system, or else the present system is still capitalist, in which case the concept of property which Marx used in his analysis of the joint stock company as a mere 'transitional' form was faulty. I take the latter view. As Cutler *et al.* (1977) have argued, these remarkable passages from 'Capital' show that Marx was unable to distinguish clearly *personal* private property in the means of pro-duction, and exclusive possession by capitalist enterprises. The former was characteristic of the earlier stages of capitalist development but is in no way essential to the concept of capitalist property relations. It is true that in most cases the shareholders of a joint stock company do not exercise any substantive powers of direction over the company's resources. What they 'own' in effect is merely a marketable financial asset — the share — which offers them the prospect of a dividend depending on the firm's ability to pay. But this does not imply that the means of production are about to pass into the hands of the 'associated producers' as collective social property. The means of pro-duction remain the object of an exclusive possession, by the capitalist enterprise (stock company) itself. Capitalist enterprises remain separate legal subjects and separate units of possession, producing commodities for the market and bound by the requirements of profitability, and the 'producers', whether manual workers or managers, can gain access to the means of production only if they are able to conclude a wage contract with a capitalist enterprise. In this light, the joint stock com-pany may be seen as a *form* of capitalist property, a form distinct from personal ownership, but in no way representing the 'abolition of the capitalist mode of production'.

What then of the Poulantzian view of the managers, and Olin

Wright's differentiated powers of possession within the managerial hierarchy? We have seen that Poulantzas' position is in a sense at the opposite extreme from that of Marx. For Marx the managers represent 'a specific type of skilled labour' and are 'divorced from the ownership of capital'. The emphasis is on the *discontinuity* between the business run by an owner/manager and the stock company. For Poulantzas, if we strip away the legal fictions then the managers can be seen as exercising the powers of economic ownership and/or possession, so that 'In all cases, therefore, the managers are an integral section of the bourgeois class' (Poulantzas, 1975, p. 180). Here it is the essential *continuity* between personal ownership and the joint stock company which is stressed, a continuity which extends to the fact that a particular category of individuals (the managers) can still be seen as the 'bearers' of private ownership, regardless of the complications introduced by the discrepant attribution of juridical ownership to shareholders. Marx's view was criticised above, but the concept of exclusive possession by *capitalist enterprises* which was outlined in that context also provides a means of criticism of Poulantzas. It is the enterprise, as legal subject, which has possession of the means of production and in an important sense this is not a juridical fiction: certainly the enterprise must hire managers to make effective that possession, yet the managers as individuals do not have unconstrained custody of the means of production, nor do they have the right to alienate the firm's assets. There are two points here: first the individual manager is a salaried employee and while his 'job security' may be greater than that of the shop-floor worker it is quite possible for him to be dismissed. Such powers as he does exercise are conditional upon the salary contract. Second, in the case of large enterprises under 'managerial' direction it may be more correct to attribute the decision-making power to the 'managerial apparatus' rather than to managers as individuals. Aside from the continuity of the management structure while individuals are appointed or leave, I mean by this to emphasise the importance of the network of departments within the company, collecting and processing information and preparing recommendations, and the prevalence of boards and committees as units of decision-making. Cutler (1978) has argued along these lines that individual managers are 'responsible' for certain decisions not in the (existential) sense that they are the unique authors of those decisions but in the sense that they are *accountable* for those decisions, as a matter of administrative procedure.

On this view, capitalist property in the means of production is an increasingly impersonal institution. Cutler *et al.* have argued through to the logical conclusion: to a significant extent the class of agents exercising exclusive possession of the means of production is made up not of human persons but of capitalist enterprises as such, and the salaried recruits to the managerial apparatus of such enterprises are 'separated' from the means of production in the classic sense. This conception is given a further twist by the fact that increasingly even the *shareholders* in public joint-stock companies are non-human individuals, principally financial institutions which themselves have their own legal and economic identities. The extent and pace of this 'depersonalisation' of capitalist property are examined comparatively, but with emphasis on the British economy, in the following chapter. In the present context the problem is to assess the implications of impersonal exclusive possession for the theories of class which I have been discussing. If one maintains the basic conception of 'economic' classes as defined by property relations then the implications appear disturbing: the capitalist class includes institutional 'individuals' as well as human individuals, and the managers of modern stock companies, as salaried employees separated from the means of production, form part of the working class. The objection may be made that this conception spirits away a distinction that is socially and politically 'obvious', between, say, managerial employees and manual industrial workers. I have already argued, in the company of Olin Wright and Colliot-Thélène, that Poulantzas misses the mark in using the productive/unproductive labour distinction as a criterion for differentiating classes within the broad category of wage or salary earning employees. Now it appears we have undermined even property relations as a basis for such a differentiation since it was claimed, against Olin Wright, that the managerial employees of a joint-stock company cannot properly be conceived as the economic owners or possessors of the means of production. But the intention behind these arguments concerning property relations is not to reduce the theory of classes *ad absurdum*. Echoing the conclusions of chapter 1, the intention is to make a clear distinction between 'economic classes' defined at the level of property relations, and socio-political collectivities. If one rejects the notion of 'correspondence' between the two, in favour of an examination of the always-specific connections between them, then the conclusions derived from the analysis of property relations become less odd, and more useful, than they may appear at first sight. This argument is developed in the final part of this chapter. But first, lest I should be accused of neglecting an important contribution to the debate, I shall briefly consider one other attempt to draw a line of class division within the ranks of wage and salary earning employees — that of Carchedi.

Carchedi: the function of labour and the function of capital

Carchedi (1977) employs a similar conceptual framework to Poulantzas, in that he too defines social classes in terms of a series of overlapping dichotomies, but he gives this position a rather different slant. He attempts at the outset to derive his three dichotomies as 'aspects' of capitalist relations of production:

1st aspect: capitalist relations of production bind together the *owner*, the *non-owner* and the means of production.

2nd aspect: they bind together the *producer* (typically exploited), the *non-producer* (typically the exploiter) and the means of production.

3rd aspect: they bind together the *labourer* (who performs the 'function of labour') and the *non-labourer* (who performs the 'function of capital').

The first aspect, ownership and separation, refers to a Poulantzian conception of real economic ownership. According to Carchedi this is the 'determinant' aspect of the relations of production and the other two are in some sense subordinate. The second aspect refers to the production of surplus value, and hence the distinction between productive and unproductive labour. But in fact this latter distinction is redundant in Carchedi's analysis. He does not make productive labour into a necessary condition of proletarian status. Only productive workers actually create *surplus value*, and are exploited in the strict sense, but many other wage-earners are 'economically oppressed' in the sense that they perform more hours of labour for their employers than are embodied in their wage. Even if their labour does not create value, Carchedi does not want to exclude these 'economically oppressed' workers from the proletariat.

It is the analysis of the 'third aspect' of the relations of production, the separation of the 'function of labour' from the 'function of capital', which is Carchedi's most distinctive contribution to the debate. In Carchedi's view the 'pure' classes of the capitalist mode of production are defined by a correspondence between the owner/non-owner division and the function of labour/function of capital division: the bourgeoisie both own the means of production and perform the function of capital, while the proletariat are both separated from the means of production and perform the function of labour. But the 'hybrid' new middle classes are defined by a non-correspondence: they do not own the means of production but they nonetheless perform certain functions of capital. Carchedi's definition of the 'new middle class' is therefore quite distinct from Olin Wright's definition of 'contradictory locations', it does not depend on the proposition, criticised above, that managers participate in the economic ownership or possession of the means of production. Rather Carchedi puts the emphasis on the 'functions' performed by different categories of non-owners. So let us examine the basis for this division of functions. Carchedi traces it back to the two-fold nature of management and supervision. The capitalist production process is the 'unity-in-domination' of the labour process (production of use-values) and the process of production of surplus value, with the latter 'dominating' the former. Correspondingly, capitalist management has a double function: (i) in relation to the labour process, management is concerned with the technical co-ordination of production; (ii) In relation to the exploitation process, management carries out control and surveillance of the workforce to ensure the extraction of surplus value. The functions of technical co-ordination, design, etc., while they may fall within the job-titles of 'management' or 'supervision', are in fact functions of the collective labourer, but the function of control and surveillance is purely a function of capital. It is a part of the surplus value producing process, but quite external to the labour process. The agents performing this 'capital function' are by definition 'non-labourers' and excluded from the working class. On this basis, Carchedi distinguishes two categories of 'new middle class' agents: (i) those who do not own the means of production, but whose function is exclusively that of control and surveillance, (ii) those non-owners whose job includes a mixture of certain labour functions alongside certain capital functions.

These arguments are presented by Carchedi as a clarification and expansion of what is implicit in Marx's discussion of the double nature of supervision and management in 'Capital', and it is useful to refer to that discussion as assessing Carchedi's views. In 'Capital', Marx conceives capitalist production as a process in which the production of use-values, or real appropriation of nature, *takes on the form* of the production of value and surplus value. Enterprises produce goods and services, but only if the selling price is right and there is a prospect of profit. There is no question of two *separate* processes going on, rather the production of commodities for profit is the social form of the appropriation of nature in a capitalist economy. By the same token, Marx's conception of the two-fold nature of management and supervision does not imply a separation between two distinct functions:

'The labour of supervision and management, arising as it does out
of an antithesis, out of the supremacy of capital over labour, and
being therefore common to all modes of production based on class
contradictions like the capitalist mode, is directly and inescapably
connected, also under the capitalist system, with productive functions which all combined social labour assigns to individuals at their
special tasks' (Marx, 1972, p. 386).

Or again:

'The control exercised by the capitalist (nowadays typically by
management A.C.) is not only a special function arising from the
nature of the social labour process, and peculiar to that process,
but it is *at the same time* a function of the exploitation of a social labour
process...' (Marx, 1976, p. 449 — emphasis added).

Co-ordination and control of production is a necessary task in any social
form of production. In capitalism it is often organised in a despotic
manner, but it is no less a necessary moment of the real production
process for that.

'Moreover, the co-operation of wage-labourers is entirely brought
about by the capital that employs them. Their unification into one
single productive body, and the establishment of a connection between their individual functions lies outside their competence. These
things are not their own act, but the act of the capital that brings
them together and maintains them in that situation' (ibid.,
pp. 449-450).

On this view, it is highly problematic to try to separate out the 'function of labour' from the 'function of capital', *with the latter conceived as
external to the actual production process* and purely concerned with the
exploitation of labour. Marx reinforces the point in a striking passage
from the 'unpublished chapter' of 'Capital' ('Results of the Immediate
Production Process'). The context is the move from the 'formal subsumption of labour under capital', the stage at which the capitalist
form of property is imposed on a pre-existing artisanal labour process,
to the 'real subsumption' in which the production process itself is
fundamentally altered through the use of machinery, the application
of science to production, and the increased scale of industry:

'This entire development of the productive forces of *socialised labour*..., and together with it the use of science... in the immediate process of production, takes the form of the *productive power of capital*. It does not appear as the productive power of labour...' (Marx, 1976, p. 1024).

In a sense the whole production process becomes a 'function of capital', since it is the capitalist enterprises which organise the collective labourer and carry out the application of new technologies. In relation to the earlier stage of 'manufacture', in the narrow sense (corresponding to Marx's concept of the merely formal subsumption of labour), it may make sense to talk of a *distinct* 'function of capital', since at that stage the actual production process still had its traditional form and the intervention of the capitalist was largely restricted to enforcing discipline on the workforce:

'The work may become more intensive, its duration may be extended, it may become more continuous or orderly under the eye of the interested capitalist, but in themselves these changes do not affect the character of the labour process, the actual mode of working' (ibid., p. 1021).

But this was before the 'specifically capitalist form of production' had come into being. In the latter form of production the *external* relation between exploitation and production proper is abolished. I am not, of course, arguing that Carchedi is wrong merely because he is in disagreement with Marx. I do wish to contest the claim that Carchedi is merely making explicit a conception which is already implicit in Marx, but the more important point is that I find Marx's version more convincing.

If one accepts this view then Carchedi's concept of the 'non-labourer', the agent involved purely in the exploitation process and quite apart from the labour process, must fall. To avoid misunderstanding: Carchedi admits that certain individuals may perform both the function of capital (of the non-labourer) and functions of labour. Indeed his second category within the 'new middle class' is defined as those non-owners who perform this mixture of functions. Yet his concept of the 'non-labourer' requires that these functions be kept distinct, and he claims that in the case of mixture of functions we are dealing with a juxtaposition of temporally discrete tasks. One can perform both functions, but *not* at the same time (Carchedi, 1977, p. 8). If, on the other hand, the despotism of the factory is the *social form* of the organisation of productive labour in capitalist enterprises then the Carchedian concept of the 'non-labourer' is undermined. It is quite legitimate to describe *rentiers* as non-labourers, living off their property income, but Carchedi wants to use the term to include employees whose work involves control and supervision and in this context it misses the mark.

Now it could be argued that although Carchedi's particular attempt to theorise the function of labour/function of capital dichotomy is flawed, nonetheless there is some potential mileage in some form of 'functional' distinction. It is indeed true that managers within capitalist enterprises, and top managers in particular, are charged collectively with a 'special function': coordination and control of labour, means of production and finance with the aim of securing the reproduction of the enterprise as a successful (therefore, at least in the long run, profitable) concern. In respect of this function lower levels of management are accountable to the higher levels, and the top management is in the last instance accountable to the major shareholders and creditors of the enterprise. Also, the top managers in particular may have a personal stake in the successful reproduction of the enterprise, insofar as their own career prospects are more closely tied to that reproduction than is the case for most workers. (Rank and file workers, 'manual' or 'non-manual' may have difficulty getting other work if the enterprise employing them fails, but the fact that their previous employer failed will not in itself count against them. Higher level managers, on the other hand, may be held responsible for the failure of the enterprise which they managed.) Equally, there is no doubt that the exercise of this function can, and often does, lead to conflict between the objectives of management and the demands of the rank and file workforce regarding wage levels, pace and conditions of work, continuing operation of particular plants and so on. The managers represent to the rest of the workforce the 'interests of the enterprise', as it were, and the rest of the workforce may refuse to accept these interests as their own.

Two points must be made here. First, as argued earlier, the performance of this 'special function' (which is a specific social form of a universally necessary function, i.e. securing the reproduction of the units of production) does not make managers into 'non-labourers' or possessors of the means of production. So if one's definition of class is based upon possession/separation, the managers (other than owner-managers in the old style) must fall into the separated (working) class. Second, the distinction drawn above, between managers who are concerned with the reproduction of the enterprise and rank and file workers who are not, is not as absolute as it may seem. It can be drawn in stark black and white only if one regards as paradigmatic a particular despotic strategy of management. One might argue to the contrary that the most successful modern capitalist enterprises, in the advanced capitalist economies, are often those in which management works to enlist the active support of the rest of the workforce for the objectives of the enterprise, in part by making the welfare of the workforce an enterprise objective. Of course there are examples in which the attempt to win the allegiance of the workforce can be represented as a mere ploy (e.g. 'profit-sharing' remuneration schemes in the absence of any substantive participation of workers in the decisions affecting enterprise performance).[6] Yet there are other examples in which this attempt to get rank and file workers to recognise the interests of the enterprise as their own amounts to more than clever manipulation. One thinks, for instance, of the practice of lifetime employment on the part of the Japanese industrial combines, or the attempt to increase the dignity of workers through avoiding social segregation and petty privilege at work, or the practice of listening to, and rewarding, suggestions from workers at all levels regarding improvements in working methods, processes and products. I am not suggesting that modern capitalism has turned all benevolent, but I do claim that the *essential* distinction between 'management interests' and 'worker interests' must be questioned.[7]

Reprise

The contemporary writers discussed above have all, in one way or other, been concerned to mark out a 'middle' place within the class structure of capitalism. This project has shown up in sharp relief the principle of definition of classes — not surprisingly, since to mark out such a middle place is at the same time to mark the boundaries of the bourgeoisie and the working class, and that depends on precise definitions. It may be useful at this stage to summarise my critical comments on the various criteria which have been advanced for defining the places of the different classes.

1 . **Productive labour/unproductive labour:** I argued that this distinction is somewhat problematic within Marx's writing. In particular if one holds to Marx's 'first' definition of productive labour as labour *employed by capital*, regardless of its material content, then the designation of labour of circulation as unproductive appears arbitrary. But

even if we leave aside that criticism, the use of productive labour as a necessary condition of membership of the working class was regarded as arbitrary by all the writers considered, except Poulantzas. There was little evidence that Marx intended the concept of productive labour to be used in that way, and Poulantzas produced no compelling arguments as to why even the humblest (or for that matter, most militant) 'unproductive' clerical worker or council road-sweeper should be denied the 'working class' designation.

2. **Mental labour/manual labour:** Taken literally this dichotomy is practically useless, since there are no labours which involve either pure physical manipulation unaccompanied by any brain processes, or pure ratiocination without any material implementation. But if the distinction is given an 'ideological' interpretation, as with Poulantzas, it again appears to license arbitrary exclusions: typists, for instance, can't be working class because their work involves 'know-how' which is denied to industrial workers; all employees of the service industries are excluded from 'manual labour' in Poulantzas' sense. The use of this criterion leads to a 'class map' which has little to do with the supposedly fundamental issue of property relations. Nonetheless certain of the phenomena which Marxist writers have condensed under the concept of the 'mental/manual' division are of considerable importance; this point will be taken up below.

3. **Property relations:** Position with respect to the property relations of capitalism gave a basic means of defining the bourgeoisie (owners of the means of production as capital) and working class (separated from the means of production and obliged to work for a wage or salary). Olin Wright tried to use property relations to mark out a middle place ('contradictory location') by arguing that ownership/possession is a matter of degree, a spectrum extending from top to bottom of the managerial hierarchy. I argued against this that it is capitalist enterprises and not the managerial employees that have exclusive possession of the means of production.

4. **Function of labour/function of capital:** Carchedi argued that the middle place is occupied by employees (non-owners) who nonetheless perform the function of capital: promoting the exploitation of others without taking a real part in the production process themselves (non-labourers). I argued that this notion depended on an external relationship between 'exploitation' and 'production' which has not existed since the early days of the formal subsumption of labour under capital. There *is* a viable distinction between

the managerial employees' function of directing the operations of an enterprise with a view to securing its reproduction and the rank and file workers' function of working the means of production within that direction, but this distinction does not imply that managers are 'non-labourers'.

All these criteria seem to be flawed in some way as bases for defining class boundaries. One is not, however, denying that there are significant socio-economic distinctions to be made within the broad category of wage and salary earning employees. It is not possible to draw a precise line in the abstract, but there are certain obvious dimensions of differentiation, some of which have already been noted: level of autonomy at work; level of remuneration; degree of control over the labour power of others; degree of access to information regarding enterprise performance and plans; degree of participation in, and responsibility for, enterprise decision-making; degree of intellectual or 'skill' content of work. These kinds of differentiation form an important object of attention for socialists, since the socialist project involves major changes on all counts: democratisation of decision-making in the enterprise, wider and more equal access to information, greater equality of remuneration, abolition of despotic forms of control over labour, extension of the intellectual scope of work and minimisation of repetitive humdrum tasks.

Certain points regarding this differentiation among employees should, however, be noted. First, it is not an exclusively capitalist phenomenon. A similar differentiation is to be found in the Eastern bloc economies (although inequality of income is much less than in the West). The institution of state property and central planning does not automatically eliminate these distinctions and it cannot, therefore, be argued that they are purely an 'effect' of capitalist relations of production.[8] Second, the degree of differentiation differs among capitalist economies, as does the degree to which it is crystallised into a dichotomous division between distinct categories of employees within the enterprise (e.g. 'staff' vs. 'shop-floor') and the extent to which differentiation of work situations correlates with broader cultural and political divisions. The often-made comparison between the UK and Japan is relevant here. Such variations depend on the particular history of the social formation, again it is not possible to deduce the form of differentiation or its political consequences from the bare existence of capitalist production relations.

The tendency of these observations is the following: it is not that Poulantzas, Olin Wright and Carchedi have just failed to come up with the 'right criterion' which would generate a 'correct' general definition of the new petty bourgeoisie/middle class, but rather that this project is mistaken. It is not possible to define such a boundary in the abstract. The concept of the new 'middle class' of employees, in all its variations, is not at par with the traditional Marxist concepts of class (bourgeoisie, proletariat, peasantry, landowners, petty bourgeoisie) which are based on forms of property-holding. In terms of the basic property relations the 'new middle class' employees are members of the working class, since they do not possess any means of production and are therefore constrained to sell their labour power. Marxists have been reluctant to accept this conception, in view of the undoubted divisions within the 'working class' so defined, but in their attempts to define certain categories of employees out of the working class they have been pushed into a kind of conceptual gerrymandering. Better to admit that the divisions within the working class, in the broad sense, are not such as to permit a conceptual segregation at the level of the 'capitalist mode of production', or even 'modern capitalism', but have to be investigated more specifically in the context of particular social formations. Certainly, one can find common features, but in reducing all the aspects of differentiation to a single dichotomy of universal application (proletariat/new middle class or proletariat/new petty bourgeoisie) one loses too much information which is relevant to questions of socialist strategy.

To return for a moment to Poulantzas, there is a nice irony here, in that whilst he refused to accept a broad economic definition of the working class, as wage or salary earning employees separated from the means of production, on the grounds that such a definition fails to grasp politically important differentiations, he actually recognised that even his own complex theorisation of class boundaries does not enable one to draw any definite political conclusions. This recognition is embodied in the 'escape clause' which he provides, that is, his distinction between (structural) class 'place' and (conjunctural) class 'position'. To explain: we have noted Poulantzas' insistence that 'economic' criteria alone (property, productive labour) are insufficient for distinguishing social classes, and that 'political' and 'ideological' relations must enter into the definition (basically authority relations within the enterprise, and the mental/manual labour divide respectively). But Poulantzas makes a firm distinction between these political and ideological 'structural features' which enter into the definition of classes, and the actual political or ideological stand taken up by individuals or groups at any given moment. He argues on two levels.

In the first instance there is a 'structural determination' of social classes by the structure of social relations. This structural determination assigns the 'class places' of the agents in the social formation. On a second level there is the question of the 'class positions' adopted by the agents. By 'class position' Poulantzas means position on the current economic, political and ideological issues in a definite social formation. The idea is that the structural determination of class *places* in some sense fixes the limits of variation of class *positions* in the conjuncture, but this proposition is effectively subverted by the following qualification.

> 'A social class, or a fraction or stratum of a class, may take up a class position that does not correspond to its interests, which are defined by the class determination that fixes the horizon of the class's struggles' (Poulantzas, 1975, p. 15).

For all the effort he expends on the structural demarcation of proletariat and new petty bourgeoisie it transpires that, according to the theory of 'class positions', a 'petty bourgeois' employee might well take up a 'proletarian' class position in the conjuncture, or vice versa. In a sense, Poulantzas is well advised to provide himself with such an escape clause. Certainly the alternative available within the Marxist tradition, a thorough-going reductionism in which actual popular struggles are simply an effect of the structure, is unattractive. As we have seen in the Introduction to this work (section entitled 'Some concepts of structure in Marxism') such a position means either (a) recourse to a Hegelian type of teleology to dynamise the structure or (b) a lapse into a kind of immobilism of self-reproducing structures. On the other hand, Poulantzas' qualification is clearly unsatisfactory. It gives rise to a dislocation between a theorised domain of structures and a domain of 'conjunctures' which seems to fall below the level of theorisation, an area of brute complexity which may or may not reflect structural determinations. Yet in this Poulantzas is not alone. Hindess (1977) has argued that on this point Poulantzas' mode of escape is rather similar to that of Lukács, with his distinction between the 'class consciousness' supposedly deducible from the structure of class relations and the empirical 'consciousness' of the members of social classes at any particular time. Again, the latter may in fact fail to correspond with the former (see Lukács, 1971, p. 79). Carchedi ends up in much the same equivocation when he writes that class consciousness is determined 'by the objective position agents have in the class structure and by the way the awareness of such a position is modified, distorted, crippled, etc. by the economic, political and ideological struggle' (1977, p. 30). The 'struggle', it seems, can make mincemeat of the objective structures.

Class analysis seems to announce its impotence at the very point where it might become directly relevant to political calculation and practice. Why should the members of certain structurally-defined classes take up certain definite political and ideological positions? How can socialists best detach workers and others from anti-socialist ideologies and foster popular support for socialist politics? Silence. All we know is that, *a priori,* true class consciousness (Lukács), or the adoption of class positions in correspondence with structural class interests (Poulantzas), exists as an objective possibility. It appears that the dominant traditions within Marxist class analysis offer us Hobson's choice: either a structural reductionism, simple or complex, or else a disjunction between structure and political behaviour which produces a theoretical indeterminancy at the crucial point.

I have argued in favour of a different mode of analysis — one which moves at several levels (investigation of economic classes at the level of property relations, investigation of social and cultural collectivities, investigation of political forces) unencumbered by the *a priori* assumption of correspondence between these levels and able to identify the specific connections in particular social formations. Each strand of such an analysis has a contribution to make to the development of socialist thinking and socialist politics. The investigation of property relations makes it possible to specify more closely what is at stake in political struggle in the long term, and to pose more accurately the problem of what attitude and policies should be taken up in relation to the organisation and accountability of enterprises and the question of the planning of production. The analysis of social and cultural collectivities, and forms of shared experience and organisation, helps in the identification of potentially fruitful modes of approach to different social groups in the attempt to develop a popular socialist politics. The analysis of political forces, their policies and their bases of support helps to identify opportunities for undermining the support for anti-socialist forces, breaking up reactionary alliances, and confronts socialists with the problem of finding the appropriate 'vehicle' for advancing socialist politics.

It is hoped that the following chapters will at least make a start in demonstrating the validity of these claims.

3
Property relations and the impersonal capital

'In the last instance capitalism aims at the expropriation of the means of production from all individuals' (Marx, 1972, p. 439).

In this chapter and the next my focus is on the economic class structure, defined at the level of property relations. In the preceding chapter I argued that the institution of private property in the means of production has undergone a progressive 'depersonalisation' with the rise of the joint stock company. This chapter is concerned with investigating the conditions which have given rise to this depersonalisation, and the particular forms it has taken. The first section gives a broad historical outline of the development of the impersonal capital and draws some comparisons between the USA and Britain, then the second section concentrates more specifically on the developments in post-war Britain. The last part of this chapter deals with the 'second order depersonalisation' of capitalist property, i.e. the trend towards the replacement of individuals by financial institutions as the dominant holders of shares in industrial and commercial enterprises, and examines the principal forms of relationship between financial institutions and other enterprises. The following chapter then extends this analysis to comprehend the broad issue of 'classes and the financial circulation', preparing the ground for an examination of the consequences of the depersonalisation of property, in terms of the constraints placed upon, and opportunities opened up for socialist politics.

The conditions for the rise of impersonal property

Marx's 'Capital' maintains a strong link between the changing forms of capitalist property and the process of concentration of capital. Capitalist production exhibits an intrinsic tendency towards increased concentration: the development of the productive forces under the impulsion of competition between capitals takes the form of a progressive socialisation — production on an ever larger scale and informed by an increasing application of scientific knowledge — and this mobilisation of the productive power of social labour demands

94

ever larger blocs of capital. The larger, progressive, capitals prosper and grow while the smaller businesses are undercut and driven into bankruptcy or taken over. The personal or family fortune becomes an increasingly restrictive limit to the possible size of capital blocs, just as management by the sole owner or traditional partnership becomes increasingly inappropriate to the complexity of the leading enterprises. But the development of a system of credit makes it possible to centralise the capital of many wealthy individuals or families, and the development of a market for skilled managerial labour means that the operations of large centralised capitals can be directed effectively.

As a rough outline of the historical trend this is not inappropriate, but one should be careful to identify the limits of this form of explanation. The emergence of new forms of capitalist property is not simply the effect of a pre-given tendency towards concentration: the credit system, the managerial labour market, and the legal forms which are necessary conditions for the development of impersonal capitals are not secured by any autonomous dynamic of the productive forces. Also the particular form in which these conditions have been met has differed between national economies, with important effects on the pattern of control over resources and on industrial performance, and further, the *incentives* for increased concentration (in terms of the competitive advantage it affords) have differed between national economies, between branches of industry, and over time in response to technological and social change. So the image of an inexorable and uniform tendency is misleading. The following pages (which draw on the research collected by Chandler and Daems, 1980, as well as Hobsbawm, 1969, Pollard, 1969, and Landes, 1969) chart the development of the modern 'managerial' enterprise — or impersonal capital — in more detail than is conventional in Marxist analyses, in the hope that this will permit a more concrete and fruitful analysis of the economic class relations it sustains and of the implications for socialist objectives.

We may begin this account with the USA, generally acknowledged to be the birthplace of the large-scale integrated capitalist enterprise. Chandler (1980) dates this birth in the latter half of the nineteenth century. In the earlier part of that century American businesses experienced considerable growth, but this was mainly of an *extensive* nature: an expansion of the number of firms rather than of their average size. At this stage there was an increasing specialisation ('division of labour in society' in Marx's terms) and most of the enterprises dealt with a single line of goods and had a single function within the overall reproduction process (i.e. wholesaling *or* retailing *or* production). Co-ordination between these enterprises was principally achieved through market mechanisms. There were very few middle managers employed at this time, and the top managers were generally owners, either part-ners or major shareholders.

From the 1850s onwards, however, new forms of enterprise begin to appear, characterised by a multidivisional structure: one enterprise comprises a number of operating units and the transactions between these units are internalised within the firm. A new hierarchy of mid-dle and top salaried management supervises the work of the operating units and coordination is increasingly achieved by means of this hier-archy, rather than through decentralised market mechanisms, although this trend does not, of course, abolish competition between the large enterprises. Such enterprises tend to develop where managerial co-ordination offers a competitive advantage over market coordination, and this competitive advantage can stem from a variety of sources: by routinising transactions between operating units it may be poss-ible to reduce transaction costs; by integrating production, purchas-ing and distribution the cost of information on markets and supplies may be reduced; 'economies of speed' — the more intensive use of labour power and fixed capital — may be obtained through the schedul-ing of flows and standardisation; administrative coordination makes possible a more ready adjustment of product specification and market services to meet market demand; a steadier cash flow can lower the cost of credit. These potential advantages only become activated, however, when the development of technology and the growth of markets increases the level of economic activity to a speed and volume which runs up against the practical limits of the existing mechanisms of market coordination. It is only then that we see the rapid growth and professionalisation of the managerial strata.

Chandler isolates two broad transitional paths in the development of the large managerial enterprise from the owner-managed traditional firm, depending on the extent to which the enterprise has to rely on external financing for its expansion. What these transitional forms have in common is the recruitment of salaried middle managers with little or no share in legal ownership to coordinate the flow of products and supervise the operating units. The difference arises in that if expan-sion is financed mainly from retained earnings then the founding entre-preneurs and their families may continue to own controlling shares and participate in top management ('family capitalism'), while a reliance on external finance is likely to mean that bankers and other financiers come to participate in the top level decisions ('financial capitalism'). Both of these forms are conceived as transitional in that no family or financial institution is big enough to staff the managerial hierarchy of a large multi-unit enterprise. As salaried managers develop specialised knowledge and techniques, and as the profits generated by expansion come to sustain a greater level of self-financing, the managerial apparatus takes over even the top level decision-making from the owners and financiers. The latter either become full-time professional managers themselves or participate in top level management only in their capacity as board members, in which case they may have a 'veto power' and some control over managerial appointments, but little else.

These conceptions can be given more substance if we examine the sectors in which the large managerial enterprises first took hold: in chronological order, transport and communication then distribution, then production. The railroads became the first 'big business' in the USA, due to the need for centralised operating control and scheduling in the context of an expanding network. Middle managers, responsible to the president and directors of the railroad companies, were employed to supervise and monitor the 'divisions', which operated between fifty and a hundred miles of track each. Concentration proceeded apace so that by 1890, thirty large companies owned and operated two thirds of the US railroad mileage. Since railroad building on such a scale required large amounts of capital the companies developed links with Eastern investment bankers who had access to European funds, bringing financiers onto the boards. Along with the steamship companies, urban transport, utilities and communications, the railroads became prime examples of 'financial capitalism' in the USA.

The sphere of distribution, by contrast, provides an example of a sector which long remained a bastion of 'family capitalism'. The 1850s saw the development of full-line, full-service wholesalers relying on the new transport and communications infrastructure, and these replaced the old factors and commission agents, but by the 1880s the wholesalers were themselves being displaced by new mass retailers: the city department stores, the mail order firms, and the chain stores. These latter again had a multidivisional structure with a buying office for each major product line, and they were able to undercut the wholesaler/retailer nexus, making their profit from volume rather than mark-up. At this stage the distribution firms did not move into manufacturing to any great extent, and with their high cash flow and low capital requirements they had little need for external financing. These enterprises therefore remained under the control of the founders and their families to a much greater extent than the more capital-intensive and long-term undertakings in transport and communications.

The development of new forms of enterprise was slower in production than in the other spheres. While the cost-cutting innovations in distribution mainly involved *organisational* change, comparable innovation in production had to await the *technological* changes which would give mass production a decisive competitive advantage. An incentive for such changes was provided by the development of railroad and telegraph: if materials and products could be shifted faster then there was a premium on innovation for higher output. Again in the latter part of the nineteenth century, three mass production techniques were developed which permitted the exploitation of this new infrastructure by industrial capitals, namely large batch production, continuous flow processing, and the making of machinery by the fabrication and assembly of standard parts. The large batch and process methods became especially important in refining and distilling industries in the 1860s and 70s. In the following years process machinery was developed for consumer goods such as cigarettes, flour, breakfast cereals and canned goods. Development was not so rapid in the metal-making and metal-working industries; the processes involved were relatively highly complex. But the 1870s saw the integration of blast furnaces, Bessemer and open hearth convertors, and rolling and finishing mills at single sites, giving the advantages of lower transport costs and improved scheduling. In the metal-working industries close attention was paid to improving machinery, plant design and 'workforce organisation', the studied fragmentation and 'rationalisation' of traditional labour functions, in search of a higher 'density' of labour and increased productivity, which reached its apogee in Taylorism.

But the application of mass production methods in industry did not in itself require very large managerial hierarchies. The mass producers became fully fledged 'managerial enterprises' only when they integrated forwards into sales and distribution, and this when the existing channels of distribution could not shift and sell their products fast enough. When this form of integration did take place, in the 1880s, the enterprises concerned were to become dominant oligopolies and in a sense the leading examples of the 'modern corporation'. Enterprises linking mass production and mass distribution first emerged clustered in four industry-types: low-priced packaged goods, perishable products for national markets, new mass-produced domestic machinery (all mass consumer markets or Marx's Department II), and high-volume, complex but standardised, producer goods (Department I). Examples of the former include cigarettes, matches, flour, meatpacking, brewing, sewing machines, while the producer goods included agricultural implements and business machines. Aside from the substantial economies of scale realised by the enterprises in these branches, the integration of purchasing, production and distribution established barriers to entry on the part of potential competitors with the result that the dominant firms were able to stabilise their position as market leaders.

The Sherman Anti-Trust Law of 1890, somewhat paradoxically, gave a further boost to the formation of large-scale integrated enterprises in the USA. By outlawing cartels and trusts it encouraged such federations to take the form of holding companies, which partly accounts for the big merger movement that lasted till 1903. Over time these merged enterprises were in a sense 'selected' for their degree of real integration, in that where effective integration under the control of a managerial hierarchy was not achieved the mergers were often commercially unsuccessful. The branches of production in which mergers were most successful remained those which offered the greatest opportunities for mass production and mass marketing, so that by the time of the first world war the largest enterprises were still clustered in the industry-groups where they had first emerged, although they had also developed in the new chemical and automobile industries. By contrast the more labour-intensive industries (such as cloth, wood, leather and printing) saw a much slower development of managerial enterprises.

The merger movement had a significant effect on the pattern of ownership. Growth through mergers generally resulted in a relatively rapid dispersion of shareholdings, which advanced the position of salaried top level management. Chandler argues that by 1918 the majority of large industrial enterprises founded in the pre-war period were under managerial control. Members of their founding families continued to have an impact on top level decision-making only if they were trained as managers, and while some capitalists did make this move there was not in general much financial incentive for them to do so if they were already wealthy as rentiers.

After the first world war there were further changes in the economic structure and strategy of the largest enterprises which put an increased premium on managerial coordination. Many of them adopted a strategy of diversification, in order to make full use of their techniques and marketing apparatuses, and the operation of several product lines under one overall ownership led to a generalisation of the multidivisional structure, as described by Chandler:

'In this type of organisation the general managers of the several autonomous divisions became responsible for coordinating the flow of goods and supervising the operating units that produced and distributed one major product line to one major market; a general office with no operating responsibilities, assisted by a large general staff, concentrated on allocating resources to the various product divisions' (Chandler, 1980, p. 32).

These multidivisional enterprises achieved a relatively high rate of internal financing. Retained funds were supplemented when necessary by working capital from the commercial banks and long-term funds from the securities markets. Security issues took the form of shares (which confer part legal ownership) more often than bonds (which do not), which led to a further dispersion of the formal ownership of enterprises. The representatives of founding families or outside financial interests rarely opposed this trend since the growth which was achieved permitted a steady increase in dividends, and capital gains on the market value of shareholdings. The famous 'conflict of interest' between 'owners' and 'managers', which has become a commonplace proposition in much writing on the 'theory of the firm' since Berle and Means, was not much in evidence!

The rise of managerial and impersonal capitals was permitted by, and in turn accelerated, the professionalisation of management after the turn of the century. Prestigious universities began to set up business schools providing a flow of trained personnel into the managerial labour market, and the managerial employees formed themselves into a number of professional associations producing professional journals. In this way the managerial employees in the USA became a relatively distinct social grouping: specific common interests and ideologies were constructed.

Over the years since 1945 managerial enterprises have clearly attained an increasingly dominant position, whether this is measured by employment, assets, or value-added in production. This has gone along with a rise in diversification and an increasingly important role for international operations. All this is well-documented by Marxist, and other, writers. What is particularly interesting in Chandler's account is the demonstration that the process dates back, in the USA, to the late nineteenth century at least, and the investigation of the particular conditions which permitted the emergence of impersonal capitals/managerial enterprises. We shall have more to say about post-war developments, but first let us compare the pre-war US experience with that of Britain and Europe.

In outline, the rise of managerial enterprises has been slower and more recent in Britain and Europe. Multi-unit enterprises first appeared in the late nineteenth century in certain capital-intensive industries with a need for professional management, but mass production (and assembly in particular) was not so well represented as in the USA. Owners continued to manage their enterprises for longer; the managerial class was smaller and showed less signs of professionalisation. There was more reliance on existing market mechanisms, and less integration of mass production with mass distribution, the combination which gave rise to the most dynamic US enterprises. In seeking to explain this differential development Chandler places most emphasis on the size and nature of the markets faced by enterprises in Europe and in the States. The discrepancy in growth rates of the market between the USA and Britain is certainly striking: in 1880 the National Income and population of the USA were roughly 1.5 times greater than that of Britain; by 1900 the difference had widened to a factor of 2, and by 1920 to a factor of 3. Further, tight labour markets in the USA brought higher wages and a greater potential consumer demand. And it can be argued that the distribution of incomes was more skewed in Britain and Europe, and regional and class tastes in general more differentiated. The conditions of existence of large-scale mass production/mass retailing Department II enterprises were not met on a broad scale till after 1945. So, with the exception of the integrated food and brewing enterprises in Britain, the first large integrated enterprises in Europe were concentrated in producer goods (Department I): primary metals, shipbuilding, heavy machinery, chemicals.

The first giant European enterprises mainly supplied either non-standardised goods for industrial firms, or materials for building transportation systems and establishing basic industries in nations beginning to industrialise, or arms for the growing militarisation of the rest of the world. These latter emphases obviously reflect the relatively strong colonial/imperial interests of the European powers and Britain in particular. The production and distribution of consumer goods remained for much longer the preserve of smaller enterprises using craft techniques, and commercial middlemen. In this context 'family capitalism' continued to flourish. The case of Germany was rather different: arriving late among the imperialists it had at first smaller markets and lower cash flows which led to a greater dependency on external finance, and gave rise to a continuing strong interventionist role for the banks ('financial capitalism').

Legal conditions also played a part. Until the post war years the American preoccupation with 'Anti-Trust' and 'freedom of competition' did not form a dominant strand in European economic policy. Indeed, in Germany cartels were viewed favourably after cartellisation had proved effective in weathering the recession of 1873. As a result there was not the same incentive as in the USA to circumvent anti-trust legislation by forming large integrated enterprises: federations of family enterprises remained a legally acceptable form of organisation. Such federations, which took the form of holding companies in Britain and cartels in France and Germany, permitted some coordination of marketing and pricing while placing relatively little reliance on managerial coordination and leaving room for decision-making by individual owners or their representatives. There was possibly a greater social value placed upon such autonomy, and family identification with particular enterprises, in Europe, so that owners sometimes chose not to expand rather than losing personal control. In the British motor industry, for example, Morris and Austin resisted merger during their own lifetimes, and in the British steel industry during the inter-war years family trusts and boards inhibited the horizontal and vertical mergers required to take full advantage of the advances in production technology.

Emphasising the role of mass consumer markets, Chandler argues that the big shift towards dominance by managerial enterprises came after 1945. With relatively full employment, higher wages, and the formation of the EEC, Europe developed the markets which could sustain dynamic mass production/mass distribution enterprises. And once this condition was met the other constraints loosened: there was a large-scale takeover of US managerial structures as such enterprises outgrew control by family or financiers and 'professional management' emerged at last.

These arguments are taken up in relation to Britain by Hannah (1980). Hannah accepts the broad outline of the Chandler case but argues, on the basis of a more detailed investigation, that the rise of managerial enterprise in Britain should be dated from the inter-war years: the post-war growth of impersonal capitals started from a strong base established during the '20s and '30s. He points out that the contribution of the hundred largest firms to total value-added in manufacturing, which reached 20 per cent in the USA in 1909, reached the same proportion in Britain in the 1920s. And although the absolute size of British firms was smaller, the UK had its share of industrial giants. Overall figures for industrial concentration are not necessarily a very good index of forms of organisation of enterprises and unfortunately the evidence on corporate structure in Britain is somewhat sketchy, but Hannah shows that by 1930 the multi-unit enterprise was dominant: 136 out of the top 200 manufacturing companies (measured by market value of their capital) had a multi-unit form. It is also clear that, with regard to legal forms of enterprise, joint stock companies came to dominate industry over the inter-war years. Pollard (1969) notes that by the late 1930s joint stock companies accounted for about 85 per cent of the profits of manufacturing industry in Britain.

The multi-unit joint stock company, with a number of operating units under one overall legal ownership, is not however equivalent to the 'multidivisional' structure which Chandler regards as characteristic of modern managerial enterprises: the latter involves a high degree of managerial coordination of the operating units. While examples of multidivisional •enterprise can be found in inter-war Britain (the indigenous ICI, the US-owned Ford and Vauxhall) nonetheless many of the British multi-unit enterprises were really only loose federations of firms, which often continued to be managed separately and even to compete in the same market. In this context, the separation of formal ownership and control was less developed: in 1930, 70 per cent of the 200 largest British firms still had family board members. It has also been argued (Chandler, 1980a) that managerial *techniques* were generally much less developed in the UK in the inter-war years. Sophisticated procedures for scheduling of flows and for costing only became widespread in the post war years and then generally in imitation of established American methods. So although Hannah is correct to point out the already-high degree of industrial concentration in the UK economy of the 1930s, and the existence of certain strongly 'managerial' enterprises, it remains true that the dominance of the integrated 'impersonal capital' was not realised until after 1945.

Apart from questions of accurate periodisation, the other issue which arises from Hannah's contribution is the adequacy of Chandler's explanation for the relative 'late arrival' of managerial enterprises in the UK. Chandler's principal explanatory factors were the size, growth-rate and character of markets and the legal forms available for large-scale enterprises. As regards markets, Hannah's arguments can be seen as supporting the Chandler view. In general regional and class tastes were more highly differentiated in the UK and Europe than in the USA, reducing the scope for the mass marketing of consumer goods, but in the food market, where tastes were fairly standardised in Britain, mass production and retailing grew rapidly. Relatively low wages did limit the market for cars and electrical goods before world war two, and also affected the demand for producer goods by reducing the incentive to substitute electrical or mechanical power for labour. However, changes in this respect were incipient before the war. Deflation brought a rise in the real wages of those in employment during the '30s, electricity was installed in most homes, and the middle-income groups at least could realistically aspire to car-ownership.

While agreeing that markets are important, Hannah stresses some further points. First, the particular *character* of markets may be as relevant as their size or rate of growth. The UK market, even by the turn of the century, was highly compact and urban (in 1901 75 per cent of the British population was classified as urban), so that the cost of information and transactions would be low relative to the USA. Combined with Britain's imperial role as international centre of commerce, bringing competitive pressure for efficiency in the system of markets, this suggests that there may have been less competitive advantage for managerial as opposed to market coordination in the British case. (Again, one can contrast the German case, in which the low level of development of market mechanisms encouraged hierarchical coordination through banks, the state, and large-scale integrated enterprises.)

Second, there is evidence to suggest that even when opportunities presented themselves for mass production/mass marketing activities, British firms were less ready to take advantage of them. Before 1914, for instance, the British textile industry presented a very large market for dyes, yet it was the German chemical giants which were first to exploit it. British companies made less of a more promising market for urban electric lighting than Edison and Westinghouse in the USA. This may be partly due to the conservative bias in the British capital market, which has made it difficult to finance investment projects perceived as 'risky' or innovatory.

Third, it may be argued that the slow development of 'managerial' capitalism should not be conceived solely in terms of a lack of *demand* for managerial staffs to coordinate enterprises. Deficiencies on the supply side are also important. The substantial lack of technically or commercially trained managerial manpower can be traced in part to the low social valuation placed upon manufacturing industry by a dominant ideology which has a strong aristocratic colouring. Patronage rather than professionalism remained for longer the key to the control over enterprises in Britain. This contrasts not only with the early rise of the 'business school' and managerial professionalism in the USA, but also with the rather different professionalism of salaried management in Germany, where the emphasis was on technical rather than commercial training, and the links between universities and state technical colleges and industrial enterprises helped to foster the early development of high-technology industry (Freeman, 1974).

It would seem that the slower development of managerially-controlled impersonal capitals in Britain was 'overdetermined' by a whole range of economic, social and cultural factors. And the particular course of development in Britain has arguably left a legacy in some of the structural problems underlying the declining international competitiveness of the UK economy over the post-war years. The technological innovations necessary to secure a strong competitive position have most often been carried out by the large integrated corporations, and the British economy, with its relative paucity of such enterprises and low level of commercially applicable research and development,[1] proved to be in a weak position when the old imperial trade preferences dissolved and the domestic industry was exposed to greater competition at home and abroad.

The impersonal capital in post war Britain

In the previous section it was argued that the development of large-scale impersonally owned capitals has been relatively slow in the British economy, and that such large-scale units of ownership which existed in the inter-war years generally displayed less real integration than in the USA. The prerogatives of personal ownership of capital remained important for longer and this affected the competitive strategies and internal managerial practices adopted by enterprises, probably limiting the ability of many British enterprises to sustain a rapid pace of technological change or to adapt to more cost-effective modes of internal organisation.

The objective here is to assess the extent to which large-scale impersonal capitals have achieved dominance in the post war years. I have already pointed out that measures of industrial concentration and the size of enterprises do not in themselves indicate the mode of possession (formally large enterprises can comprise relatively autonomous operating units which preserve personal possession) but it may be useful to begin by considering these indices, which show a striking increase in the importance of large enterprises. Table 3.1 shows the estimates of industrial concentration made by Hannah (1976) and Prais (1976).

Table 3.1 *Percentage share in manufacturing net output of 100 largest enterprises 1935-1970*

	1935	1948/49*	1953	1958	1963	1968	1970
Hannah	23	21	26	33	38	42	45
Prais	24	22	27	32	37	41	41

* 1948 for Hannah, 1949 for Prais

The above measures relate to output; for employment the indices are equally striking:

Table 3.2 *Analysis of enterprises by total employment size: manufacturing industry in the UK 1972*

Size of enterprise (number employed)	Enterprises (No.)	(% of total)	Employment (% of total)
10,000 and over	85	0.12	35.02
2,000 – 9,999	375	0.52	21.75
500 – 1,999	1,047	1.45	13.77
200 – 499	1,823	2.52	7.96
100 – 199	2,852	3.94	5.55
1 – 99	66,119	91.45	15.96
All enterprises	72,301	100.00	100.01

Source: Devine *et al.* (1979).

It can be seen that companies employing over 2,000 workers, while less than 1 per cent of the population of firms, employ over half of the manufacturing workforce. The other side of the coin was demonstrated in the findings of the Bolton Committee (Bolton, 1971) which estimated that employment by 'small enterprises' (with less than 200 workers) had fallen from around 38 per cent of the manufacturing workforce in 1935 to 20 per cent in 1963.

A third measure of concentration is by ownership of assets. In this regard Aaronovitch and Sawyer (1975) have estimated that among quoted manufacturing companies with 1957 assets of £5 million or more, the 100 largest enterprises owned 58 per cent of the assets in

1957, and 73 per cent in 1968.

Giving a broad summary, the Department of Industry (1976) showed that the 100 largest private-sector manufacturing enterprises in the early 1970s accounted for around 40 per cent of manufacturing industry's net output, net assets, and employment; 40 to 50 per cent of visible exports, and 70 per cent of expenditure on industrial scientific research and development.

These indices show up clearly the importance of the largest 100 enterprises, and of large enterprises generally, in the manufacturing sector of the British economy. Although it is hard to construct comparable figures for other economies because of differing legal forms and classification of enterprises, it is generally reckoned that the level of industrial concentration in Britain is now higher than in any of the continental European countries. George and Ward (1978), working with a rather different measure, estimated the four-firm employment concentration ratios in manufacturing industry in selected EEC countries (i.e. the weighted average of the percentage of the labour force employed by the largest four firms in each of the various branches of manufacturing). The ratio for the UK, at 32 per cent, was significantly higher than in West Germany (22 per cent), France (24 per cent) and Italy (20 per cent).

All the statistics quoted above are limited in the sense that they apply only to manufacturing industry. But although such aggregated figures are not available for the financial and commercial sectors it seems clear that they have undergone a parallel process of increasing concentration. The present 'big four' London clearing bank groups have emerged from eleven independent banks since 1968, and from hundreds since the nineteenth century; among the fastest growing financial institutions the building societies have decreased in numbers from almost three thousand in 1890 to around a thousand in the 1930s, to around 480 today, while the largest ten societies account for over 64 per cent of their total assets and the biggest single society, the Halifax, for over 18 per cent. The activities of life insurance companies and pension funds have also grown rapidly over the post war years, and in this field the dozen largest companies account for over 60 per cent of long-term premium income. In retailing, the widespread development of chain stores and supermarkets demonstrates a similar trend.

As regards the legal form of property, the overwhelming majority of large scale enterprises take the form of public joint stock companies with limited liability (as against only 20 per cent of British businesses in 1914). The only major exception to this rule is in the case of the financial sector, where the building societies retain the mutual form from their origins as friendly societies, as do some insurance companies. In both the joint stock and the mutual forms the enterprise exists as a legal entity distinct from its shareholders and therefore private individuals cannot be said to own the means of production employed by the enterprise. Possession rests with the enterprise itself. In this sense, we have already said enough to show that *possession of the means of production by impersonal capital is now the dominant mode.* The question remains, however, of the importance of individual shareholders in enterprise decision-making: of whether the formally impersonal possession conceals the continued existence of a 'capitalist class' of individuals who have substantial *de facto* powers over the allocation of enterprises' resources by virtue of their participation in beneficiary ownership.

In Chandler's argument, although it was not posed in precisely these terms, the move towards large, formally impersonal capitals goes together with a real shift towards coordination and policy-making by salaried managerial employees. Shareholders become marginalised as such and can only participate in policy-making if they become specialist managers themselves. This view rests on a particular conception of the competitive advantage achieved by 'managerial' enterprises. Large scale enterprises are 'selected' for survival and growth only if they achieve significant economies over traditional smaller firms by exploiting the opportunities for coordination and resource allocation offered by professional management. Large enterprises which do not move in this direction but continue to produce or trade as a set of operating units under more personal control, are liable to disintegrate, as happened to a number of British holding companies of the 1920s. Chandler's arguments have recently been given an interesting theoretical reinforcement by Williamson (1981), who has specified more precisely the kind of economies realised by the successful managerially-coordinated large enterprises. These are not so much technical economies of scale (although they are sometimes important) as economies of 'transaction costs', i.e. the costs of negotiating, writing and executing transfers of goods or services between technologically separable economic units. Williamson has argued that it is precisely in the cases where managerial coordination would not, on *a priori* grounds, be expected to yield transaction cost economies over market coordination that large managerially-coordinated enterprises have failed.

There remains the possibility that certain features of the economic environment may 'select' large enterprises for survival and growth even if such enterprises do not justify themselves on the grounds of economies of scale and integration. Researchers investigating the very rapid rise in industrial concentration in post-war Britain, to levels in excess of the other major capitalist economies, have claimed to find such 'environmental features' in the British financial and taxation systems. Prais (1976) for instance argues that the preference for the shares of larger enterprises on the part of the financial institutions has encouraged the exceptional rounds of mergers and takeovers in the British case. This preference is seen as grounded in caution: large diversified enterprises with interests in several markets tend to show a lesser variability of profits than smaller single-product firms, a financial advantage which would appear to be independent of real integration between the operating units of the large enterprise. Devine *et al.* (1979) also cite the tax situation during the 1960s, when income was taxed relatively heavily but capital gains were not, as an incentive for entrepreneurs to capitalise their prospective profits by submitting to takeovers rather than continuing as independent owners. Financial factors of this kind can put a premium on large size which goes beyond any competitive advantage in production and trading, and studies (e.g. Singh, 1975) have shown relatively poor real integration and profitability on the part of many large enterprises which were formed in the British merger booms. The suggestion here is that some of the large British enterprises may lack centralised managerial coordination, and their operating units may continue to be directed by their erstwhile major shareholders, preserving a more personal mode of control within the legal form of large impersonal capital.

One widely-adopted approach to judging the degree of *de facto* control by major shareholders, is through analysis of the pattern of shareholdings. Berle and Means (1932) backed up their argument on the 'divorce of ownership and control' by citing the increasing dispersion of share-ownership. In their view the decline of majority shareholding on the part of individuals or families signalled a general decline in shareholder-control, since there was no longer a dominant beneficiary owner of the enterprise to contest control with the incumbent managerial employees. This line of investigation was taken up by Florence (1961), who showed that among larger British companies in 1951 there was only a small minority (around 3 per cent) in which the largest single shareholding accounted for 50 per cent or more of the voting shares. Further, in 62 per cent of companies with share capital of £3 million or more the largest twenty holdings accounted for less than 30 per cent of the voting strength. This showed a greater dispersion than the corresponding figures for 1936. Florence's findings that share-ownership was becoming more dispersed and that the concentration of share-ownership less among larger companies, were supported by Revell and Moyle (1966) in their investigation of share issues quoted on the London Stock Exchange in 1963 (Larner, 1966, also confirmed a declining concentration of shareholdings among larger US enterprises).

It has been pointed out however (e.g. by Beed, 1966) that it is not clear what conclusions can be drawn from data of this kind. The dispersion of share-ownership *may* signal a general decline of influence over enterprise policy on the part of shareholders, but it may equally give rise to a situation in which only a relatively small percentage holding of the voting stock is required to exercise dominant influence: the majority of small shareholders lack any leverage over company policy, and their shares figure as mere titles to revenue, but the decision-making power becomes centred in the hands of the larger minority shareholders. The first possibility is the Berle and Means 'separation of ownership and control', but the second is more ambiguous — a separation of shareholding as such from control, but one which preserves the dominant controlling role of the larger shareholders. It is not possible to decide this issue *a priori*.

If investigation of the pattern of shareholding does not in itself substantiate any definite conclusions regarding the direction of enterprises, the kind of analysis undertaken by Channon (1973) may be more productive. Channon's undertaking was the detailed examination of the organisational structure and business strategy of the hundred largest British industrial enterprises over the period 1950 to 1970, using a Chandlerian framework of analysis. One of his central concerns, therefore, was the question of the pattern of control over resources as manifested in the structure of the managerial hierarchy. He distinguished three models:

1. **The 'functional' form of organisation:** This is a form in which 'the enterprise is broken down into a series of specialised hierarchical functions culminating in the office of the chief executive who performs the role of coordinator and general manager of all the specialist functions'. This form offers the potential at least for overall direction of the enterprise by a single substantial shareholder or 'owning-family' representative, managing from the top the specialised functions of production, sales, finance and so on.

2. **The holding company form:** I have remarked earlier on the use of this form in the British economy. To recap, it draws together

under one legal ownership a collection of enterprises which may continue nonetheless to be managed separately. The holding company is unlikely to exhibit central policy-making, coordination or strategic functions in relation to the subsidiary enterprises. The prerogatives of personal direction of the subsidiaries may be circumscribed in certain ways, but the possibility of such personal direction is not eliminated.

3. **The multi-divisional form:** I have cited Chandler's description of this form above. Channon's definition is in the same vein. This form is one which features a 'general office, usually divorced from operations, which services and monitors the operating divisions'. The operating divisions, which may be defined on product or geographical lines depending on the character of the enterprise, have a certain autonomy and have their own specialist staff but are subordinated broadly to the strategy of the enterprise as a whole. The top managers of the divisions will generally be appointed by the general office. The establishment of this form generally marks a break with the dominance of personal or family direction, and a decisive shift towards control by a 'managerial apparatus' employing specialised salaried employees.

Tracing the developments within the population of the hundred largest enterprises, Channon shows that while in 1950 only 8 per cent had a multi-divisional structure (and most of these were subsidiaries of foreign-owned enterprises), by 1970 the figure was around 70 per cent. He periodises this development into three stages: in the 1950s the functional form was dominant; by the 1960s the former was proving too inflexible to manage effectively enterprises which were growing larger and more diversified, and the holding company form achieved dominance; by the '70s it was apparent that the holding company form was in turn too ramshackle to permit the formulation of a rational overall strategy for the enterprise in many branches, and maintained a wasteful duplication of effort among the subsidiaries. The multidivisional form acquired dominance. This last step was not, of course, achieved without difficulty. In many cases it involved recourse to outside management consultants, since although managements consciously wished to install a more rational control over the enterprise many did not have the internal resources to accomplish such a change successfully. Change also met resistance from the managers of some subsidiary units within holding companies, jealous of their own autonomy.

If this is the broad picture — one which confirms the thesis of the increasing importance of the impersonal capital — it is also possible to be more concrete, with regard to development within different groups of enterprises. For this purpose, Channon categorised the population of enterprises according to their degree of diversification, and the degree of importance of technological development to the enterprise.

1. **Single or 'dominant product' enterprises:** These enterprises, for which diversification was relatively unimportant, were found concentrated in drink, tobacco, power machinery, oil, metals and materials. These branches tended to show a high degree of concentration, and barriers to entry on the part of new enterprises, but relatively low profits. Most enterprises in these branches had only a low level of 'transferable technology'; many were processors of specific raw materials. In this context, strategic change was found to be generally rather slow, especially among firms for which 'family' influence remained important. This influence seemed to correlate with stagnation, and maintenance of the original product/market scope of the enterprise. By 1970, however, most of the enterprises in these branches had evolved some kind of multidivisional form, partly in order to cope with the limited diversification which was attempted through acquisition, and partly to organise geographically-based divisions.

2. **The 'technological diversifiers':** For these enterprises, technological expertise was the basis for diversification into new products and markets. They were concentrated in the industry-groups of electrical and electronic engineering, chemicals and pharmaceuticals, and mechanical engineering. These branches of production clearly played a leading role in the economic expansion of the post-war boom, with growth rates well in excess of the average for manufacturing industry. Large 'family' companies were rare relative to the low technology industries; most of the dominant enterprises developed thorough-going multidivisional structures, making this sector the *locus classicus* of the large-scale impersonal capital, but the breadth and openness of markets allowed space for the continuing presence of a penumbra of smaller specialist enterprises.

3. **The 'acquisitive diversifiers':** Enterprises in this category carried out significant diversification, but less by development of their own technological and marketing resources and more by acquisition and merger (main branches: food, textiles, paper and packaging, printing and publishing). In some cases the diversification was related either by market (food and packaging) or in the sense of vertical

integration (textiles and paper), but in this category we also find the 'conglomerates' whose various diversified activities bear little economic relationship to one another. In many cases the candidates for 'acquisitive diversification' were enterprises suffering relatively low growth and profitability (the main exceptions were in convenience foods, plastic packaging and synthetic fibres), and those under 'family' influence in particular tended to be narrow in their operational scope and vulnerable to competition. In this context, diversification through acquisition could be seen as a defensive move. As such, it was often a failure: profits were rarely improved, 'since the managerial and structural reorganisations that were needed to achieve the potential benefits from acquisitions were rarely made. Deficiencies in management skills, inadequate financial controls and poor rationalisation actually often compounded the earlier difficulties' (Channon, 1973, p. 194). Many of the large enterprises formed in this way remained at an intermediate stage between the holding company and the multidivisional forms, with loose control and planning systems and a poorly developed central office, especially in the case of enterprises led by a 'dominant personality' of the 'tycoon' type. We see here in more detail the roots of the poor profitability of many products of the mergers and acquisitions booms of the 1960s, as analysed by Singh.

Channon's account reinforces the thesis argued above, that there has been a distinct trend towards the impersonal capital, whose operations are directed and managed by an 'apparatus' of salaried employees, but it also permits one to qualify and render more precise that thesis. The trend has been distinctly uneven across branches of production, strongest in the 'leading sectors' of post war development (Channon's 'technological diversifiers') but relatively weak among the single-product enterprises and those that diversified 'defensively' through stock-market acquisitions. By 1970 'family connections' among the directors of the larger British enterprises, while still significant and probably more important than in other industrial capitalist economies, were diminishing. On Channon's calculation 15 per cent of directors had such links with owning families, but the vast majority had 'little or no significant equity stake in their companies', and remuneration was mainly by straight salary.

I shall return later (Chapter 5) to the implications of these developments at the level of the enterprise for socialist politics and ideology. For the present though I shall follow up my comments on the depersonalisation of capitalist property relations at enterprise level by considering in more detail the 'second order depersonalisation' noted briefly in Chapter 2. That is, not only are the means of production largely possessed by the impersonal legal subject of the joint stock company, but the shares of those companies are increasingly held by other impersonal subjects viz. joint stock, or mutual, financial institutions (and to a lesser extent governments). The investigation of patterns of shareholding, it was argued above, does not in itself lead to very conclusive results regarding the internal direction and management of enterprises. Nonetheless, in this context of the second order depersonalisation, such investigation is of considerable interest. Devine *et al.* (1979) have collected the results of research by Errit and Alexander (1977) and Moyle (1971) which show the following trends in ownership of ordinary shares quoted on the UK stock exchange:

Table 3.3   *Ownership of Ordinary Shares, by Market Value*

	% of market value			
Sector of beneficial holder	*1957*	*1963*	*1969*	*1975*
Personal	67.7	56.1	49.5	39.8
Financial Sector	21.3	30.4	35.9	47.9
Overseas	4.4	7.0	6.6	5.6
Public	3.9	1.5	2.6	3.6
Industrial and Commercial	2.7	5.1	5.4	3.0

Within the financial sector it is the pension funds and insurance companies which are the most substantial beneficiary holders, accounting jointly for 32.7 per cent of market value in 1975. That this trend has continued since 1975 is shown in the recent financial data.[2] Over the years 1975-79 the personal sector 'disinvested' in company and overseas securities at a rate of substantially more than £1,000 million per year and this has more than been made good by the net acquisition of company securities by life assurance and superannuation funds. Meanwhile the personal sector has acquired the liabilities of these latter institutions at an annual rate exceeding £5,000 million. We have clearly now reached a situation in which the majority of ordinary shares in the UK are held by the big financial institutions, and the greater part of personal wealth is held in the form of the liabilities of these institutions rather than in 'titles to ownership' of companies.

This transformation raises a number of questions of interest in the context of class analysis. These can be ordered into two problem areas: first, what is the extent and significance of intervention in the operations of companies by the financial institutions? Second, the broader 'systemic' issue which may be posed in this way: what does the rapid growth of the financial institutions which collect personal savings, and lend these to enterprises and governments, suggest about the class structure of modern British capitalism? The point about this latter question, which will be more clearly defined in the following chapter, is that it directs attention not only to the 'power relations' between financial and industrial enterprises but to the overall pattern of financial flows within which those relations are inserted.

I shall refer to the first issue under the heading of 'financing and control over the enterprise', and then address the second issue under that of 'classes and financial circulation'.

Financing and control over the enterprise

Although this issue has been raised in relation to the current pattern of shareholding in the British economy it may be useful to begin by referring back to the discussion of external financing in Chandler, and comparing the conclusions of that discussion with the views of certain Marxist writers. Note first that the shareholding relation is not the only relevant relation between financial and industrial/commercial enterprises in this context. If the financial institutions simply buy up shares *already held by the personal sector* then they are not providing any additional finance for the companies concerned, and on the other hand financial institutions may provide substantial funds for use by companies without acquiring an equity stake (e.g. in the case of bank loans). The following discussion is concerned with the broad question: do the financial institutions exercise important leverage over company policy *either* by virtue of their stake in beneficiary ownership *or* by virtue of their provision of substantial external finance (purchase of *new* shares or bonds, or provision of loans)?

Chandler has drawn out the importance of the mode of financing of enterprises in his distinction between 'family capitalism' and 'financial capitalism' as different routes to the formation of managerial enterprises. In the case of enterprises which require substantial external financing, the original owners of the firm's share capital will generally be unable to retain a monopoly over top level decision-making and representatives of financial interests are likely to be placed on the board of directors. But a high level of external financing is not a universal feature of capitalist enterprises. In the US case large enterprises could be built up in retailing without taking on board specifically financial interests, and even in the more capital-intensive branches of industry enterprises could over time outgrow the need for large-scale borrowing, thereby reducing the leverage of financiers' representatives on company policy. Besides, the increasing complexity and professionalisation of management means that the financiers' capacity for detailed intervention in company policy becomes more and more limited: financial capitalism gives way to managerial.

This analysis of the US case sustains criticisms which have been levelled at Hilferding's conception of 'finance capital'. In this conception, taken up by Lenin (1964), Hilferding generalised from the situation in Germany before the first World War and argued that increasing fusion between financial and industrial capital, under the dominance of the former, was a necessary feature of advanced capitalism. This 'unity-in-dominance' (to use more modern jargon) of financial and industrial interests he labelled 'finance capital'. While Hilferding's conception may have been applicable to the Germany of the time, his view that this showed the necessary future of capitalism in general has not been borne out. In retrospect, the dominant position of banks appears as a rather particular feature of the German case. Banks have had controlling interests in certain branches of industry at certain times in other national economies but we have seen how this was less widespread, and arguably a transitional phase, in the case of US capitalism. Sweezy (1939) made this argument within a Marxist framework, dating the transitional phase of 'banker dominance' from 1890 to 1929. More recently Hussain (1976) has argued that the Hilferding/Lenin conception of 'finance capital' has tended to block off specific analysis of modern financial institutions on the part of Marxist writers. In particular the emphasis placed by the Hilferding/Lenin tradition on the financing/domination of *industrial capitals* by 'finance capital' has obscured the increasing role of the financial institutions in collecting personal savings, extending personal credit and financing government borrowing (of which more in the following chapter).

The thrust of the foregoing remarks is not to deny the importance of the financial institutions or, more specifically, of the external financing of industrial and commercial enterprises at the present time. It is rather to clear aside one influential but misleading conception within the Marxist tradition — that of universal 'banker dominance', so as to open up some useful areas of investigation. 'Finance capital' in the fullest sense may have been a geographically and temporally circumscribed phase but it should not be concluded that full financing from retained profits is the natural state for 'mature' managerial capitalism.

In this regard Chandler may be criticised for his implicit proposition that managerial enterprise has outgrown the need for large-scale external finance. Partly, no doubt, this is an effect of the periodisation of his detailed studies: the industrial cases he considers are fully documented only up to the early post war years, when the leading managerial enterprises had a generally strong liquidity position. The Radcliffe enquiry into the British financial system during the 1950s found the leading companies placing little reliance on external financing (and drew the conclusion, now notorious to economists, that variations in the rate of interest had little effect on industrial investment plans). But from the vantage-point of the 1980s we can see that this state of affairs was not to continue indefinitely. Four points may be made in criticism of the notion of a 'natural' self-financing on the part of industrial capitalist enterprises.

First, a high rate of internal financing cannot be 'read' unambiguously. Theoretically, it can indicate *either* a strong financial position of the enterprises concerned (profits sufficient to finance a high level of investment) *or* a weak investment record (low borrowing a correlate of unambitious investment plans). British companies have shown a relatively high degree of internal financing (around 70 per cent of capital funds over the last ten years), but an increasing proportion of company funds has been required merely to 'keep going' (i.e. to cover cost of stocks and depreciation of fixed assets). Relatively low borrowing by enterprises has been associated with weak profitability in conjunction with a weak investment record.

Second, industries which at one time sustained rapid accumulation on the basis of retained profit have run into crisis. The problems of the motor industry in the USA and Britain in face of rising oil prices and severe foreign competition provide an obvious example. In such cases it is rather unlikely that the private sector financial institutions will come to the rescue with the funds required for structural change and improved competitiveness. The prospects for e.g. Chrysler in the USA and BL in Britain look too risky and in both cases it is the state which is providing the external finance, fearful of the reverberations of the collapse of such giant employers (both directly and in their capacity as consumers of intermediate output from other branches of industry). The conditions attached to state aid in these cases show up very clearly the leverage over company policy which the monopoly provision of external finance grants the state under these circumstances, although of course that leverage can be exercised in different directions (insistence on a degree of worker participation in the case of

Chrysler under Carter; strong support for a hard line management policy over work practices and wages with BL under Thatcher).

Third, impersonal capitals have become more diversified and are thus better able to maintain their dominant position even in the face of significant changes in demand and in technology. But the development and exploitation of radically new technologies still give birth to (or at least permit the birth of) *new* large enterprises. This has happened with the rise of semiconductor technology and the microelectronics industry. In this field, the investment costs of setting up in manufacture of semiconductors, or even of remaining competitive in the market, have escalated rapidly with the increasing technical complexity of the products and the production process, and the enterprises concerned are unable to finance their growth by means of their (very substantial) retained profit alone, forcing reliance on external funds. The general point here is that the emergence over time of new capital-intensive branches of industry will bring a need for large-scale external investment finance, even if established and profitable enterprises in other branches have achieved self-financing growth.

Fourth, government economic policy and world trading conditions can have an important impact on the borrowing needs of all enterprises. In Britain in 1980, for instance, the sharp and severe drop in effective demand precipitated in large measure by the government's attempts to cut public sector borrowing and tightly control the money stock has forced many otherwise profitable enterprises into trading losses and unwanted borrowing to cover costs.

We saw earlier that financial enterprises have become increasingly important as major *shareholders* in industrial and commercial enterprises. The above remarks also show that the provision of *new external finance*, both by financial institutions and by governments, is of continuing importance even for 'managerial' enterprises. Such funds may be required for expansion, for investment in new technology, for restructuring in the face of shifts in the pattern of demand, or to cover current costs when markets are depressed. It is worth noting that in the British case these two relationships between financial enterprises and industrial/commercial enterprises (acquisition of equity stake, provision of new finance) have been relatively distinct. This is shown in Table 3.4. For most of the years considered, industrial and commercial companies have relied on external sources for around 30 per cent of their capital funds but within their total external financing bank borrowing has generally accounted for a greater proportion than capital issues (i.e. sales of new shares and bonds). That is, although the pension funds and life assurance companies have taken over an increasing proportion of shareholdings it is the banks (which in Britain are not significant as shareholders) which have provided the greater part of new external finance. Generally speaking, less than half of the massive flow of funds from the personal sector into the life assurance and pension funds has been used to acquire shares and bonds issued by UK industrial and commercial companies, the balance being invested mainly in government bonds, shares of other financial enterprises, and landed property.

Table 3.4 *Industrial and Commercial Companies: External Finance*

£ billions: annual average: percentage of column totals in brackets.

	1963-66	1967-70	1971-74	1975-79
Bank Borrowing	0.5 (41.7)	0.7 (41.2)	3.2 (69.6)	2.7 (51.9)
Other loans and mortgages	0.1 (8.3)	0.2 (11.8)	0.3 (6.5)	0.4 (7.7)
Ordinary shares	0.1 (8.3)	0.2 (11.8)	0.2 (4.3)	0.9 (17.3)
Other capital issues	0.3 (25)	0.3 (17.6)	0.1 (2.2)	– (0)
Overseas finance	0.2 (16.7)	0.3 (17.6)	0.8 (17.4)	1.2 (23.1)
	1.2 (100)	1.7 (100)	4.6 (100)	5.2 (100)

Level of internal provision of capital funds

£ millions: percentage of total capital funds in the year in brackets.

1963	1966	1969	1972	1975	1978
£3,679	£3,615	£5,717	£9,971	£12,037	£19,603
(69.4)	(70.3)	(69.0)	(55.0)	(68.9)	(70.0)

Source: calculated from the Bank of England (1980)

In contrast to the Lenin/Hilferding 'finance capital' thesis, it is argued here that these financial relationships do not carry any *necessary* implications concerning control over the strategy and operations of industrial and commercial capitals on the part of financial interests. Under certain circumstances financial enterprises may use the financing relation as a means of leverage over company policy, but they often act as passive collectors of dividends and interest payments. This point may be sustained by examining in more detail the major forms of financial relationship.

1. **Shareholding on the part of non-bank financial institutions:** I have already noted the role of life assurance companies and pension

funds in this regard. It should be added that investment trusts and unit trusts are also substantial shareholders, although their rate of growth has been less dramatic than that of the former. The point about all of these institutions is that they are not really equipped to intervene in regular company decision-making. Their acquisitions of shares and bonds are geared to rather narrow financial considerations and they often behave in a speculative manner rather than entering into substantial long-term relations with particular enterprises. In their written evidence to the Committee to Review the Functioning of Financial Institutions (Wilson, 1978) the institutions stated that

'In discharging their role as owners of capital, few institutional investors would interpret this as requiring a regular detailed monitoring of a company's progress... For a normal portfolio of soundly based companies, the investor would not be able to justify on economic grounds the expenses of the necessary team of experts to do the monitoring to which should be added the costs that would be incurred to the companies' (Wilson, 1978, p. 90).

The evidence continued to the effect that 'in the ordinary way good managements should be allowed to get on with the job' although 'regular communications' should be maintained. The institutions did however, recognise certain situations in which 'other forms of action' might be taken if necessary: cases of inadequate management, contested takeover bids, boardroom disputes. In such instances the institutions generally try to keep a low profile and avoid publicity which might have an adverse effect on share prices, but from time to time a case reaches the newspapers. It has been reported (Devine et al., 1979) that the successful £400 million takeover bid by Grand Metropolitan Hotels for Watney Mann in 1972 was completed, against the wishes of most individual Watney Mann shareholders, with the help of the big institutional shareholders.

If there is not much evidence of direct intervention by the institutions other than on such occasions, this does not mean that the behaviour of the shareholding institutions is without effect on industrial and commercial capitals. I mentioned earlier the role of the financial institutions in fostering an 'artificially' high level of industrial concentration in the British economy. This effect may be seen, somewhat paradoxically, as in part due to the wish of the institutions to avoid entering into too close a relationship with any one enterprise. To the extent that they acquire shares of only the largest enterprises, the institutions leave themselves a freer hand for the speculative management of their funds, since it may be impossible to sell off a major shareholding in a smaller enterprise without driving down the market price of its shares. This preference for larger enterprises on the part of the institutions puts a premium on their shares and hence encourages mergers and takeovers even where they may not be justified on the grounds of production and trading performance.

In the ideology of the institutional investors, the capital market is a smoothly functioning mechanism for allocating resources in the best possible way. Share prices are supposed to reflect the 'quality of management' and economic performance, and a falling share price acts as a spur to increased efficiency on the part of weak enterprises in order to avoid becoming a 'takeover bargain'. With such faith in the beneficial effects of competitive markets, the institutions can blind themselves to their own economic effects.

2. **Bank lending:** It is useful here to distinguish between lending by means of the overdraft facilities granted by the clearing banks (i.e. the 'big four' of Barclays, Lloyds, Midland and National Westminster), and the provision of medium term loans by the merchant banks, or merchant banking subsidiaries of the clearing banks. Overdraft borrowing is very important as a source of marginal credit to enterprises, yet this financing relationship does not generally involve intervention by the lending bank. Overdraft loans are generally secured on the assets of the company involved so that if the company should go into liquidation the bank will be able to reclaim its funds. Beyond determining the creditworthiness of the potential borrower on this criterion it is unlikely that the clearing bank will carry out further detailed surveillance of, or intervention in, the affairs of the company.

Term loans, on the other hand, carry the implication of a more detailed inspection of the borrowing enterprise's affairs. Such loans are often secured not on the borrower's present assets, but on the cash flow expected from the investment project for which the funds are borrowed. This is advantageous for the borrower since it implies a broader view of creditworthiness and may make possible access to external finance on a larger scale. From the lending bank's point of view such loans must involve making a critical assessment of the company's trading prospects. This may extend to offering advice or setting conditions. Term loans have become a very substantial source of funds for companies, particularly over the 1970s. On the calculations of Revell (1973) the position in 1970 was one in which almost all clearing bank advances to companies took the form of overdrafts and the greater part of secondary bank[3] advances were term loans. On this basis the ratio of clearing bank advances to secondary bank advances gave a rough index of the relative importance of overdrafts and term loans. This ratio stood at around two to one, indicating that the overdraft was the dominant form of bank loan but that term loans were already substantial. By the end of the '70s, the Bank of England reckoned that term loans accounted for 40 per cent of total clearing bank advances. Meanwhile, the relative magnitude of secondary bank advances to the UK private sector had also increased. Repeating Revell's calculation, this suggests that around 60 per cent of bank sterling advances to the UK private sector now take the form of term loans.[4] Insofar as term loans imply a closer relationship between financier and borrower this at least suggests an overall shift in the pattern of bank lending favouring a closer engagement of the banks in the affairs of other enterprises.

There are signs that the severe deflation pursued by the Conservative government since 1980 is forcing the banks to consider accelerating this shift. In this context it is worth quoting a leader from the 'Times' business news of 30/1/81, which reflects both the pressure for change and the traditional arm's length relationship between banks and industry in the British case.

'In the German slump of the '20s the banks became deeply embroiled in industry. This has not always been a successful partnership but at the same time it was felt essential for the survival of German industry. With bankruptcies mounting and the recession continuing such strategy might even become part of discussions on the sort of problems which the banks and their industrial customers are now facing, though it would of course run quite counter to traditional prudential banking practice in this country.'

With many industrial customers collapsing into ruination, more 'interventionist', longer term lending policies 'might even become part of discussions'!

Aside from the pattern of lending, there are other relevant relationships between the merchant banks in particular and industrial and commercial enterprises. The merchant banks, with their important position in the City of London financial network, can act as 'Issuing Houses', giving advice to enterprises on new capital issues. Further, Minns (1980) has argued that although the pension funds own a high proportion of company shares, the control over their share portfolios often reverts to the merchant banks which contract to manage many funds under only the most general guidance from the funds' trustees. Minns suggests that about two thirds of pension fund assets are under external control, and that merchant banks control 65 per cent of such assets. The merchant banks also have strong overseas connections and conduct a high proportion of their banking activities in currencies other than sterling. This reflects their early involvement with empire trade and overseas investment (during the nineteenth century this formed the basis of their business; at the time British manufacturing industry was in the main self-financing from the personal wealth of the owners, according to research cited in Scott, 1979) but in present conditions it puts them in a strong position for providing financial services for multinational enterprises operating in Britain.

Given all these relationships between the merchant banks and other enterprises it is hardly surprising to find channels of communication and influence formalised in 'interlocking directorships', with representatives of the merchant banks sitting on the boards of other financial institutions and top industrial companies. Such links have been investigated by Aaronovitch (1961), Barrat Brown (1968), Stanworth and Giddens (1975) and Overbeek (1980), and their evidence suggests that the links have grown closer with the increase in overall economic concentration since the Second World War. But Scott (1979) has argued that while the interlocking of personnel does indicate the existence of 'spheres of influence' of strategically-placed financial enterprises it does not sustain the notion of banking 'empires', according to which the allocation of productive resources is determined by a few dominant banking concerns pursuing policies of active intervention in relation to the financially dependent enterprises.[5] Scott's position squares with that of Chandler, who took the view that the 'banking empire' was no longer an appropriate form of control over large-scale managerial enterprises although such 'empires' may have existed as a transitional form particularly in the USA and Germany, as well as with the conclusions of my own discussion above.

3 . **Government grants, loans, and shareholding:** In contrast to private-sector financial institutions, governments rarely enter into financial relationships with industrial and commercial enterprises merely for the sake of the revenues to be gained in the form of interest payments and dividends. If financial capitals may be content not to intervene in the affairs of their industrial and commercial clients providing that their flow of revenue is not seriously threatened, the rationale for governments acting as financiers is generally to affect the behaviour of enterprises according to the priorities of economic or social policy, and to produce an allocation of resources which 'market forces' would not otherwise produce. In other words, government financing of enterprises is usually explicitly a means of leverage over company policy whether it be employment policy (e.g. provision of Temporary Employment Subsidy or subsidy of short-time working), location of industry (finance available as part of government regional policy), furtherance of new technology (e.g. finance for development of microelectronics) or cushioning the demise of industries whose market has collapsed.

The general tendency of the leverage exercised by the state-as-financier has depended on the political complexion of the government and on the political constraints it has faced. For instance the Industry Act of 1975, which set up the National Enterprise Board (NEB) was originally intended by the Labour left as a means of gaining control over the activities of large capitalist enterprises and subordinating them to a form of planning which would promote 'industrial regeneration' along with a measure of industrial democracy. Financial leverage, as well as the possibility of sanctions against uncooperative firms, and further nationalisation, was to be used to push industrial development in a socialist direction. In the event, the proponents of this strategy did not manage to articulate their objectives sufficiently clearly, and mobilise sufficient popular support for them, to be able to avoid the watering-down of the NEB and the associated planning agreements. Plans for a thorough-going reallocation of productive resources and restructuring of social relations in industry went by the board, and although the 1974-79 Labour government continued to provide finance for industry through various channels this provision was shaped in response to *ad hoc* political pressure: to protect employment in particular sectors; to shore up important but financially-ailing enterprises such as BL; to be seen as not ignoring the need to promote certain new technologies (Microelectronics Applications Project, NEB funds for INMOS).

The Conservative government elected in May 1979 clearly found itself embarrassed by even the level of intervention-through-financing bequeathed by Labour. The Tories claim to believe in the 'unfettered working of market forces' and saw, in principle, no role for state financing of industry. They did, all the same, devote more state funds to INMOS after a long period of indecision on the part of the Industry Secretary, and even used that provision as a means of leverage over the siting of that enterprise's new microelectronics factory (South Wales rather than Bristol). They also continued to fund BL's losses, in this case making it plain that finance was conditional on the success of a hard-line policy against militants within the BL unions. That is, even an 'anti-interventionist' government finds it very hard to relinquish the option of state financing of industry at least as a means of staving off disastrous industrial collapse or of making good the blatant short-fall in private sector finance for 'risky' but strategic industries.

The pressures operating on the Thatcher government in relation to the financing of industry, and the possibilities for using state finance as part of a programme of transformation of industry and society in a socialist direction, will be considered in greater depth in later chapters. In the present context the point being made is that although public sector financing of private industry is small in relation to financing by private sector financial capitalist enterprises, the former is by nature more 'interventionist' than the latter.

Reprise

Let us take stock of the foregoing arguments concerning financing and control over enterprises, in the context of the theme of this chapter, i.e. the rise of the impersonal capital as the dominant mode of posses-sion of the means of production in modern industrial capitalism and more specifically in Britain. I have charted the increasing importance of fewer and larger enterprises in the spheres of both industry and finance. I have pointed out that the larger enterprises almost exclusively take the legal form of joint stock companies, meaning that the actual means of production are possessed not by individual persons but by impersonal legal subjects. I have also examined the arguments of Chandler, Channon and others concerning the direction of the larger joint stock enterprises and their managerial structures, arguments which indicate that impersonal possession is in the main not merely a convenient juridical fiction: the leading enterprises have generally outgrown the possibility of genuine control by founding families or narrow banking oligarchies, and are highly dependent on the recruitment of salaried management. Further, the provision, or lack of provision, of definite forms of education and training of managerial employees in different national economies has had a significant impact on the trading success of enterprises in those economies.

I have argued against the Leninist conception of 'finance capital' in which industrial enterprises are taken to be under the control of dominant banking interests, but at the same time I have stressed that the 'impersonal capital' or 'managerial enterprise' in industry or commerce is not an autonomous centre of decision-making. Self-financing by such enterprises is not in the natural order of things and industrial capitals maintain definite links with the financial enterprises which can provide funds either through acquisition of shares or the extension of credit. By reference to the pattern of shareholding, I have noted that a second order depersonalisation of capitalist property is well under way and is likely to continue. Individual persons own a decreasing fraction of company shares and more and more tend to accumulate wealth in the form of claims against financial institutions. In the British case it is the life assurance companies and pension funds which have tended to take up the company shares relinquished by the personal sector, although it is the banks which have provided most of the new capital funds for companies over recent years.

Marx was right in his judgement quoted at the start of this chapter: capitalism has indeed aimed at 'the expropriation of the means of production from all individuals', in a process which calls into question the traditional Marxist conception of the capitalist class as a category of persons owning the means of production and employing wage labour. The following chapter examines what is, in a sense, the obverse of the rise of the impersonal capital, i.e. the expansion of the broad working class of wage-earning and salaried employees. At this stage the focus is still on the specifically economic aspects of the class structure. I shall discuss the effects at the level of the financial circulation process and then develop some implications of that discussion with regard to arguments over capitalist economic development.

4
Classes and the financial circulation

This chapter deals with the economic ramifications of the dominance of the impersonal capital and the advanced separation of individuals from the means of production. I examine the increasing importance of personal saving on the part of employees separated from the means of production and therefore unable to carry out real accumulation. I then draw out some of the implications for the financial circulation process, for aggregate profits and for the Marxist theory of surplus value. The following chapter takes up some of the implications for the socialist project of the analyses of chapters 3 and 4.

First of all, it should be noted that if the formation of impersonal capitals, analysed in the previous chapter, is a significant feature of the development of the economic class structure, the other side of the coin is the increasing proportion of the economically active population appearing as employees (or unemployed) as opposed to employers or self-employed. In 1975 in the UK out of an estimated labour force of 25.6 million, 1.9 million or 7.4 per cent were employers or self-employed. For a detailed breakdown of this category we have to go back to the 10 per cent sample of the 1971 census.[1] In 1971 the overall percentage of self-employed and employers out of the economically active was also 7.4, but only 2.9 per cent were employers, i.e. the other 4.5 per cent were strictly petty bourgeois: small traders or producers hiring no employees. Further, employers directing establishments with 25 or more workers were a mere 0.06 per cent of all of those in employment. Most of the employers were operating on a very small scale, and were concentrated in those branches of the social division of labour which have succumbed least to what Marx referred to as the 'real subsumption of labour under capital': almost 30 per cent were in small-scale retailing; many of the others were either in farming, small-scale construction work, the service sector, or in the professions, especially law, medicine and accountancy. The overall picture is one in which the overwhelming majority of the working population is made up of wage or salary-earning employees. The category of employers and self-employed receive a disproportionate share of personal income, but as a fraction of personal income from employment and self-employment this has fallen from 14.5 per cent in 1951 to 11.8 per cent in 1978. If the term 'working class' is used in an economic sense to denote the class of individuals in a capitalist economy who possess no means of production and are constrained to sell their labour power for a wage or salary, then one can say that the vast majority of the economically active population in Britain is working class. If one took this to imply that socialism has a crushing built-in majority in Britain, albeit not yet 'realised', then one would indeed fall foul of Poulantzas' strictures against the notion of the 'wage-earning class' as politically misleading. No presupposition is made here that the common economic position of sellers of labour power has necessary unifying effects at the political level. Indeed, even setting aside lines of political and cultural differentiation the class of employees is divided by further 'economic' factors: possession of property other than means of production e.g. housing; degree of development of labour power through education and training; level of income; security of employment; access to information and to decision-making at work... this list is by no means exhaustive. All the same, it is analytically useful to identify the 'working class' in this broad sense, i.e. at the level of property relations. Although it is not a category which displays any political or cultural homogeneity, its development as the obverse of the impersonal capital is of great importance for the financial circulation process, and hence for the process of economic development in general.

The point is that except for the increasingly marginalised private capitalists it is impossible for individuals to carry out real accumulation of capital (in Marx's terminology) or real investment (in Keynes' terms). To the extent that personal income is greater than current expenditure individuals can do nothing else but *save* the balance, and with rising real incomes over most of the post war years the volume of personal savings has expanded enormously. This is shown in a particularly striking manner by the figures for the personal savings ratio (i.e. the proportion saved out of personal disposable income) in Britain, given in Table 4.1.

Table 4.1 *Personal savings ratio in Britain (%)*

1949	1953	1957	1961	1965	1969	1973	1977	1978
0.9	3.8	4.7	8.6	8.8	7.9	11.0	13.9	15.2

Source: Economic Trends Annual Supplement, 1980.

These figures are not greatly out of line with those for other industrial capitalist economies. In the late 1970s the personal savings ratio in France and Germany was within a percentage point of the British figure, although the Japanese figure was considerably higher (24.5 per cent in 1977) and that for the USA was much lower, at 5.0 per cent in the same year (Falush, 1978).

This rise in personal saving, combined with the trend towards the impersonal capital examined in the previous chapter, signals a substantial transformation of the economic class relations represented in traditional Marxist conceptions of capitalism. Those conceptions involve a capitalist class of individuals who own the means of production and employ wage-labour, and whose savings out of their profits are used to finance real accumulation, along with a class of workers whose wages are just sufficient for their reproduction and who therefore cannot save. Marx recognised the possibility of a partial separation between saving and real accumulation, in the case of the joint-stock company which employs the savings of rentiers under the direction of salaried managers, but, as we have seen, he thought this was only a transitional phase towards socialism and his analysis of its effects remained underdeveloped. He certainly did not envisage a situation in which saving on the part of employees would become far more important than rentiers' saving.

Now, of course saving on the part of capitalist enterprises (i.e. undistributed profits) remains important for the accumulation process. I have noted the degree of reliance on 'retained earnings' in the financing of British enterprises in particular. Impersonal capitalist enterprises, that is, are able to save and invest in the one movement in a similar way to the traditional individual capitalist-manager. But by the late 1970s in Britain the volume of saving carried out by the personal sector was actually greater than that carried out by industrial and commercial companies, and the development of such large-scale saving outside of the enterprise raises certain fundamental issues. Such saving may, under certain conditions, be successfully channelled into the financing of real accumulation; it may, however, cause stagnation in the accumulation process and at the same time create severe problems for the state's finances. I therefore consider it important to examine in some depth the phenomenon of employees' saving. In the following pages I propose to investigate the reasons for a high level of personal savings, the make-up of savings and the ways in which they are channelled to borrowers, and the implication for the accumulation of capital. I shall begin by giving a brief consideration to the main strands of economic theory concerning personal saving, although as we shall see these turn out to be inadequate for illuminating the role of saving in advanced capitalist economies.

Theories of saving

The breakdown of personal income into consumption on the one hand and saving on the other was one of the key elements of Keynes' economic theory, and Keynes' theory of the 'consumption function' (Keynes, 1936) forms the starting point for modern theories of personal savings. Keynes acknowledged that the 'propensity to consume' out of personal income (and therefore also the propensity to save) would be influenced by a wide range of factors including the level of personal income; the prevailing level of interest rates; social practices and institutions relating to consumption; the 'psychological propensities and habits' of individuals, and the distribution of income. But all the same he maintained that it was a reasonable simplifying assumption that consumption would be a fairly stable function of income in a given economy, if there were no 'revolutionary' changes in social habits:

'... men are disposed, as a rule and on the average, to increase their consumption as their income increases, but not as much as the increase in their income' (Keynes, 1936, p. 96).

On this view, rising incomes will lead to an increase in savings, and further, an increase in the proportion of income which is saved (there is also the implication that higher income groups within the population will tend to have a higher propensity to save, so that, e.g. greater equality in income distribution will tend to lower the overall savings ratio). Keynes presented this principle as a 'fundamental psychological law' in grand ahistorical manner. Let us examine its adequacy in accounting for the movement of savings in the post war period.

Over the 1950s real personal disposable income (PDI) rose at an average annual rate of 3.1 per cent, and only fell in one year of exceptionally rapid inflation, 1950-51 (the 'Korean War boom'). Over the 1960s, the average annual rise was 2.6 per cent and there was no year of falling real PDI.[2] Therefore it is not surprising, on Keynesian grounds, to find a gradual rise in the personal savings ratio over these decades. It is clear enough that, in broad terms, the substantial post war rise in real personal disposable income has been at least a necessary condition for increased personal saving.

Problems of explanation arise in the 1970s, however, when change in the level of real PDI became much more erratic, with sharp rises over 1971 to '73 followed by relative stagnation then falls from 1973 to '77 while the savings ratio remained at an historically high level, as shown in Table 4.2.

Table 4.2 *Personal disposable income and savings in the 1970s*

	Real PDI (£ million)+	% rise in PDI over previous year	Savings ratio
1970	63,352		9.0
1971	64,585	1.9	7.8
1972	69,597	7.8	9.5
1973	74,069	6.4	11.0
1974	75,051	1.3	14.2
1975	74,707	− 0.5	14.7
1976	74,773	0.1	14.6
1977	73,560	− 1.6	13.9
1978	78,682	7.0	15.2

+ at 1975 prices.
Source: Economic Trends Annual Supplement, 1980.

Keynes' simplified consumption function does not provide an adequate explanation for this, and neither does Friedman's modified version (Friedman, 1952). The main point of the latter theory is actually a development of a qualification which Keynes made in relation to the short run behaviour of savings:

'... a man's habitual standard of life usually has the first claim on his income, and he is apt to save the difference which discovers itself between his actual income and the expense of his habitual standard... Thus a rising income will often be accompanied by increased saving, and a falling income by decreasing saving, on a greater scale at first then subsequently' (Keynes, 1936, p. 97).

Friedman's 'permanent income hypothesis' follows this suggestion, maintaining that consumption will be not so much a function of *current income*, but rather of an agent's perceived 'permanent' or long-term income. Therefore the observed propensity to save may be more erratic than Keynes' simplified theory suggested. This principle perhaps offers some explanation of a rising savings ratio during the early 70s when the rise in real PDI was considerably 'above trend', but it also carries the counter-factual implication that the ratio should have fallen substantially in the years to 1977 when real PDI was stagnant or falling. Faced with the behaviour of savings over the years to 1975, the OECD admitted that it was difficult to do more than 'hazard guesses' as to their determination (OECD, 1975). Factors which were reckoned to be disrupting the more predictable behaviour of earlier years included rising unemployment (which could induce 'precautionary' savings), accelerating inflation, in particular following the oil price rises of 1973-74, and exceptionally high interest rates.

Over recent years an alternative theory of saving in times of inflation has been proposed (e.g. Bean, 1978). The suggestion is that since inflation reduces the real value (purchasing power) of the financial assets held by savers, it may induce a higher level of savings as agents attempt to rebuild their stock of financial assets in 'real' terms. Households, that is, may be considered as taking a view of an appropriate 'real' stock of savings relative to their real income. As a basis for this claim, it may be pointed out that despite the high savings ratio, the ratio of financial assets held by the personal sector to PDI has been on a falling trend since its peak in 1969. Over the years from 1972 to 1976 it fell from 2.73 to 1.7 (CSO, 1978). As we shall see, this attempt to build up the real value of accumulated savings by saving a higher proportion of current income is deeply ironic since increased savings have contributed to falling profitability and weak real investment, retarding the growth of output of goods and services over which financial assets are a deferred claim.

Another possible link between inflation and personal savings is that mediated by government economic policy. Personal saving is calculated as total personal disposable income minus personal sector expenditure on goods and services (consumers' expenditure).[3] Now, a part of the latter is financed by borrowing so when governments have reacted to rapid inflation by raising interest rates and/or restricting the availability of consumer credit, and this has led to a fall in the amount of consumers' expenditure financed by borrowing, this has led to a rise in the savings ratio.

The pattern of savings

The theories of saving considered above take us some distance, but share a common weakness: they all deal with savings as an *aggregate*, and attempt to construct some kind of function relating this aggregate to disposable income, inflation or some other macroeconomic variable.

In so doing, they ignore a good deal of relevant information. We can get a better picture of the dynamics of personal sector savings by considering the various different kinds of assets acquired by different groups within the personal sector rather than just the overall savings ratio. Broadly speaking if agents in the personal sector are able to save, i.e. are in receipt of an income in excess of current consumption requirements, then there are two possibilities: they can either accumulate *financial assets* or else acquire property in the form of housing. Let us first consider the acquisition of financial assets. This can be broken down into the accumulation of *liquid assets* on the one hand (e.g. cash, deposits with banks and building societies) and *illiquid assets* such as claims against life assurance companies and pension funds, government bonds and company shares, on the other. The latter forms of savings (payment of life assurance premiums, contributions to pension funds) may be labelled 'contractual savings' since in this case individuals enter into a definite contract to set aside a part of their incomes and pay this to the financial institution concerned. It is clear that contractual saving has become increasingly important in Britain.

Take life assurance. Originally, this was not so much a means of saving but a means of providing for dependents should the wage or salary earner in a family meet an early death. But more recently the big growth area of life assurance business has been in endowment policies — in this case premiums are paid over an arranged term and at the end of that period (or on prior death) the sum in the endowment is paid to the policyholder. Further, 'with profits' policies are available, whereby the sum paid out reflects the income earned by the assurance company on the financial assets which it in turn acquires using the funds subscribed by its policyholders. The 'endowment policy' still functions as an insurance against the financial consequences of early death, but in addition it provides a means of accumulating a financial claim for the purposes of, for instance, provision for retirement, paying children through the education system, or passing on wealth intergenerationally. Superannuation — contribution to a pension scheme — is also obviously a means of providing for a level of income greater than the basic state pension in retirement. The increasing participation in pension schemes, and increasing holding of life assurance policies, over recent years is shown in Table 4.3.

The financial importance of these forms of saving may be gauged by the £7.7 billion, or 41.2 per cent of total personal savings which flowed into life assurance and superannuation in 1978. The full breakdown

of personal sector acquisition of financial assets for that year is shown
in Table 4.4.

Table 4.3 *The spread of life assurance and pension commitments 1966-78*

a) Estimated total membership of pension and life assurance schemes:

	1966	1968	1970	1972	1974	1976	1978
Millions	5.02	5.56	6.24	6.83	8.02	8.72	9.76
as % of working population	19.6	21.9	24.7	27.1	31.3	33.4	37.0

b) Ordinary life assurances in force at end year:

	1966	1968	1970	1972	1974	1976	1978
millions	11.4	12.3	13.9	15.1	17.0	18.5	19.7

Sources: 'Life Assurance in the UK' (London, Life Offices Association), various issues, and Economic
Trends Annual Supplement, 1980.

Table 4.4

Personal sector savings in 1978	*(£ billion)*
Personal savings	17.2
Net sales of stocks and shares	1.5
	18.7

Acquisition of financial assets	*(£ billion and % of total savings)*	
Bank deposits	3.2	(17.1%)
Building Society deposits	4.9	(26.2)
Life assurance and superannuation	7.7	(41.2)
Public sector debt	1.7	(9.1)
Notes and coins	0.6	(3.2)
Deposits with other financial institutions	0.6	(3.2)
	18.7	(100)

Source: 'The Economist', December 8, 1979.

But aside from using the excess of income over current consumption
needs to accumulate *financial* assets, wage and salary earners do have
one other option which has become increasingly popular: the acquisition of physical assets, not in the form of means of production but

in the form of housing. For most people it is not possible to buy a house outright, but it is possible to take out a mortgage loan from a building society. Thereafter, a part of their income is earmarked for repayment of the principal plus interest. The end-point of this process is the full repayment of the mortgage loan, but even before this it may be possible to sell the house and realise any gains arising from increase in the market value of the property above its purchasing price. This can seem especially attractive when house prices are rising faster than the general price level, as has been the case over the 1970s. The extent of owner-occupation of the UK housing stock, much of it financed through the building societies, is one indicator of this trend: in 1914, only 10.6 per cent of the housing stock was owner-occupied, by 1950 the figure was 29.5 per cent and by 1979, 54.6 per cent. In international terms this is a high proportion, exceeded only in the USA, Canada and Japan.

The repayment of mortgage loans to the building societies occupies a somewhat ambivalent position in relation to the savings/expenditure balance of the personal sector. In one sense mortgage repayment may be regarded as similar to the payment of rent to a landlord, but while rent payment can legitimately be seen as 'consumer spending' (in exchange for the use value of housing), mortgage repayment is more than that. It is not merely a payment for enjoyment of a use value, but rather a progressive writing-off of a liability to the building society, which eventually results in full ownership of the house. Now it is clear that the house itself is not 'consumed'; rather it is a durable physical asset ('bricks and mortar') which may be seen, to some extent, as a substitute for paper financial assets. In 1978, in addition to the acquisition of financial assets noted above, the personal sector paid £6.3 billion in mortgage repayments to the building societies. The substantial acquisition of building society deposits shown in table 4.4 is also in part linked to personal sector 'investment' in the proverbial bricks and mortar: a building society deposit as such is a financial asset, and a fairly close substitute for a bank time deposit, but within the life-cycle of housing finance it can function as a means of establishing a favourable credit-rating with the society.

The importance of housing as a locus for the accumulation of property is further demonstrated if we consider not just year-by-year financial flows but the *stock* of assets held by the personal sector. At the end of 1978 housing accounted for 37.5 per cent of this stock, as against 41 per cent in the form of financial assets (the balance being made up of consumer durables and other physical assets).[4]

Before assessing the implications of substantial personal saving for economic development it is necessary to address two further preliminary questions: who precisely is doing the saving, and why should it take these forms? On the first question, it is unfortunate (and somewhat surprising) that there has been no proper official survey of savings. The personal sector balance sheets published in 'Economic Trends' (CSO 1978) do not give any breakdown by level of income or social status. One can, however, make a rough inference from (a) the distribution of income and (b) the distribution of wealth-holding, both areas in which government statistics are available. A priori it seems likely that saving year-by-year will be more unequally distributed than income (the Keynesian 'consumption function' cited earlier suggests that higher income groups will save proportionately more) but less unequal than wealth-holding (since the latter is a cumulated effect of saving over the years, and will therefore lag any tendency towards greater equality of income). In addition, the data from the Department of Employment's Family Expenditure Survey give an idea of the incidence of various important forms of saving within different income groups, although the authors are careful to point out that this survey cannot be taken as a basis for calculating savings ratios for different groups since the income and expenditure figures given do not refer to a standardised accounting period.

As regards income distribution, we can build up a picture from Central Statistical Office and Department of Employment information. The broad distribution of income by 'tax unit' (married couples or single people over school leaving age and not in full-time education) has not changed very markedly over the post war years, although there has been a slow and fairly steady fall in the shares of the top 1 per cent and the next 9 per cent, mainly taken up by the increasing share of the next 40 per cent, i.e. those above the median. This left a situation in 1976-77 in which the top 1 per cent accounted for 5.5 per cent of income pre-tax (3.8 per cent after tax), the top 10 per cent accounted for 26.2 per cent of income (23.1 per cent after tax), and the next 40 per cent accounted for 49.8 per cent (50 per cent after tax).[5] It can be seen that the tax system does not make income distribution greatly more even, in fact it has acted to cushion to some extent the fall in pre-tax income share of the top 1 per cent and the next 9 per cent of tax units. This distribution, however, does not tell us much about the social characteristics of the 'tax units' involved or give any direct idea concerning their saving behaviour. More information on this score can be drawn from the Family Expenditure Survey and this is presented in Table 4.5.

Some comments on the table. The payments included in row (1) are the following: life assurance premiums, including those for mortgage endowment policies, and contributions to pension and superannuation funds deducted by employers. The average weekly payment (for all housholds) in this category was £3.69. The payments included in row (2) should not all, perhaps, be regarded as 'savings': payments for house purchase, including deposits; mortgage capital and interest repayments; and payments for structural alteration. Nonetheless this figure gives an index of the accumulation of property in the housing stock. The average weekly payment was £4.90. Row (3) includes purchase of savings certificates and bonds, premium bonds, stocks and shares, unit trusts etc., deposits in savings banks, building societies etc., and contributions to Christmas, savings and holiday clubs. The average weekly payment was £1.25. The relative magnitude of these average weekly payments shows up again the importance of life assurance, pensions and housing as opposed to other forms of saving.

Now let us consider the profile of the different income groups shown in Table 4.5, drawing upon all the statistical sources cited:

i)   Those households with a pre-tax weekly income of less than £60: In this category fell about 30 per cent of households, accounting for only 10 per cent of income. Among this group, wages and salaries were a minor source of income compared to social security benefits, and the average number of workers per household was less than 0.4, indicating the predominance of elderly households living on state pensions, along with large families only partly supported by a low-paid wage worker. As can be seen, these households accounted for only a tiny share of savings.

ii) Households in the income range £60 — £110 per week: This category also contained about 30 per cent of households, receiving around a quarter of household income. Wages and salaries accounted for the major part of income, with the relative importance of social security falling towards the top of the range. We are evidently dealing with workers' households in the main (the range straddles the mean and median weekly earnings of both 'manual' and 'non-manual' male workers). Many households in this range must sustain a significant level of saving, since the table shows that this category contributed over 20 per cent of the forms of saving noted.

iii) Those in the income range of £110 — £170 per week: here we find about one quarter of households, accounting for one third of income and with wages and salaries representing over 80 per cent of income. According to the New Earnings Survey[6] we are well past the peak of the frequency distribution of male manual earnings, although by no means out of reach of a houshold including one male 'manual' worker and one 'non-manual' working woman. All the same, many of the earners in this category will be salaried 'non-manual' males. As can be seen, households in this range are responsible for a substantial fraction of total savings, proportionally greater than the fraction of total household income received.

Table 4.5   *Distribution of income and some forms of saving, by income group, 1978*

Range of household's gross normal weekly income	(i) less than £60	(ii) £60- £110	(iii) £110- £170	(iv) over £170
% of all households	29.4	29.1	26.3	15.2 (100*)
% of all household income received	10.2	23.5	33.7	33.5 (100)
(1) % of total payments to life assurance and pension funds	4.3	20.8	36.1	38.8 (100)
(2) % total payments for 'purchase or alteration of dwellings including mortgage payments'	1.7	25.4	40.6	32.4 (100)
(3) % of total payments for 'saving and investments'	3.2	20.0	41.2	35.7 (100)

* components may not sum to totals because of rounding.
Source: calculated from Department of Employment (1979).

iv)   Households with an income in excess of £170 per week: these were the top 15 per cent of households, receiving a further third of income. Wages and salaries were again the dominant source of income (although among those with an income in excess of £200, 'self-employment' contributed 10 per cent). At least at the lower end of the range, the income level is not unattainable by manual men with working wives (the average number of workers per household was in excess of two in this range) although households comprising non-manual workers must predominate. This 15 per cent of households account for more than a third of the forms of saving considered here, despite the facts that the households are on average larger than others, and that their share of income after tax will be a few percentage points lower than the 33.5 per cent quoted in the table.

Checking the profile above against the distribution of wealth, one finds that the latter is much more unequal. As regards marketable wealth in 1977 the top 1 per cent accounted for 24 per cent of the wealth, the top 10 per cent for 61 per cent of wealth, and the next 40 per cent for 34 per cent of wealth. All the same, these figures are considerably less unequal than those for 1966, which supports the idea that the rise in the savings ratio over the 1970s has been relatively broadly based. Further the Royal Commission on the Distribution of Income and Wealth has shown that the measurement of *marketable* wealth alone may be misleading. If one includes non-marketable assets such as state and other pension rights in measuring the distribution of wealth this nearly halves the 1976 share of the top 1 per cent, and nearly doubles the share of the bottom 80 per cent.[7] It might be objected that the Royal Commission's 'correction' of the wealth figures is itself misleading, since pension rights are not at par with, say, company shares or country houses. But the point here is to find an index of saving on the part of different strata, and pension rights indicate that the holders of those rights have saved in order to acquire them.

The significance of these statistics is that while saving is, rather obviously highly skewed towards the upper earning groups, it is by no means the preserve of the very rich alone. It appears that a not inconsiderable fraction of salary, and even wage earners are accumulating financial assets and a stake in the housing stock. Saving on the part of the economic class of wage-earning and salaries employees is actually quite broadly based.

Investigation of the second question noted above (why should saving take the particular forms it does?) leads to results which reinforce this conclusion. There is one major and rather obvious pecuniary factor promoting saving in the form of building society deposits, acquisition of houses, and acquisition of life assurance and pension claims in the British case: the tax-favoured status of these forms. It has been estimated that in 1978 a taxpayer claiming the main personal allowances who takes advantage of mortgage, superannuation and life assurance allowances could cut his real tax liability from 30 per cent to 19 per cent if he earned twice average earnings, and from 46 per cent to 34 per cent if he earned five times average earnings (Kilroy, 1979). This provides a powerful incentive to save in these particular forms for higher income groups, but it should also be noted that these forms of saving are more characteristic of the 'middle classes' (to use a descriptive tag without prejudice to subsequent analysis) and even 'affluent workers' than of the very rich. Inland Revenue (1975) investigations suggest that life policies form a higher proportion of asset holdings for those towards the bottom of the wealth distribution, and dwellings are also most significant as a proportion of wealth for those in the middle to lower wealth ranges.[8] By contrast, those at the top of the wealth distribution still hold a major, if dwindling, fraction of their wealth in the form of company shares and bonds. The 'middle class' salaried employee or highly paid wage worker who finds household income to be in excess of current expenditure is not, in Britain at any rate, likely to wish to play the stock market and gamble on speculative gains. He or she will have little or no knowledge and expertise regarding stock market 'investment', will not have a large reserve of personal wealth sufficient to write off speculative losses as 'bad luck' with equanimity, and will rather save in the 'safe and solid' forms of bricks and mortar or life assurance and pension claims. That is, the fact that these forms of saving have been made attractive to even the highest earners because of open-ended tax concessions should not hide their greater relative importance to a broad stratum of salary and wage earners some way further down the income/wealth pyramid.

A further point should be stressed here. The importance of contractual savings, which emerges strongly from the discussion above, is a point of particular relevance to the assessment of the standard economic theories of saving considered earlier. Those theories, formulated at the level of macro-economic variables, tend to leave out of account the definite social factors which govern the level of contractual saving, yet if one is looking for an explanation of the trend rise in the personal savings ratio in post war Britain, these factors cannot be ignored. Consider the fraction of personal disposable income (PDI) devoted not to current consumption but to pension contributions and mortgage repayment: it may well be that rising PDI is a *necessary* condition for the increase in such payments, but to explain *why* such payments should have increased it is necessary to go beyond the psychologism of the 'consumption function'. The first point to notice is that for many employees contributions to a pension scheme are deducted from 'disposable' income by the employers at source — these payments are therefore not a residual at all. Second, to the extent that people do enter voluntarily into endowment, annuity or other schemes, one must enquire why they feel this is necessary: here one has to consider the effects of earlier retirement and longer life expectancy, leading to a longer period of retirement for many people, coupled with the breakdown of the 'extended family' which previously cared for old people to a much greater extent. Also one has to consider the adequacy or otherwise of socialised provision for the elderly. Third, once people have entered into such contractual commitments then there is considerable pressure to maintain them. The 'cashing in' of a life assurance policy prior to its maturity generally entails substantial losses, and people will often maintain their level of current consumption by means of consumer credit, bank overdraft and so on rather than break their contractual savings commitments, if they find themselves financially squeezed.

Similar arguments apply in the case of mortgage repayments. I have already pointed out that mortgage repayments are in one sense a substitute for rent payments (an element of 'consumption') although they also lead to the eventual acquisition of a durable asset comparable in some ways to a financial asset. Why should so many people decide to buy houses by means of building society loans rather than rent? Again psychologism cannot provide a satisfactory explanation: here one has to refer to the taxation policies of successive governments, to the balance between public and private sector building programmes (also subject to political determination), to the availability and quality of rented accommodation and so on. And again, once mortgage commitments are acquired they may be difficult to break even if current real income falls, or fails to rise as expected, particularly if rented accommodation is hard to come by.

If these points are taken into consideration, it is hardly surprising that theories of saving which operate at the level of functional relations between personal consumption and other macroeconomic aggregates have only limited success in 'explaining' or predicting the behaviour of savings.

Savings and financial flows

I have considered above the pattern of savings carried out by agents separated from the means of production, yet receiving an income in excess of current consumption needs. This section is concerned with analysing the effects of such savings on the pattern of financial flows, and on the prospects for real accumulation.

A first point to notice is that the important financial circuit bound up with house purchase is mainly internal to the personal sector (mediated by the building societies). That is, some agents save in the form of building society deposits and the societies then use the funds raised in this way to extend credit to other (or even the same) agents who wish to buy houses.[9] Given the very high ratio of the existing housing stock to any year-by-year additions to the stock in response to additional demand, and given that credit extended for new building forms only a small fraction of total building society credit, a strong inflow of funds to the societies and consequent increase in available mortgage credit acts as a powerful means of inflating house prices. Here the attempt to accumulate is self-defeating: the inflation of house prices is possibly advantageous to some speculators but positively disadvantageous to first-time buyers and of no real benefit to the majority of owner-occupiers who will never 'realise' the market value of their property since they will only sell to buy again, either elsewhere or up-market. This effect is not lost on these responsible for managing the financial system. The Deputy Governor of the Bank of England was reported in the 'Times' (14/1/81) as noting that 'tax incentives originally designed for the best of motives... have created or magnified distortions in the process of saving and investment which are later found to require corrective measures'. The problem is that if the 'best of motives' involved a bi-partisan appeal by governments to the rising stratum of savers — at least appearing to facilitate their acquisition of property in the housing stock — then the required 'corrective measures' may be highly unpopular with that stratum. This would be the case if tax concessions were reduced in the absence of an accelerated house-building programme and a mechanism for controlling house prices — a calculation particularly to be borne in mind by the Tories, given their electoral base.

The other major flow of personal sector savings — into the life assurance companies and pension funds — gives rise to a rather different financial circuit. We have already seen that these institutions deploy most of their funds in acquiring the liabilities of the corporate sector (i.e. capitalist enterprises) and the public sector (i.e. the state) as well as landed property. To analyse the implications of this, it is necessary to develop an adequate theory of the financial circulation process, and its relationship to real accumulation. Volume Two of Marx's 'Capital' contains many suggestive insights into this matter, but not a coherent and adequate theory. The following exposition

draws on the theories of Keynes (1930 and 1936) and Kalecki (1968).
Kalecki based himself on the insights of 'Capital' but developed these
into a lucid and coherent whole; Keynes may be faulted from a Marxist
standpoint for having an inadequate conception of production (this
he largely carried over from neoclassical economics in the Marshallian
tradition) but this does not detract from the brilliance of his analysis
of the savings/investment nexus.

First, the point may be established that total saving must equal total
borrowing, so that net saving on the part of the personal sector implies
an equal amount of borrowing by the other sectors of the economy.
This follows from the formal properties of monetary transactions. Let
us distinguish between transactions involving the exchange of money
against use values whether consumer goods or means of production
— the 'industrial circulation' — and those involving the exchange of
money against financial assets, which may be referred to as the 'financial circulation'. Consider the industrial circulation: any transaction
within this circulation can be viewed from two sides — for the recipient
of the money it constitutes income while for the other party it
constitutes expenditure. Because money is not destroyed during the
transaction the income of one party must equal the expenditure of the
other. But what holds true for each and every·transaction will also
hold true for all transactions in aggregate: Income and Expenditure
are just two ways of looking at the one monetary flow.

If Y = total income and E = total expenditure then we have:

$$Y = E \text{ (Identity 1)}$$

But it is clear that for many economic agents their expenditure does
not equal their income. If the economy is viewed as a set of agents
engaging in monetary transactions then it may be partitioned into three
disjoint (separate) subsets.

a) Those whose income and expenditure are equal.

b) Those whose income exceeds their expenditure: the 'savers'. If
   income exceeds expenditure within the industrial circulation, then
   these agents must either be accumulating money balances, acquiring financial assets, or repaying debt contracted previously. For
   convenience I shall refer to all of these activities as 'saving'.

c) Those whose expenditure exceeds their income: the 'borrowers'.
   If expenditure exceeds income within the industrial circulation, the
   agents must finance the balance of their expenditure either by new
   borrowing (bank credit or new issues of financial claims), by running down their accumulated money balances (if any), or by selling
   financial assets previously acquired (if any). For convenient exposi-

tion I shall refer to all this as 'borrowing'.

Let Ya, Yb and Yc be the incomes of the respective sectors and let Ea, Eb and Ec be their expenditures. It follows that:-

$$Ya + Yb + Yc = Ea + Eb + Ec \text{ (from Identity 1)}$$

But by definition $\quad Ya = Ea$

so $\quad Yb + Yc = Eb + Ec$

thus $\quad Yb - Eb = Ec - Yc$

but $\quad Yb - Eb = Saving$

and $\quad Ec - Yc = Borrowing$

so $\quad$ *Saving = Borrowing*

This can be seen to be the principle behind the national financial accounts published by the Central Statistical Office, where any divergence between recorded saving and borrowing is attributed to the 'residual error' due to inaccuracy in compiling the Income and Expenditure figures.

So saving and borrowing must be equal. But what are the implications of this under different economic conditions? To conceptualise fully the relationship between saving and borrowing one has to make a distinction between the actual, realised level of saving/borrowing at any point in time *('ex post')* and the planned or desired level of savings and borrowing *('ex ante')*. It is clear that although *ex post* saving and borrowing are always equal, the desired level of saving at any given time need not equal the desired level of borrowing. It is, however, a fundamental conclusion of the economics of Keynes and Kalecki that if the desired level of borrowing does not equal the desired level of savings then forces come into play which tend to bring them into equality. Since we know that actual saving always equals actual borrowing, a discrepancy between the desired or planned levels must mean that some agents' intentions are frustrated (they find themselves borrowing or saving more than they planned). The argument is that the agents concerned will respond in such a way as to alter the level of income, output and employment, bringing the planned magnitude of saving and borrowing into line.

Let us consider first the 'Keynesian case', in which we abstract from the existence of government and overseas trade. In this case the relevant form of financing identity is simple. The only economic sectors considered are households and firms. If the household sector is a net saver and the corporate sector a net borrower, then it follows from the exposition above that net personal savings = net borrowing by firms.

A. Assume an autonomous rise in the desired level of savings, so that *ex ante* savings exceeds borrowing. The extra saving will mean that less income is passed back to firms (consumer spending/sales revenue) than they were expecting. Faced with unexpectedly weak demand firms either drop their prices or suffer an unplanned rise in stocks. Either way income falls further short of expenditure than planned, and involuntary borrowing rises. Firms then respond by cutting back on their expenditure (therefore also on output and employment, the latter being a lagged effect). As a result the personal sector finds its income reduced, and so, according to the Keynesian 'consumption function', settles for a lower level of savings. Planned savings are brought back in line with planned borrowing through the mechanism of a fall in the level of income. This effect is often referred to as the paradox of thrift: the individual saver imagines that he can increase his wealth by saving a larger fraction of current income, yet if savers in aggregate attempt to do this, the net effect is likely to be recessionary, merely reducing current income without stimulating any increase in accumulation. *If* savers were able to carry out real investment in place of current consumption the effects would be very different, but as we have argued above the agents responsible for saving are separated from the means of production so that their *saving* decisions do not have any direct and positive influence on the *investment* decisions of capitalist enterprises.

B. Assume an autonomous 'investment boom' (financed, say, by new bank credit) so that *ex ante* borrowing by firms exceeds savings. The extra expenditure in this case increases the pressure of demand for commodities, which will lead to 'windfall' profits and/or destocking on the part of firms. In either case this provides a stimulus to expand output and employment. Income rises and (the consumption function again) the planned level of saving also rises. Here the *ex ante* discrepancy is overcome through a rise in income which raises planned saving to meet planned borrowing. In effect, additional investment is self-financing since it will generate savings to match.

These Keynesian arguments are interesting from a Marxist viewpoint, in that they draw out the consequences of the continuing separation of individuals from the means of production. Perhaps the owner-manager of earlier years could channel his own savings directly into real accumulation within his own enterprise, but once the 'saving strata' have lost this option then their savings become a possible source of stagnation in real accumulation. The important question is whether enterprises are *willing* to borrow, for investment purposes, the funds which the personal sector wishes to save at a level of income and demand consistent with rapid accumulation. Neoclassical economists imagined there was a mechanism to ensure this, in the rate of interest. The rate of interest was conceived as the price of 'loanable funds'[10] and was supposedly set, like all prices, by the balance of supply and demand. An increase in saving would increase the supply of loanable funds which would lead to a reduction in the interest rate, which would in turn increase the demand for loanable funds on the part of enterprises. One of the great merits of Keynes' and Kalecki's arguments was the demonstration that saving and borrowing were always and necessarily equal regardless of the rate of interest, and that the rate of interest, insofar as it has a general determination, is the 'price' which balances the 'demand' for *money* holdings against the stock of money in existence. There is a mechanism which brings the desired level of saving and borrowing into equality, but it operates through variation in the level of income and output and may well be inconsistent with rapid accumulation.

So far I have been using a model in which the personal sector and the corporate sector are the only participants in the circulation process. This model demonstrates the possibility of stagnation induced by a high level of personal savings, but it does not follow that personal saving always produces that effect. In Japan, for instance, a savings ratio higher than that in Britain co-exists with rapid capital accumulation. To take the inquiry further we must consider a more developed model in which the state finances and international transactions are given consideration.

The state in the circulation process

I established above the identity of total saving and total borrowing. In the simplified model, the only net borrower was the corporate sector, but if the public sector (state) is also a net borrower then the financing identity becomes:

Personal Saving = Corporate Borrowing + Public Sector Borrowing

That is, the borrowing imposed on the other sectors by virtue of personal sector saving may be shared between capitalist enterprises and the state. To a certain extent, capitalist states over the post war period have willingly accepted financial deficits in the pursuit of 'Keynesian' demand-management policy: if the economy showed a tendency towards recession the government could expand demand by either increasing public expenditure or reducing taxation so as to stimulate private expenditure. This mode of thinking attained the status of conventional wisdom in place of the earlier doctrine of 'sound finance' (i.e. the state should make all efforts to avoid a financial deficit, except of course in the prosecution of war). It is possible to dispute whether government-engineered variations in the level of demand were particularly effective in a counter-cyclical sense, indeed it has been suggested that because of timing problems (information lag, delays in implementation of policy, lag between introduction of policy and its full effects) these variations may have exacerbated rather than damped the fluctuations in economic activity (Dow, 1965). Also, of course, there has been the notorious 'stop-go' cycle of alternating fiscal expansion and balance of payments crises (the political dimension of which will be considered in Chapters 6 and 7). But aside from *discretionary* variations in expenditure and tax rates, the pattern of state finances established in the 'post war settlement' has produced an *automatic* mechanism for expanding the state's financial deficit in times of recession. I refer here to the combination of generalised income tax and the principle of income maintenance for the unemployed: if recession involves a fall in private spending and rise in unemployment then it simultaneously reduces the state's tax base and increases the amount payable in unemployment benefit and social security. This effect (known to economists as the 'built-in stabiliser') can offset to some extent the recessionary tendencies implicit in the rising personal saving ratio and analysed in the Keynesian 'Case A' above,[11] but although it moderates the fall in demand it does not necessarily stimulate accumulation. Borrowing to support the unemployed is not at par with borrowing to finance real investment.

This latter point was clearly recognised by Keynes. Contrary to widespread misrepresentation, Keynes was not exclusively concerned with 'short run', conjunctural questions of demand management. He saw a dangerous secular tendency in capitalist development: rising income would raise the level of savings which the personal sector would wish to carry out, and there was no guarantee that borrowing for investment on the part of capitalist enterprises would keep pace with this. Borrowing for real investment would be expanded only if its prospective marginal profitability were greater than the marginal cost of funds (interest rate) and there were two problems here: the marginal profitability of investment might fall due to diminishing returns as the capital stock expanded (a version of the 'tendency for the rate of profit to fall'), and there were likely to be severe difficulties in engineering a fall in the interest rate sufficient to offset this. If the level of investment continued to be determined by calculations based on comparison of the prospective yield of real capital assets as against paper financial assets, then there was a real danger of secular stagnation, not merely 'cyclical fluctuations'. For this reason, Keynes advocated 'a somewhat comprehensive socialisation of investment' (Keynes, 1936, p.378) as a means of sustaining an adequate pace of accumulation.

In the practice of British governments, 'Keynesian' economic policy has fallen a good way short of this kind of radicalism. Insofar as public sector borrowing has been expanded as a policy measure this has been merely conjunctural. A favourite means of boosting demand has been a cut in the rate of personal taxation — a ploy which has obvious attractions in terms of electoral calculation but which has generally led to an unsustainable growth of imports, and does very little to promote the longer term growth of productive capacity. The general point here is that state borrowing for socialised investment could in principle absorb rising personal saving and avoid stagnation, but it has not played this role in the British case. The state sector has indeed been saddled with a high level of borrowing, through the automatic mechanism sketched above, but its real investment programme has been cut to the bare minimum. Increasingly the borrowed funds have been used merely to finance the unemployment, and the losses sustained by state industries, consequent upon stagnation or recession (Bain, 1980).

The role of the 'overseas sector'

The case of the Japanese economy, where high savings are combined with rapid accumulation, has been mentioned above. The differences from the British case can be partly explained by a higher level of voluntary borrowing for investment on the part of Japanese enterprises, and partly by a state economic policy which, despite the relatively low level of public expenditure, has concentrated successfully on developing strategic investment in key sectors of industry. But at the level of the financial circulation there is another crucial difference: the trade surplus run by the Japanese economy has absorbed a major part of Japanese savings. If we return to the financing identity and include the 'overseas sector', i.e. other economies, then the saving/borrowing equivalence becomes:

Personal Saving = Corporate Borrowing + Public Sector Borrowing
+ Overseas Sector Borrowing

If economy A runs a trade surplus with others, then it is effectively lending to the other economies, and this 'overseas sector borrowing' reduces the level of borrowing which would otherwise be borne by the corporate sector or the state. The deficiency of demand within economy A which might otherwise be the consequence of the excess of personal sector income over expenditure is redressed by the excess of other countries' expenditure (on A's exports) over income (from A's imports). Conversely, a trade deficit corresponds to a financial surplus on the part of the overseas sector, so that for any given level of personal saving the financial deficit to be borne by the corporate and public sectors is increased.

In seeking to explain the Japanese trade surplus one is, of course, led to consider factors beyond the financial circulation: the institutional arrangements which act as 'import controls' for Japan; the rapid growth of productivity in Japanese factories which has enabled them to compete so successfully in export markets. This latter phenomenon is related both to the long-term lending policies of the Japanese banks, which encourage investment in technological innovation, and to the social relations within Japanese enterprises: the active involvement of much of the workforce in raising productivity and quality; the relative absence of 'management'/'workforce' antagonism and trade union 'defensive' strategies, which in part depends on the life-time employment policy of the big industrial companies.[12] The analysis of the social relations of Japanese capitalism would be a massive task in its own right; the point here is simply to emphasise that the financial identities considered above only show the formal possibilities arising from a substantial personal sector financial surplus, while the actual distribution and effects of the corresponding financial deficit depend on the overall development of the national economy in question, including the social relations at the 'point of production'.

Kalecki: saving and profits

Before leaving this question of the effects of the savings of employees on the financial circulation, it will be useful to adapt the model employed above to take account of the implications for aggregate profits. For this task it is appropriate to refer to Kalecki's version of the Income/Expenditure equivalence thesis.[13] It was determined above that

$$\text{Income} = \text{Expenditure (Identity 1).}$$

If we consider an economy composed exclusively of impersonal capitals employing wage and salary earning workers, then the only categories of net income are enterprise profits (P) and wages-plus-salaries (W). Similarly, the only categories of net expenditure are consumer spending by employees (C) and investment spending by enterprises (I). It follows that

$$P + W = C + I \ (2).$$

If we assume that all wages and salaries are spent on consumption (i.e. $C = W$) then equation (2) reduces thus:

$$P = I \ (3).$$

The profits made by capitalist enterprises depend on the investment expenditure which they carry out. This should not be surprising: since the capitalist class has exclusive possession of the means of production, the only net 'cost' to that class is the purchase of labour power. Any expenditure by capitalists over and above the purchase of labour power (i.e. 'investment') must flow back to the capitalist class as profit (i.e. income in excess of costs).

If employees save part of their incomes, this model shows the effects:
Let employees' saving = S
then $S = W - C$.
But we can re-arrange equation (2) to give

$$P = I + C - W$$
$$\text{so} \quad P = I - (W - C)$$
$$\text{so} \quad P = I - S \ (4).$$

For any given level of investment, profits will be reduced by the amount of employees' savings. This is because the full price paid for labour power is no longer returned as income to the capitalist class.

If the state sector is included, then the income/expenditure equation must be modified to take into account state expenditure (G) and revenue (T):

$$P + W + T = C + I + G \ (5)$$
$$\text{so} \quad P = I + (G - T) - (W - C)$$
$$\text{so} \quad P = I + (G - T) - S.$$

That is, the state's budget deficit will increase aggregate profit, *ceteris paribus*. In the same way that employees' saving represents an excess of expenditure over income from the point of view of the capitalist class, a budget deficit represents an excess of income over expenditure for the rest of the economy. This effect should make Marxists rather more cautious than they have been in going along with the 'New Conservative' proposition that 'state expenditure squeezes profits' (cf Rowthorn, 1980, Ch. 4). State expenditure in excess of revenue can *sustain* aggregate profit in the face of high personal savings, while state spending balanced by revenue will be neutral in its effect on profit, *ceteris paribus*.

To complete the picture the overseas sector must be included in the income/expenditure model, adding overseas income (M) and expenditure (X). Then we have:

$$P + W + T + M = C + I + G + X \quad (6)$$

$$\text{or} \quad P = I - (W - C) + (G - T) + (X - M)$$

$$\text{or} \quad P = I - S + (G - T) + (X - M)$$

(X — M), the excess of expenditure by the overseas sector over income, represents the trade surplus of the economy in question. As Kalecki remarks, 'it follows directly that an increase in the export surplus will raise profits *pro tanto* if other components are unchanged' (1968, p. 51). The full picture is one in which the mass of profit is determined by investment, diminished by workers' savings but augmented by both a state budget deficit and an export surplus. Two points emerge: first, state expenditure in excess of revenue will boost profits *unless* it causes a fall in investment, rise in savings or fall in trade surplus/rise in trade deficit. Second, one can trace both 'vicious' and 'virtuous' circles relating investment and international trade: if a strong export performance stimulates further investment (and vice versa) then profit will tend to rise, while if a high import penetration and poor export performance reduce the incentive to real investment (and vice versa) profit will tend to fall.

Some implications for the theory of surplus value

I have described a situation in which saving by employees has become a significant element within the financial circulation, and have analysed the possible effects of this within the framework of an income/expenditure model of the circulation process. We may now take stock of the implications for the classical Marxist theory of surplus value in capitalism.

Marx operated, in 'Capital', with a theory in which the price paid for labour power by capitalist enterprises was tendentially equal to the 'value of labour power', i.e. the wage would just cover the subsistence and reproduction needs of the workers: '...the value of labour power is the value of the means of subsistence necessary for the maintenance of its owner' (Marx, 1976, p. 274). Marx's views on whether this 'subsistence' level would tend to fall towards the minimum 'biological' requirement, or would rather have a *social* determination over and above the former, changed over time (Rowthorn, 1980, Ch.7). In

'Capital' he took the latter view:

> '... the number and extent of (the worker's) so-called necessary
> requirements, as also the manner in which they are satisfied, are
> themselves products of history, and depend therefore to a great
> extent on the level of civilisation attained by a country; in particular
> they depend on the conditions in which, and consequently on the
> habits and expectations with which, the class of free workers has
> been formed' (Marx, *op. cit.*, p. 275).

Unlike the value of other commodities, therefore, the value of labour
power contains an 'historical and moral element'. All the same, Marx
did not envisage a situation in which the wages or salaries of a broad
stratum of sellers of labour power would be *more than sufficient* to cover
current consumption needs, leading to the acquisition of financial assets
and durable property other than means of production. When Marx
did consider the question of workers' savings, in the 'Grundrisse', he
claimed that although *some* workers individually might be able to
accumulate money balances by exceptional industriousness or frugality,
it was impossible that workers *in general* could save, for this would contradict the idea of the wage as tendentially equal to the 'value of labour
power':

> 'If they all save, then a general reduction of wages will bring them
> back to earth again; for general savings would show the capitalist
> that their wages are in general too high, that they receive more than
> its equivalent for their commodity' (Marx, 1973a, p. 286).

It seems that in present circumstances, and on Marx's definition, the
existence of saving on a broad scale shows that the aggregate payment
of wages and salaries is considerably in excess of the aggregate 'value
of labour power'.

What are the consequences for the concept of surplus value? Let
us first recall the role of this concept in Marx's theory of capitalism.
The essential feature of any class society, according to Marx, is the
existence of a *social surplus product*, i.e. a product over and above that
(the 'necessary product') required to maintain and reproduce the
'direct producers', the disposition of which is vested in the hands of
a class distinct from the direct producers. (In pre-class societies either
there was no surplus product or else such surplus product as did exist
was appropriated communally. In communist society there will still

be a surplus product — required for consumption by those unable to work and for augmentation of the stock of means of production — but this is to be appropriated through social planning by the 'associated producers'.) The labour required to produce the necessary product may be designated as the necessary labour, while the labour embodied in the surplus product is surplus labour. Class societies differ in their modes of extraction of surplus labour — the social means by which the direct producers are compelled to produce a surplus product. In capitalist society, as a consequence of its particular property relations, both the necessary and the surplus product assume the form of collections of commodities, produced for exchange against money. The necessary product is purchased with the wages of workers while the surplus product is purchased with the profits of capitalist enterprises (which may or may not be owned by individuals). This can be represented schematically as below:

universal	necessary product	: surplus product	(1)
	necessary labour,	surplus labour,	
	aggregate labour-time N	: aggregate labour-	
		time S	(2)

specific	necessary commodities,	surplus commodities,	
to	aggregate monetary value W_1	: aggregate monetary	
capitalism		value P_1	(3)
	wages, aggregate	: profits, aggregate	
	monetary value W_2	monetary	
		value P_2	(4)

The labour-times (2) are embodied in the products (1), in general. In capitalism the products (1) take the form of commodities (3) which are purchased with the incomes of the two classes (4). In 'equilibrium' (Marx does not use the term, but the concept is often implicit in his analysis), $W_1 = W_2$ and $P_1 = P_2$. Further, W_1 maps onto N and P_1 maps onto S: this can be interpreted in the sense that W_1/P_1 is equal to N/S. In this context, the concept of 'surplus value' can be seen as effecting an essential expressive relationship between all the levels (1) to (4) above: surplus labour 'takes the form' of surplus value, and profit in turn is the monetary 'expression' of surplus value.

My argument is that *to analyse adequately workers' savings one has to drop the 'expressive' relationship between the levels (1) to (4) embodied in the concept of surplus value.* Money incomes must be conceptualised as *claims* over output which may or may not by fully exercised in any given period, and which may be augmented through borrowing. If workers save, then W_2 is greater than W_1, and part of workers' current income is not used to claim current output but may instead be used to purchase financial claims against financial institutions which in turn acquire financial claims against other capitalist enterprises (and states). This introduces two discrepancies between profit on the one hand and disposition of the surplus product by capitalist enterprises on the other. First, part of the gross profits of enterprises is channelled through the financial institutions (in the form of dividends, rent and interest) and distributed to the holders of life policies, pension schemes and other financial claims. In this case the final claim over the surplus product may be exercised by retired wage-earners, as well as the 'idle rich' rentiers (i.e. the product disposed of by the capitalist class falls short of P_1 above). Second, retained profit does not set a limit to the appropriation of the surplus product by capitalist enterprises. To the extent that they finance real accumulation by means of borrowed funds (either *ex ante* personal savings or new bank credit which will generate *ex post* saving to match, as analysed above), real appropriation by enterprises can outrun their profitability even in aggregate (i.e. the part of P_1 above disposed of by capitalist enterprises exceeds P_2).

Now, if the payments made by workers currently employed into savings schemes were exactly matched by payments made out to retired workers then one could conceptualise this by saying that the *aggregate* payment of wages and salaries was actually equal to the aggregate consumption needs of the entire working class (employed and retired). Saving would merely be a means of transferring current wages and salaries to retired workers, and in terms of the schema above W_2 would be equal to W_1 plus that fraction of P_1 required to support retired workers. But this is not the case. In 1978, for instance, contributions to life assurance and superannuation schemes amounted to £8.9 billion, while pensions and other benefits paid out amounted to only £4.6 billion. In addition, the life assurance and pension funds received an income from rent, dividends and interest of £4.6 billion, and had administrative and tax costs of £1.5 billion, leaving an overall surplus for further 'investment' of £7.4 billion.[14] In other words, saving out of current income was greatly in excess of real appropriation by retired workers (both measured in money terms), and W_2 was greater than the total monetary expenditure by workers employed or retired.

Should one then say that, insofar as they save, the working class receive part of the 'surplus value' in the form of their wages and salaries? I am inclined to resist this formulation, for it would seem to imply that employed workers are able to appropriate part of the surplus product. The only sense in which workers can be said to appropriate the surplus product is by continuing to consume when they are no longer employed; their separation from the means of production means that they cannot appropriate the surplus product in the sense of disposing of means of production as capital. I would rather say that wage and salary earning employees receive a 'surplus income' (in the sense that W_2 is greater than W_1), but there is no guarantee that this 'surplus income' will be channelled by the financial institutions into the real accumulation of capital. Rather, as I have already indicated, it is more likely under the present arrangements to be channelled into the acquisition of landed property or state debt.

This mode of analysis also allows us to take further the comments made above on the relationship between the state finances and profits. I showed that, *ceteris paribus*, an increase in the state's budget deficit (or reduction in its surplus) will increase aggregate profit, unless it leads to an equivalent rise in savings, deterioration in the trade balance or fall in investment. More formally, one can say that provided the sum of the marginal propensity to save and the marginal propensity to import is less than unity (surely the case), and provided the enlarged public sector financial deficit does not reduce investment, then the net effect of an increase in the budget deficit must be to raise profits. But profit is a *monetary* magnitude: this analysis does not immediately tell us about the capacity for real appropriation of the social product on the part of capitalist enterprises. The effects of an increase in the budget deficit at the latter level depend on the degree to which means of production and labour power lie idle, and on the responsiveness of employment of these to an increase in monetary demand. If productive resources are currently not fully utilised, and can be brought into use by means of increased monetary expenditures, then the increased profits will permit an increased appropriation of real output. But if the rise in demand merely gives rise to an inflation of prices and money incomes then the rise in profits will be offset by a decline in the purchasing-power of money. The only condition, however, under which a rise in state expenditure (greater than or equal to any change in state revenue) could actually *reduce* the 'real value' of total profit as a claim over output on the part of capitalist enterprises, would be if it gave rise to a price inflation of Department I commodities in excess of the rise in money profits. This effect may occur, but we can see that it is highly over-simplistic to assert in general terms that 'state expenditure squeezes profits'.

The analysis above deals with monetary magnitudes (the state's budget deficit, total profits) on the one hand, and with real appropriation of the social product on the other. But what of the Marxist focus on labour-times? In relation to this question it might appear 'obvious' that labour-time appropriated by the state is labour-time which cannot be appropriated by capitalist enterprises, so that there is indeed a trade-off between state expenditure and profits: the greater the proportion of social labour-time appropriated through state expenditure, the less the surplus value available to capitalist enterprises. But this argument rests on a conflation, a conflation which is encouraged by the use of 'value' concepts. Certainly, the labour-time available within a given national economy in a given period is finite, and therefore the greater the appropriation of social labour by the state the less, in principle, is available for appropriation by capitalist enterprises. But two points have to be made. First, this argument tells us nothing about causality. It cannot legitimately be inferred, for instance, that increasing state employment in Britain has reduced the appropriation of labour-time on the part of capitalist enterprises below what it otherwise would have been. It may be argued, on the contrary, that workers employed by the state would otherwise have been unemployed; there is only a direct trade-off if full employment is assumed. Second, even if it is argued that workers employed by the state would otherwise have been employed by capitalist enterprises, this point concerns state *employment* and not state *expenditure* — and this is the crucial conflation. Part of state expenditure takes the form of payment of wages and salaries to state employees, and in this case state expenditure functions as a means of appropriating social labour-time, but to the extent that state expenditure takes the form of purchases of commodities from capitalist enterprises, or indeed grants and subsidies to the latter, it does not function as a means of appropriating labour-time. In this case state expenditure figures directly as revenue for capitalist enterprises, without diminishing the fraction of social labour-time available for exploitation by those enterprises: there is no diminution of the available labour force. Transfer payments to households have a similar role, since most of the money paid out by the state in this form is passed on to capitalist enterprises as consumer expenditure.

I consider it important to make these points (and to insist on the distinctions between monetary magnitudes within the circulation process, the appropriation of the social product by different categories of agent, and the distribution of social labour-time between sectors) because of the role they play in the following arguments. Positively,

I wish to argue in favour of an 'economic strategy' involving state investment expenditure, and to maintain that such expenditure will not cause a self-defeating decline in profits which would restrict private sector investment (although there are certainly *political* problems associated with such a strategy; these will be considered later).

Negatively, I shall argue later that the Thatcherite economic programme, with its heavy emphasis on cutting state expenditure, is in no sense consonant with the supposed 'needs' of capitalism.

5

Economic class relations and the socialist project

Chapter 3 outlined the development of the impersonal capital as arguably the dominant mode of possession of the means of production in the contemporary British social formation. Chapter 4 extended the analysis to consider in economic terms the position of the 'personal sector' wage and salary-earning employees, and the effects of the saving of this sector on accumulation — the expansion of the salaried strata in particular being, at least in part, the obverse of the rise of the impersonal capital. Given my concentration so far on the possession/separation issue, and its relation to the circulation process, and given my earlier insistence that economic class relations at the level of possession/separation cannot be conceived as the underlying 'essence' of social and political collectivities and movements, which demand analysis in their own right, I am not yet in a position to draw full 'political conclusions' (the following chapters will take us some way further in this direction). But although the realm of political forces and their support blocs — the realm of political *agency* — remains to be investigated, the foregoing analysis of the economic class structure does yield certain implications in terms of what is *at stake* in socialist transformation. It will therefore be appropriate to offer in this chapter an account of some of these implications.

It will be argued that the developments of the economic class structure noted in the previous two chapters open up certain opportunities for socialism, but also place certain constraints on what a socialist movement can hope to achieve. But before investigating these opportunities and constraints it is necessary to outline what one takes 'socialist objectives' to be, in broad terms. Some comments on this score have been made above (in particular, see the final section of the Introduction); for present purposes I can summarise my view of these objectives as follows:

1. The development of economic *planning* directed towards the well-being of workers and their families, retired workers and those unable to work, both immediately — in terms of material living standards — and in the longer term (planning of investment in industrial

capacity, social 'infrastructure' and social amenities; avoidance of long-term environmental degradation). This may be conceived in terms of constructing a 'socialised appropriation' of the social product and progressively restricting the sphere of *commodity* production and circulation, and monetary calculation based on profitability (although the elimination of the latter may be an unattainable theoretical limit).

2. The development of participative *popular democracy* both 'at work' and in a broader social context — in itself a distinction the sharpness of which socialists wish to reduce by such means as Marx's 'polytechnic' education and the creation of closer links between industry and community.

3. As an integral condition of democracy at work and beyond, the progressive *reduction of social hierarchy in the division of labour*, whether this hierarchy is thought in terms of mental/manual labour (Poulantzas), function of capital/function of labour (Carchedi), 'conception' versus 'execution' (Braverman), or in some other way. Linked with this, also the compression and restructuring of income differentials. (Although, again, the complete abolition of hierarchy, whether of function or income, may be an unattainable theoretical limit.)

These points are not exhaustive,[1] but they will serve my purpose. The object now is to analyse the implications of the current structure of economic class relations for these objectives, and therefore also to render more precise the objectives. I shall consider first the issue of socialisation of production and planning, then address the question of industrial democracy/workers' control at the level of enterprise.

Socialisation and planning

It is a central thesis of Marxism that the accumulation of capital creates certain of the economic conditions of existence of socialism. In 'Capital' Marx wrote that the 'immanent laws of capitalist production itself' lead to 'the growth of the cooperative form of the labour process, the conscious technical application of science ... the transformation of the means of labour into forms which can only be used in common, the economising of all means of production by their use as the means of production of combined, socialised labour' (1976, p. 929). The concentration and centralisation of capitals (growth and merging respectively) lead to a 'constant decrease in the number of capitalist magnates' and increasingly the 'monopoly of capital becomes a fetter upon the mode of production, which has flourished alongside and under it' (ibid.). Production, that is, becomes progressively *socialised* under capitalism, and hence progressively incompatible with the 'capitalist integument'.

At the same time there also grows the 'revolt of the working class', which is 'trained, united, and organised' by capitalism itself (ibid.). In Marx's more 'deterministic' formulations these two tendencies — socialisation of production, growth of the working class revolt against exploitation — together *guarantee* the historical triumph of communism, 'capitalist production begets, with the inexorability of a natural process, its own negation' (ibid.).

I have already argued (Chapter 1) that capitalist development does not of itself lead to the political unification of the working class. Marx's arguments for this position, as elaborated in the 'Communist Manifesto', were examined and found to be seriously problematic. And this discussion will be taken further in the following chapters. Within the present context, however, I shall concentrate on the question of the socialisation of production. If capitalist development does not lead automatically to the formation of a united opposition class determined to 'expropriate the expropriators', does it not at least lay the 'economic' foundations for socialism, constructing a system of socialised production in relation to which capitalist property becomes increasingly inappropriate?

But this question, which Marx answers in the affirmative, is badly posed. 'Socialisation' is the problematic concept: for Marx socialisation of production stands in inevitable contradictory tension with capitalism. We have seen above how he conceptualised the joint stock company as a mere 'transitional' form, an unstable half-way house between capitalism and its abolition: this was because the joint stock form represented the socialisation of capital itself, which had to be a 'self-dissolving contradiction'. Modern Marxist writers as far apart in other ways as Poulantzas and Cutler *et al.* have stressed against this view that there is socialisation and socialisation. The new capitalism of the impersonal multidivisional enterprises and the financial institutions deploying employees' saving has produced a specifically *capitalist* 'socialisation' of production, embodied in social forms and practices which in many cases will have to be deconstructed before socialism can be developed.[2] This is a powerful criticism. It does indeed seem as though Marx's concept of 'socialisation' was too general and too poor. It was linked with a general philosophical theme deriving from Hegel: socialisation within capitalism was the 'negation of the negation' (Marx, loc. cit.). As Bachelard (1972) argued for the case of the natural sciences, general philosophical conceptions can often function as 'epistemological obstacles', providing a simple and apparently clear answer where there should be a series of well-defined *questions*. In the spirit of this observation, however, it is not enough to argue that Marx's views have been shown to be false by the continuing development of capitalist socialisation. One must try to locate the precise questions with which to replace Marx's schematism.

Let us therefore re-pose the problem. Considering the particular forms of 'socialisation' which have emerged with the development of the impersonal capital, to what extent do these increase or limit the opportunities for socialist transformation of the economy? How can socialists develop their arguments and strategies to gain the maximum purchase over the reality of contemporary capitalist property relations? In what ways can planned and democratic economic forms be presented as a feasible and superior development/transformation of existing forms? If it is clear enough that capitalist development brings social planning of the economy closer to the realms of possibility than, say, peasant and artisanal production it should also be clear that socialists must pose and answer these questions if they are to intervene effectively in politics.

At the outset it may be noted that the development of large-scale impersonal capitals, integrating purchasing, production and marketing within a multidivisional form, substantially increases the element of 'planning' within capitalism. As Chandler has it, the 'invisible hand' of market relations between independent enterprises is progressively displaced by the 'visible hand' of managerial coordination. And if 'planning' is now possible at the level of the giant enterprise, perhaps straddling several branches of production, then the planning of the economy to meet social objectives is at least 'put on the agenda': what was only a long run historical speculation in the era of smaller-scale entrepreneurial capitalism begins to look like an economically feasible proposition.

But this general remark has immediately to be qualified, in two important ways. First, neither the development of the 'visible hand' in coordinating 'vertical' flows from the extraction of raw materials through to final sales, nor the rise of the diversified corporation carrying out a planned allocation of resources between different product divisions, abolishes competition between capitalist enterprises. In fact, contrary to a persistent theme in neoclassical economics, competition between giant 'dominant firms' is often fiercer than the competition between small enterprises in unconcentrated markets: increasing scale often goes along with the development of a keener rationality of profit. Planning on the part of large-scale enterprises, that is, remains a planning directed towards the production of commodities at a profit, in competition with other large enterprises.

Second, the development of capitalist integration and planning in the pursuit of profit cuts across national boundaries. The rise of the 'multinationals' has received much comment[3] and I shall not go into great detail here. What is of particular interest is that direct investment overseas by such enterprises has become increasingly important over the post war years (as opposed to portfolio investment, of which British capital has a long tradition), and that this phenomenon is especially important for the British economy. In 1971 the UK was second only to the USA as a home base for multinational companies; overseas production by British-based multinationals as a proportion of domestic output in 1977 was, at 40 per cent, higher than the corresponding figure for any other national economy except Switzerland; and in 1971 nearly 20 per cent of UK output was produced by overseas based companies. Both 'foreign' multinationals operating within Britain and British enterprises with substantial overseas production facilities can 'plan' the international distribution of their profit-making taking into account comparative costs, the state and growth rate of national markets and the degree of militancy or subordination of labour. They can also play off national governments against one another, taking advantage of discrepancies of company law and taxation policy, and governmental competition to attract investment through regional and industrial policy.

The point that capitalist planning is increasingly conducted on an international scale poses problems for the socialist project. A question must be raised concerning the appropriate level at which socialist planning can take place: can it be national in scope or must it be international? A lengthy discussion of this issue is beyond the scope of this work but given its importance in relation to the socialist project I shall make some comments.

A useful starting point here is Rowthorn's discussion (1980, Chapter 3). Rowthorn suggests that the continued existence of large scale capitalist enterprises possessing production facilities in several countries could render impossible the development of planning for social need in one particular national economy, so that a determined left government would be forced to break up such capitals and transfer the possession of the principal means of production to a planning authority at the level of the nation state. That is, one aspect of the

'socialisation of production' under capitalism — the international
capitalist enterprise — would have to be dismantled to permit a socialist
'socialisation'.

This can be represented schematically as below:

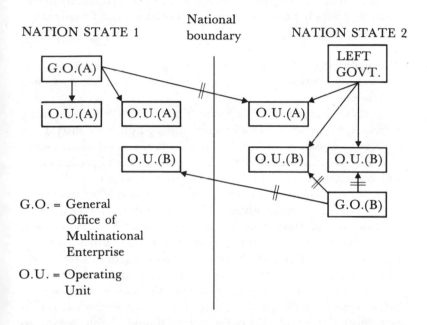

NATION STATE 1   National   NATION STATE 2
                        boundary

G.O. = General
       Office of
       Multinational
       Enterprise

O.U. = Operating
       Unit

The Left government in nation state 2 may be obliged to sever the
relations of possession linking the operating units of the multidivisional
international firms to their general offices (indicated by crossed arrows)
in order to gain control over the allocation of resources within the nation state. According to Rowthorn, multinational B's operating unit
in nation state 1 might be appropriated by the left government and
sold off to help provide funds with which to compensate multinational
A for the appropriation of its operating unit in nation state 2 (in order
to reduce the chances of direct counter-revolutionary intervention by
other states).

    There is, however, a further problem here: even if the required
'nationalisation' of possession were accomplished, it would not be possible to opt out of the international division of labour with other capitalist
economies. Many of the production facilities currently possessed by
international enterprises are integrated within a Europe-wide plan of
production.

'A substantial part of Britain's trade takes place within multinational firms; components produced in one country are shipped to a subsidiary of the same firm in another country, Ford motor cars, for example, are produced on a European-wide basis. If a foreign subsidiary in this country were nationalised its parent company might refuse to supply necessary components or purchase its output...' (ibid., p. 89).

'Nationalisation' of capitalist property does not abolish the real economic interdependence of units of production in different national economies.

Rowthorn's argument is important, in that it highlights an irony of capitalist socialisation. Traditionally, among British socialists at any rate, 'nationalisation' of industry has been conceived as an unambiguously socialist aim.[4] By transferring the means of production to state ownership, nationalisation represents a broadening of the scope of economic calculation beyond the limited horizon of private profit. But the type of argument advanced by Rowthorn carries the implication that nationalisation of modern international enterprises represents, in one respect, a *restriction* of the scope of economic calculation by tying it to *national* objectives. If multinational companies were wholly sinister organisations, purely instruments of sophisticated exploitation, then one need not have any qualms about the project of 'nationalising' and therefore dismantling them. But if such enterprises can in part 'justify' themselves on economic grounds, with regard to economies of scale and of transaction costs, then matters become trickier. There could be real economic costs involved in nationalisation.[5] Although it will not do to assume that political developments in different nation states will ever be sufficiently 'synchronised' to avoid entirely the problems of advancing the socialist project in one country, or a restricted group of countries, this consideration does point to the vital need for maximum international coordination in the pursuit of socialist objectives. Given the difficulty of constructing international institutions *ex nihilo* I believe that this means British socialists must give more serious attention to the opportunities at EEC level. The chances of successful socialist planning would be greatly increased, and the scope for multinationals to play governments off against one another reduced, if European socialists could make a more effective collective impact on the making of EEC policy and legislation.[6]

So constraints, and opportunities, at the international level are important. Nonetheless certain advances can be made at the national level, and given that politics and governmental power are still largely national in scope certain advances *must* be made at that level if they are to be made at all. If I have begun by stressing the difficulties connected with the internationalisation of large-scale impersonal capitals, I shall now try to identify certain *points d'appui* offered for socialist argument by the development of capitalist property relations.

The historic opportunity of investment planning

'... There is no doubt that the credit system will serve as a powerful lever during the transition from the capitalist mode of production to the mode of production of associated labour...' (Marx, 1972, p. 607).

To recall the conclusions of my earlier analysis: we now have a capitalism in which the greater part of the means of production is possessed by impersonal capitalist enterprises — legally distinct subjects employing salaried managerial labour — the majority of whose shares is held by further impersonal enterprises. And the latter enterprises (financial institutions) have drawn the funds to acquire this equity stake from the savings of the personal sector, that is mainly wage and salary-earning employees. This veritably 'socialised' capitalism may be construed ideologically in a variety of ways. In the USA Peter Drucker has talked of a 'pension fund socialism': the workers, through their pension funds, 'own' a large part of private business and profits have become pensions, or 'deferred wages', so that surplus value has disappeared. Sir Harold Wilson has gone along with this view, saying that trade union members control 'some 50 per cent of the equity capital of the 250 or so biggest industrial companies, through pension fund trustees in the main accountable to them' (quoted in the 'New Statesman' 24/10/80). This amounts to a form of nationalisation, and represents 'the biggest social revolution we have had in this country'. Tories such as Sir Keith Joseph put a different slant on the phenomenon, talking of a 'people's capitalism' or 'property-owning democracy' rather than 'pension fund socialism', but the basic conception is the same: shareholding on the part of the financial institutions which collect personal savings and pay out pensions, annuities or endowments gives everyone, trade unionists included, a stake in the production of commodities for profit. There is no longer really a 'propertyless class' who might have nothing to lose but their chains. When enterprises plan their production on the criterion of profitability they are only honouring their obligation to their shareholders —

to earn them a reasonable return on their money — and if those shareholders are institutions which are in turn merely trustees of the people's savings ... well, evidently notions of class struggle and exploitation must be out of date.

But this ideological construction is highly vulnerable, one might even say feeble. There has been a real enough change in the form of capitalist property but the notion that the workers 'control' industry through their pension funds or life assurance contributions is manifestly absurd. Most workers have no idea of what is done with 'their' savings, even in the case of pension funds which are not farmed out to the merchant banks for management. They do not know where the money is 'invested', whether in British enterprises or overseas, in speculation on property or 'art treasures', or in lending to the government to finance unemployment. All they are interested in — all they are generally *permitted* to be interested in — is whether they get a reasonable pension at the end of the day. And the financial institutions, subscribing fully to the ideology of the 'smoothly functioning capital market', take it for granted that the best interests of their personal sector customers are served by placing funds where they can get the 'best' and 'safest' monetary returns, regardless of the consequences for productive investment. So the right to a pension or endowment is a far cry from any power of possession over means of production, or positive influence over the allocation of resources.

This blatant discrepancy between the actual structure of property relations and its ideological appropriation in 'pension fund socialism' or 'people's capitalism' should form an excellent starting point for socialist argument and propaganda at a number of levels. Workers and trade unions could be encouraged to insist that the management of their massive savings should be made accountable to them, and should be directed towards employment-creating, socially useful investment. Of course, if the financial institutions were forced to explain themselves we know what they would say. They have already said it to the Wilson Committee: we are doing our best to preserve the value of the funds entrusted to us, and any attempt to force us to invest in projects offering sub-optimal returns for 'social' reasons is an attempt to make us break faith with our customers. This shows the importance of attacking the ideologies of British financial capital, and in this attack Keynes is a valuable ally of Marx. Even from the point of view of 'saver', let alone 'worker', conservative/speculative management of funds can be shown to be damaging: savers' interests lie in ensuring that when they retire, or reach a specified age, the pensions, endowments or annuities they receive will support a reasonable standard of living. But this fundamentally depends on the level of output of the economy when the savers reach old age. Simply setting *money* aside now does not in any way guarantee the output of goods and services x years hence to meet the needs of old people; neither does lending money at a profit. That future output depends on real *investment* in productive assets now and in the future, while the piling-up of financial assets in excess of real investment can only be inflationary in the long run (a 'long run' which is already with us). So any changes in the financial system which promote a higher level of productive investment will permit a higher living standard for today's savers in the years to come. Thus far, the effective popularisation of basic Keynesian arguments would help strengthen a socialist case for the social planning of investment as in the interests of workers, both immediately (in terms of employment prospects and living standards) *and* in their capacity as savers for the future.

From a socialist viewpoint, however, the argument must be taken further than Keynes. Keynes imagined a socially painless 'euthanasia of the rentier' which would be 'nothing sudden, merely a gradual but prolonged continuance of what we have seen recently in Great Britain, and will need no revolution' (Keynes, 1936, p. 376). The 'functionless investor' would fade away in face of the eminent reasonableness of social planning of investment. He did not foresee the rise of the new rentiers — the financial institutions collecting workers' savings — yet these are more organised, powerful and ideologically-armed than the old-style rentiers (even they haven't faded away). It will take a fight, not merely a debate and the passing of time, to disarm the financial institutions and restructure the control over investment funds. Notice, though, that the socialist case can be advanced on stronger ideological ground than ever before. Within the British political culture it is rare for workers (even manual industrial 'proletarians') to consider the wholesale expropriation of the property of another class as a reasonable political option, but if the financial institutions insist they are only guardians of the people's savings then why should the 'people' not call them to account? This argument will not force the financial institutions to surrender, but it can help to 'legitimate' the case for investment planning and develop the popular support which would be needed in the ensuing political battles.

Broad political support will not, of course, be won merely by appealing to the inherent rationality of planning as opposed to the profit-oriented allocation of resources. Socialists will have to say more about how such planning would operate: its mechanisms and the criteria employed for allocating resources. It is a serious *lacuna* in socialist thought to imagine that the virtues of 'planning for social need' are self-evident, that the only grounds for doubt must be vested interest in the workings of the 'free market'. It is all too easy to counterpose 'need' versus 'profit' as the criterion for production — in fact it is just the mirror-image of the apologetic proposition that production for profit is essentially the same thing as production for need. Many people who are not committed to the market mechanism as the 'best of all possible worlds' nonetheless feel a justifiable scepticism about planning. What is to ensure that the allocation of resources is not arbitrary, subject to the sway of *ad hoc* political pressure? Even if the planners are enlightened, how will planning actually work? Marxists have often been reticent on these questions. This is partly because of Marx's strictures on Utopian socialism. Marx argued, quite correctly, that any broad change in the property relations of a society would involve sharp political, if not military, struggles and that the course of such struggles could not be legislated in advance according to the blueprints of some would-be social reformer. He therefore made a radical break with the French socialist tradition of speculation on the details of a socialist society, in favour of developing the real working class movement against capitalism which would work out the 'details of socialism' in the process of struggle. But if Marx's arguments were valid in their historical context, they should not be allowed to block the development of concrete proposals which, although not acting as historical blueprints, could help to more accurately define, and hence mobilise support for, socialist objectives.

So the question is this: if the developing property relations and pattern of financial flows within British capitalism increasingly open up a space for socialist argument in favour of planned investment to benefit both 'workers' and 'savers' (substantially overlapping categories), how is that space to be exploited? What credible proposals can be advanced to catalyse support? What means can be used to isolate the implacable opponent of such a change?

As regards the appropriation of funds for the purposes of planned provision, a first point is that the financial institutions could be short-circuited to some extent by increasing taxation of the wealthy. We have perhaps conceded too much to 'pension fund socialism': although workers' savings are very important it remains true that income (and hence saving) is highly unequally distributed. The flow of funds from the personal sector to the financial institutions does not only represent workers providing for their retirement, but also represents the accumulation of wealth whereby socially privileged strata transmit their cultural patrimony (e.g. saving through endowment policies to provide for private education).[7] This latter aspect of personal saving could be reduced by instituting a more steeply progressive income tax and/or a wealth tax. In the long run it may be possible to go further than this, to appropriate in the form of tax revenue a large part of the income which workers would otherwise have put into long-term savings schemes, and to expand commensurately the *socialised* provision for retired workers (state pensions plus appropriate social amenities). More immediately, however, this may be politically inopportune, and widely resented as 'robbing the people of their savings'. It would be possible instead to preserve the relationship between the financial institutions and the personal sector savers but to alter substantially the deployment of funds by obliging the institutions to contribute to a national investment bank, giving them in return bonds with a rate of return linked to the real growth rate of the economy.[8]

Probably more important than the detail of how a left government could *appropriate* personal saving, is the question of *deployment* of the funds. It is after all the effectiveness (or otherwise) of the socialised deployment of the personal sector surplus which would over time build support for (or resentment against) any such scheme. If one is to present a credible case for investment planning as a progressive development one has to consider the problems raised by the choice of criteria of operation for a national investment bank.

To start with a relatively easy issue, part of the funds raised could be channelled into public sector investment projects, of which there is presently in Britain a substantial backlog (e.g. modernisation of the railways, energy conservation measures, renewal of urban sewage systems, accelerated house-building programme). There could be problems of ranking priorities here, becoming more acute as full employment of labour and means of production is approached. These would best be resolved by a form of cost-benefit which pays close attention to the social 'externalities' involved in investment projects,[9] which compares the time profiles of return on projects competing for resources at non-usurious rates of discount,[10] and which does not operate with the technocratic pretension that all factors in an investment decision can be rigorously quantified (i.e. which does not disguise as purely technical questions matters which should properly be open to political debate).

Apart from public sector projects, the more difficult question of providing investment funds for private sector enterprises also arises. Of course, if one envisages the nationalisation of all the major enterprises ('top monopolies'), then the problem becomes internalised within the 'public sector', but two points here: first, the present discussion is predicated on the hypothesis that there is a fruitful ideological space within which to argue for socialist investment planning — it does not depend on the (counterfactual) proposition that there is wide popular support for sweeping nationalisation of enterprises. Second, even if the major private capitalist enterprises were nationalised this would not abolish the problem of allocating resources between the kind of 'infrastructural' provision, and social services, which are already within the public sector in Britain and those areas of commodity production which are at present the domain of 'private enterprise'. It is widely accepted that one of the main factors contributing to the relative decline and adverse trading position of the British economy is a shortfall of investment in private industry, and socialists cannot afford to be indifferent to this since the employment prospects and livelihood of millions of workers are at stake. A national investment bank deploying a major part of personal savings would have to find means of channelling funds to private industry, and develop control measures to ensure that the funds are used productively. When the TUC representatives on the Wilson Committee argued along these lines, the financial institutions poured scorn on them: how can you 'force-feed' industry with investment funds? If capitalist enterprises see the prospect of adequate profits then they will borrow investment funds without any government having to insist, and if they do not see investment as profitable then it is useless to try to force them. And it is not only the financial institutions which present this objection; it has also been put forward by Cutler *et al.* (1978, Conclusion) in criticism of the TUC/Labour left 'Alternative Economic Strategy'.

In answer to this, there are cases in which the notion of force feeding is very wide of the mark. The conservatism of the British financial institutions biasses them against 'high risk' investment projects which nonetheless may have a strategic importance for the development of the national economy. INMOS in the late 1970s was an obvious case in point: this enterprise was very willing to invest state funds, but unable to raise sufficient capital privately. All the same there is a strong argument that low investment in the British economy is not just a matter of funds being unavailable; there is a reluctance to borrow for investment purposes on the part of many enterprises.

So let us examine this problem of 'force feeding' more closely. It is true that capitalist enterprises will invest only if they expect an 'adequate' rate of return on capital. But what conditions are required for a given investment project to offer such profitability? Cutler *et al.* (1978, Chapters 10 and 11) have argued forcefully that the calculation of profitability is by no means a transparent and unambiguous exercise, and that the method and effects of such calculation can vary between enterprises. All the same it is useful here to set up a paradigm of the profitability calculation against which to assess the prospects for investment planning, while accepting that there is considerable scope for variation in the actual calculations performed by particular enterprises. Leaving aside the problems of precise definition of revenues and costs, we can say that the profit accruing to an enterprise equals revenue minus costs. Most investment projects, however, will involve substantial initial costs and will generate sales revenue over an extended period, so the problem arises of comparison of present costs and future prospective revenues. The method of comparison which is increasingly accepted as most 'rational', at least by large-scale enterprises with sophisticated calculation procedures, involves discounting future revenues (or costs) at a rate of discount equal to the 'cost of (money) capital' to the enterprise. The Net Present Value calculation, for instance, yields a figure of merit for an investment project which effectively shows whether the rate of return on a project is in excess of the compound interest to be paid on the money capital required to finance it. If the Net Present Value is positive, this shows that an enterprise borrowing funds at the given interest rate would make a profit after meeting interest payments, or alternatively that an enterprise possessing surplus money capital would make a better return on the funds by carrying out the investment project rather than lending the funds at interest.

If a given investment project within the domain of operation of capitalist enterprises were considered desirable as part of an investment plan (to satisfy a definite 'social need', to gain export revenue, to develop a 'growth industry', to preserve employment) and yet the capitalist enterprises concerned were unwilling to invest then the investment planning authorities would have two broad options: either nationalise the enterprises and force them to invest on criteria other than those of profitability, or 'distort' the market to render the project sufficiently profitable to appeal to the enterprises. Without wishing to rule out the first option I should like to consider the second, to examine the possibilities of indirect leverage over investment decisions. First, note that there are two general factors influencing the profitability calculation which could be substantially altered by the institution of a national investment bank appropriating the personal sector surplus and also promoting large-scale *public sector* investment projects. On the one hand the cost of money capital could be reduced, by offering funds for projects consistent with the overall investment plan at low interest rates, and on the other the level of aggregate demand could be boosted by the public sector projects. This latter effect would directly influence the calculations of suppliers of commodities to the public sector, and indirectly influence other enterprises through its 'multiplier' repercussions. In this way, many investment projects which enterprises are at present unwilling to undertake could be made attractive: the cost of capital would fall while the prospective returns rise. Far from 'force feeding', the problem would be to assess selectively the enterprises deserving investment funds.

These effects would be real enough, but it would be naive to suppose that cheap loans and the raising of aggregate demand would render all socially desirable investment projects in the sphere of commodity production sufficiently profitable to make capitalist enterprises come clamouring for public funds. The closure of the Talbot works in Linwood in Scotland, announced in February 1981, with its resulting localised mass unemployment, is a pointed reminded of the limitations of cheap loans or grants as a means of maintaining the allegiance of capitalist enterprises to given investment projects. And in this case it seems likely that even if it were not for the depressed state of aggregate demand in the British market, the commodities produced by Talbot at Linwood would not have generated 'sufficient' profit for Peugeot. We have to identify the factors other than usurious interest rates and deficiency of aggregate demand which can make investment projects unattractive to enterprises. First, it may be that some commodity-producing projects deemed socially useful are unprofitable because the 'social need' which they are supposed to answer fails to find expression as a monetary demand on the market. If the 'need' can be clearly justified on social grounds then there is a *prima facie* case for either altering the distribution of income (if that would permit the need to be translated into monetary demand) or producing the product for social non-commodity distribution (which would presumably involve nationalisation of the enterprises concerned). The second obvious point here is competition. The 'cost of capital' may be low enough and there may be a strong demand for the type of commodity which the investment project aims at producing, but if other competing enterprises are able to supply the same commodity or a close substitute more cheaply (or of a higher quality) then the project will not be 'commercially viable'.

At this point it is necessary to ask on what grounds socialists would wish to see an investment project of this nature (i.e. unprofitable in the face of market competition) supported within the framework of investment planning. Without claiming to treat the question exhaustively, we can identify some possible reasons. First the competition may be from 'cheap imports'. It is rather too easy to rally chauvinistic backing for the support of industries against foreign competition but nonetheless there may be good grounds for protection. The 'cheap imports' may be the result of an over-valued exchange rate for the national currency. If that is the only problem faced by certain investment projects then it can be solved fairly easily by an interventionist government willing to regulate international capital flows in order to adjust the external value of the currency (it is *upward* adjustment of the exchange rate which may be very difficult). But even if the exchange rate is at a 'realistic' level certain industries may still face severe problems of international competition. In some such cases specific protection, in the form of import controls, subsidies or state purchasing, may be justified on socialist grounds, for instance if the industry is a struggling 'infant' with good future prospects ('good', that is, in respect of the efficient satisfaction of social need), or even a struggling 'geriatric' which stands a good chance of reviving its fortunes through a thorough re-investment programme. And in cases which merit protection, if that is still not enough to induce voluntary investment of funds offered by the national investment bank there is again a *prima facie* case for nationalisation. On the other hand there may be industries within the national economy in which enterprises stand to be progressively undercut by their international competitors in the long run. In such cases protection may be justified in the short term to alleviate the employment effects of a rundown of the industry but long run protectionism would reduce the potential material living standards of the working population. In such cases there has been a shift in the pattern of 'comparative advantage' on an international scale. Even if this shift is due to the availability of cheap labour power in other countries it is by no means obvious that socialists should support long-run protectionism: it may represent considerable progress for a 'Third World' worker to be exploited by capital in the production of labour-intensive commodities rather than by a landlord. Here there is a good case for devoting social funds to retraining programmes and the development of new enterprises (public sector or cooperative) on a scale properly commensurate with the problem, rather than trying to 'force feed' the industry with investment funds.

I have discussed international competition, but of course there are also competitive pressures within the national economy. In principle, such pressures could be abolished by means of widespread nationalisation but again even if this had sufficient political support the problem of optimising the allocation of resources would remain. However unpalatable, socialists have to consider the idea that profitability may function *to some extent* as an indicator of relative efficiency in the use of resources, especially as between substitutes for meeting a given social need. Of course, differential profitability may reflect differential exploitation of labour: in this case a left government could intervene to the advantage of enterprises which were less profitable because of less intensive and oppressive working and/or better wages by, for instance, minimum wage legislation or fostering union organisation in the more oppressive enterprises.[11] Consider, though, a case in which a given enterprise is unwilling to invest because of low expected profitability, yet this low prospective profitability can be traced neither to faulty managerial calculations, nor to foreign competition of a kind justifying protection, nor to the failure of an identified 'need' for the enterprise's product to register as monetary demand, nor to internal competition from other enterprises operating a more intensive exploitation of labour. The 'bourgeois economist' would certainly claim that such an enterprise was not using resources efficiently to satisfy consumers' wants and therefore would not merit investment funds and we have to ask whether he would be wrong.

Well, there could still be a case for investment in such an enterprise if it were shown that the lack of profitability was the result of higher costs than competitors stemming from locational disadvantages. Say, for instance that transport costs are high relative to competitors', but yet if the enterprise were to be run down this would cause large-scale local unemployment. Then one could argue for stable long-term subsidies to be granted to offset the higher transport costs, recognising that the higher resource cost of delivering the commodities to their consumers should be borne by the state which would otherwise have to bear the cost of unemployment (and which is also in a position to take account of the 'social cost' to the community involved). But if it is not possible to identify any factor such as this, then the economist's verdict is probably correct: the enterprise is socially inefficient. This may be due to managerial incompetence, in which case the state (having taken over the investment side of the financial institutions' business) could exercise its prerogative as 'trustee of the people's savings' to force managerial changes. This could involve the institution of worker management (discussed more fully in the following section) with access to a state 'management consultancy' service.[12] On the other hand, the low prospective profitability could be due to the enterprise becoming trapped in a clearly sub-optimal line of production, i.e. one in which consumers were simply not willing to pay a price for the commodity sufficent to cover its costs of production (including the opportunity cost of investment funds expressed in the rate of interest charged by the national investment bank). This poses a problem similar to that of enterprises being progressively undercut by international competition but where long term protectionist measures are not justified: the best response may be to seek means of re-deploying the workers involved.

The intention behind the preceding arguments was not to examine exhaustively the investment criteria to be employed by a national investment bank with socialist pretensions. It was rather to identify some of the concrete problems which would have to be faced in any such exercise. I hope the discussion has this value: it addresses the question of intervention to further social objectives within the system of commodity-producing enterprises and, rather than positing nationalisation as panacea (a theme with a pronounced minority appeal), it identifies certain cases in which nationalisation could be argued as necessary to further social objectives as well as cases in which nationalisation might be of no obvious advantage. The starting point was the issue of the opportunities offered to socialists by the current form of capitalist property in Britain, and my conclusion is that the socialised deployment of the personal sector financial surplus would permit a greatly accelerated rate of productive investment, yielding dividends in terms of socially useful output and employment, provided that the deployment of funds be carried out according to fairly well-defined criteria of rationality rather than merely in response to *ad hoc* political pressure.[13] At present the non-bank financial institutions collect the greater part of the personal sector financial surplus — the 'surplus income' which individuals are unable to use to finance real accumulation due to their separation from the means of production — and channel this into financing the government's deficit, acquiring company shares, investing in property or overseas, all under the guidance of a speculative mode of calculation. Despite their increasing equity stake in capitalist enterprises they provide relatively little new investment finance and for much of the time act as passive collectors of dividends. Their mode of calculation has definite *effects* on industrial enterprises, but they do not generally intervene actively in the determination of company policy. In contrast, a state investment bank under the guidance of a planning apparatus could make funds available for socially useful investment projects, and where these projects were demonstrably in the interests of working people, yet were not profitable enough to attract capitalist enterprises, the state could either adjust the parameters of the market to make them profitable (not always easy, but the state does have considerable means at its disposal to effect such adjustments) or failing that, nationalise the enterprises concerned, on relatively strong ideological ground. I believe that by arguing along these lines socialists may be able to raise more popular support than by arguing for 'nationalisation' and 'planning' in the abstract.

Some criticisms considered

I accept that in arguing in this way one must be aware of the general objections which socialists are likely to raise. It may be argued that these proposals amount to no more than state capitalism. True enough, insofar as the state provides investment funds for commodity-producing enterprises within this scheme 'state capitalism' is an accurate tag. Only it is not clear that the identification of such a project as state capitalism is damning.[14] My argument is that state capitalism of the kind outlined above would be a highly progressive development. It could sustain a more rapid development of the 'productive forces', contribute to the greater satisfaction of social needs and produce a high level of employment which would increase the social power of the working class. In the long term such a state capitalism could develop towards a more fully socialised appropriation incorporating the physical planning of production, as political and economic circumstances permitted. In this respect, my analysis can be located close to the 'Alternative Economic Strategy' (AES) — which has been given its most lucid expression by the CSE London Working Group (1980) — in its acceptance of the need for socialists to offer constructive and credible proposals for regenerating economic growth and reducing unemployment even if these appear to fall short of 'true socialism'.

Apart from the objection of principle that this is merely state capitalism I shall consider three further points. First, if the foregoing appears to ignore questions of democracy within the enterprise that is only because of the order of exposition. I fully accept that socialism is not just about productive investment and full employment, and questions of democratic enterprise organisation are considered in the final section of this chapter which is complementary to the foregoing.

Second, and more substantial, there is the kind of objection to proposals linked to an Alternative Economic Strategy which has been raised by Cutler *et al.* Their objection is actually twofold. Discussing the proposals of Holland and Benn designed to rectify the short-fall in investment in the British economy they make this point:

'We would argue that these positions which tie socialist politics to the success of a programme of "industrial regeneration" are not a viable basis for socialist strategy. This is for two reasons: first, these strategies largely ignore the *political conditions of their implementation*, and second, they fail to answer the question of whether such a "regeneration" is possible and whether, if possible, it can take place under conditions which will be of benefit to socialist politics. Holland and Benn stake their politics on the prospect of particular outcomes of the practice of management of capitalist national economies' (1978, p. 277).

The first objection, concerning the political conditions of implementation of AES-type proposals, is a telling one. In elaborating such proposals there is admittedly a strong temptation to indulge in political rationalism: they are by nature proposals which give an important role to action on the part of a 'socialist government' or the 'state' within which a socialist government is installed, yet it is often unclear what such a socialist government would look like, how it might come into being and from where it would draw its mass support. Likewise it is often not sufficiently recognised that the 'state' which would supposedly execute the progressive measures might be very much disinclined to do so and anyway may be the object of considerable public mistrust.[15] I have attempted to guard against this temptation by qualifying the foregoing arguments, and pointing ahead to the later chapters in which the particular social forces (as opposed to economic classes) active in British society will receive a fuller treatment. My arguments concerning the broad possibilities and constraints given by the present structure of capitalist property are not supposed to have the status of a ready-made political programme, and in discussing the possibilities for investment planning as a fruitful avenue for socialist argument I make no pretence to have identified the means of conversion of 'social reason into social force' (to use Marx's formula[16]). But although I cannot do so systematically at this juncture some limited anticipatory comments may be in order. My hypothesis is that there is a space for a socialist argument in favour of investment planning; that such an argument could be presented in such a way as to appeal to organised labour and even to broader strata of the population concerned about employment prospects and their standard of living in retirement; that if organised workers were to support the proposal they could use their union organisation to press for social accountability of their savings funds; and that if the proposals were not linked to a 'dogmatic' pursuit of nationalisation they would stand a chance of recruiting some support from the more progressive elements of the state and corporate salariat — those whose technical expertise would be required in any such project, even if it is overlaid with oppressive 'professional' and 'managerial' ideologies — helping to isolate, so far as possible, reactionary financier elements. And one institutional point in this context: it would be crucial in any socialist investment planning project to bypass the control over state finances on the part of the Treasury. The Treasury is not a reactionary monolith, but the combination and interpenetration of the upper echelons of private financial capitalist enterprises and the Treasury sets up a formidable obstacle to radical change in the management of financial flows. Even given substantial popular support, a socialist government/movement would have to give very careful thought to the development of a competent planning cadre able to hold its own against Treasury influence.

The latter part of the objection raised by Cutler *et al.* i.e. their agnosticism concerning the *possibility* of a broad economic 'regeneration' on terms favourable to socialism, is based on weaker ground. In expanding on this point they do develop some important arguments concerning the constraints which would face a socialist government attempting to advance an AES (for instance, the problems of 'forcing' investment referred to above, and the potential conflicts between such a government and the trade unions, given the need to raise labour productivity in order to develop a tenable trading position for the national economy) yet ultimately their position tends to a form of defeatism. They set up a dichotomy thus: 'Rather than scheming as to what a Left-Labour government should do, it is vital to consider the political basis on which such a government will become a possibility.' They then argue that this means starting at a 'more basic level' by considering the following three sets of issues:

'the political obstacles to advance within the practices of the Labour

Left and the labour movement itself; ... broadening the base of mass support, creating institutions and organisations which extend the socialist movement beyond the minority of organised labour; ... fighting for specific reforms in the organisation of capital that will create new positions of struggle and control for working people (limitations of shareholders' and managements' powers, workers' representation etc.) and fighting for reforms in non-commodity areas such as health, education, and welfare that introduce elements of popular administration and control' (Cutler *et al.*, 1978, p. 283).

I have quoted these latter points at length because I can readily agree with them, and consider them important, but what I find politically weakening is the dichotomy between promoting socialist developments which do *not* depend on the existence of a socialist government and the stigmatised 'scheming' as to what such a government should do. The point is that working people are bound to be concerned about issues which cannot be tackled effectively without central government involvement, issues such as mass unemployment, inflation, industrial decline, poverty, the social effects of government expenditure cuts. These are important to a great many people, whether they are perceived in terms of localised effects impinging on their everyday lives or in terms of the national picture which emerges from news media coverage and wider reading. If socialists aim at the formation of a government as a part of their strategy they must be ready to make their views known on these issues: how to reduce unemployment? how to avoid inflation? where the money would come from to provide better social services? Granted, if socialists merely develop a list of pat answers to these questions (nationalisation, 'planning') while failing to fight for more immediately realisable socialist gains outside of government they will not get much of a hearing, but equally to write off the macroeconomic questions as too difficult to speculate about is to forego the right to contest the policies of a reactionary national government. At the level of parliament, the news media and opinion poll data, management of the national economy has been the dominant issue in British politics for much of the post-war period and however important it is for socialists to insist that 'the political' be given a broader definition, they cannot afford to be silent on so important a concern. I therefore contend that 'scheming as to what a Left-Labour government should do' — in the sense of attempting to elaborate credible options for policy at a national level, while recognising the real problems involved — is actually a rather important part of developing 'the political basis on which such a government will become a possibility'. This, in brief, is the framework of political calculation within which I have found it useful to investigate the idea of investment planning as a means of appropriating within socialist argument the changing structure of capitalist property in Britain. The next section of this chapter will now extend this investigation to consider the complementary issue of the development of democratic forms of control within the enterprise.

Democracy at the level of the enterprise

One of the most basic features of capitalism is the separation of the workers from the means of production and one of the most basic aims of socialism is to abolish that separation, to regulate the allocation of resources and the expenditure of labour time according to the 'republican and beneficent system of *the association of free and equal producers*' (Marx, 1974, p. 90). It is clear, however, that the socialist abolition of the separation of workers from the means of production cannot take the form of re-establishing the personal property of the individual worker in his/her own means of production on the model of peasant or artisanal conditions. Small-scale production may have a certain place within a socialist economy[17] but as a general *alternative* to modern large-scale industry it is merely utopian. As Marx argues,

> 'This mode of production pre-supposes the fragmentation of holdings and the dispersal of the other means of production. As it excludes the concentration of these means of production, so it also excludes cooperation, division of labour within each separate process of production, the social control and regulation of the forces of nature, and the free development of the productive forces of society. It is compatible only with a system of production and a society moving within narrow limits which are of natural origin' (Marx, 1976, pp. 927-8).

In the context of large-scale industry, I have already shown that a substantial part of the means of production is the object of possession by impersonal institutions — capitalist enterprises — and the object of socialism must be to reconstruct this impersonal possession in such a way that enterprises both follow a plan of production consistent with the maximum satisfaction of the democratically-constructed 'needs' of the working population as a whole, and are open to democratic participation, on equal footing, of the workers within the enterprise. The foregoing discussion of investment planning represents an essay in definition of the first of these conditions within the context of British capitalism; I now turn to the second condition, and the relationship between the two. Following the same pattern as before, I shall approach this in terms of the possibilities and constraints connected with contemporary capitalist property relations.

To begin with a general point of caution, concerning the relationship between socialised economic planning and enterprise democracy: I have claimed these to be complementary features of the socialist project, and in an important sense they are, yet there is an inherent tension between the two which must be faced up to. This tension surfaced in particularly acute form on the morrow of the first proletarian revolution as the Bolsheviks attempted to construct a system of coordinated workers' control over industry in face of the proliferation of relatively independent factory committees. As Bettelheim notes (1974, p. 125):

'The task was not easy because along with the rise in numbers of factory committees each one had a tendency to multiply its prerogatives and to treat each factory as an independent unit of production, the collective property of its own workers, determining by itself production, sales and pricing, while the *social domination of the working class* over the means of production required that the atomised and contradictory powers of the factory committees be subordinated to a common political end' (my translation A.C.).

We know how this tension was eventually resolved: the exigencies of 'War Communism' demanded the abolition of the authority of the factory committee and its replacement by a centralised authority. We also know the long-term political cost of the suppression of the kind of 'spontaneous' workers' initiative represented by the rise of the factory committees. Of course, the conditions of Russia in 1917 and the following years posed 'special problems' for the Bolsheviks, but it must be recognised that the tension between the tendency to treat each factory as the 'collective property of its own workers' and the need to ensure the subordination of production to a 'common political end' is in no way unique to the Soviet experience. Neither can this tension be ascribed to 'false consciousness' on the part of workers, 'failing to recognise' the identity of their own particular interests and the general interests of their class: that line of thought leads to a variety of utopianism with strongly oppressive overtones. So long as production is carried on in units of production which have a degree of real economic autonomy and 'employ' distinct groups of workers (despite their general interdependence in terms of input/output relations) there will exist real grounds for conflict between particular groups of workers and the 'social interest', however democratically the latter is generated. For instance, where labour is either particularly demanding or is not in itself particularly fulfilling or interesting one could reasonably say it is in the interests of the workers concerned to work short hours and/or work at a relatively low intensity of labour. Also so long as consumption is not fully socialised (surely an impossibility) particular groups of workers will have an interest in raising their own particular level of consumption. But both of these points can conflict with the interest of the rest of the working population. Shorter hours of labour and less intensive working will, *ceteris paribus*, reduce the volume of output, while raising consumption standards means making a larger claim over available output, leaving less for personal consumption on the part of other groups or for investment and social provision. This kind of conflict cannot be legislated out of existence.

If this point is conceded, it has important implications for one's view of the future of politics. Even under 'socialism' there will be scope for quite genuine conflicts of interest between regions, localities and enterprises. It is naive to imagine that all social conflict is 'class' conflict at root and that socialist planning can be a wholly harmonious process. It is therefore wrong to counterpose 'politics' under capitalism (i.e. realm of conflict of interests) against 'administration' under socialism is to find a satisfactory mode of institutionalising conflict Marx and Engels' formulations suggest.[18] One general problem of socialism is to find a satisfactory mode of institutionalising conflict over the allocation of resources within the context of planning, and minimising the antagonisms it could generate.

This is, however, a long term consideration, given that neither social planning of the economy nor enterprise democracy exists in Britain. Let us return to the question of the possibilities for enterprise democracy under present circumstances. I have discussed earlier two salient features of the developing forms of impersonal capitalist property at the level of the enterprise: the increasing *scale* of enterprises and rising level of industrial concentration; and the increasing adoption of the *multidivisional* form of enterprise as a means of control over geographically-and/or product-diversified operations. I shall consider the implications of these points in turn.

1. The question of scale: Marx identified the rise of large-scale industry as one of the progressive features of capitalism. Increasing scale of the enterprise was a necessary condition for the development of the productive forces, and it also (a) put social planning on the agenda and (b) produced an increasingly concentrated and homogeneous workforce. I have already cast some doubt on point (b), or at least on the political effects which Marx assumed would be consequent on the concentration of labour (Chapter 1), while in the discussion of planning I argued that although point (a) may be broadly accepted it is by no means unproblematic, particularly given the fact that large-scale enterprises increasingly straddle national boundaries. But what of the potentiating/constraining effects on democracy within the enterprise? Tomlinson (1980) has developed an interesting discussion of this point in relation to the ideas of Cole (1917), arguing that large-scale enterprises can pose severe problems for enterprise democracy. Cole had written '... it is at least a half-truth that the measure of control he (the worker) will have will vary inversely to the total number of votes, so in the workshop the control of the individual will be real in most cases only if the workshop is small, unless, as in the coal mine, only the simplest and most uniform questions have, as a rule, to be decided' (Cole, 1917, p. 233). Tomlinson in his commentary argues that this notion need not lead to a simplistic 'small is beautiful' position.

'Instead it can, for example, be based on the argument that any particular agent's capacity to absorb information is finite, and that broadly therefore the smaller the unit to be controlled the greater the likelihood of competence sufficient to make the necessary judgement. Of course such conceptions do not yield any simple size limit to organisations which can be democratically controlled. This will depend, as Cole suggests, on the basis of decisions which are pertinent to any particular production process, and is therefore not a simple function of the number of agents involved' (Tomlinson, 1980, p. 170).

Despite this qualification, however, Tomlinson is prepared to argue that 'smallness of operation in production and distribution is something socialists should generally favour' (ibid.). Interestingly, this position is backed up by the experience of the Mondragon cooperative enterprises in the Basque region of Spain. As Campbell (1980, p.13) has pointed out 'the Mondragon planners have decided that there is a limit to the number of people able to make industrial democracy work "under one roof". They now put this figure at around 400 people.' If one accepts this point, that effective democratic mechanisms within the enterprise may depend, in many branches of production, on having a relatively restricted number of agents involved in decision-making, then a rather awkward question arises: does enterprise democracy then come into conflict with the exploitation of economies of scale and the progressive development of the productive forces? Is increasing industrial concentration an obstacle rather than an opportunity as regards this socialist objective? Perhaps one can shed some light on this by being rather more precise in defining both 'the enterprise' and 'economies of scale'. First, if the enterprise is defined as the unit of legal ownership then it is clear that enterprises may comprise a number of operating units, plants, sales outlets and so on. And although the dominant *enterprises* in this sense have undoubtedly grown considerably in size, by any measure, over the post-war years it is not obvious that the *operating units* have grown in the same way. For instance, according to the calculations of Prais (1976) the share in total manufacturing output of the largest 100 manufacturing plants (i.e. single geographical entities, producing predominantly one product) has remained fairly static over the last fifty years. In some branches of production technical economies of scale have led to significant increases in plant sizes (e.g. process production of chemicals), while in others technical changes such as the development of small cheap electric motors, and the partial displacement of metal casting by plastic moulding, have favoured or at least permitted smaller-scale production.

In Tomlinson's argument, this discrepancy between the marked growth of the dominant enterprises and the relatively static overall position as regards plant size is taken as throwing doubt on the notion that the growth of the dominant enterprises has been based on the exploitation of economies of scale. Economies of scale are seen as operating at *plant* level and it is therefore argued that the growth of the multi-plant enterprise reflects narrowly financial considerations rather than any 'progressive development of the productive forces'. The implication is that if effective democracy at the enterprise level depends on the existence of relatively small units, there may be a case for dismantling large-scale capitalist enterprises. As Tomlinson (*op. cit.,* p. 167) puts it, 'building on the technological achievements of capitalism does not necessitate a defence of enterprises on the scale currently common in capitalist countries'.

I believe that the earlier discussion of the multidivisional enterprise in the USA and Britain (Chapter 3) permits a more differentiated and rigorous judgement. It is true that the increasing scale of certain enterprises in post war Britain can be traced to speculative financial considerations (primarily among those which Channon identifies as 'acquisitive diversifiers'), and that many such enterprises have failed to exploit economies of scale and have shown a poor record even in terms of profitability. But on the other hand many large multidivisional enterprises probably can 'justify themselves' in terms of economies of scale and integration, if these are given a broad interpretation. Tomlinson operates with a very narrow conception of 'economies of scale', effectively restricting the notion to cover the technical advantages to be gained by scaling-up a given production process, but the arguments of Chandler, Channon and Williamson enable one to identify other important economic advantages of large-scale integrated enterprises: economies of efficient scheduling of internal transfers; advantages of linking purchasing to production and production to marketing, the latter providing a feedback mechanism for changing the product-specification; economies of 'horizontal' coordination of output plans and reduction of wasteful duplication; economies of administration; advantages of technology-transfer. Different large-scale multidivisional enterprises may exploit these advantages in different degrees, according to the form and degree of diversification they have developed and according to the particular effectiveness of their management, but the general point here is that these advantages cannot be written off as financial/speculative considerations.

If one takes a broader view of economies of scale along these lines then one must also take a more differentiated view of the large-scale enterprise. Some conglomerates may be unwieldy economic units with a primarily speculative rationale, which could usefully be dismantled, but the dismantling of other large enterprises (one example: full-line chemical companies) might involve genuine losses in productive efficiency even if plant sizes, and hence purely technical scale economies, are not affected. Referring again to the Mondragon experience, it is clear that the planners there recognise the economic advantages to be gained from the formation of larger units. These larger units have taken the form of 'cooperative combines' run by nominees from the control committees of member cooperatives. Since the formation of the first such combine in 1968, comprising six units of production with a total of around 6,000 individual members, the Mondragon planners have made it a recommended practice to group individual cooperatives into such units. They judge that this form of organisation permits the cooperatives to obtain advantages of scale at the level of administration, coordination and planning while retaining the benefits of relatively small operating units i.e. maximum scope for democratic accountability (Campbell, 1980, pp. 12-13). The question arises as to what extent such arrangements can provide a model for the democratisation of the multidivisional capitalist enterprise.

2. **The multidivisional enterprise:** The tendency of the argument here is the following: *if* the exploitation of economies of scale on the part of capitalist enterprises primarily involved the development of ever larger units of production, in the technical sense, concentrating progressively larger numbers of workers into massive factories, then there could indeed be a conflict between the wish to retain the benefits of economies of scale on the one hand and the requirements of 'manageable' enterprise democracy on the other. I am, however, suggesting that many significant economies of scale have been realised at the level of the large enterprise comprising a number of units of production rather than at plant, or operating unit, level. Further, recall Channon's argument that many such multi-unit enterprises in Britain have, over recent years, found the 'functional' model of organisation — i.e. the monolithic top-down hierarchy — to be too inflexible and have quite deliberately changed over to a *multidivisional* form, reforming the managerial apparatus to restrict the role of the general office and permit a greater degree of autonomy for the management of the operating units. Certainly, examples can be found where the growth of the enterprise has involved the creation of massive technical operating units (in the car industry and the shipyards for instance) but it is not clear that this trend will continue, and in some cases technological change is already undermining the competitive advantage of those enterprises operating very large-scale units.[19] The prospects may therefore be good for a long-term strategy which aims at both restricting the scale of most *operating units* and granting them a reasonable degree of operational autonomy in order to make participative democracy a feasible proposition, while developing further the economies of administration, co-ordination, etc. which are at present realised by large-scale enterprises. This would mean re-examining the *current* grouping of units of produc-

tion into larger enterprises, but the point is that 'enterprises', as groupings of operating units, would be reconstructed rather than simply dismantled into small independent components.

This position requires a more differentiated conception of 'enterprise democracy'. Democratic mechanisms must be conceived as operating at different levels: within the operating units there may be scope for direct participative democracy perhaps also involving factory committees in close touch with the workforce; at the level of the enterprise, direct democracy would probably be impractical and some form of representative mechanism would be required. It is not possible to say in the abstract what kind of decisions would be taken at these different levels, or at least not with any precision, since this would depend on the character of the economic relations between the general office of the enterprise and its operating units, and between the operating units themselves, quite apart from the particular forms of struggle at local and national level which would be required to implement any such scheme. All the same, some general remarks may serve to give this conjecture more substance. One could argue, for instance, that the conditions of work and the forms of division of labour within the operating unit should be the subject of democratic decision-making within that unit while the general investment policy of the enterprise should be decided at the 'higher' level, by means of a mechanism involving representatives from the operating units, central enterprise staff and national planners (assuming, that is, the kind of investment planning referred to above). Such decision-making at enterprise level could, of course, involve encouraging the development of 'workers' plans' from the 'bottom upward' — only rational planning would require that the implementation of these be considered in the light of broad social objectives.

What is envisaged here is a 'pincer movement' for democratising the operations of large multidivisional enterprises and subjecting them to popular accountability. From 'above', a left government could attempt to gain control over the deployment of investment funds, in particular the surplus income of the personal sector, while from 'below' workers could struggle for democratic control over the particular enterprises which employ them, breaking down the managerial hierarchies and commercial secrecy of these enterprises. If the 'pincers' were to meet then the space for conventional capitalist 'management' — i.e. the hierarchal direction of enterprises in the pursuit of profit, recognising some form of responsibility to 'shareholders' but not to working people — would be at least severely restricted and at best eliminated. It is clear, however, that our two 'pincers' are not at par. The institution of national investment planning would certainly require broad and determined popular support, but by nature it would depend on the formation of a socialist government and would give an important role to organisations operating at a national level. Enterprise democracy differs from this in that (a) workers can begin to fight for such an objective in the absence of a socialist government and (b) it is by nature impossible for even the most 'socialist' of governments to develop enterprise democracy 'from above'. Any such development depends crucially on popular initiatives and cannot simply be legislated (there are, however, important ways in which a socialist government could help to *foster* enterprise democracy, by making changes in company law, e.g. turning shareholders into mere bondholders, granting the *right* to set up democratic mechanisms where this was approved by the workforce, and by means of preferential funding for democratic enterprises and 'workers' plans').

So investment planning and enterprise democracy stand in rather different relations with national politics. In the absence of a left government, developing the objective of investment planning is *primarily* a matter of developing ideas, policies and strategies and attempting to win broad support for these. Developing the objective of enterprise democracy, while it too involves theoretical/ideological activity, can also be a matter of practical struggle. The following section offers some comments on this point.

Enterprise democracy and industrial democracy

In the preceding arguments I have deliberately used the term 'enterprise democracy' to refer to democratic control by workers over the enterprises which employ them, within the context of the socialist project. Enterprise democracy, that is, was presented as the complement to social planning of investment at a national or even supra-national level. 'Industrial democracy' on the other hand is a term which is generally taken to refer to particular practices of management already operating in certain capitalist economies (e.g. West Germany) or specific proposals such as those of the Bullock Committee (Bullock, 1977), practices and proposals which give some role to workers or their representatives in enterprise decision-making, but which are not necessarily linked to the overall social planning of the economy in the interests of working people. The problem now is to assess the relationship between enterprise democracy (as socialist objective) and 'Industrial Democracy' (as object of current struggle and debate). Broadly speaking, socialists appear to be divided into two camps over this question. There are those who argue that 'Industrial Democracy' as it exists and as it is proposed by Commissions of Inquiry and certain trade unions, is a dangerous diversion. So long as the broad configuration of the economy remains capitalist, with enterprises producing commodities for profit, 'Industrial Democracy' is bound to function merely as a means of incorporating workers' representatives into a capitalistic rationality. Clarke (1977) gives a clear presentation of this view, marshalling the support of Mann (1973) the TUC (1974) and Mandel among others. His case depends on the constraints placed upon any enterprise attempting to survive in the market:

> 'The capitalist market would immediately overwhelm any formal redistribution of authority at the enterprise level: *reform of the authority relations of the factory is impotent in the absence of structural reform of the production relations of society*' (Clarke, 1977, p. 364 — emphasis in the original).

Clarke goes on to argue that Industrial Democracy as currently envisaged would actually tend to suppress industrial militancy and weaken entrenched working class resistance to capitalist control, thereby reducing the chances of 'genuine' workers' control over production at some future date. On this view, then, there is a sharp dichotomy between workers' control at enterprise level — as an element of socialism — and Industrial Democracy. The latter does not offer a route to the former, and should be strenuously opposed as a mere manipulatory gambit on the part of 'capital'. It would probably be fair to say that views of this kind have been dominant among British socialists from the Labour-left leftwards, but over recent years they have come under increasing criticism, on both theoretical and political grounds. Let us examine some of this criticism.

First, there has been criticism of the role of the 'market' in the theoretical position of writers such as Clarke. In this position the forces of market competition impose a basically unitary practice of management onto individual enterprises, rendering workers' participation and even workers' cooperatives nugatory. This view of capitalist management can be traced back to Marx's conception of the individual capitalist as the mere 'personification of capital'. As Cutler *et al.* (1978)

point out, this leads to the denial of any specific effectivity on the pa
of the management of particular enterprises: each enterprise will fun
tion according to a uniform mode of calculation, as a mere 'aliqu
part of the total capital'. This kind of universalism has been strengtl
ened more recently by the work of Braverman (1974) who argued th
'Taylorism' represents the essence of capitalist management, the pr
foundly anti-democratic invariant to be found within all branches
capitalist production, imposed by the rationality of profit. It is the
conceptions which have come under attack. Cutler *et al.* have argue
that Marx's 'personification of capital' thesis depends on an untenak
conception of the capitalist economy as a rational totality, a conce
tion which obliterates the real distinctions between particular branch
of production, markets and enterprises. Enterprises are constraine
by the need to make 'adequate' profits, but there is more than o₁
way to make profits and the general constraint of market competitic
by no means exhaustively determines the calculations of management
Tomlinson (1980a) has drawn out the implication that there may l
a space to begin to develop democratic and cooperative forms of ente
prise management, even given the continuation of the production
commodities for profit. Cressey and MacInnes (1980) have also co₁
tested the determinism of market forces, which they describe as tl
'wicked uncle' of socialist demonology. They identify a certa
circularity in the classical Marxist view that market competitic
necessarily enforces the real subordination of labour to capital:

> 'Once labour is formally subordinated, then its real subsumptic
> *has* to follow — it occurs as the realisation of capital's "essence"
> the "inversion" at the heart of capitalist society imposed by the log
> of competition. Yet such market forces are *produced* by ... the in
> manent tendencies of capital!' (Cressey and MacInnes, 1980, p. 17

Rejecting the conception of the 'immanent tendencies of capital
mediated by market forces, imposing a unitary subordination of labou
these writers are also led to the conclusion that it is not futile for worke
to contest hierarchical and oppressive managerial structures. 'Industri
Democracy' is the site of a potentially fruitful struggle, not merely
manipulatory diversion.

Second, there is the political criticism which can be levelled at tl
dichotomous view which makes 'structural reform of the productic
relations of society' a *precondition* for any meaningful democratisatic
of the enterprise. The nub of this criticism is that such views give ri

to a kind of political paralysis: everything must wait until the revolutionary moment in which the production relations are transformed; until then labour must play a purely *oppositional* role, a role which precludes struggle of a 'prefigurative' kind. It becomes very hard to see'how the 'revolutionary moment' will ever arise in the absence of struggles to construct alternative forms of social organisation of production which might 'prefigure' and win support for socialist objectives unless, in a surely discredited formula, oppositional industrial militancy has an intrinsic tendency to revolutionary socialism. This kind of criticism has been made by the writers mentioned above, and has also been amplified by Rowbotham *et al.* (1979).

Taken together, these criticisms have important implications for the question of Industrial Democracy. 'True' workers' control will never spring into existence in fully fledged form and socialists must fight, within the present society, for democratic measures which can help to 'de-mystify' management and raise radical questions concerning the organisation of work and the goals of production, whether these measures involve the accountability of managerial agents or the promotion of workers' plans. If workers should be encouraged to resist the blandishments of managements offering responsibility without power, in an attempt to 'regain control by (ostensibly) sharing it', they should also be encouraged to reach beyond the status of a 'permanent opposition' to managerial control. 'Enterprise democracy', as the decentralised aspect of the socialist control over production by the associated producers, will never be realised unless workers begin to struggle *under capitalism* for control over the policy and operations of enterprises, and this means exploiting rather than rejecting outright the kind of 'Industrial Democracy' proposals raised by the Bullock Commission, and more recently by the EEC. This is not to say that such proposals must be accepted at face-value but they should be subjected to specific criticism rather than rejected in toto as merely a device for getting workers to 'participate' in their own exploitation. In later chapters I shall make some comments on the importance of incomes policy in the development of the socialist project. I shall not anticipate the arguments here, but it is worth pointing out that in a context of incomes policy, struggles over enterprise policy and operations would assume an increased importance: if wage-determination were conducted on a more centralised basis then the focus of collective bargaining at *enterprise* level would have to change. The shop stewards movement, contrary to the arguments from some quarters, would not necessarily be demobilised in a context of incomes policy, but would be able to use its bargaining strength at enterprise level to insist on measures of control over the broader issues of enterprise policy. This would imply that any particular 'Industrial Democracy' proposals which attempted to bypass or undermine the strength of the shop stewards should be resisted, but such particular resistance would be quite different from a total rejection of the supposedly malign effects of accepting any responsibility for the operation of enterprises under capitalism.

Reprise

In this chapter I have been concerned to draw out some of the implications for socialist politics of the analysis of capitalist property relations given earlier. I have concentrated on two main issues: the possibilities for social planning of investment, by means of a state appropriation of the working class and rentiers' surplus income at present channelled through the private financial institutions; and the possibilities for enterprise democracy in the context of the economic dominance of large multidivisional enterprises. It has been suggested that these two projects could form a pincer movement to circumscribe the operations of hierarchic managements pursuing the profitability of the enterprises which employ them without regard to the interests of working people, and therefore to reconstruct the impersonal possession of the means of production in the direction of (socialist) social appropriation. The two projects were seen to have differing conditions of implementation and are therefore unlikely to be synchronised in a 'revolutionary moment', but nonetheless they can be seen as mutually supportive: struggles for democratic forms within enterprises may help to build support for broader democratic planning, while a sympathetic government pursuing the latter project could also greatly expand the opportunities for enterprise democracy by means of legal changes and financing. Government industrial policy could make all the difference between a demoralising defeat for workers' initiatives taken at enterprise level, and the development of inspiring examples of 'workers' plans' for socially useful production, popular accountability of management and workers' self-management.

It may be useful at this stage to attempt a schematic synopsis of some of the points raised in the preceding discussion, a map showing certain potentially fruitful sites of struggle. The diagram below shows certain relationships between economic agents, and enables one to identify some lines of reconstruction of those relationships.

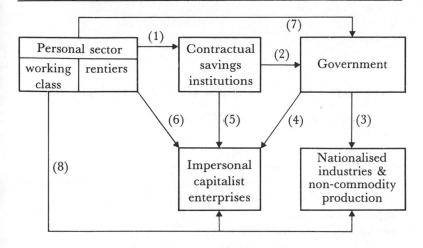

Relation (1) shows the flow of savings from workers and rentiers. This relation could be maintained, or replaced by tax revenue (7) bearing particularly on the rentiers. Relation (2) represents lending to the government, which could be transformed by a system of compulsory subscription of funds to a national investment bank, which would provide funds on a planned basis for both public projects and commodity-producing enterprises (3 and 4). Relations (5) and (6) represent shareholding on the part of financial institutions and individual rentiers respectively. The prerogatives attached to shareholding at present would have to be broken to permit the development of social planning and enterprise democracy. Relation (8) represents the provision of labour power by the working class. This relation would have to be transformed in the sense that workers would not merely provide labour power but also participate in the management and planning of enterprises. While this transformation depends fundamentally on workers' initiatives it could be aided by a government using the financing relation (4) as a means of leverage.

Many important *political* questions are, of course, left unanswered in this presentation, and it would be naive to suppose they are readily answerable; I have made some qualifications to this effect in the course of the argument. To reiterate the point, the main concern of this discussion has been to locate certain strategic possibilities, as well as constraints, in relation to the currently dominant structures of capitalist property, or in other words to argue the mutability of the economic class relations of possession and separation from the conditions of production in what one might call a 'non-millenarian' manner.

6
Classes, social collectivities and political forces

Chapters 1 and 2 presented arguments in favour of 'disaggregating' the classical Marxist conception of social classes. In place of the attempt to produce a synthetic totalising definition of classes it was argued that an analysis which respects the specificity of economic class relations (defined at the level of property-holding), social collectivities and political forces is likely to be more fruitful. Chapters 3 and 4 followed this up by investigating the principal forms of capitalist property, with particular reference to the British case, and Chapter 5 drew out some of the political implications of that investigation. I now turn to the question of social collectivities and political forces. This question will be approached in two stages: this chapter develops the conceptualisation of social collectivities and the relations between these and political forces, and attempts an historical outline of the development of these relations in Britain since 1945, while the following chapter is a fuller essay in the analysis of the specific relationships between economic class structure, social collectivities and political forces in the period of emergence of Thatcherism and of Thatcher's government 1979-1982.

To expand on the plan of the present chapter: I shall begin by discussing the notions of 'social collectivity' and 'political force'; the relevance of the division of labour to the formation of social collectivities will then be considered; the content of the notions of 'middle class' and 'working class' (in the British context) will be explored in this light, and finally I shall offer an overview of the development of the dominant political forces and their constituencies in the post-war period.

Some preliminary definitions

By 'social collectivity' I shall mean a category of agents broadly sharing some aspect of culture and orientation to politics, susceptible to organisation into a political constituency of some kind. This definition is necessarily somewhat open-ended: the existence of social collectivities will be a matter of degree, and what is more, such collectivities may cut across one another — there will be no unique map of social collectivities such that each agent is a member of one and only one. Nonetheless, certain collectivities acquire a certain salience or pertinence in relation to the dominant political issues of a given period. To refer to this phenomenon I shall use the term 'pertinent social collectivity'. By 'political force' on the other hand I shall mean specifically political parties and movements, or tendencies within these, with explicitly shared objectives. Another generic term will be useful: I shall employ the term 'corporate body' to refer to a formal grouping of agents such as a trade union, staff association, or employer's organisation.

These preliminary definitions of concepts may be given some more substance by considering the relations between them, and also their relations with the concept of economic class. We have already seen (Chapter 1) how Marx conceptualised the formation of the 'proletariat' into an active political force, in the 'Communist Manifesto'. In terms of the concepts outlined above we could express Marx's views thus: the economic class of proletarians (propertyless sellers of labour power) will necessarily become increasingly homogeneous in respect of income levels and conditions of life and work; this will result in the increasing 'non-pertinence' of social collectivities based on branch of industry, religion, nationality, sex etc., and the increasing pertinence of the social collectivity coterminous with the proletariat itself; eventually as a result of the process of struggle this social collectivity will become organised into a corporate body — the trade union movement — and a political force: the communist movement or party. In schematic form:

The arrows indicate an order of determination which is supposed to operate on a long historical time scale. Marx clearly did not formally abandon this schema even in his later writings. In Volume Three of Capital (Marx, 1972), in the tantalising unfinished fragment on 'Classes', Marx notes that even in England, where 'modern society is indisputably most highly and classically developed in economic structure ... the stratification of classes does not appear in its pure form. Middle and intermediate strata even here obliterate lines of demarcation everywhere' (1972, p. 885). But immediately the pertinence of this point is denied:

> 'However, this is immaterial for our analysis. We have seen that the continual tendency and law of the development of the capitalist mode of production is more and more to divorce the means of production from labour, and more and more to concentrate the scattered means of production into large groups, thereby transforming labour into wage-labour and the means of production into capital' (ibid.).

I noted earlier that Marx recognised the social and political 'materiality' of lines of demarcation *other* than those of property holding in the 'Eighteenth Brumaire': nonetheless what is striking in this passage is that he never settled accounts with the general theory which denied such factors any pertinence in the long run. Unfortunately the 'obliteration of lines of (economic class) demarcation' is still highly material *despite* the undoubted continuing transformation of 'labour into wage-labour and means of production into capital', and a theory which asserts 'correspondence' of economic classes and political forces as the norm can only block specific politically relevant analysis. Now, it is in the nature of the critique of this aspect of classical Marxism which has already been proposed that it is not possible to erect an alternative 'general theory'. I have emphasised that the relations between economic classes, social collectivities and political forces must be investigated specifically, in a given historical context. All the same it will be useful to outline some of the more important possible forms of relationship.

For instance:

i) Political forces may crystallise and channel 'inputs' from social collectivities and corporate bodies, in the sense of recruiting personnel from the latter, developing relatively amorphous social ideologies into a focused political project, and 'processing' policy-recommendations from corporate bodies. On the other hand, at particular junctures political forces can 'break loose' from the social collectivities and corporate bodies which traditionally support them, either in pursuit of an autonomous political project or in the face of intolerable contradictions among the demands of their 'constituents'.

ii) Political forces may build (or attempt to build) support for their objectives by fostering the development of certain pertinent social collectivities (e.g. 'the nation', the 'anti-monopoly alliance', the 'revolutionary proletariat'), unifying their own supporters in specific ways while dividing or confusing their opponents.

iii) The actions of political forces and corporate bodies, within the resistant medium of social collectivities over which they have some influence but which they cannot shape *ex nihilo*, may either conserve or transform in various ways the system of economic class relations. The character of this conservation/transformation effect may or may not correspond to the intentions of certain of the forces involved. Political forces and corporate bodies may be more or less able to calculate the likely effects, *ceteris paribus*, of the implementation of their policies and demands, and the conservation/transformation effect is anyway likely to appear as the 'resultant vector' of non-coherent activities on the part of a whole range of such forces and bodies (although, for instance, dominant positions within a government may give one political force more leverage than others).

Note that economic classes are nowhere in this account presented as 'actors'. It would indeed be the exception if the pertinent social collectivities were exclusively formed on economic class lines (even though this may be the plan of certain political forces), as it would be if such social collectivities were to appear on the 'political stage' as political forces in their own right.

It should be clear how far from a general theory such remarks take us: to progress any further one must be more specific. The first step in this direction will be by way of a discussion of the division of labour within capitalist economies, and the possibilities for the formation of social collectivities connected with this. This problem is selected because of the importance given to the division of labour within modern Marxist discussions of social class[1] and also within more orthodox sociological analyses of class (i.e. 'occupational classes'). It will be argued that the division of labour does not *determine* the pattern of pertinent social collectivities but along with certain other factors constitutes a complex grid of social differentiation within which social collectivities may be formed.

The division of labour and social collectivities

Discussion of the division of labour in Marxist theory has been rendered somewhat opaque by the development of various conflicting terminologies. I propose to begin therefore with a terminological clarification. One of Marx's fullest accounts of the various aspects of the division of labour is contained in 'Capital' Volume One (Marx, 1976, pp. 470-80). In this context he distinguishes the 'division of labour in manufacture' (i.e. the detailed division of tasks between workers employed by a single capitalist) from the 'social division of labour' (i.e. the division of social production as a whole into various distinct 'branches'). He then goes on to develop a more detailed schema:

'If we keep labour alone in view, we may designate the division of social production into its main *genera* such as agriculture, industry, etc. as *division of labour in general*, and the splitting of these broad divisions into species and sub-species as *division of labour in particular*. Finally, we may designate the division of labour within the workshops as *division of labour in detail*' (Marx, 1976, p. 471 — emphasis added).

What Marx here calls the 'division of labour in general', I shall refer to as the *division of labour by sectors or by branches*, as appropriate. What he calls the 'division of labour in particular', I shall refer to as the *division of labour by enterprises*, or *enterprise-groups*, as appropriate. Finally, what he calls the 'division of labour in detail' will here be referred to as the *division of labour within the enterprise*. These terminological changes are not made merely for the sake of variety but because I believe the substitute terms convey their meaning more pointedly than Marx's originals.

The main point of potential confusion, however, arises because of the quite distinct meaning attached to the term 'social division of labour' by modern Marxist writers. Whereas Marx often used this term to refer generally to what I have called the division by sectors or branches many recent writers have used it to refer to the division of functions, found within all branches in a capitalist economy, between the 'exploiters' or 'controllers' of labour power and the direct production workers. In this sense, it is opposed to the 'technical division of labour' between different productive tasks. For instance Balibar (1970, p. 214) writes that the 'double function' of the capitalist (at once exploiter of labour power and organiser of production) 'is an index of what I shall call the double nature of the *division of labour* in production (the 'technical' division of labour and the 'social' division of labour).' This formulation has been taken up by Poulantzas, Carchedi and others. It usually goes along with the claim that the 'technical' division of labour, i.e. the actual distribution of tasks, is in some sense subordinate to the social division. For instance, Poulantzas (1975, p.21): 'it is the social division of labour, in the form that this is given by the specific presence of political and ideological relations actually within the production process, which dominates the technical division of labour.' I do not propose to employ this terminology. The notion of the 'technical' division of labour is much too poor, and elides Marx's interesting discussion of the different levels and forms of division of labour. The notion of the social division of labour as employed by these writers will, however, be reconstructed below under the name of *division of labour by strata.*

Let us now examine the characteristics, and possible effects on the formation of social collectivities, of the various aspects of the division of labour which have been identified.

1. **The division by sectors or branches:** This, as Marx points out, is an ancient principle of division. It can be traced back, for instance, to the rudimentary sexual division of labour between hunting (male) and horticulture (mainly female) in certain 'primitive' societies (Terray, 1972, pp. 108-110). At a 'later' stage of social development, this division by branches becomes the basis for commodity exchange between the units of production within the different branches. For Marx, the further development of this form of division of labour in society appears as a prerequisite of the division of labour within the enterprise under capitalism:

> 'Since the production and circulation of commodities are the general prerequisites of the capitalist mode of production, division of labour in manufacture requires that a division of labour within society should have already attained a certain degree of development' (1976, p. 473).

Once established, capitalist commodity production then pushes yet further the division of labour by branches:

> 'Inversely, the division of labour in manufacture reacts back upon that in society, developing and multiplying it further. With the differentiation of the instruments of labour, the trades which produce these instruments themselves become more and more differentiated' (ibid.).

If the division of labour between branches is conserved and extended within capitalist economies, it can form the principle of a particular kind of social collectivity which cuts across 'class' lines and inhibits the formation of class based collectivities. That is, common interests can be formed on the basis of the branch of production, which in some respects unite wage-workers, managers and employers in a particular branch, possibly in opposition to the interests of wage-workers in other branches. Witness for example the common front of workers and employers in the textile industry in Britain in 1980/81 calling for import controls, which, although they may be justified, would raise the price and restrict the choice of clothing for other workers. If one recognises the materiality of the division of production and labour by branches, it is no good writing off such conflicts as 'false consciousness'. The possible divisions between workers considered as car workers, textile workers, railwaymen etc., are not merely the product of a Machiavellian manipulation on the part of 'capital' (although of course managers and politicians may seek to exploit and amplify such divisions).

2. **The division by enterprises:** I have earlier remarked on two features of the development of the enterprise in modern capitalism — increasing scale and diversification. While the increasing scale of many enterprises means that more workers are grouped under a single 'employer' it clearly does not abolish the divisions between enterprises, which again can form the basis of social collectivities. Given diversification, this principle of division can cut across branches of production, adding a further complexity to the social differentiation of labour. In many cases, identification of workers with the enterprise which employs them may be only weakly formed but again a community of interest *may* be established at this level, depending perhaps on the degree of 'paternalism' of the management, the character of employment conditions in the enterprise, and the degree of craft skill or other interesting aspect of work within the enterprise. A striking example of the formation of pertinent social collectivities on enterprise lines is found in the Japanese industrial/commercial combines which provide lifetime employment for many workers as well as extensive 'welfare' and social services. As Hirschmeier and Yui (1975, p. 300) remark:

'It is sometimes held that Japanese would be ideal Marxists considering the importance of group-centredness and the tendency to follow the masses. But one could argue against this that Japanese groups have nothing to do with classes. A Japanese worker at Mitsubishi feels closer to his own manager than to a co-worker at Hitachi.'

Of course, there are unions and parties within Japan which cut across enterprise identification, but the point made by Hirschmeier and Yui is that for many workers, for much of the time, the enterprise is a more strongly pertinent collectivity.

3. **The division within the enterprise**: As Marx argues, this division of labour is of a different kind from the others. He takes Adam Smith to task for conflating the division of labour in society with the division within the enterprise. For Smith, the difference is 'merely subjective': the division within the enterprise is confined to one location and can be surveyed synoptically while in the case of the division of labour in society 'the spreading-out of the work over great areas and the great number of people employed in each branch of labour obscure the connection' (paraphrased by Marx, 1976, p. 475). For Marx on the other hand the difference is more material: the division of labour between branches exists on the basis of the interchange of products as *commodities*, whereas within the enterprise the specialised worker produces no commodities — 'It is only the common product of all the specialised workers that becomes a commodity' (ibid.). The point at issue here is the form of connection between the divided labours:

'The division of labour within society is mediated through the purchase and sale of the products of different branches of industry, while the connection between the various partial operations in a workshop (or more generally, in an enterprise — A.C.) is mediated through the sale of the labour-power of several workers to one capitalist, who employs it as combined labour-power' (Marx, 1976, pp. 475-6).

The latter is a 'planned and regulated' system while the former is established '*a posteriori*' through the workings of the market. What Smith's conflation effectively conceals is the authority of the capitalist over his employees, who are 'merely the members of a total mechanism which belongs to him' (p. 477).

In Marx's view, this 'total mechanism' or regulated system of division of labour within the enterprise develops in two stages: those of manufacture proper, and large-scale machine industry. Within manufacture, the precise form of division depends in the first instance on the historical precursors of the capitalistic form of production in the given branch of industry — whether the 'manufacturer' (a) draws together previously separate trades into one workshop to produce a common product or (b) splits up a previously unified craft production process into its component tasks. But over time a certain common rationality is imposed, as 'capital' seeks both maximum control over labour power and its progressive cheapening. Here Braverman (1974) buttresses Marx's case by reference to the 'Babbage principle'. Babbage had argued that one of the main reasons for the cheapness of manufactured articles was

'that the master manufacturer, by dividing the work to be executed into different processes, each requiring different degrees of skill or of force, can purchase exactly that precise quantity of both which is necessary for each process; whereas, if the work were executed by one workman, that person must possess sufficient skill to perform the most difficult, and sufficient strength to execute the most laborious, of the operations into which the art is divided'.[2]

In commentary on this principle Braverman claims that it is

'fundamental to the evolution of the division of labour in capitalist society. It gives expression not to a technical aspect of the division of labour but to its social aspect. Insofar as the labour process may be dissociated, it may be separated into elements some of which are simpler than others and each of which is simpler than the whole. Translated into market terms, this means that the labour power capable of performing the process may be purchased more cheaply as dissociated elements than as a capacity integrated in a single worker' (Braverman, 1974, pp. 81-82).

Alongside the technical advantages of the division of labour noted by Adam Smith (specialised dexterity, time saving, development of specialised means of production) the 'Babbage principle' imposes, it is argued, a specifically capitalist form of division.

In Marx's second stage — large-scale machine industry — the craft skill of the worker in handling his tools 'passes over to the machine' (Marx, *op.cit.*, p.545). This 'destroys the technical foundation on which the division of labour in manufacture was based' (ibid.), but it does not destroy the advantages which the division of labour offers the capitalist in terms of controlling and cheapening labour power:

> 'Thus although, from a technical point of view, the old system of division of labour is thrown overboard, it hangs on in the factory as a tradition handed down from manufacture, and is then systematically reproduced and fixed in a more hideous form by capital as a means of exploiting labour power. The lifelong speciality of handling the same tool becomes the lifelong speciality of serving the same machine. ... In this way not only are the expenses of (the worker's) reproduction considerably lessened, but at the same time his helpless dependence upon the factory as a whole, and therefore upon the capitalist, is rendered complete' (ibid., p. 547).

Within large-scale industry, the crippling specialisation of the individual machine-minders is one aspect of the division of labour. The others are (i) the 'separation of the intellectual faculties of the production process from manual labour' and (ii) the division of the workers into 'manual labourers and overseers, into the private soldiers and the N.C.O.s of an industrial army'.

In Braverman's analysis, this 'separation of the intellectual faculties of the production process from manual labour', or division between 'conception' and 'execution', is taken as the fundamental and enduring feature of the capitalist division of labour. Already rationalised by Babbage, it was later given its most explicit and systematic expression by F.W. Taylor, whose project was to eliminate the autonomy of the worker by appropriating for management any remaining knowledge or skill involved in the direct production process, to analyse and codify the components of the labour process and thereby to permit the management to lay down standard rules for the expenditure of labour power. 'Taylorism' is seen as the quite self-conscious pursuit of what Braverman calls the 'general law of the capitalist division of labour', according to which

> 'Every step in the labour process is divorced, so far as possible, from special knowledge and training and reduced to simple labour. Meanwhile, the relatively few persons for whom special knowledge and training are reserved are freed so far as possible from the obligations of simple labour' (Braverman, 1974, pp. 82-3).

Most of Marx's comments on the division of labour are concerned with industrial production, but Braverman sets out to show that the capitalist division of labour between 'conception' and 'execution' is to be found equally in routine clerical work and in fact within any developed capitalist enterprise.

To summarise this conception: for both Marx and Braverman the developed form of the division of labour within the capitalist enterprise is not so much a technical division of tasks — as in early manufacture — but a socially determined structure, reflecting the exigencies of the production of surplus value. It has a dichotomous aspect, in that most workers are degraded to the status of mere machine minders while a restricted cadre is invested with the scientific/technical knowledge necessary for the development of production. We see why Marx felt it important to attack Smith's generalised conception of the division of labour, and to insist on the different conditions governing the division of labour *between* and *within* commodity producing enterprises.

However, in emphasising the specifically capitalist form of the latter division, both Marx and Braverman exaggerate what they take to be its essential features: rationality and authoritarianism. Their conceptions can be challenged at two levels. First, it is not clear that a 'rational' capitalist would necessarily wish to subordinate and cheapen the mass of labour to the greatest possible extent. Other more 'enlightened' strategies are possible, and may in the long run prove more profitable. Second, even if straightforward authoritarianism and minimisation of wages are assumed to be universal features of capitalist rationality, it is difficult to claim that this 'rationality' is uniformly imposed in practice as a function of the 'undisputed authority of the capitalist' (Marx). The specific claims of Marx and Braverman in this regard have been contested in a number of recent writings. Lazonick (1979) argues, for instance, that when Marx took the self-acting mule as a prime example of a technology permitting the increased subordination of labour to capital he was in fact relying, at second hand, on the claims made by the machine's manufacturers, and that in practice the mule-spinners held a relatively superior position in the division of labour. More's study (1980) of skill levels among engineering workers in England over the period 1870-1914 comes to the conclusion that it is not possible to sustain a definite 'deskilling' thesis on the evidence available. Cressey and MacInnes (1980) argue more broadly that Taylor's project of minute and exact control over labour was actually a failure, and that Braverman's tendency to take Taylor at face-value is a case of confusing the 'fetish of capital' for its reality. Gershuny (1978) provides a counter-example to Braverman's law of job degradation for the majority, by showing that over the 1960s in UK manufacturing industry the proportionate decline in skilled manual employment was significantly lower than the proportionate *increase* in the 'administrative and technical' section of the workforce.[3] The recent study of US manual workers by Hull *et al.* (1982) suggests that technological advance in industry has been associated with reduced job dissatisfaction. Employees have often found their work with new machines less physically demanding and have often regarded it as more skilled. Such studies do not settle the issue definitively, but they do bring out the problems facing a simple 'deskilling' or 'degradation of work' thesis.

This kind of qualification is of considerable importance for the problem of the formation of social collectivities. The sense of outrage on the part of both Marx and Braverman at the crippling effects (physical or spiritual) on many workers of the division of labour within capitalist enterprises is fully justified, but their unitary and rationalistic conception of the total subordination of labour to capital leads them to an overestimation of the role this division of labour must play in the formation of social collectivities: the extraction of any 'skill' content from labour for the mass of workers; the homogenisation of 'simple labour' in all branches of production; the cheapening of labour power; increasingly intolerable oppression — these tendencies are bound to overwhelm any secondary differentiation of the workers by branch or by enterprise and lead to the formation of a revolutionary proletariat. But the division of labour within the enterprise is not a juggernaut which crushes out all trace of 'skill' or peculiarity in the wage-labour of each and every branch of production, and neither can the 'capitalist' attain the Taylorist ideal of total control over labour. Homogeneous 'simple labour' is not inexorably established as the norm for wage-labour in capitalist economies, and by the same token it is not inevitable that a uniform structure of division of labour within enterprises will progressively undermine any ties of social identification other than those of 'class'. While not inevitable, it is however clearly *possible* that a broadly common position within the hierarchical division of labour forms the basis for a corporate body or social collectivity embracing workers in different enterprises and branches. I refer to this below as the 'division of labour by strata'.

4. **The division by strata:** This concept refers to the broad division
among all employees of capitalist enterprises (and state apparatuses)
into different hierarchical categories, in respect of character of labour
power (more or less skilled/qualified)[4], role within the functioning
of the enterprise (autonomy/restriction of work, control powers,
access to information), and conditions of employment. If the division
of labour within the enterprise were as (tendentially) uniform as
Marx and Braverman suppose then there would be little problem
in specifying this 'division by strata': it would simply be the
paradigmatic division within the enterprise (mass of simple labour,
restricted cadre of intellectual workers and N.C.O.s) writ large.
If on the other hand the form of division of labour within enterprises is not homogeneous then the concept of 'division by strata'
must be more nebulous and approximate. We may talk of such
categories as 'professionals', 'managers', 'technicians', 'foremen'
and 'manual workers' (and sub-gradations of these), but we have
to recognise that these terms do not have homogeneous referents,
and the degree of real social distinctiveness and cohesiveness of these
categories may be highly variable. Despite the emphasis placed on
this aspect of the division of labour by Marxists and non-Marxist
sociologists alike, it cannot be said that the division by strata forms
the 'naturally' pertinent basis for social identification in capitalist
societies.

It is now possible to draw together the comments made above on the
various aspects of the division of labour. The divisions by branches
and by enterprises, within the enterprise, and by strata, form a grid
or matrix of differentiation within which social collectivities may be
formed, collectivities whose political pertinence is not given in advance,
but is always constructed in historically specific ways. Let us take just
a few examples of strongly formed collectivities with a broadly socialist
orientation to illustrate the point.

First, Bologna has argued that the remarkable political vitality of
the International Workers of the World (IWW) can be traced in part
to the character of the American proletariat which it organised, in the
early years of the twentieth century, as a 'mobile proletariat ... completely against identification with any task or skill' (Bologna, 1976,
p. 72). In this context the IWW could 'exploit the extraordinary level
of communication and coordination allowed by a mobility-based
struggle.' In a lyrical passage Bologna describes the 'absolutely original
type of agitator' which the IWW succeeded in creating: 'not the mole
digging for decades within the single establishment or proletarian

neighbourhood, but a type of agitator who swims within the stream of proletarian struggles, moves from one end to the other of the enormous American continent and calculates the seismic wave of the struggle ...' (ibid.). In this case the *weakness* of the division of labour between branches or enterprises as a principle of social collectivity, on account of the substantial movement of US workers, both geographically and in and out of various kinds of work,[5] is a condition of existence of a strongly formed radical proletarian collectivity cutting across branch or enterprise lines. On the other hand, the British National Union of Mineworkers (NUM) has developed as a strongly formed collectivity in a very different way. The sources of its solidarity and strength lie in part in the continuity of tradition in the (relatively closed) mining communities — the opposite of the mobility of the proletariat organised by the IWW. The NUM is firmly based within a definite branch of the division of labour, although it cuts across enterprise (i.e. colliery) boundaries and although its political interventions often find an echo in other branches. The contrast between these two cases should warn us against generalising propositions which make either fluidity and mobility of the working class, or tradition and community within particular branches, into uniquely favourable conditions for socialist organisation (the first is perhaps Bologna's temptation; the second appears to be the temptation of the work done under the auspices of the 'History Workshop').

A third contrasting example of collectivity can be found in the Scottish Trades Councils in the latter part of the 19th Century, which formed a much stronger focus for working class politics than national trades unions at that time. Here a collectivity was developed on a regional or local basis, drawing together workers from the various trades, rather than in a national body for the members of a single trade. Fraser (1978, pp. 1-2) explains this by reference to the particular position of Glasgow within the Scottish economy:

'The stress on local autonomy arose fairly naturally from the structure of the Scottish economy. Glasgow had a dominating position, both in population and in concentration of industry. Clydeside workers were unwilling to accept decisions emanating from Aberdeen, Kirkcaldy or wherever, or to subordinate their own needs to those of other parts of the country. As soon as any efforts to form national unions were made, they came up against the imbalance between Glasgow and the rest of the country.'

The local Trades Councils were nonetheless able to organise quite effectively around demands for city improvements and municipalisation of utilities, campaigned against excessive salaries for local bureaucrats, and had an important role in discussing and pushing for parliamentary reform. Here the principle of collectivity cut across trade and enterprise boundaries, but did not surmount what Marx called the 'territorial division of labour' between regions.

These examples show something of the variety of ways in which social collectivities can be formed, 'within' some aspects of the division of labour grid while cutting across others. But the stress so far on the division of labour is somewhat one-sided. The matrix of social differentiation which can form the basis for collectivities includes other dimensions, such as parentage, region, religion, income level, form of housing tenure. Where these latter principles of differentiation are coterminous with certain aspects of the division of labour (and with each other), the chances of formation of a politically pertinent collectivity within the 'division of labour grid' may be increased (e.g. 'working class' catholics in the west of Scotland as a traditional Labour Party support-base); where they cut across the division of labour the chances may be diminished (the difficulty of developing 'class' politics in Northern Ireland).

The 'working class' and 'middle class' as social collectivities

I have built up a conception in which the agents belonging to a given economic class (defined at the level of property holding) may be distributed in various ways into more or less strongly formed social collectivities of various degrees of political pertinence. It is not possible or useful to provide an encyclopaedic account of the collectivities existing 'within' the economic classes in Britain but this section pursues the analysis of two rather broad and vaguely defined, yet nonetheless politically and culturally important, social collectivities: the 'working class' and the 'middle class', as these terms are used by 'ordinary people' and formalised by sociologists. This analysis is necessary to an understanding of politics in Britain, and yet it is too often dismissed by Marxists, at least implicitly, as irrelevant. The kinds of theorisation of classes discussed in Chapter 2, theorisations concerned with demarcating the working class and the new middle class/ new petty bourgeoisie on Marxist criteria, do not address the problem of assessing the importance of the 'classes' (broad collectivities, in my terms) which are taken to exist in particular social formations — the 'classes' which are (more or less consistently) recognised by the people as such, and to one or other of which many people regard themselves as belonging. There can be no presumption that these collectivities correspond to the classes of Marxist theory (however conceived), and where they fail to correspond it will not do to reject them as unimportant. I am not arguing that there are no uses for a conceptual demarcation of classes quite distinct from the demarcations present within popular ideology — on the contrary, I have used such a demarcation in previous chapters — but I am arguing that the latter demarcations have a real importance and should not be dismissed as merely 'subjective'.

We may begin by considering the meaning which the notion of 'class', and the 'working class'/'middle class' distinction in particular, has within popular ideology in Britain. Here one has to rely on the indices produced by survey techniques, which do not provide unambiguous definitions and which are open to a variety of interpretations but which nonetheless do provide a starting point for analysis. One important qualification here is, however, that answers to survey questions are variable over time and the fullest surveys available are now somewhat out of date: one must be alert to the changes since the late 1960s when the surveys of Butler and Stokes (1974) and Townsend (1979) were conducted (these form the basis of the following discussion). Nonetheless, one can get some useful mileage out of the 1960s surveys, before moving on to an historical account.

A first question is the extent to which some notion of 'social class' is pertinent to people; whether it forms a part of their everyday conceptual apparatus. Here the variability of survey responses immediately becomes apparent. In answer to the question 'do you ever think of yourself as belonging to a particular social class?' Butler and Stokes got a 50 per cent positive response in 1964 and a 43 per cent positive response in 1970. With a rather different question Townsend's survey team in 1968-69 found around 80 per cent of respondents willing to assign themselves 'spontaneously' to a social class. In both cases, however, it was clear that among those respondents who thought in terms of 'class' the most common designations were 'working' and 'middle'. Further, with a little prompting (i.e. respondents presented with a standard list of classes and asked to place themselves) the overwhelming majority of respondents were willing to assign themselves to the 'middle' or 'working' classes or some sub-division of these. If quantification is risky, it does at least seem that the two-class, middle/working conception is quite deeply rooted in popular ideology. When questioned on the *basis* for class determination, however, Townsend's respondents were not surprisingly rather vague: 'Way of life' came first among the principles which Townsend offered, followed by family and occupation, with money and education also being mentioned. Interestingly but not surprisingly, a higher proportion of men than women took occupation to be the principal factor determining class.

If the popular conception of 'class' does not involve any rigorous or well-elaborated notion of class determination, it is of interest to examine whether people's self-assignation correlates strongly with certain 'objective' features of their economic and social location. It is often assumed that what I have earlier called the 'division of labour by strata' is the prime objective content of the British 'class' system but there are severe methodological problems in investigating this hypothesis, since the schemas proposed for the classification of occupations are not actually independent of the phenomenon to be explained. Occupational classifications, from the Registrar General's of 1911 to the Hall-Jones scale (Hall and Jones, 1950) and all its variants, involve some kind of ranking by 'prestige' or 'standing in the community'. They are therefore nearer to being attempted *systematisations* of popular ideology than objective scales which could be used to *explain* that ideology. As Townsend (1979, p. 371) aptly remarks of the 'grading' of occupations 'the whole procedure is ... a mixture of presupposition and the partial representation of social perceptions.' It is interesting, however, to see the extent to which occupational classifications *fail* to 'correspond' with self-assigned social class. Two examples of this are shown, in Tables 6.1 and 6.2.

Table 6.1   *'Occupational class' and self-rating according to Townsend*

Occupational class*	Self-rating			
	Middle		Working	
	Men %	Women %	Men %	Women %
Professional	81	86	15	12
Managerial	69	72	29	26
Supervisory-High	62	68	38	30
Supervisory-Low	50	55	47	43
Routine non-manual	45	47	54	51
Skilled manual	22	30	76	68
Partly skilled manual	16	23	82	74
Unskilled manual	11	15	86	82

* Women classified according to husband's occupational class.
Source: Townsend (1979).

Table 6.2   *Occupation and self-rating according to Butler and Stokes*

Occupational class	Self-rating	
	Middle %	*Working %*
I Higher managerial or professional	80	20
II Lower managerial or administrative	60	40
III Skilled or supervisory non-manual	57	43
IV Lower non-manual	46	54
V Skilled manual	26	74
VI Unskilled manual	20	80

Source: Butler and Stokes (1974).

What is clear from these comparisons is that 'occupational status' is not the only factor which individuals consider when assigning themselves to a given 'social class'.[6] For instance, nearly 30 per cent of the men in Townsend's sample in 'managerial' occupations regarded themselves as working class, and at the other end of the scale 20 per cent of Butler and Stokes' 'unskilled manual' workers regarded themselves as middle class. What one finds is a continuum extending from top to bottom of the occupational scale; the 'lower' on the scale, the lower the proportion identifying as middle class and the higher the proportion identifying as working class. But there is one 'break' in the continuum, in that there is a relatively sharp rise in the proportion of 'working class' identifiers when we reach the 'manual' occupational categories. I argued earlier that there are problems in attempting any rigorous theoretical definition of the 'manual work/mental work', or 'manual/non-manual', distinction but all the same this classification, conceived as a socially constructed principle of division, has a certain social validity, as least as it applies to male workers. 'Manual' workers within the British classification, although their precise work situations may vary quite widely, have in general considerably less job-security and less access to various benefits provided by employers than 'non-manual' workers. Despite this, it is worth noting that in Townsend's sample 31 per cent of men assigning themselves to the middle class had 'manual' occupations, and 25 per cent of men assigning themselves to the working class had 'non-manual' occupations.

A fuller account of the factors active in people's class identification would no doubt have to consider income, wealth, housing tenure, education, style of consumption, social origins, family and local connections. For some groups, for instance, it is clear that a relatively high income, and the style of consumption which accompanies that, can induce a 'middle class' self-identification despite having a 'manual' occupation.[7] Butler and Stokes found that income level was particularly important in individuals' self-image by class for their occupational groups III, IV and V (for the meaning of these see Table 6.2). The particular importance of housing tenure has been noted already: Townsend found that among respondents renting council accommodation only 20 per cent rated themselves as middle class while among owner-occupiers 40 per cent did so. It seems likely that the spread of owner-occupation may undermine the 'working class' identification of some 'manual' groups.

It is not being suggested here that the various factors bearing on class identification are totally independent variables. The correlations between occupational status, income, educational opportunity and attainment have been well-established (see for instance Westergaard and Resler, 1975), and it can be politically important to stress these systematic connections when opposing the notion that 'class inequality' is disappearing. It is clear that individuals in the 'higher' occupational groupings are far more likely to have high incomes and to be owner-occupiers than those in the lower groupings, and it is also clear that children of higher category parents have a much better chance of extending their education beyond the minimum, and of qualifying for higher status occupations themselves (Goldthorpe, 1980, Halsey et al., 1980). Nonetheless, these linkages are not so tight that one can read off class self-identification from the hierarchical classification of occupations, in any of its variants: there is an area of overlap between manual and non-manual earnings; many manual workers are now owner-occupiers; many individuals in the higher occupations have come from manual backgrounds. The general point here is that 'class' as a cultural phenomenon in British society, as a form of broad and loose social collectivity, is not only quite distinct from the classical Marxist conception in which classes are defined on the basis of property relations — neither is it reducible to the sociological conception of 'occupational class'. In fact it is futile to search for a rigorous definition which will 'correctly' locate the division between the 'working class' and the 'middle class' in Britain. It is more appropriate to regard these social collectivities as based on what Wittgenstein called 'family resemblances'. Wittgenstein (1968, pp. 31-32), exploring the philosophy of language, posed the question of what was common to all the things which we call 'games':

'What is common to them all? — Don't say: "There *must* be something common or they would not be called 'games' " — but *look and
see* whether there is anything common to *all*. For if you look at them
you will not see something that is common to *all*, but similarities,
relationships, and a whole series of them at that ... I can think of
no better expression to characterise these similarities than "family
resemblances"; for the various resemblances between members of
a family ... overlap and criss-cross in the same way.'

The same might be said of the individuals in Britain considering
themselves members of the 'middle class': there is not an *essential*
characteristic common to them all, which could be discovered by
theoretical reflection.

At this point it will be useful to take the measure of the dislocation
between the economic classes defined on the basis of capitalist property relations and the working class and middle class collectivities
in Britain. First, the 'working class' in Britain may be seen as a *subset*
of the economically defined working class (i.e. wage and salary earning employees separated from the means of production), although it
probably also includes sections of the petty bourgeoisie (in the strict
sense of small-scale producers and traders employing their own means
of production and labour power) who regard themselves as 'working
for a living'. The 'working class' collectivity is, in a sense, centred
on manual industrial labour, at least for the adult male members of
working class families, although (a) by no means all people who consider themselves working class are employed in that sphere and (b)
a not insignificant minority of people employed in that sphere do not
consider themselves working class. The British middle class, on the
other hand, includes large sections of the economically defined work
ing class (especially salaried employees) as well as sections of the petty
bourgeoisie proper and sections of the 'individual bourgeoisie' (i.e.
personal owners of means of production and employers of the labour
power of others).[8] These are the two basic 'classes'; in addition there
is the 'upper class', which designation is generally restricted to the
hereditary aristocracy and rich rentiers. To look at the matter differ-
ently, one could say that the members of the economically defined
working class in Britain are divided between the 'working class' and
'middle class' collectivities, with this division depending on a range
of factors including place within the division of labour by strata, parentage, education, home-ownership, and income. In a sense, the paradigm (male) member of the 'working class' will be a manual industrial

worker, born of a father who was also a manual industrial worker, with minimal education, living in rented accommodation. The paradigm 'middle class' employee on the other hand will have some kind of 'white-collar' job, will come from a non-manual background, will be educated beyond the minimum and will expect his or her employment to have the trajectory of a 'career', and will own a home. The fact that such consistent 'paradigm' cases are becoming increasingly rare (this will be discussed later) explains in part why there is no clear boundary between the 'classes'.

We have seen that the social collectivities often known as 'classes' in British society are reducible neither to economic classes in the Marxist sense nor to the sociologists' occupational classes. We have also seen that these collectivities have a considerable pertinence within popular ideology. I shall now examine the relationship between these collectivities and politics, first by a further reference to the surveys of the 1960s cited earlier, then by developing a broader historical perspective.

'Class' and politics: the partisanship surveys of the 1960s

In this section I shall consider two aspects: the broad question of the relationships, within popular ideology, between 'class' division and the political, and the narrower question of the relationship between 'class', party affiliations and voting patterns. The work of Butler and Stokes, and other subsequent research within the same analytical framework, has shown that 'middle class' and 'working class' identification have a considerable relevance as regards support for the two main political parties in Britain. The same research also shows, however, that the 'class' basis of support for the parties is now weakening significantly, and that even at its peak this phenomenon fell a long way short of the Marxist conception of political 'class consciousness'. Let us examine these points.

In a 1963 survey, Butler and Stokes found that among those with a 'middle class' self-image and who also considered themselves partisans of the major parties 79 per cent were Tory and 21 per cent Labour supporters. Among 'working class' identifiers 72 per cent were Labour supporters and 28 per cent Tories. The correlation between 'class' and party support is even more striking if one considers subdivisions within the broad classes, with the self-confessed 'upper classes' showing 100 per cent Tory allegiance and the 'lower working class' showing 77 per cent Labour partisanship. Within the six 'occupational status' categories (see Table 6.2) the pattern of partisanship was also quite clear, although in fact at the 'manual'/'non-manual' divide there was a clearer break in terms of partisanship than in terms of 'class' identification, as can be seen if Table 6.2 is compared with Table 6.3.

Table 6.3   *Party self-image by occupational status 1963*

	I	II	III	IV	V	VI
Conservative	86%	81	77	61	29	25
Labour	14	19	23	39	71	75

Source: Butler and Stokes (1974).

The discrepancy between 'working class' identification, which showed a relatively continuous rise across the occupational categories and Labour partisanship, which displayed an abrupt rise from class IV to V is ascribed to the somewhat 'anomalous' position of the class IV (lower non-manual) individuals: in this category there was a majority of 'working class' identifiers, yet also a majority of Tory partisans. In all the other occupational categories, however, identification with one class or other carried with it a tendency to identify with the 'corresponding' party.

These correlations, while of interest, do not tell us much about the political substance of the 'class'/party link, but Butler and Stokes pursued this further by soliciting 'free' responses concerning the reasons for identification with one or other party. These responses could be organised under four general headings: first, those showing an appreciation of politics as a domain of representation of opposed class interests; second, those viewing politics in terms of a 'simple representation of class interest' without any elaborated notion of *conflict* of interests; third, those showing a simple 'cultural partisanship' without any definite conception of class interests being involved; and fourth, those seeing no 'interest-related' or normative class content in party support. The results of this categorisation show that the bulk of 'working class' labour partisans viewed politics in terms of the 'simple representation' principle (i.e. Labour was 'out to help the working class'; working people vote Labour 'because it's their party'), although a quite substantial minority reckoned in terms of opposed class interests (39 per cent). Among 'middle class' Tories on the other hand, a substantial majority (65 per cent) took the fourth view, thinking in terms of 'national interest', 'competence' and so on rather than in class terms. This latter result is only to be expected: the Tories have assiduously cultivated the image of the defender of the 'national interest' as opposed to the supposed trade union 'sectionalism' of the Labour Party, and militant 'class conscious' organisations within the middle classes have never made much headway (John Gorst's 'Middle Class Association' for instance). What is perhaps more surprising from a Marxist viewpoint is the restricted provenance even among working class Labour supporters of a developed conception of politics as 'class conflict' (let alone any revolutionary conception of the possibility of an alternative social order). The very names of the 'classes' in Britain are symptomatic here: 'middle' and 'working'. The 'middle class' designation logically implies a three-class model, featuring an *upper* class, yet as Townsend noted 'practically nobody claims to belong to such a class' (1979, p. 374). If the 'upper class' is generally reckoned to be marginal or vestigial and the two principal classes are seen as *'middle'* and 'working' then it is clear that the British 'class system' of popular ideology is not equivalent to a ruling class/dominated class dichotomy. 'Working class' people may wish to see their interests favoured over those of the 'middle classes' but they are unlikely, in general terms, to see this conflict as a struggle to displace a ruling class.

I have taken these surveys from the 1960s as a useful starting point. They provide quite a full 'snapshot' of popular conceptions of class, and of the class/politics relationship, some of the elements of which remain relevant today. But to progress any further one must consider the 'class'/politics relationship in Britain in a broader historical context. To remain with Butler and Stokes for a moment, these writers argued, in the book based on the results of their survey, that the pattern of party support is the result of three distinct processes: the physical replacement of the electorate through birth, coming of age and death; the formation of enduring party alignments on the basis of religion, class or long-term issues; and response to immediate events and issues. On the basis of this schema it can be argued that the high-water mark of class/party correlation in the 1960s, registered above, was not so much related to the current policies of the political parties, as to the 'delayed' effect of the social conditions of the interwar depression years and the substantial shifts within popular ideology and political alignment during and immediately after the second world war. From 1945 until the 1960s the *replacement* of the electorate strengthened the 'working class' support for the Labour Party, but at the same time the *current* basis for such an alignment was weakening:

'The newer cohorts entered a politics that was dominated by the class alignment and divided their loyalties along class lines more completely than did their elders, those who had entered politics half a century before. But the new cohorts felt much less keenly the social conditions from which the class alignment arose in the first place. Moreover, the social evolution of Britain, as well as certain political factors, tended to weaken the class alignment in the electorate as a whole and not only in the young' (ibid., p. 193).

A fine illustration of Althusser's conception of 'differential temporality', and the impossibility of reducing historical time to an 'essential section'! (Althusser and Balibar, 1970, Pt.II, Ch.4). This quotation points us towards an historical account of both the 'social evolution of Britain' and the 'certain political factors' which have weakened the 'class' alignment in British politics.

The intention here is not to construct a full history of the post-war period but it will be necessary to examine some of the main developments in the class/collectivity/political force relationships over the post-war years, even at a cost of some over-simplification, in order to establish a basis for the fuller discussion in the following chapter of these relationships under the Thatcher government. My scope here is necessarily limited, and I propose to concentrate on the relationships between the political parties and the social collectivities which have furnished their support blocs. The remit which I set myself is to examine in outline the ways in which the political parties have both responded to and helped to shape the pertinent social collectivities in Britain over the post-war years, and how the activities of political forces have been constrained by, and have served to maintain or transform, the economic class relations of British capitalism.

Class and politics since the war: an overview

I have already mentioned that the decisive electoral victory for the Labour Party in 1945 reflected a substantial shift of political and ideological alignment in the later years of the second world war, a radicalisation of which Calder (1969) gives an eloquent account. It is clear that by 1945 there was widespread popular support for the extension of state welfare provision, for a measure of nationalisation of industry and 'planning' and for a governmental commitment to the maintenance of full employment. Much of this consensus, at least nominally, cut across party lines: Beveridge, who formalised the project of 'welfare' expansion, was a Liberal; the 1944 White Paper on employment policy was produced under the war-time coalition; Butler's educational reforms were also decided in 1944, but many people thought that the Labour Party was more likely to live up to the promise of reform. Butler and Stokes argue that the main source of new electoral strength for Labour in 1945 was the mobilisation of manual workers who had grown up in homes without a long tradition of participation in electoral politics. However, the reformism of this period did not appeal only to manual workers, and among men of the 1945 cohort of voters middle class electors were in fact more likely to be Labour than working class electors were to be Conservative.

I shall not enter into a detailed discussion of this Labour government, its programme and effects, but it should be noted that over the years to 1951, as more and more of the party's electoral pledges were realised, there occurred what is ofen interpreted as a 'weakening of commitment' of both party and people to 'socialism', and a progressive exhaustion of the political impetus for social and economic change. In 1946 the mines were nationalised with the vigorous support of the miners after sixty years resistance by the coal-owners, and shortly afterwards the petty bourgeoisie of the medical profession were organised into a National Health Service. In terms of 'class struggle' this was perhaps the high point of the government's achievements. It is particularly notable that neither in the mines nor in the other industries nationalised at that time was there any substantial movement towards workers' control. 'Management' remained in place, only now it was responsible to a government-appointed Board of Directors and ultimately to Parliament, rather than to shareholders' representatives. The Labour leadership was sceptical about workers' control, indeed Cripps is reported as having said 'I think it would be almost impossible to have worker-controlled industry in Britain even if it were on the whole desirable' (Coates & Topham, 1975, p. 60). But it would be quite wrong to ascribe the failure to take socialist transformation further at this stage by establishing workers' control in the nationalised industries to 'betrayal' on the part of the parliamentary leadership. As Nina Fishman (1980) has pointed out, despite the undoubted idealism and enthusiasm of committed trade unionists in these industries there was considerable reluctance among NUM members to go over to the National Coal Board, to run 'their' industry. There was also a reluctance to attempt the *transformation* of the unions which would have been required to turn them into instruments of workers' control, since this would clearly have introduced an element of responsibility which was foreign to the previous practice of trade unionism, and would have meant taking on board the awkward problem of reconciling, within a reconstructed union framework, the interests of workers in the given nationalised industry and the interests of working people as a whole, as regards the running of that industry. Some miners wanted to take up this challenge, but there was not sufficient determined popular support to make the break with a more conventional trade union practice.

Further, at the 'macroeconomic' level, the fiscal and monetary management of aggregate demand gradually displaced physical planning as the favoured mechanism for control over the economy (this shift is charted quite precisely by Budd, 1978). Again, this did not so much represent a 'betrayal of socialist ideals' as a response to the evident absence of any developed thinking on the part of socialists as to how 'planning' should be conducted in a peacetime economy, without the overriding and generally agreed common objective of victory in war as the guiding principle and without the continuation of 'dictatorial' direction of labour.

Meanwhile the Conservative Party was regrouping its forces after the defeat of 1945, building up better-organised and larger constituency parties and reorganising its ideology. In 1947 the party's 'Industrial Charter', a result of the work undertaken by the Conservative Research Department under Butler, registered the Tories' acceptance of the 'welfare state' and the 'managed economy'. In the 1950 election the Tories' share of the vote recovered significantly, with Labour losing support among the middle classes of the southern suburbs in particular, although the Labour Party could still rely on enthusiastic working class support (the turnout at the 1950 election was the highest ever). Between 1950 and 51, however, the 'political exhaustion' of Labour became more apparent. The nationalisation of iron and steel-making was one of the few 'socialist' measures remaining on the party's agenda. Further, the acceptance of the need for rearmament connected with the Korean war on the part of the parliamentary leadership led to a damaging split within the party, with Bevan and Wilson resigning over Gaitskell's budgetary measures designed to pay for the arms. Finally the sterling crisis resulting from the surge in imports induced by the rearmament programme provided the occasion for the expiry of the administration. In the 1951 election campaign, Labour was on the defensive, trying to arouse fears of Tory warmongering and mass unemployment, while the Tories promised more housing and less taxation. In the event Labour received marginally more votes than the Tories, in an election in which the two parties took a larger share of

the total votes than ever before, but because of the geography of electoral support in relation to constituency boundaries it was the Tories
who gained the majority of seats in Parliament and formed the next
government. Labour support tended to be concentrated in already safe
seats while the Tories swung many of the southern marginals, as many
of the managerial, professional and small business strata registered
Tory votes where they had previously voted Liberal or not voted at
all (Bonham, 1954).

It would seem that by this stage there was relatively little 'class
content', in Marxist terms, to the rivalry of the main political parties.
Clearly the majority of working class voters saw the Labour Party as
'their' party and wished to see it remain in government, while the
majority of middle class voters supported the Tories, but in neither
case did the party or the 'class' have a radical and distinctive programme for the transformation of social relations in Britain. The Tories
had broadly accepted 'Attlee's consensus', although Churchill was
already critical of 'socialist bureaucracy' and 'loss-making nationalised industries' and his party promised a further relaxation of wartime
controls on workers, consumers and private capital; the Labour leadership had basically achieved what they had set out to achieve in the
initial round of nationalisation and formation of the National Health
Service and had no new radical project to present to their working
class supporters, while the broader 'labour movement' in the country
was not unified around any radical demands for further government
action. If there was still a profound cultural divide between the parties, related to the social collectivities which furnished their support,
there was little corresponding clash of definite 'class projects' for social
development.

Tory government 1951-64

Once established as the party of government in 1951, the Tories
benefited greatly from the subsequent rapid development of capital
accumulation and rise in living standards in Britain. From 1951 to
1955 manufacturing output rose 14 per cent, car production 87 per
cent and steel production 21.5 per cent. Apart from in 1952 employment grew continuously and unemployment rarely rose above 300,000.
Real personal disposable income rose 15 per cent over the period.[9]
The marked improvement in the terms of trade for Britain over the
early '50s permitted a rise in real wages despite a decline in Britain's
exports, while a substantial inflow of American direct private invest-

ment helped to boost capital accumulation.[10] In the chemicals and electrical engineering industries multidivisional enterprises such as ICI and Associated Electrical Industries carried out large investment programmes — the chemicals industry stimulated by the removal of German competition during and shortly after the war combined with a world shortage of chemicals, and electrical engineering stimulated by the rapid growth of electricity generation under Citrine (Shonfield, 1958). The industrial expansion of the period was reflected in the sectoral division of labour, which showed an increase in the proportion of the workforce in 'secondary' (industrial) employment from 39.7 per cent in 1948 to 41.6 per cent in 1951 and 42.2 per cent in 1956 (Gershuny, 1978).

The fears raised by Labour in the 1951 election campaign therefore remained unrealised, and the Tories were able to approach the 1955 election, following Churchill's replacement by Eden as prime minister, with considerable confidence. The Labour Party was deeply divided — principally over foreign policy and rearmament, issues on which the Bevanite left was fighting a losing battle against the alignment of Britain with the USA, without mass popular support[11] — and was unable to present its supporters with a convincing programme. The manifesto, 'Forward with Labour', left the direction of putative advance vague in the extreme. By early 1955 the result of the forthcoming election seemed a foregone conclusion and this was reflected in a substantially reduced poll in which the Tories increased their parliamentary majority. Following this election victory, however, Tory fortunes were more mixed: Butler's electioneering budget, with substantial tax-cuts, rebounded as imports rose sharply and the exchange rate of the pound came under pressure, forcing the introduction of 'stop' measures; Eden's popularity waned rapidly even before the ignominy of attempted intervention at Suez in 1956, which then shook the 'Great British' imperial ideology that provided a pole of attraction to Toryism for sections of all classes in society. In 1957 Macmillan inherited the leadership of an unpopular government, lagging behind Labour in the opinion polls, but the policies pursued over the years to 1959 managed eventually to retrieve the party's position: Macmillan's nuclear 'defence' policy seemed at the time a plausible way to reclaim the status of a world power on the cheap; the formation of EFTA was negotiated; Macmillan sacked the deflationary Chancellor Thorneycroft and substituted Heathcoat-Amory who instituted another convenient bout of pre-election tax cutting. Prior to the 1959 election the Tories carried out a highly expensive campaign, by previous standards, backed up by a business campaign against Labour nationalisation plans. Labour, vilified as likely to spoil the Tory prosperity, remained a weak and uninspiring political force. Despite the disarming of the Bevanite left with Bevan's shift of position on nuclear weapons, unity was not forthcoming under Gaitskell's leadership. The left called for more nationalisation; the 'traditional' right wing of the party argued that this 'needed more research' and conveniently forgot about it, while the new 'revisionist' current represented by Healey, Jenkins and Crosland saw public ownership as irrelevant and raised 'equality' as the prime goal of socialism — a position formalised in Crosland's 'Future of Socialism' in 1956. The document 'Industry and Society' adopted by the 1957 party conference reflected a compromise with this 'revisionist' tendency. The continuing failure of Labour to present a distinctive alternative to the Tories was indicated strikingly in the opinion poll finding that 40 per cent of electors believed it made no difference which party was in power. Lacking more substantive arguments for voting Labour, Gaitskell promised an extravagant 'electioneering'-type budget if returned to office, a ploy which the Tory leaders were able to ridicule despite the fact that they had started that particular game. So in the 1959 election Labour support ebbed further and the Tories' parliamentary majority was again increased.

This run of Tory election victories over the 1950s prompted the speculation at the time that the Tories had managed to establish themselves as the 'natural party of government'. It was suggested that increasing 'affluence' and the growth of the 'middle class' meant the decomposition of the social base of the Labour Party (e.g. Abrams and Rose, 1960). The right wing of the party took this to heart: Gaitskell talked of the need to shed Labour's 'cloth cap' image and attempted to ditch the famous clause four of the party constitution, the charter for nationalisation, as an electoral liability. The latter gambit failed, since many in the party who were sceptical of the benefits of further nationalisation saw the removal of clause four as an unnecessarily provocative step, 'removing Genesis from the Bible' as Harold Wilson put it. Besides, the Gaitskellite strategy for Labour was more deeply problematic: if the implicit criterion for political acceptability was resemblance to the Tories, what was there to convince voters that Labour was preferable, and what was there to motivate the party activists to build support? The standard left response to the kind of argument put by Gaitskell was that the party should be 'more socialist' and would thereby gain more working class support, but it is not clear that the left opposition within the party had a political project which could have commanded mass popular support among the working class in the 1950s. The foreign policy issues on which the left fought were of great importance to the activists but of relatively little salience to the mass of the working class, while nationalisation had faded in popularity — quite understandably, given the failure to develop a popular democratic alternative to conventional managerial practice in the nationalised industries, and to develop a coherent set of criteria for allocating resources with which to counter the charge that they were 'inefficient loss-makers'. The propaganda onslaught by the Tories and private business interests must have helped to discredit nationalisation, but this cannot be the whole explanation. Even Bevan reckoned that if the Labour Party were to campaign on a programme fully reflecting the aspirations of the rank and file party activists 'we could say goodbye to any Labour government being elected again in Britain'.[12]

Fortunately for the Labour Party, the position of the Tories as the party of government was less secure that it appeared to be in the late '50s. First of all, it is useful to make a distinction between the party's parliamentary majority and its share of the popular vote. We have already noted that the Tories received fewer votes than Labour in 1951: although they increased their share of the vote in 1955, this share was actually falling by 1959. The party's greatly increased parliamentary majority in '59 masked a decline in popular electoral support as the Liberal Party enjoyed the beginnings of an electoral revival. In fact over the 1950s the Tories never won as much as half of the popular vote, and were never more than a few percentage points ahead of Labour — percentage points which are nonetheless crucial within the British electoral system.

It is clear that the Tories enjoyed fairly solid electoral support from the 'middle classes', but given the relative numerical strength of the 'classes' in Britain, this was never enough to win an election, and a substantial minority of the working class provided around half of the Tory vote. As Butler and Stokes pointed out, the replacement of the electorate was working against this kind of 'cross-voting' as more cohorts from 'working class'/Labour homes entered the electorate, but evidently the Tories managed to counter this trend. This maintenance of a working class Tory vote sufficient to return the party to office can be thought of as having two components: first the reproduction of relatively stable social collectivities having a principle of identification outside the conception of 'class' which prompted most 'working class' people to vote Labour, and second a more conjunctural conversion of voters. In the first category one can group, for instance, the traditional Toryism of the working class in mid-Lancashire, in an area of high home ownership; the traditional anti-Irish protestant Tory vote in the cities of Liverpool, Manchester and Glasgow, where the Labour Party had become identified with Catholicism; and the weakly unionised workforce of the West Midlands engaged in small and relatively paternalistic businesses. Certain of the policies pursued by the Tories during the '50s served to strengthen such stable 'non-class' social collectivities. Particularly important here was the shift in housing policy from Bevan's overriding emphasis on council housing to Macmillan's stress on 'private enterprise' and owner-occupation, fostered by the extension of local authority mortgages. There is strong evidence from Butler and Stokes' surveys that housing tenure over-determines party support, in relation to 'occupational class': in council housing only 51 per cent of those in occupational classes I-IV with a partisan self-image were found to be Tories, as against 76 per cent in owner-occupied housing. Conversely, in owner-occupied housing 42 per cent of those in classes V and VI had a Tory self-image as against 28 per cent in council housing (Butler and Stokes, 1974, p. 109). This correlation is not of course self-explanatory but three plausible connections can be identified: the differential formation of 'class self-image' in the presence or absence of property-owning; the rational calculation of self-interest on the part of the occupants of the different forms of housing, with regard to the tax and rent policies likely to be pursued by the parties; and the flow of political information within the cultural milieu of the residential area. At the same time as the evolution of housing tenure was strengthening one base of working class Tory support, however, certain other bases were being eroded, for instance paternalistic relations within industrial enterprises were in many cases being undermined by the growth of industrial concentration and rise of large multidivisional enterprises, and the development of trade unionism within these.

To move to the more 'conjunctural' factors in working class support for the Tories: it is not plausible, in retrospect, to ascribe all the votes necessary to the preservation of Tory government over the '50s to stable and definite 'Tory' social collectivities. In addition, the Tories recruited crucial marginal support on two major grounds which affected the mass of the electorate: the continuing ideology of Britain's imperial greatness and the rapid increase in national prosperity. And as the 1950s ended time was running out on both of these scores, as became increasingly evident during the later years of Macmillan's premiership.

As regards 'imperial greatness' or 'world power status', the Tories made a brave job of trying to patch this up after Suez but in the early '60s Labour leaders were able to ridicule the so-called 'independent British deterrent' which had run into the now familiar conflict between resources available and military pretensions; the attempted re-orientation of British trade towards Europe was ignominiously thwarted by the rejection of Macmillan's application for EEC membership; the process of 'decolonisation' was becoming increasingly uncontrollable and chaotic as many British-established federations of post-colonial states fell apart.

As regards national prosperity, the 'stop-go' cycle of populist tax-cutting budgets followed by balance of payments crises and deflationary measures to protect the exchange rate was becoming increasingly vicious. Heathcoat-Amory's election budget was followed in 1960 by the 'stop' measures of credit restriction and high interest rates. Selwyn-Lloyd, installed as chancellor in '61, continued the deflation but this time added a 'pay pause' designed to counter wage inflation. This pay policy, for which there had been no attempt to establish wide political support, bore particularly hard on certain groups of relatively weakly organised workers such as nurses, teachers and hospital workers whose case commanded considerable public sympathy, and when the defla-tionary measures had checked the run on the pound trade union antagonism to the government remained. The unions refused to co-operate in Selwyn Lloyd's National Income Commission, and the chancellor continued to pursue deflation in 1962. The emerging compe-titive weakness of the economy was demonstrated by the fact that while the deflationary measures pushed unemployment up sharply over the winter of 1962-63, the balance of payments remained in deficit. With the replacement of Selwyn Lloyd by Maudling, Tory economic policy changed back to 'go' again, this time with the spurious rationalisa-tion that fiscal expansion would of itself produce a virtuous circle of increased growth of GDP, increased productivity, increased exports and a further increase in growth. The game was up when the resulting record deficit on the balance of payments current account was registered, and well publicised by Labour, before the 1964 election. It became possible to argue that although the GDP had undoubtedly continued to grow under the Tories, and more rapidly than in Britain's past, the jerky 'stop-go' process was helping to weaken the relative position of the British economy on the world market, a position which had become exposed with the dismantling of the imperial trade preferences and the progressive liberalisation of world trade after

Bretton Woods. Further, the 'excessive' commitment to military expenditure (by the standard of other capitalist national economies) was diverting resources away from much-needed industrial investment.

Labour in the 1960s

With the ground shifting beneath both 'imperial greatness' and unproblematic prosperity the Tories' electoral bloc showed increasing signs of weakness. It became evident that the Tory success of the '50s had owed more to the 'conjuncture' of that decade and less to an irreversible shift in class/political alignment than had been thought earlier by political commentators such as Abrams. It was not obvious, however, that Labour would be the main beneficiary of this change. It was the Liberals, under Grimond's leadership, who picked up many of the disaffected Tories in the by-elections of 1962 and '63 — a party with a less strong 'class' identification than the Tories or Labour. But over 1963 and '64 the Labour Party made a comeback as a distinctive and relatively unified political force. Wilson succeeded Gaitskell as leader and proved himself a much more astute politician, able to make considerable capital out of the scandals of Macmillan's last years (the Profumo affair, Rachmanism). Also a rather 'contingent' factor gave Labour a political windfall: Macmillan's controversial selection of Douglas-Home as his successor. This both demoralised the Tory 'progressives' such as Powell and McLeod (who denounced this selection as a victory for the 'magic circle' of Tory politics) and gave Wilson a golden opportunity to campaign against the Tories as an anachronistic party out of tune with the 'realities of modern Britain'. This was somewhat ironic since within the Tory Party as a whole the early '60s saw a marked decline in the proportion of Eton-educated aristocratic MPs and a rise in the proportion of the 'professional middle classes' and career politicians, but with the fourteenth Earl of Home as figurehead, Wilson's charge seemed plausible. The obverse of Wilson's attack on the 'grouse-moor' Tories was his promotion of the Labour Party as 'modern' and 'scientific', as poised to release the 'technological revolution'. This gambit, drawing on the rapid growth of the science-based industries such as electronics, chemicals and nuclear power over the previous years, proved a successful means of unifying the party. As Sked and Cook (1979, p. 215) put it,

'Wilson had provided the Labour Party with exactly the right means to revive itself. For science not only offered the movement an image of modernity which it had recently lacked; it also provided a vocabulary with which Labour's traditional divisions could be obscured.'

The rising 'middle class technocratic' element in the party could believe this to mean that Labour would support modern managerial private industry while the left could imagine it meant the nationalisation of profitable growth industries in the name of state-sponsored technological advance.[13] Along with 'science', 'planning' was an important catchword in building a support bloc for Labour. Again, this had some appeal both to the industrial managers of the Federation of British Industry, who had called for 'planning' at their 1960 conference as a way out of the damaging 'stop-go' cycle (Jessop, 1980), and to the party activists for whom 'planning' meant increased government *control* over industrial enterprises. The kind of planning which the FBI had in mind — 'indicative planning' involving the gathering and exchange of information on the development of the economy and the improvement of co-ordination, rather than the formulation and compulsory implementation of a central plan — had already been attempted under the Tories with the formation of the National Economic Development Council (NEDC) in 1962 but had effectively remained subordinated to conventional stop-go demand management practice: Labour promised a form of planning which would be 'purposeful' and 'effective', which would 'have teeth in it somewhere' (Budd, 1978, Chapter 6).

If the ambivalent Wilsonian 'science' and 'planning' programme was useful in obscuring divisions within the Labour Party and among its supporters, it could not provide a basis for a determined and purposeful popular political movement. In fact, even in electoral terms there was only a modest revival of Labour support from 1959 to 1964 (from 43.8 per cent to 44.1 per cent of the vote). Labour's rather narrow parliamentary majority in 1964 was chiefly an effect of a slump in Tory support and continuing electoral revival of the Liberals (who received over 10 per cent of the vote for the first time since the war). Once installed in government, however, the Labour Party embarked upon an energetic legislative programme including the establishment of the Department of Economic Affairs (DEA) under George Brown with the remit of formulating a national plan, and the Ministry of Technology under Cousins, a leading light of the leftward movement in the trade unions since the '50s; the repeal of the 1957 Rent Act attacked by Labour as a 'landlord's charter' and associated with 'Rachmanism'; the development of comprehensive education; the development of regional policy in an attempt to alleviate the relatively high unemployment and slow growth of the depressed areas of the UK dependent on declining industries; the 1965 Trade Disputes Act, which gave union leaders full legal protection from actions over breach of employment contract; and the Redundancy Payments Act. This activity was quite widely popular, with the exception of the changes in trade union law which had only minority support. Despite the use of fiscal deflation in the attempt to maintain the exchange rate of the pound, and the difficulties experienced by the new National Board for Prices and Incomes in controlling inflation, which led to a slump in Labour support in mid-1965, Labour's electoral support had increased markedly by 1966. A main theme of the Labour campaign was 'planning' (The 'National Plan' had been published in late 1965), along with an expansion of the state educational and medical services. Also, interestingly, Labour was trying to claim for itself the new prospective owner-occupiers with a promise of low interest mortgages for low income earners.

As for the Tories, Heath had replaced Douglas-Home as leader in the party's first leadership election in '65, and was campaigning on the basis of EEC entry, Trade Union reform and reduction in direct taxation. Heath, 'the grocer', showed the Tories in a truer light than Home had done, as an increasingly 'middle class' (as opposed to aristocratic) party. Possibly because of this the party forfeited some of its patrician appeal to its traditional supporters. At any rate, the party's share of the vote continued its slide, giving Labour a large parliamentary majority.

Despite this electoral success for Labour, the years following the 1966 election showed up starkly the inability of this government to hold together a determined support bloc which could accomplish substantial social and economic changes. Cracks appeared in the 'planning' and social expenditure programmes, and in the relations between the parliamentary Labour Party, the trade unions, and the party activists.

The 'National Plan' was first to go. This exercise had never had much substance: the government had carried out an 'Industrial Inquiry' by questionnaire and had collated the results concerning investment trends, production, manpower requirements, expected exports and imports and so on, then used this as a basis for formulating some ambitious forecasts of growth to 1970. Given that previous periods of rapid growth had been brought to a halt in the face of escalating deficits on the balance of payments, largely because of the

high marginal propensity to import manufactured goods, the improvement of the balance of payments figured prominently in the plan. But
the plan's 'Check List of Action Required' in this regard (HMSO,
1965, p. 17) was hardly adequate to produce a rapid improvement,
and in many cases the 'action' was deferred: 'studies will be made,
industry by industry of ways of increasing exports'; 'Plans will be
made, industry by industry, to save imports' (ibid.). This could mean
a lot, or very little, depending on the urgency of the 'planning' and
the effectiveness of the control mechanisms in the hands of the government. In practice, the central feature of 'indicative planning' was that
government had no effective control mechanisms over private capitalist
enterprises. As Jessop argues:

' ... The indicative voluntary nature of planning in this period
expresses a fundamental problem at the heart of state intervention
in Britain. For, whereas organised labour has considerable 'veto'
power at the point of production and monopoly capital has considerable scope for international mobility, the 'social partners' of
government in the management of the economy are weak, decentralised, and fragmented' (Jessop, 1980, p. 41).

The TUC is a relatively loose confederation of craft, general and industrial unions; there was no single peak organisation representing the
management of industrial enterprises until the formation of the CBI,
sponsored by the Labour Party, in 1965. This means that even if the
government, the TUC and CBI were able to agree on a particular
course of development of the national economy 'the state and the social
partners alike are unable to enforce compliance with such a plan at
the micro-level' (ibid.).
   If the DEA was unable to organise rapid growth in conjunction with
a stable balance of payments, then one of the objectives had to give,
and in 1966 it was the growth target which was abandoned. Leruez
represents this as a misguided political choice: 'Yet again, as under
the Conservatives but in even more striking fashion, the defence of
the pound was put above expansion' (Leruez, 1975, p. 179). The
assumption here is that if the pound had been devalued earlier on this
would have made it possible to adhere to the growth path of the plan,
but in the light of the comments made above this view is open to doubt:
it gives the plan more credibility than it merited. Further, if the pound
had been devalued in 1964 or 1966, it is likely that the trade unions
would have resisted the cut in real wages which devaluation implies,

as they did after 1967. Both the 1965 'plan' and devaluation can be seen as technocratic measures, equally inadequate to abolish the competitive weakness of the UK economy — a weakness which is inscribed in its industrial structure, and the slow growth of productivity which is linked to the development of social relations within enterprises as well as the shortfall of investment.

In the absence of both the 'political will' and the social forces which would have been required to go beyond the merely 'indicative' and technocratic attempt to alleviate the balance of payments constraint, the Wilson government used the only effective levers at its disposal to maintain the external balance: the old standby of fiscal deflation; incomes policy, to hold down both labour costs of British firms and consumer spending on imports; and then eventually devaluation of the currency which, although it did not abolish the trade constraint, at least temporarily pre-empted speculative pressure on the pound and brought a period of increased price competitiveness. None of these measures, of course, were popular with Labour's political constituency. Deflation put a brake on the much-heralded planned growth; the application of wage restraint lost the government the support of the union leaders such as Cousins, Scanlon and Jones as well as many union members; devaluation, as Callaghan pointed out in orotund fashion prior to his resignation as chancellor, involved 'a reduction in the wage levels and the real wage standards of every member of the working class of this country'. By 1968, the TUC and the Labour Party conference overwhelmingly opposed the government's wages policy and, ironically for the government, this policy was helping to provoke strikes which were damaging the balance of payments.

The damage to internal party, and party/union, relations was carried a stage further with the abortive 'In Place of Strife' proposals of 1968/9. These were Wilson and Castle's response to the 'unoffical strike problem' which had been building up over the '60s but had acquired particular prominence in 1968 with the publication of the Donovan Commission's report. This 'problem' reflected the increased power of the shop stewards movement in a macroeconomic context of sustained relatively full employment and an industrial context of increased concentration of labour in the mass production of standardised commodities,[14] and was probably exacerbated by the restriction of real wages over the late '60s: it was by no means unique to Britain. Donovan had taken a fairly low-key approach, refusing to accept the view (promulgated by the CBI) that legal restrictions on unofficial strikes would achieve the desired industrial peace, but Wilson and

Barbara Castle convinced themselves that penal sanctions were necessary and justified, and in accordance with public opinion. Wilson had borne a personal grudge against 'politically motivated' militants ever since the seamen's strike of 1966 had spoiled his incomes policy and the attempted revival of the balance of payments upon which he had staked so much of his credibility. For Castle and others, unregulated shop-floor militancy marred the rational, state-controlled Fabian landscape. But although 'In Place of Strife' was in accord with majority public opinion, it was certainly not in accord with Labour Party and union opinion, and although that in itself has not always blocked the parliamentary leadership, this time it became obvious that sufficient Labour MPs would reject the proposals to make it impossible to establish them as law. Wilson and Castle had to back down, but not before the credibility of the leadership had been further dented.

The struggles over incomes policy and trade union legislation were part of a more general worsening of relations between the Labour Party, organised labour and the 'intellectual left' over this period. As regards Labour's traditional connection with the industrial working class, this was being called into question by the changing social composition of both the parliamentary party and the constituency organisations. In 1945, 50 per cent of Labour MPs and half of the cabinet had come from a 'working class' occupational background, but by 1970 the proportion had fallen to 25 per cent of MPs and one out of twenty-three in the Cabinet (Butler and Stokes, 1974). This shift went well beyond the general decline of the traditional working class in the electorate (discussed below) and reflected the increasing selection of 'more educated candidates' with 'administrative aptitudes' under the conditions of electoral competition, and within the dominant technocratic conception of politics, which had held sway since the rise of 'Butskellism' in the mid '50s.

At constituency level as well, relations between the party and its traditional supporters were breaking down. Hindess (1971) analysed this in detail for the case of Liverpool, and although the detailed studies of other areas which might support a definite generalisation were not carried out, it seems plausible that a parallel evolution was taking place in other city Labour parties. The core of Hindess's argument concerns the differential orientation to politics according to the definite zones of living conditions within the city. Within the 'middle class' zones of owner-occupation of housing, politically active people tended to see politics as an arena for establishing the broad outlines of policy; the 'details' of execution of policy could be left to suitably qualified experts and were not really the business of politics. On this view, politics provides the background or environment within which individuals pursue their own 'chosen' careers, living in their own 'chosen' houses. The material conditions of life support a marked separation of the personal and the political. Within the 'working class' zones such as council estates, by contrast, this separation of the personal and the political is less tenable. If people have very little choice in matters of housing then the details of planning and the execution of policy become very important, and are not just to be left to the 'experts'. The government is experienced not merely as providing background amenities against which individuals pursue their choices, but as an external constraining and coercive organisation. There is an unavoidable personal involvement in the consequences of political decisions and therefore the details of policy execution are, or ought to be, 'political matters'. With the decline of private rented accommodation and growth of public housing programmes these orientations, and the political demands connected with them, became progressively more differentiated, and this differentiation was reproduced within the Labour Party. 'Middle class', owner-occupier, Labour activists pursuing a more 'humane' and 'equal' society by means of general legislative change confronted 'working class' council tenants deeply concerned with the 'parochial' and 'trivial' issues arising from their everyday interactions with state apparatuses. And in this confrontation, the evolution of the parliamentary party strengthened the hand of the former:

> ' ... in general, the pressures on the Labour Party from the institutional environment towards the increasing bureaucratisation and centralisation of decision-making, the employment of and dependence on, specialists and the emphasis on professional administration, have been entirely consistent with the basic orientation of party activists in the middle class areas' (Hindess, 1971, p.140).

This process analysed by Hindess runs deeper than disagreement over *policy*. The 'middle class' activists did not necessarily support all the actual policies of the national party, but what they did support was the *form of policymaking*, and the right of the leadership to make policy. If this analysis is correct, then although many 'working class' people continued to think of the Labour Party as 'their' party in some vague sense, it was actually losing contact with their day-to-day political concerns and subsequently losing active working class support at a local level.

As regards left intellectual radicalism, the party was also losing its attraction, especially for the young. The Wilson government had supported the expansion of the universities following the Robbins Report, but the radicalism which the universities harboured in the late '60s was not generally translated into active support for Labour. Hardly surprising, since one of the main components of that radicalism was opposition to the Vietnam war, and although nominally defeated at the party conference in 1967, Wilson's basically pro-US stand defined the party's position in the eyes of many young radicals. Also, of course, the ferment in the universities was in part a revolt against the technocratic role which they had been assigned in the Wilsonian scheme of things.

It must be said, however, that despite the forfeiture of much active and committed support among the industrial working class and the intellectual left, popular support for the Labour Party, as registered by the opinion polls, had not collapsed by 1970. In April and May Jenkins' style of fiscal management was widely approved, and a Labour election victory was widely expected. Part of the explanation must be that many of those who were deeply disappointed by the government's record and lack of 'Socialism' still regarded the party as the lesser of two evils. But apart from this, two other points have to be considered. First, the banal but important point that things were not that bad over the 1960s for the mass of the electorate, so that those Labour voters who had neither expected not desired revolutionary socialism had no real reason to feel betrayed. Despite the successive sterling crises, deflationary fiscal packages and wage restraint, real personal disposable income per head had risen by around 12 per cent from 1964 to 1970. By the end of the period, paid holidays were longer, life expectancy had increased, accidents at work were reduced and the public services had been expanded considerably (although as Townsend has argued the benefits of this expansion went disproportionately to the 'middle class').

The second point, which requires a more lengthy discussion, concerns the changing social composition of the electorate. The reduction in active and committed Labour support has to be seen in the context of a more general weakening of the 'class'-party alignment, a tendential replacement of solid electoral support (for both main parties) by more volatile behaviour. The polls before the 1970 election may have registered broad support for Labour but as the election result itself showed this support was conditional and unreliable. Schematically, there are two sides to the weakening of the 'class'-party link, the specifically political and the sociological. So far I have mainly stressed the directly political side of the weakening of active Labour support (i.e. the policy, performance and organisation of the Labour Party). It will now be useful to consider the other side of the issue, and in the following section I shall examine the changes in the division of labour and social collectivities which help to explain the general weakening of 'class'-party associations.

The division of labour and social collectivities: changes in progress over the 1960s

One can get a first indication of these changes from the statistics on the division of labour between sectors of the economy. Table 6.4 shows that there appears to be a turning point around 1960: before then manufacturing employment, and the broader 'industrial' employment, had been growing faster than overall employment, whereas over the period 1960-64 (which, taken as a whole, shows a rapid growth of overall employment) the manufacturing and industrial sectors showed only a marginal growth of employment, therefore accounting for a declining share of the total. Of course, neither the 'industrial' nor the 'non-industrial' sectors were homogeneous in this respect. From 1954 to 1960 the net expansion of industrial employment was the result of rapid growth in sectors such as chemicals, mechanical and electrical engineering, vehicles, paper, printing and publishing, and metal manufacture, set against decline in shipbuilding, textiles, clothing and footwear, and mining and quarrying. From 1960 onwards the relative decline reflected a slower growth of employment in the 'growth industries' and an accelerating decline of the 'traditional' industries. Equally, the relative expansion of the non-industrial sector was uneven, with a net decline in transport and communications, with growth in the distributive trades tapering off from 1960, and with both 'Insurance, banking and finance' and 'Professional and scientific services' showing an accelerating growth of employment over the period.

Following the trends further, we find that over the decade 1961-71 manufacturing employment began to decline absolutely (employment in 1971 was 95 per cent of the 1961 level), while the faster-growing non-industrial sectors accounted for a substantially increasing proportion of the workforce. The composition of this 'tertiary sector' expansion is shown in Table 6.5.

Again, the pattern is uneven. The workforce in distribution began to decline with increased concentration in retailing, rationalisation and

Table 6.4 *Employment Trends 1954-1964*

	Average annual percentage increase in employment 1954-60	1960-64	Employment at mid-1964 1000s	% of total
Manufacturing	0.9	0.1	9,016	35.5
Mining & Quarrying	– 2.3	– 3.7	659	2.6
Construction	0.6	1.3	1,802	7.1
Gas, Electricity & Water	–	2.0	410	1.6
All Industry (total of above)	0.6	0.2	11,889	46.7
Agriculture, Forestry and Fishing	– 1.4	– 2.8	947	3.7
Transport and Communications	– 0.5	– 0.2	1,693	6.7
Distributive Trades	1.8	1.1	3,459	13.6
Insurance, Banking and Finance	2.8	3.3	647	2.5
Professional and Scientific Services	2.7	3.6	2,352	9.2
Miscellaneous Services	– 0.1	1.6	2,190	8.6
Public Administration and Defence	– 2.9	– 0.3	1,730	6.8
Total Economy	0.5	0.7	25,432	

Source: adapted from National Plan, 1965, pp. 27-32.
Components may not add to totals because of rounding.

Table 6.5 *Change in employment in the 'Tertiary Sector' 1961-71*

	1971 as % of 1961 employment	% of G.B. Workforce 1961	1971
Distribution	95	13.9	12.9
Financial	166	2.5	4.1
Professional & Scientific	137	9.2	12.4
Miscellaneous Services	97	9.9	9.6
Public Administration	146	4.9	6.3
All Tertiary	114	40.4	45.8

Source: Gershuny (1978, p. 96).

the development of larger stores. The financial sector showed particularly rapid growth, connected with the growth of financial transactions implied by the vast expansion of saving and borrowing (analysed in Chapter 4). The 'professional and scientific' category also grew rapidly, reflecting the expansion of both professional services for business and the development of education and the NHS in the state sector. The 'miscellaneous services' sector declined in importance, reflecting a switch in popular expenditure patterns — away from cinemas and theatres and towards television; away from domestic help and laundries and towards domestic appliances; away from transport services and towards the use of private cars.[15] Finally, the workforce in public administration showed a marked rise, connected with the expansion of public expenditure programmes and the development of state apparatuses concerned with industrial consultation and intervention.

As regards the decline in employment in manufacturing, mathematically speaking this is equal to the growth rate of labour productivity in manufacturing minus the growth rate of output from that sector. The decline can therefore by thought of as, broadly, the result of the pursuit of higher productivity (in face of declining profit rates and the weakening competitive position of British industry on the world market) in a context of constraint on the growth of output. The balance of payments provided such a constraint, of increasing tightness over the 1960s.[16] More specifically though, the sharpest decline in employment in manufacturing within this period came in the later 1960s, with the 'shake-out' associated with the merger boom and the accompanying 'rationalisation' of enterprises' activities, a process which was in part stimulated by fiscal deflation and in part actively sponsored by quasi-state agencies such as the Labour government's Industrial Reorganisation Corporation.

The discussion above relates to the relative expansion of various forms of *non-industrial* employment (division of labour by sectors). There is, however, another aspect to the changing composition of the workforce over the 1960s: a shift in what I referred to earlier as the 'division of labour by strata'. Tables 6.6 and 6.7 give two views of this shift, considering different time periods and employing different classifications. Table 6.6 shows the growth rate of certain major 'socio-economic groups' (the official nomenclature) over the decade 1961-1971. Note that it is confined to males only, but includes retired people as well as those economically active (relevant to the composition of the electorate as a whole).

Table 6.6   *Selected socio-economic groups of males classified by own occupation, economically active and retired*

	1961 *(Thousands)*	*1971* *(Thousands)*	*% change* *1961-1971*
Employers and Managers	1691	2086	23.4
Professional employees	500	703	40.6
Intermediate non-manual	685	965	40.9
Junior non-manual	2252	2158	– 4.2
Manual workers (excluding supervisors)	9774	9017	– 7.7

Source: adapted from Social Trends No. 6 1975 Table A.1 p. 30

The contrast between the rapid growth of the 'professional' and 'intermediate non-manual' groups (as well as the 'employers and managers' category where the growth is slower but the starting point higher) and the decline of not only the 'manual workers' group but also the 'junior non-manual', suggests a substantial change in the balance of these strata among the male population, and reinforces the idea of a decline in the 'traditional' male working class.

Table 6.7 has a different focus,[17] dividing the employed workforce according to form of payment as well as by strata (for the salary-earners) and sector (for wage earners). It also gives some indication of the pattern of the sexual divison of labour as it was developing in the late 1960s.

Table 6.7   *Wage and salary earning categories (as percentage of those in employment), 1966 and 1971*

	1966	*1971*
Salary Earners	32.9 (53.2)*	36.7 (52.1)*
Managerial	6.4 (83.8)	7.5 (83.8)
Technical and Professional	9.8 (60.8)	11.6 (59.9)
Clerical	16.7 (37.0)	17.7 (33.7)
Wage Earners	67.1 (68.0)	63.3 (67.1)
Industrial	47.3 (81.2)	43.7 (81.1)
Non-Industrial	17.5 (29.9)	17.7 (30.4)
Agricultural	2.3 (86.6)	1.9 (85.6)

* Figures in brackets refer to the percentage in each category who are male.
Sources: Calculated from sample Census 1966, Economic Activity Tables. Part III Table 34, and Census 1971, 10% sample Economic Activity Tables, Part IV Table 34.

The importance of the salary/wage distinction goes beyond the mere periodicity of payment, since broadly speaking it correlates with the 'staff'/'worker' demarcation, with salaried employees generally having higher 'status', greater continuity of employment and greater access to benefits such as pension rights. It is therefore interesting to find such a marked increase in salaried employment even over this five-year period. As can be seen from the table, the fastest growth of salaried employment was in the (male-dominated) managerial grades and the technical and professional grades (which were rather more open to women). Salaried clerical labour showed a small proportional increase, along with a reduction in the proportion of male employees. As would be expected from the previous discussion, the main decline in wage-earning employment came in the (male-dominated) industrial sector, while the non-industrial wage-earning category, which includes a substantial majority of women, showed a slight increase.

The overall picture which emerges from the various statistics considered is that of (a) a sectoral shift from industrial to non-industrial employment, plus (b) a shift in the balance of the 'status' categories of employment, towards salaried employment in the various managerial, technical and professional grades in particular. Further, these shifts took place in the context of (c) a change in the sexual division of labour as a higher proportion of women took up (at least part-time) paid employment: both non-industrial waged employment, and salaried clerical labour are sectors where a substantial majority of employees are women.

If the combined effect of these rather complex changes in the distribution of social labour between sectors and strata was to reduce the size of the 'traditional' industrial working class, it was also to render the 'traditional' British conception of the middle class more problematic. As Raynor (1969) noted, the first use of the term 'middle class' in Britain was probably in the early years of the nineteenth century (Raynor quotes the Oxford English Dictionary's date of 1812), and it was during the nineteenth century that the 'middle class' developed into an identifiable and vocal, if rather vaguely defined, social collectivity. In the early period, the designation 'middle' marked out an intermediate place between the industrial proletariat and servant classes on the one hand, and the landed and financial aristocracy on the other — a place occupied not only by the rising industrial and commercial bourgeoisie, but also by the traditional professions and the civil servants, clerks and school teachers. Ever since then the term 'middle class' has continued in widespread use, but its referent has undergone radical changes. At the 'top end' the peculiarly British mutual accommodation and interpenetration of the bourgeoisie and aristocracy has licensed an extension of the term 'middle class' until there is only a vestigial 'upper class' against which to draw a contrast, while at the same time there have been successive waves of new recruits which have enlarged the base of the 'class': the new groups of professionals, managers and technical experts which expanded from the latter half of the nineteenth century onward with the development of capitalist industry and trade; the more recent expansion of salaried employment in education, research, health, social welfare, administration and planning. As Raynor (1969, Chapter 2) argues, the 'middle class' was never homogeneous (in particular it has never been equivalent to Marx's 'bourgeoisie'), but nonetheless its degree of heterogeneity has been greatly increased over the post-war years, and the shift in the distribution of social labour analysed above has accelerated this process. The fissures between the employers (large and small), the self-employed, and the rentiers, and between these categories and the 'salariat'[18] of employed professional, managerial and technical workers, have been added to by the fissure between the private sector business salariat and the more newly expanding public sector salariat, so that the notion of the 'middle class' has virtually reached bursting point. The 'middle class' designation has retained some validity for so long, covering such disparate socio-economic categories, largely because of the remarkable tenacity of the amalgam of cultural values which characterised the nineteenth century middle classes: part bourgeois (thrift, independence) and part acquired from the aristocracy and gentry (respectability, 'gentlemanly' behaviour). But this ideological cement began to crumble with the accelerating influx of people from working class backgrounds into new non-industrial and salarian positions, and the development of 'white collar unionism'. It becomes less and less feasible to equate the relative contraction of the industrial proletariat with the relative expansion of the 'middle class'.

There are two analytically distinct points at issue here: first, the nature of the social positions which have been created by the expansion of non-industrial employment and the relative expansion of technical and administrative employment within industry, and second the recruitment of agents to fill these positions. As regards the first point, I have suggested that the 'tertiary sector' expansion has increased the heterogeneity of non-manual/industrial positions within the division of labour. Particularly important here is the expansion of the public sector salariat connected with the 'welfare state'. This category, in contrast with the business salariat, owes its existence to the social democratic expansion of state services under the sign of an ideology of state-sponsored social improvement, and is therefore less likely to subscribe wholeheartedly to the traditional middle class values of personal independence and responsibility, or to go along so readily with the middle class complaints against 'wasteful state spending' and 'excessive taxation'. Further, as Jenkins and Sherman (1979) point out, the public sector has been a relatively fruitful domain for 'white collar' union organisation since the early years of the present century. Aside from the development of a public sector salariat, however, there is also the point that many private sector salarian posts have been 'routinised' in the search for cost-effectiveness, eroding the previously valued autonomy of the middle class occupations (Braverman's analysis of clerical labour, Oppenheimer, 1975, on professionals, Crompton, 1979, on insurance clerks), and providing conditions under which union organisation could be developed.[19] This development has introduced a definite tension between the (still widespread) 'middle class' aspirations of many salaried and non-industrial employees, and the forms of collective organisation and action which have been employed to defend their economic position. As argued earlier, I do not consider it useful to debate the significance of these phenomena in terms of an essential theoretical designation of the new strata as either 'new working class' or 'new petty bourgeoisie' (although I have argued that in terms of *property relations* alone they are working class). But what is of interest in the present context is the particular ramifications of these developments within the British social formation, i.e. the weakening hold of the 'middle class' designation within popular ideology, and of the middle class/Tory nexus.

As regards the second point (the recruitment of agents to the salaried and non-industrial positions), the investigations conducted by Goldthorpe (1980) are of considerable interest. Goldthorpe shows that, contrary to the 'closure' and 'buffer zone' theses, there has been a very substantial recruitment of males from manual working class family backgrounds into even the 'highest' strata of salaried employment.[20] This does not reflect a radical social openness or free circulation of agents between social positions, since the offspring of the higher occupational grades still have a much greater relative chance of ending up in those grades than people from lower occupational backgrounds, but all the same it represents *de facto* social mobility on a large scale. Given the rapid expansion of demand for managerial, technical, professional and administrative labour, it was quite impossible to restrict recruitment to the offspring of the existing middle classes. Writers of a Marxist persuasion have often denied the importance of social mobility as a factor in class analysis. Within the English tradition of radical, 'Marx-influenced', sociology the tendency has been to concede that social mobility is *in principle* important (large-scale mobility *would* make a difference to one's analysis), but to deny that really significant social mobility has taken place. According to Goldthorpe's study, this denial is just empirically wrong. Poulantzas, on the other hand, characteristically refuses to debate on the empirical ground of 'bourgeois sociology' and denies that *any* degree of social mobility could have a material bearing on the Marxist analysis of the class structure. Contrary to the 'bourgeois problematic of social mobility', he avers,

'... it is clear that, even on the absurd assumption that from one day to the next, or even from one generation to the next, the bourgeoisie would all take the places of workers and vice versa, nothing fundamental about capitalism would be changed, since the places of bourgeoisie and proletariat would still be there, and this is the principal aspect of the reproduction of capitalist relations' (Poulantzas, 1975, p. 33).

If one takes this as a statement obliquely concerning the Marxist political project, it has a certain validity, in that it brings out the difference between Marxism and 'meritocratic', or social-democratic notions of 'equality of opportunity': the Marxist project is not merely to allow access to the privileged classes for the most 'able' individuals from all sections of society, but to transform the class *structure* (to eliminate private possession of the major means of production and hierarchical management, and to institute a democratically socialised appropriation). But otherwise, Poulantzas' assertion is bizarre; the *social* and *political* consequences of his hypothetical periodic interchange of classes (e.g. in terms of the constitution of political parties and their constituencies) would be incalculable, and certainly 'fundamental'. Surely we can maintain that the existence of social mobility does not undermine the Marxist critique of capitalism, without feeling obliged to insist that it is really of no consequence. Marx, although he did not have a great deal to say about the movement of individuals between classes, did on several occasions note the possible effects of such movement. For instance, his remarks in the 'Eighteenth Brumaire' and in correspondence with Weydemeyer, relating the 'immaturity' of the American working-class movement in the mid 19th century to the 'flux and interchange' whereby American proletarians were able to convert themselves into independent self-sustaining peasants.[21] Or, in his discussion of the banking and credit system, this interesting passage concerning the ability of individuals without their own capital to borrow funds and set up businesses:

> 'Although this circumstance continually brings an unwelcome number of new soldiers of fortune into the field and into competition with the already existing individual capitalists, it also reinforces the supremacy of capital itself, expands its base and enables it to recruit ever new forces for itself out of the substratum of society. In a similar way, the circumstance that the Catholic Church in the Middle Ages formed its hierarchy out of the best brains in the land, regardless of their estate, birth or fortune, was one of the principal means of consolidating ecclesiastical rule and suppressing the laity. The more a ruling class is able to assimilate the foremost minds of a ruled class, the more stable and dangerous becomes its rule' (Marx, 1972, p. 600-601)

But even without Marx's *imprimatur*, it would still be clear enough that large-scale movement of individuals between positions in the social division of labour, inter- or intra-generationally, can have important consequences for the formation of social collectivities and the development of politics. In this regard, it is relevant that the 'places' created by the expansion of non-manual/salaried employment were in many cases filled by the sons of manual wage workers, providing them with an avenue for social advancement, rather than, say, by more rapid breeding on the part of previously privileged strata.

Goldthorpe argues that in the British case the effects have been strikingly asymmetrical: the expanding upper occupational strata show a low 'demographic homogeneity' (i.e. a low proportion of members whose fathers were members of the same stratum or class), while the manual wage-earning classes, dwindling in size, show a very high level of demographic homogeneity: there has been little pressure for recruitment of manual workers from beyond the ranks of existing manual workers' families.

For the 'middle classes', then, heterogeneity of social origin must be added to heterogeneity of socio-economic position as another factor tending to render problematic any clear 'class' designation[22] (or in other words tending to reduce the degree to which the term 'middle class' identifies a pertinent social collectivity). For the manual working class the pattern of mobility has had a double-edged effect, on the one hand increasing the possibility of 'social advancement' (although this remains slim for men who have passed their mid-20s), while on the other reducing the influx of people from other backgrounds. One should beware the temptation of 'reading off' from the high demographic homogeneity of this category any necessary political homogenisation (a temptation to which Goldthorpe appears to give way). The manual working class may not be divided by social origin, but it remains divided by industry, region, housing tenure and other factors, which are not politically irrelevant. Equally, however, the substantial *de facto* mobility out of the manual working class has not dissolved its traditional collectivist propensities, at least so far as trade unionism is concerned. This mobility probably helped to 'legitimise' and stabilise the hierarchical structure of social relations, and to pro-mote the ideology of individual career advancement, but it by no means terminated the struggle for collective advancement.

Party politics once more

The starting point for this discussion — of the changing division of labour by sectors and by strata, and of the social pattern of recruit-ment of individuals to the positions within these divisions — was the condition of party politics as the 1960s ended, and in particular the position of the Labour Party, which had forfeited the active support of important sections of its 'traditional' partisans yet had not apparently suffered a collapse of electoral support (as indicated by opinion polls before the 1970 election). I suggested that the latter point could be explained in part by reference to the change in the social composition of the electorate which had been in progress over the '60s. This sug-gestion can now be justified. If serious strains were emerging within Labour's main traditional active support bloc, the expansion of the salariat and accompanying transformations within the 'middle class' were also tending to undermine the 'middle class'/Tory axis. The proportion of the electorate having a strong partisan identification was on the decrease, and the electorate becoming more 'volatile'. Elec-toral studies of the period show that an increasing number of people were making their support for one or other of the main parties condi-tional upon the calculation of 'rational self-interest' or 'governmental competence', rather than basing their voting upon a 'class reflex'. The net effect was that while Labour's electoral support did not collapse,

it became less deeply rooted, and more liable to be swayed by conjunctural influences. In 1970, Labour identification was not necessarily
tied to support for the party's 'traditional' concerns, or at least the
concerns of the left-wing: only 39 per cent of Labour identifiers were
in favour of nationalising more industries; only 40 per cent did *not*
believe that trade unions had too much power; and although 60 per
cent were in favour of spending more on social services this represented
a marked decline from the 89 per cent recorded in 1964 (Crewe *et al.*,
1977).

In this respect, the opinions of the parliamentary leadership were
not dissimilar to those of the majority of Labour supporters, but this
congruence does not invalidate the claim that Labour's substantive
and definite electoral support bloc was on the decline, and was being
replaced, at least at the margin, by a more conditional and circumspect
form of popular support. In 1970, Wilson appealed to be judged on
the government's record, on its competence in dealing with 'the country's problems' and in particular the balance of payments. If it is true
that the publication of figures showing a deficit shortly before the election was a significant factor in Labour's 'last minute' loss of support,
it is surely fitting — a case of Wilson being hoist by his own technocratic
petard. The irony is only compounded by the fact that in retrospect
those trade figures turned out to be misleading and only a statistical
'blip'.

One can get a further perspective on the development of the
class/politics relationship in the period of the Wilson government by
asking the question of whether matters *could* have turned out very dif-
ferently, and in particular whether a 'socialist alternative' was there
for the taking. Consider Glyn and Sutcliffe's epitaph on the period:

> 'Between 1964 and 1970 the Labour government tried to serve two
> masters. It would not challenge capitalism, so it tried to support
> it; but it could not make its policy acceptable to the trade unions
> on whom it depended. Such contradictions are bound to beset a
> working class party in power, if it does not oppose capitalism, but
> tries instead to make it run more efficiently and more humanely'
> (Glyn and Sutcliffe, 1972, p.213).

The problem with this conception is that neither 'capitalism' nor the
'working class' are preconstituted masters which it is possible merely
to 'serve'. The Labour government 1964-1970 did not abolish capitalist
relations of production in Britain, for sure, but it did not merely serve

a pre-defined capitalist class interest either. Social and economic relations were modified in a whole range of ways over this period, some of them to the advantage of the working class. Of course the government did not 'challenge capitalism' outright in the sense, for instance, of attempting massive nationalisation under workers' control. But what precisely would it have meant to 'serve the working class' over this period? Did the industrial militants in the car industry and the docks, the union leaders disaffected by incomes policy and the council tenants by the local state apparatus, the left intellectuals in the universities, add up to a social bloc capable of achieving sweeping changes in Britain's insertion within international economic relations and the relations of production in the domestic economy, even if the Labour leadership had wished to lead such a movement? I doubt it. Beynon points out that the militancy in the car industry had no clear political issue:

'the slogan ''the mines for the miners'' meant something. That no similar slogan has come from the car workers is important, and is tied up with the fact that ''the car plants for the car workers'' makes no sense to the lads who work on the line. They hate the car plant in a way that the miners never hated the pit. They can see no obvious salvation in the nationalisation of the car industry, be it under workers' control or not' (Beynon, 1975, pp. 318-9).

Hughes (1960) noted what he called 'a failure of initiative and imagination on the part of trade unions' concerning workers' control in the nationalised industries generally, a 'failure' which was not really made good over the '60s. In the universities, anti-imperialist students were discovering Marx but generally had little of substance to propose as regards the development of the domestic economy, or at least little which found a resonance among the masses.

If the Labour Party had announced, in 1964 or 66, its intention to 'oppose capitalism' fundamentally and had explained what this was likely to involve in terms of dislocation of international trade and payments (even Callaghan's mildly redistributive budget of 1964 was enough to cause a run on the pound), and the onus which would have to be placed on the trade unions in running industry, given the likely non-co-operation of many among the managerial strata, it is quite implausible to say they would have been elected to office. They would undoubtedly have alienated much of their 'middle class' support, and would not have won over any working class Tories. That would have lost them the election, even supposing that such an announcement would not also have alienated any working class Labour supporters. This is not to whitewash the actual political practice of the Wilson government, or to deny any element of political contingency. The *feasible* political choices confronting Labour could doubtless have been handled in a way which would have produced greater benefit for working people, and lost Labour less active support. Only this: it is misleading to suggest that a socialist alternative qualitatively different from the actual record of 1964-70 existed *in potentia* and merely went by default, on account of a failure of political will.

Heath and after

I have argued above in terms of a discrepancy between Labour's electoral success in 1964 and more particularly 1966, and the failure of the party to hold together a decisive social bloc capable of accomplishing radical change in a socialist, or even a Croslandite, direction (a failure which was not, however, merely a matter of will). But if the Wilsonian rhetoric went well beyond what Labour was able to achieve, Heath's 'mandate' for change was even flimsier than that of Labour in the '60s. In the 1970 election the Tories received the votes of 33.2 per cent of the electorate (as against 36.4 per cent for Labour in 1966), and although this was enough to give them a safe parliamentary majority, it did not reflect massive and determined popular support for the 'Selsdon' programme of trade union reform plus 'rolling back of the frontiers of government' (the promised direct tax cuts were popular, but that does not prove much). Butler and Stokes' surveys even suggest that part of the electoral swing to the Tories was for no more substantial a reason than the belief among some electors in the 'circulation of the parties', i.e. the sentiment that 'it's time the other party had a go'.

The discrepancy between the Heath government's pretensions, and presumed mandate, and its actual powers can be shown up by considering, first, the famous 'U turn' and second, the circumstances of its electoral defeat in 1974.

The U turn

The intentions of this government in the 'Selsdon' phase are well known: to regenerate a profitable, fast-growing, internationally competitive British capitalism by creating 'incentives' (direct tax cuts), outlawing the 'disruptive' activities of industrial militants, and reducing state 'interference' in the workings of the market: no more support for 'lame ducks'; no more detailed quantitative restriction on credit; no more incomes policy. These policies were fairly soon in disarray, for a number of reasons. Relations with the trade unions deteriorated rapidly, as could only be expected. Heath was attempting to break with the politics of accommodation, the 'triangular system' of government/union/employer consultation which had been growing up at least since the war. Wilson had tried this first, with 'In Place of Strife', but fortunately for Labour these proposals had never reached the statute book since union opposition was internalised within the party. The Tories had no such mechanism for demonstrating in advance the unworkability of their Industrial Relations Act. As Middlemass (1979, p. 443) remarks of the Act, the TUC 'could hardly have accepted such a reversal of the terms of politics as they had been understood for a generation.' Having chosen confrontation with the unions the Heath government went down to important defeats: the resolution of the miners' strike by the Wilberforce Report in 1972; the official solicitor's intervention to free the 'Pentonville Five' in the context of demands for a general strike, after which the Industrial Relations Act was virtually a dead letter. If the 'labour movement' was not in a position to enforce a socialist alternative on the Labour government between 1964 and 1970, it was well able to resist Heath.

Two factors bolstered this resistance. In the first place Heath's break with the previous 'Keynesian' consensus on macroeconomic policy (in the minimal sense of nominal adherence to 'full employment' as a policy-goal) was less than complete. So when unemployment approached one million in early '72, following fiscal deflation in earlier budgets, the government went for reflation by means of substantial tax cuts — a course of action which had the full support of most economic commentators including the 'Times'. One of the effects of this reflation was a huge surge in imports and a record trade deficit, but it did also restrict the growth of unemployment. My point here is that a further rapid increase in unemployment might have weakened the unions' power of resistance (one can draw a comparison with the Thatcher government), but playing according to rules which prohibited blatant mass unemployment tied the government's hands. A second factor weakening the Heath government's attempt to dictate to the unions on the basis of its 'mandate from the nation' was the rather agnostic attitude taken up by large employers. The CBI, and large companies in particular, refused to use the new powers of the Industrial

Relations Act for fear of stirring up even more trouble, leaving them for smaller maverick employers to exploit, and discredit, in highly contentious situations. The strident anti-union bloc of small businessmen, outraged sections of the middle classes, and probably also elements of the non-union working class, was not a sufficient counterweight to organised labour, given the tendency for the management of large enterprises to stand above the fray.

Aside from the policy of confronting union power, other aspects of the Selsdon programme were under severe strain by 1972. The non-intervention policy with regard to 'lame ducks' was effectively abandoned with the politically inescapable rescue of Rolls Royce and Upper Clyde Shipbuilders, and the 1972 Industry Bill marked a return to the kind of industrial policy which had been evolving over the 1960s with the formation of NEDC and IRC. Two other areas of the market were also to succumb to 'intervention'. In the case of wage bargaining, the Tories had earlier ruled out incomes policy but as inflation accelerated, following the boom-induced rise in world commodity prices and the downward 'float' of the pound on the foreign exchanges from 1972, Heath imposed a statutory pay and prices standstill. In the case of the financial system, the Heath government had been sympathetic to the Bank of England's 'Competition and Credit Control' proposals of 1971 which, while incoherent, promised more freedom of market competition. It was not long before the effects of this 'freedom', in the form of rampant property speculation and massive growth of the money supply, forced the government into re-imposing restrictions on the volume and direction of credit. Heath was even led to castigate, in his famous phrase, the 'unacceptable face of capitalism', and to berate industrialists for failing to take up industrial investment opportunities.

As a result of these multiple features in the attempt to implement the Selsdon programme the government was forced away from its original 'free market' radicalism into what Middlemass (1979) has called the 'politics of crisis avoidance'. But despite the various aspects of his 'U turn', Heath had by this stage burned his boats, so far as the re-creation of a 'corporatist accommodation' was concerned. Despite the imposition of price controls, his government could not win acceptance for its pay restraint policy on the part of the TUC. When confronted by the miners' pay claim in 1973, well in excess of the government's stipulated maximum, Heath therefore reverted to the doctrine of the national mandate. The miners' strike was presented as a direct challenge to the authority of the government, and was made into a sticking-point beyond which the government would not be pushed. Here was a sectional interest dictating to the democratically-elected representatives of the people, and since it had proved impossible belatedly to accommodate that sectional interest through the mechanism of 'tripartism', it had to be challenged. Hence the election of February 1974, to answer the question of 'Who governs Britain?', in the context of a state of emergency.

The elections of 1974

The results of the February election provide an interesting commentary on the state of the nation after four years of Heath's rule.[23] Heath was calling for a decisive mandate to put the unions in their place, but the most striking feature of the results is that they offered no party any decisive mandate whatever. For the first time since the war, the two major parties each received the votes of less than 30 per cent of the electorate. Compared with 1970, the Liberal vote nearly trebled: at over six million, this vote represented more than half of the votes going to each of the main parties against little over a sixth in 1970. In Scotland, the nationalist vote doubled relative to 1970. In terms of parliamentary representation, Labour — although receiving less votes than the Tories — became the largest single party; the Tories had five seats less than Labour; the Liberals, with their geographically diffuse support, were grossly 'under-represented' relative to their share of vote, having only fourteen seats; while the Scottish Nationalists, benefiting from the concentration of their vote, increased their parliamentary contingent from one to seven. Labour, as the largest party in this first 'hung Parliament' of the post war years, formed a government, but parliament remained dominated by the prospect of another election.

What can we read in this voting pattern, in relation to the political developments in the preceding period? First, there is the point that Heath signally failed to get his popular backing against 'union blackmail'. The 29.5 per cent of the electorate who did vote Tory under the circumstances of February 1974 must have known what they were doing — contesting the 'unconstitutional claims of the disruptive sectional union interests' — but they did not form a sufficiently large social bloc. Too many potential Tory voters were scared off by Heath's dangerous practice of confrontation, and also bewildered by the effective abandonment of the brave 'Selsdon' ideals in other respects. (The Selsdon-type beliefs, that the trade unions had too much power and that public spending was too high, remained strong among the electorate.) As Middlemass (1979, p. 445) puts it: 'As in 1944-45, employers and managers in a sense detached themselves from the dangerous appeal to the nation, over the heads of the nine million voters who were also affiliated to the TUC'. The CBI, which had been vocal enough in calling for 'curbs on unofficial strikes' in the late '60s, was alarmed by the massive popular resistance to the Heath government's stand, and its leader Campbell Adamson suggested that a Tory victory in February 'would not solve Britain's problems'. If the Tories' supporters in 1970 had liked the sound of anti-union radicalism, a significant number had decided by 1974 that it threatened to bring the house down around their ears.

Second, there is the question of Labour support. The resistance to Heath on the part of the union movement clearly had mass support, but equally clearly this resistance movement was not able to constitute itself, as it were, into a hegemonic political force capable of securing a workable parliamentary majority through the Labour Party and imposing a radical alternative course of social development (it was much less able, of course, to constitute itself as the nucleus of an alternative state power in an extra-parliamentary manner). The Labour vote suffered a double slippage. On the one hand the party lost 'middle class' support, so that a higher proportion of its votes came from the working class (i.e. manual workers) than ever before. But at the same time the party received the votes of a smaller proportion of working class electors than ever before since the war. Only 44 per cent of manual workers voted Labour, as against 25 per cent for the Tories, 14 per cent Liberal, 3 per cent Nationalist and 14 per cent abstaining 24 (the abstention rate among the electorate as a whole was considerably higher). The gains for the labour movement in the shipyards, at the power stations and on the streets were not therefore translated into electoral support for the Labour Party, on a broad enough basis. Too many electors evidently wished to reject the terms of Heath's question, wished for neither Heath-style confrontation nor a politics dominated by trade union power.

Neither did the remaining reduced core of electors identifying with the Labour Party subscribe with any unanimity to the proposals of the party's left wing, which were designed to capitalise on anti-Heath radicalism and extend it in an anti-capitalist direction. According to studies cited by Crewe et al., (1977), 50 per cent of Labour identifiers supported more nationalisation of industry, 61 per cent were in favour of spending more on social services, and 44 per cent did *not* believe that trade unions had too much power. Opinion poll findings of this kind raise a problem. Marxists too often tend to take a cavalier attitude towards the findings of such polls — anything which people ought not to think, according to socialist ideology, is regarded as the product of 'media manipulation' and cannot really be people's own considered view. But this is just the mirror image of the bourgeois view that whenever workers take a militant stance this must be due to manipulation by agitators, and again does not reflect people's considered judgement. Each view is essentially contemptuous of popular judgement, relying on the idea that people are dupes, unable to form their own ideas and easily swayed by press magnates/communist agitators. But if one rejects this view and credits people with a capacity to judge matters for themselves this does not mean that one should take an uncritical attitude towards poll findings. These findings are *products* with definite conditions of production. Pollsters generally face people with questions in the abstract and in this situation may elicit responses different from those which people might give when faced with an issue of direct practical concern to themselves. For instance people may express themselves against the trade unions in general terms, yet support the claims submitted by their own union on their behalf. And insofar as the media do 'mould' opinion their influence is probably greater the less the issue is one of direct practical concern. People are not merely dupes, but are more likely to accept uncritically a line which is constantly propagated by the media if it doesn't touch them personally; otherwise they are more likely to insist on making up their own minds. Either way, the low level of support for left Labour policies and the trade union movement (in general terms) which is indicated in the findings cited above, is of real importance. That is, to the extent that the responses were the result of critical reflection they clearly show that left policies were lacking in credibility and attractiveness, yet insofar as the responses represented an uncritical carrying over of the 'media' line this would seem to suggest that the concerns of the left failed to strike the masses as of immediate practical importance; the left policies cannot have appeared to meet the practical needs of the working class, or else the Labour identifiers polled would not have been content to reiterate the media line with regard to those policies. I believe, therefore, that it is not implausible to infer from these findings that a substantial fraction of Labour voters reckoned merely that the party would be able to form a more competent and moderate government, and would be better able to defuse the crisis, although one should not discount the continued existence of a 'class reflex' vote owing little to any elaborate political calculation.

Then there is the question of 'third party' support. The main development here was the spectacular rise in electoral support for the Liberals, and for the Scottish National Party. To take the Liberals first, it had been a commonplace of political analysis over previous years to regard the Liberal vote as largely a product of temporary disillusion with the Tories following on periods of Tory government, as a protest vote. Certainly there was good reason for erstwhile Tories to protest in 1974, but the scale of the Liberal revival suggests that something more fundamental was involved. I argued earlier that profound changes in the division of labour by sectors and by strata had been tending to unsettle the 'working class'/'middle class' partition of the population in certain respects, over the 1960s. These trends continued in a broadly similar pattern over the Heath years (continuing decline of manual employment in manufacturing and expansion of the salariat accompanied by continuing social mobility) so perhaps one can understand the revival of the Liberal Party (with its relative lack of symbolic 'class' connections, and lack of political 'dogmatism') as reflecting this trend 'de-alignment' as well as the conjuncture of 1974. That is, the evident polarisation on the plane of government/organised labour relations was dislocated from a *reduction* of 'class' polarisation as regards the political perspectives of an important section of the electorate.

As for the other main intruder into the parliamentary arena, the support for the SNP at this time was a more complex phenomenon. I cannot analyse it fully here, but shall attempt a few remarks. First, 'nationality', ever since the union with England, had continued to exist as a basis of collectivity in Scotland: in Scotland's distinctive cultural patterns and traditions, distinct legal and educational systems, distinct administrative apparatus, and industrial structure. Only the *political pertinence* of that collectivity was variable, and for much of the time its pertinence was low. That the SNP managed to exploit nationality — to make it politically pertinent — in 1974 must be seen against the background of Scotland, and West Central Scotland in particular, as one of the relatively 'depressed regions' of the United Kingdom. Pressure from the STUC and the Scottish Labour Party over the 1960s had helped to channel considerable regional aid to Scotland, which partly reversed the country's relative economic decline (Begg and Lythe, 1977) but did not eliminate high unemployment, and at the same time brought recognition of a 'Scottish dimension' to economic policy. Then in the '70s the development of North Sea oil off Scottish

shores provided the nationalists with a populist gambit of major pro-
portions: the prospect of an oil-rich independence helped to bring
together elements of the nationalistically-minded middle classes (who
furnished most of the leadership) with certain sections of the Scottish
working class (who voted SNP in considerable numbers). But if the
support for the SNP was, like the Liberal vote, a substantially 'cross-
class' phenomenon it cannot so easily be categorised as a flight from
'class' as pertinent social collectivity, since it must be recognised that
the 'national distinctiveness' of Scotland is overdetermined by the differential balance of classes in Scotland as opposed to England.[25] Even
though the official ideology of the SNP posited a technocratic non-
class Scottish national politics (Hyslop, 1979), many of the party's
supporters were reckoning in terms of cutting adrift from *Tory* England;
settling accounts with the 'Tartan Tories' could come later.

To return to the fortunes of the government: between February and
October, the minority Labour government settled the miners' strike
and abolished the Pay Board. In July compulsory wage restraint was
ended, but the Price Commission was retained. The immediate
industrial crisis had been resolved, but inflation, which had been
substantially boosted by the rise in world oil prices, continued to
accelerate, and the discrepancy between price rises of 8 per cent and
wage rises of 16 per cent over the six months stored up an acute problem of squeezed profitability. The 'social contract' arrangements,
whereby the Labour leadership hoped to secure voluntary wage
restraint in exchange for the repeal of the Industrial Relations Act,
food subsidies, a rent freeze and other measures, were developing in
somewhat shaky manner.[26] In October the decision was taken to go
to the polls in an attempt to get more decisive support for a Labour
government: more popular authority and a workable parliamentary
position. The net effect of the October election was to give Labour
the narrowest of parliamentary majorities (four seats) but in terms of
the popular vote the question of mandate was hardly resolved. Between February and October the Labour and Tory votes *both* fell, and
Labour's parliamentary success was merely the result of a greater
slump in the Tory vote. In fact, the SNP was the only party to pull
out a higher vote in October.[27] Labour was in government and had
to make the best of it, but the party was with a less numerous support
bloc than even the Selsdon Heath of 1970.

Labour 1974-1979

The Labour government sought from the start to construct and hold together a support bloc around the theme of a 'social contract', and I propose to organise my account of the development of political forces in this period around that same theme. To start with the lowest common denominator, all sections of the Labour Party could agree that the object was to cement a good working relationship between the government and the trade unions, and thereby also to secure widespread political support, to develop a hegemony which would contrast sharply with both the Heath phase and the bitterness and disillusionment which followed compulsory wage restraint and 'In Place of Strife' in the late '60s. Beyond this, however, the 'social contracts' according to the left and according to the parliamentary leadership diverged markedly. Let us first consider the social contract according to the left.

For the left, the social contract was to be intimately connected with the industrial policy which had been taking shape under the auspices of the National Executive Committee over the early '70s. This originally developed from critical reflection on the failure of 'planning' over 1964-70, and on the Italian model of state enterprise, Stuart Holland's 'The State as Entrepreneur' (Holland, 1972) being an influential contribution. In the context of the mobilisation and assertiveness of organised labour under Heath's government, the industrial policy proposals became charged with a stronger element of workers' control which was seen as an essential component of the 'planning agreements' to be made with large enterprises, and vital to their enforcement. These proposals were embodied in the NEC 'Action Programme' of 1973, and then also in the party manifesto of February. As Prior (1980, p. 3) summarises:

'The policy in these documents centred around industrial policy with a call for the creation of a National Enterprise Board, which would by selective nationalisation and investment establish a state presence in all major manufacturing sectors, and for the use of planning agreements to achieve a new degree of worker involvement in company planning.'

Prior further claims that union support for such an industrial policy was a central plank of the social contract, which therefore 'represented the first British attempt within a framework of parliamentary democracy to build in a process of extra-parliamentary mobilisation around the policies of a Labour government' (ibid., p. 4).

As is clear in retrospect, however, the radical industrial policy of the Labour left failed, at this time, to provide the focus for a hegemonic movement, either in the Party, the unions or beyond. That this was due not merely to right-wing and civil service sabotage is clearly recognised by the left MPs who were most involved at the time. Michael Meacher and Frank Field have stressed that only a limited circle of people were actively involved in formulating the industrial policy proposals, and that beyond this circle, understanding of the proposals was rather minimal. Meacher has said of the unions:

> 'If they had been involved in the kind of ideas that led to this distinctive industrial policy of '73-'74 they would have demanded as a quid pro quo for the successive incomes policies of 1975-6-7 the other side of the social contract, that these various aspects of industrial policy and worker participation in its various forms should be implemented' (1980, p.7).

In a similar vein, Stuart Holland noted that 'it takes time to win the intellectual appreciation by some trade unionists that these policies would be useful and to achieve that gut reaction by trade unionists that they are absolutely essential. And that process certainly didn't happen' (1980, p. 20). Holland also accepts in retrospect that the left damaged its prospects in this regard by hitching its industrial policy to opposition to the EEC, so that the pro-EEC verdict of the 1975 referendum reduced the credibility of the left generally. Holland argues that withdrawal from the EEC was not an essential component of the strategy for the domestic economy, since the EEC member-countries are, de facto, able to pursue a wide range of industrial policies.

For the parliamentary leadership of the Labour Party, the notion of a 'social contract' was never tied to an industrial policy of the kind which the left envisaged. If there was not much coherent intellectual opposition to the left's proposals, this by no means signified tacit support but rather a belief that the pressure of 'realities' in government would soon dispel the fancies of opposition. This much is plain from Harold Wilson's comments:

> 'Sub-Committees and Sub-Sub-Committees (of the NEC) had produced grandiose proposals for nationalising anything and pretty nearly everything. In the more difficult political conditions in which

a Labour leader has to operate when in opposition, appeals for restraint were less likely to be effective...' (Wilson, 1979, p. 29).

Or again, the left's Department of Industry White Paper produced in 1974 is described as a 'sloppy and half-baked document, polemical, indeed menacing, in tone' (ibid., p. 33). Wilson was particularly pleased when, in the re-drafting of this document at his behest, the section on planning agreements was 'cut down to size' and it was made plain that the NEB would have no 'marauding role'.

On the Wilsonian view, the social contract was primarily an arrangement 'between government, industry and the trade unions, on the basis of mutual sacrifices to reach agreement on a strategy to curb rising prices' (ibid., p. 44). Part of the 'price' was to be redistributive fiscal policy, and policy aimed at producing increased industrial investment, but as regards the latter aim the NEB was conceived as a state merchant bank, a broker in the tradition of the Industrial Reorganisation Corporation rather than a 'rogue elephant' wreaking industrial havoc on the basis of leftist dogma. Far from being an instrument of struggle against the prerogatives of private capital, and the multinationals in particular, the contract was to provide a means of national reconciliation. The power of the trade unions was to be recognised, and channelled into a realistic programme of social-democratic reforms, thereby defusing, rather than exploiting, the aggressive industrial mood. When articulated in this way the Wilsonian social contract appears very close to what Sir Ian Gilmour (1978) has claimed is the essence of true and wise Toryism: the avoidance of 'dogma'; the balancing of opposed social forces; the concession of reform where reform is due in order to hold together a 'national' constituency (despite the fact that Gilmour viewed the 1974/75 legislative programme as a dangerous concession to sectional union interests and a threat to the constitution — true Toryism is only recognised as such well after the event!). In his memoirs, Wilson makes no bones of placing himself in the line of succession of Baldwin, Churchill and Macmillan.

It was, of course, the latter version of the social contract which predominated, despite continuing dissent on the part of the left of the party and certain of the unions. Initially, at any rate, it was not without genuine benefits to the unions and the working class — the changes in labour law and the reform of pensions in particular. It could not otherwise have achieved its conciliatory aim. But over the years from 1974 the project of incorporation of union power within a consensus of 'national' dimensions was very severely tested.

Two points are of particular importance here. First, the external conditions were extremely unfavourable, given the record trade deficit generated by the 'Barber boom' and added to by the subsequent massive rise in oil prices. The trade deficit had to be either financed or reduced: the former course meant courting the international financial institutions with their implicit or explicit power of veto over domestic policy, while the latter meant either fiscal deflation in excess of the deflation of demand *already* induced by the OPEC financial surplus (in paradoxical combination with cost-inflation) or setting up stringent import controls. Since import controls on the necessary scale were regarded as out of the question,[28] a precarious combination of international borrowing and expenditure-restriction was embarked upon.

Second, also connected with the dual impetus of the Tory boom and the oil-price rise, inflation was accelerating rapidly over 1974-75. The 'threshold payments' scheme introduced under Heath before the oil-price rise -- a scheme supported by the then Labour opposition — was tending to generate a runaway wage-price spiral, but since prices were to some extent constrained by continuing state controls there was also a severe squeeze on company liquidity, with its threat to employment. Under these circumstances some kind of pay restraint was a clear political necessity, not merely to placate 'capital' domestic or international but because millions of workers and their families were fearful of the consequences for their livelihood. (The apparent failure of the left to recognise this was one reason why the left's economic programme lacked a mass following.)[29]

These related constraints at the international and national levels left the government with very little room to manoeuvre, and selling corporate peace under the given conditions stretched the Labour leaders' powers of statesmanship to the utmost. Grudgingly and haltingly, the trade unions were brought into line on incomes policy without any actual government *diktat*, and with increasingly little being offered in return, by means of emotive appeals to the national interest. Meanwhile international loan finance was secured, but the inflow of funds to London had the effect of holding the exchange rate at a level which, given the British inflation rate, made British enterprises increasingly uncompetitive and hence worsened the corporate liquidity position. Then in 1976 when the sterling bubble burst[30] the constraint took another twist, with a falling exchange rate helping to boost the inflation rate and depress real wages. If one interpretation of the social contract was that it promised the development of the 'social wage' of state benefits and services in exchange for sacrifice on the side of wages and salaries, this became increasingly problematic after the government turned to the International Monetary Fund to help finance the balance of payments and bolster the pound. The IMF could offer secure finance, in contrast to the holders of short-term sterling balances, but it could also exact a price. It is well known that part of the price of IMF finance was curtailment of the government's public expenditure plans, which was to increase the tension between the party leadership on the one hand and the left and the unions (particularly in the public sector) on the other, over subsequent years. What is less clear, however, is the extent to which the IMF was shoulder-charging an open door in this respect, that is, whether Labour leaders had already lost their faith in public expenditure.[31]

The theme of public expenditure is obviously of great importance to the development of politics under the subsequent Tory government, and will be discussed more fully in the following chapter, but some comments at this stage are in order. The main point here is that not only did the Labour leaders reject the left's version of the social contract with its new emphasis on a radical industrial policy, but also they increasingly came to question even the Crosland/Fabian/'Keynesian' version of socialism, so that their politics in the latter half of the 1970s became more and more of a mere holding operation — mere 'government' lacking any social purpose with a broad popular appeal. The questioning of public expenditure was an integral part of this process. In the mid '70s public expenditure was under attack for a variety of reasons. The Institute of Economic Affairs had for a long time been polemicising against the extension of state activity on the grounds that it restricted choice, led to dependency and reduced the motivation to work, and fostered economic inefficiency in comparison with 'private enterprise'. These arguments had not at first cut much ice with social democrats,[32] but two further ideological strands came to prominence in this period which helped to put the advocates of social progress through public spending and 'welfarism' onto the defensive, or even convince them of the folly of their ways: the monetary theory of inflation, and the 'too few producers' thesis of Bacon and Eltis (1976). The first of these strands, taken up vigorously by many economic commentators in the press and the City, undermined confidence in the 'Keynesian' approach to demand management and employment policy by suggesting that in the 'long run' government deficit-financing merely led to higher inflation and was impotent to control employment. Its intrusion into the thinking of the Labour leadership was

registered in Peter Jay's speech for Callaghan at the 1976 Party conference. The second strand, the Bacon and Eltis thesis, took up a theme
which had long been forgotten by all but Marxist economists, the
distinction between 'productive' and 'unproductive' labour. It was
argued that the non-commodity producing sector of the economy ('non-
marketable' in Bacon and Eltis' terms) and the public services sector
in particular, was pre-empting resources from private commodity production, and the manufacturing sector in particular. This was the basic
reason for Britain's poor investment record and profitability,[33] and
what was needed was the release of resources from the unproductive
areas in order to rebuild the productive base. This influential view
suggested that social democracy in the mixed economy had to *reculer
pour mieux sauter:* it was necessary to call a halt to the expansion of public
sector service expenditure to allow an industrial regeneration, which
would then, at some later stage, permit social objectives to be given
priority again.

Once these views were accepted by the Labour leaders, the social
democratic cupboard was bare. Callaghan, Healey and company could
only 'govern': holding the line against inflation through incomes policy;
bemoaning the 'intolerable' level of unemployment; waiting for an
expansion of world trade to lead a recovery and for North Sea oil to
give room for manoeuvre on the balance of payments. The Labour
left, meanwhile, did not manage to mount a convincing enough case
for its 'alternative strategy'[34] (the far left had no half-way credible
strategy to propose), while the trade union movement was not united
in pushing for any positive *quid pro quo* in exchange for wage restraint,
having rejected the Bullock proposals for Industrial Democracy, but
was increasingly tugging for a return to 'free collective bargaining'.

If this makes it seem inevitable that Labour's electoral support
should slump, it has to be pointed out that, according to the opinion
polls, Labour might well have won had an election been called in 1978.
From a socialist point of view the government was barren, yet incomes
policy and fiscal restraint were beginning to produce their intended
effects and the expansion of world trade was benefiting the economy.
In the third and fourth quarters of 1978 the annualised rate of increase
of the Retail Prices Index was only 6.8 per cent and real incomes were
rising again following the sharp falls of 1976 and 77; unemployment,
while still very high by post-war standards, was beginning to fall from
its peak in 1977 and job vacancies were on the increase; the balance
of payments current account showed a substantial surplus.

Further, the political alternatives on offer were far from inspiring.

The 'Economist', in March '78, doubted whether Thatcher could 'forge a new majority of the right' and reckoned that her 'crusade to balance the books and roll back the government' was not finding much popular resonance. In fact it took a series of political blunders on Callaghan's part to spoil Labour's chances of being re-elected, *faute de mieux*, as the responsible and sober 'party of government': the seemingly endless postponement of the election while the party's parliamentary position crumbled, requiring the prop of transparent chicanery; the unenforceable wishful thinking of the 5 per cent pay limit, the last straw for the unions. Even if the media did inflate the 'winter of discontent', even if Callaghan was unlucky when the Scottish National Party chose to commit political suicide in revenge for the failure of Labour's devolution proposals, by supporting the Tories' 'no confidence' motion in the Commons, Callaghan's procrastination and the effects of his autocratic dealings with the unions were surely the main factors weakening the credibility of Labour between 1978 and 79.

The scene was set for Labour to lose (more than for Thatcher to *win*) the election of May 1979.

Reprise

My object in this chapter has been to provide a transition between (i) the analysis of economic class relations, in the sense of possession of and separation from the means of production, and the strategic opportunities for the socialist project connected with the current forms of these relations, and (ii) the *politics* of taking up these opportunities in modern Britain. I began with some general considerations on the division of labour and social collectivities, then offered an account of the development of political forces and their support blocs over the post-war years. In the latter account I have described a situation in which the major parties each have a reservoir of virtually guaranteed electoral support, based on the traditional connection between the parties and the two 'classes' of British society (which I have termed 'social collectivities' to distinguish them from classes defined at the level of property relations), the 'middle class' and the 'working class'. On the other hand, these 'core' support blocs have never been sufficient to ensure either party a parliamentary majority, and although they are still important they have been increasingly eroded at the margin, in part because of the changes in the division of labour which have loosened the hold of the 'two-class system' within popular ideology.

It appears that an increasing number of people are calculating their political support on the basis of the plausibility of the parties as governing parties, asking whether they seem to have the answer to the 'country's problems' (whether these be inflation, unemployment, taxation, law and order, trading position or whatever) rather than voting, and engaging in political activism, on the basis of a deeply-felt class identification. The consistent appeal of the major parties to the 'nation' and their attempt to project an image of governmental competence (and also to brand their rivals as incompetent) has both reflected and reinforced this trend among the electorate. At the same time, however, the parties have found it increasingly difficult to build and sustain popular confidence in their capacity to 'solve the country's problems', as these problems have become more acute and intractable.

Consider in this light the succession of governments in the post-war period up to 1979. Labour from 1945 to 1950 pushed through a programme of social and economic reform which was widely popular, although bitterly resisted by sections of the professional middle class and industrial bourgeoisie. By 1950 the party was able to win a second general election with an increased vote. Then when Britain's political geography gave the Tories a parliamentary majority in 1951 they too were able to sustain popular support in more than one election. Popular participation in electoral politics began to flag after 1951 but arguably this was because most people felt less urgency as regards political change; there was no strong and deep-going popular reaction against the government. The economic class relations of British capitalism were sustaining rapid accumulation, and in this respect the rise of the large-scale impersonal enterprises discussed in chapter 3 was particularly important. The emergence and expansion of new industries provided relatively full employment and made available a whole range of new consumer goods, while real disposable incomes rose fairly steadily. Meanwhile, tax revenue was sufficiently buoyant to sustain an expansion of social service provision. Despite all the shortcomings of British society in this period from a socialist point of view, and the alarming prospects raised by nuclear armament, it has to be said that capitalism was 'too successful', in developing the productive forces and meeting popular aspirations, for political forces supporting a radical transformation of social relations to make much headway. And of course British capitalism was by this stage a very different capitalism from that of the inter-war years: a social formation in which the organised working class, as organised in the trade unions, was at least consulted and listened to by governments as a matter of course, and in which the major political forces took for granted the obligation to minimise unemployment and to preserve and expand the welfare state.

By the 1960s, however, the 'success' of the existing social formation was beginning to be called into question in various ways. We have seen how Labour made its re-emergence as a governing force in 1964 on the basis of a need for sweeping 'modernisation' and planning, pulling together a support bloc spanning the left and managerial technocrats, and how the expectations raised in the early Wilson period were substantially frustrated. The popular endorsement of Labour in 1966 was the last time to date that the party in government has been re-elected. Thereafter, in 1970, 74 and 79, the governing party has been rejected without however any great surge of popular support for the alternative party, at least by the standards of earlier years. It is appropriate here to step back from the detail of party politics and to attempt to draw out in general terms the conditions producing this weakening hold of governments over popular support.

First, ever since the war governments had willingly taken responsibility for the management of the national economy and by the late 1960s it was clear that this 'management' was becoming much less successful: inflation and unemployment were emerging as serious problems and the balance of payments position, upon which Wilson laid such stress, was increasingly precarious. But can we go 'deeper' than this and pinpoint the conditions of existence of these problems? The trading position of the British economy is one crucial factor here, not only as expressed in the *ex post* trade balance but also in the constraint posed on expansionary demand management. The conditions producing weakness in this respect are highly complex but at a risk of oversimplification one might say that the balance of payments constraint reflects a relative 'industrial ossification' of the British economy — a failure to restructure and reinvest on a sufficient scale to maintain the position of the national economy on the world market. Behind this there are two interlocking sets of causes, the relative conservatism of British capital and the strongly entrenched defensive position of the British working class. As regards the first set of causes one can point to the conservative/speculative behaviour of British financial institutions (discussed in chapter 3); the failure to develop fully the advanced multi-divisional forms of capitalist enterprise; the continuing low social valuation of 'industry' relative to the 'liberal professions'; and the relative paucity of commercially-relevant research and development. The effects of these factors included a low level of investment, or at least a low efficiency of investment, and a lack of 'dynamism' in industrial management.

That, however, is only one side of the picture. On the other side is the organised working class: by the end of the 1960s, after a long period of relatively full employment, the trade unions were in a strong position both in terms of wage bargaining and in terms of the defensive 'veto power' which they were able to exercise over changes at the point of production seen as threatening workers' interests. The competitive weakness of the British economy was truly overdetermined: even if the financial institutions had been more disposed towards promoting industrial investment, even if managements had been more competent and imaginative, the restructuring of industry would still have run up against the formidable defensive conservatism of the organised working class. Governments over the '60s and '70s, as I suggested earlier, have not had the capacity, even when they have had the will, to launch a frontal assault on the organised working class and force through a radical restructuring in spite of its resistance. But at the same time the leadership of the organised working class has had neither the imagination nor the capacity to attempt to force a radical restructuring of the national economy on working class terms. To schematise, the British working class has not been ready to run the risks of attempting to constitute itself as the ruling class, of putting forward concrete proposals for working class control over industry and finance and fighting seriously to achieve them. Whether any alternative leadership could have gone further in this direction in the 1960s and 1970s is an open question, but I have argued that it is not useful to conceive of the record so far as merely one of 'betrayal'. The problems of the British social formation were sufficiently pressing to demand at least rhetorical radical solutions from the parties (Wilson's 'planning', Heath's 'free market'), and governments' failures to match their promises were of sufficient concern to the people to breed a serious disillusionment with party politics, yet I submit that for most people of all classes the problems were *not* considered so urgent as to demand a really radical questioning of existing social relations, with all the risks that would entail. The parties in government have not found the social forces with the potential of making revolution (or counter-revolution) pressing to be shaped and led. Labour governments have been able virtually to ignore the demands of the left without provoking massive popular protest (albeit at a cost of running down the party's membership and activist support) while the Heath government found that its tough anti-union stance, however much in accord with 'public opinion', was unworkable, with the electorate recoiling from its practical consequences.

In a word, governments have made themselves unpopular with their manifold 'failures', those failures are traceable to their basic failure to restructure the social relations of British capitalism, and yet there has been no social force with the 'will' and capacity to enforce any radical restructuring against the opposition which any such move must encounter. There has been a kind of stalemate in the class struggle which has placed governments in the position of tackling deep-rooted problems with technocratic instruments of strictly limited effectiveness: they have held the line on the balance of payments by means of periodic deflation, which has not really solved anything; they have periodically checked inflation and attempted to rebuild industrial profitability by means of *ad hoc* incomes policy but have been unable either to maintain popular support for such policies or to push forward to a comprehensive planning of prices and incomes, investment and consumption.

Against this background, the magnitude of the *political* problem facing the socialist project becomes apparent. In chapter 5 I outlined some of the major objectives which seemed feasible given the constraints and opportunities posed by the development of capitalist property relations, under the two headings of investment planning and enterprise democracy, recognising the importance of a 'left government' in relation to these while admitting that the conditions of formation of such a government were another matter. In the light of the discussion above, it is possible to present the objectives of investment planning and enterprise democracy not merely as desirable from a socialist point of view, but as potential means of tackling the basic problems reflected in the sorry history of party politics since the '60s: investment planning as a means of breaking through the conservative/speculative mode of calculation of the financial institutions and restructuring industry; enterprise democracy as a means of transforming the 'veto power' of the working class into a positive influence over the direction and management of enterprises. Not a complete programme by any means, but necessary and crucial components of a restructuring on socialist terms which would break the stalemate. Nonetheless, the politics of support for such a transformation of economic class relations are complex and problematic. Some of those on the left have assumed that there is an inherent socialist majority in Britain which has failed to surface only because successive Labour governments, in pursuing a policy of managing rather than opposing capitalism, have never given that majority its political cue. But on the basis of what I have said in this chapter concerning the formation and power of governments, this comforting view is not plausible. Governments can mount a radical and effective challenge to the existing social formation only if they have definite, credible proposals commanding the active support of a substantial social bloc, a hegemonic force spanning a whole range of social positions (as Labour did in 1945, for all the weaknesses we can see in retrospect). And the problem is that the left, inside and outside the Labour Party, and the trade union movement, have not yet measured up to that historic requirement. To imagine that the Labour leaders could have thwarted and de-mobilised such a force for all these years is to attribute to them superhuman powers.

Without doubt, the construction of such a hegemonic bloc for socialist objectives must involve winning the support of many people who regard themselves as 'middle class' or of no class, many who have never considered themselves socialists, many who are not members of trade unions, by colonising and re-defining the notion of the popular or national interest (while avoiding chauvinism and the opportunistic erasure of real social differences). If this is the general challenge, it is always faced under specific historical conditions. The following chapter presents a contribution, in the spirit of Marx's 'Eighteenth Brumaire', to the analysis of the 'specific historical conditions' — the particular relationships between economic class structure, social collectivities and political forces — leading to Thatcherism, and under the Thatcher government. For it was of course Thatcher from the right, and not the left, who seized the initiative in attempting to break the stalemate of class forces and carry through a radical restructuring of the British social formation.

7

Thatcherism, classes and politics

In this chapter I shall address three main questions: first the question of 'where Thatcherism came from'; second, the question of the feasibility of the central economic programme of Thatcherism; and third, the question of the politics of Thatcherism in practice. Let me begin by expanding briefly on the substance of these three questions. First, I use the term 'Thatcherism' to refer to the ideology and political practice of the dominant faction within the Conservative government elected in May 1979. So by the question of 'where Thatcherism came from' I mean to enquire into the conditions of formation of 'Thatcherist' ideology, the conditions under which this tendency could come to dominate the Tory party, and the conditions under which such a party could win a large parliamentary majority in 1979, and retain considerable, if diminished, support thereafter. In these enquiries I shall draw on the arguments of the previous chapter. Second, in considering the economic feasibility of the Thatcher programme I intend to make use of the results derivéd in chapters 3 and 4 concerning the development of capitalist property relations. I shall argue that Thatcher's economic programme is contradictory and unrealisable in face of the dominant form of capitalist property. On the third question, it must be recognised that although Thatcher's basic economic programme is not realisable, nonetheless Thatcherism has had real economic and political effects, and even if Thatcherism fails politically as well as in economic terms there will be no wiping the slate clean and acting as if nothing had happened since 1979. I shall offer a contribution to the debate over the political effects of developments in the Thatcher period as far as late 1982, and the effects on the prospects for socialism.

7.1 Where Thatcherism came from

As mentioned above, this question breaks down into a number of narrower questions — those of the conditions of formation of Thatcherist ideology, and of the conditions of dominance of that ideology within

266

the Tory party and subsequently in the realm of electoral politics. The answers to these questions are necessarily interwoven and I shall not attempt to answer them in strictly serial fashion, but it should be borne in mind that we are dealing with a complex issue — one which involves processes at the levels of parliamentary politics, international economic relations and popular ideology — and, to echo the conclusions of earlier chapters, not an issue which is reducible to the 'expression' of a pre-given class interest.

First consider the main strands of Thatcherist ideology. Thatcher and her close associates subscribe to a very definite and clear-cut vision of the problems of British society and the economy, and an equally definite vision of the solutions to those problems. The central problem is seen as state interference, bureaucracy and waste, a cancer which has been developing almost continually at least since the war, enfeebling the economy and popular morality alike. In order to finance its wasteful bureaucracy and misguided charitable programmes the state has levied taxes on a scale which has crushed out incentives for personal effort. Running up against the limits of taxation, the state has also borrowed and 'printed' money on an excessive scale, the former squeezing out more worthy private sector investment and the latter generating uncontrollable inflation. This cancerous growth of the state is given the name 'creeping socialism', but it is a 'socialism' which even Conservatives have connived in. In seeking to break with it, Thatcher also seeks to break with much of the tradition of Conservatism in Britain. Other major problems which have grown up in the shade of the meddling socialist state include the excessive power of the trade unions and the breakdown of respect for law and order. Within Thatcherist ideology, the solution is to restrict the role of the state, concentrating its powers on matters which are rightfully the business of the state such as defence, policing, formulation of general laws (including laws to put the unions in their proper place), and control over the supply of money. The counter-productive pretensions of the state to preserve employment, restructure industry and adjust aggregate demand, incomes or prices (directly) must be rejected. The market must be allowed to function freely within a framework of sound law and sound money and the individual must be presented with sufficient incentives to make it worth his while to succeed in the market. Further, individuals must be encouraged to accumulate private property, in the housing stock and preferably also in the means of production so as to realise the dream of a true 'property owning democracy' (Howell, 1978). As many people as possible should have more to lose than their chains. Respect must also be re-established for the institutions of family and state. This will provide the social and political stability which is the necessary complement to the competitive working of the free market system.

This, roughly speaking, is the message which was developing within the Tory party from 1974 onward, which was presented to the electorate in 1979 and which has been constantly reiterated from the heights of government ever since, in various different formulations, although it cannot be said to have guided every action of the Tory party in office. This message has, as Hall (1980) has said, a 'hegemonic thrust' or 'global character'. It is not just a matter of new *policies* but of a new 'ethic' and a new 'commonsense'. In a sense, the Thatcherist message is greater than the sum of its parts. But to investigate the conditions of formation and 'success' of Thatcherism, we have to return to those parts and see how each could develop, and how they could be fused into an effective ideological and political force in the late 1970s. We can distinguish within Thatcherism a programmatic economic element and a social-philosophical element, although the two are interwoven. The programmatic economic element owes a great deal to two connected developments in the field of theoretical ideology – intellectual developments — the rise of monetarism and the rise of the 'social market economy' doctrine[1] — while the social-philosophical side rests upon the popular attitude that has been called 'anti-statism' (by Hall, 1980, Leonard, 1979 and others) as well as upon classic petty bourgeois ideology and moralism. In all these aspects, the development of Thatcherism must be considered negatively as well as postively, in terms of what it attacks and rejects as well as what it supports and affirms. Thus, for instance, the rise of monetarism must be connected with the 'failure of Keynesianism', the rise of the social market doctrine with the 'failure' of state industrial intervention and corporatist accommodation between government and unions, the development of anti-statism with the unpopularity of bureaucracy and the 'tax burden'. I have already put forward (in the previous chapter) some arguments which are relevant in this context, but in the following section I propose to examine each of these couples in more detail, and the conditions under which the pre-Thatcher orthodoxy could be presented as a failure and the Thatcherist doctrine as a plausible alternative.

The 'failure of Keynesianism' and the rise of monetarism

One has to be careful here. There is a convergence, tempting for Marxists, between the tide of monetarist opinion which claims that Keynesianism was only ever a temporary palliative, and the view that Keynesianism merely displaced the contradictions of capitalism onto a different plane.[2] There is also a temptation on the left to avoid any substantive treatment of Keynesian economic theory as such by extending the term 'Keynesianism' to refer generally to the 'social democratic consensus' the crisis of which, it is claimed, brought Thatcher to power (the notion of the 'Keynesian mode of domination' put forward by the London Edinburgh Weekend Return Group, 1979). Keynes' ideas and the practice of Keynesianism merit more careful attention than this.

We saw earlier (chapter 5) that Keynes himself recommended, on the basis of his theory, a 'more or less comprehensive socialisation of investment' — a policy much more radical than those put into practice by post-war social democratic governments.[3] But at the same time there is undoubtedly a serious weakness in the Keynesian view of the capitalist economy. Keynes challenged what he called the 'classical theory' on the question of the determination of aggregate demand, but he did not doubt the ability of competitive markets to produce an optimal allocation of resources (or as near optimal as possible) within the context of state regulation of aggregate demand:

> 'But if our central controls succeed in establishing an aggregate volume of output corresponding to full employment as nearly as possible, the classical theory comes into its own again from this point onwards. If we suppose the volume of output to be given, i.e. to be determined by forces outside the classical scheme of thought, then there is no objection to be raised against the classical analysis of the manner in which private self-interest will determine what in particular is produced, in what proportion the factors of production will be combined to produce it, and how the value of the final product will be distributed between them' (Keynes, 1936, pp. 378-9).

This formulation points to a theoretical and practical dislocation between 'macro' and 'micro' economics: classical theory can claim its own in the matter of freely functioning markets, provided that a governmental practice based on Keynes' theory ensures the correct volume of demand overall. It was this view, with its 'moderately conservative implications' (Keynes), and its provision of a limited yet important role for enlightened government career economists, which found favour in the Treasury and the Universities in the post-war years. It was, however, a view which was increasingly seen as deficient, if not 'in crisis', from around 1960 for reasons associated with stop-go and the balance of payments. The expansion of domestic demand consistently produced unsustainable deficits on the balance of payments, forcing fiscal policy into reverse and therefore reproducing unemployment. What was needed, apparently, was a mechanism for alleviating the balance of payments constraint, for making it possible to expand domestic demand without creating an unbalanced surge of imports. On the most minimal interpretation, this meant merely improving the technical competence of demand management: getting the timing of fiscal changes right and avoiding electioneering budgets. But the emphasis on industrial policy, 'planning' and productivity over the 1960s showed that both governments and industrialists felt there was something more fundamental at stake, so that even the most competent and politically disinterested management of demand would not be sufficient to produce full employment and rapid growth in conjunction with balanced trade. The tendency to move into deficit on the balance of payments current account with rising GDP reflected a structural weakness of the UK economy, and this structural weakness could not itself be abolished by the practice of demand management. Whatever the precise diagnosis of this 'structural weakness' (lack of industrial investment, poor design or marketing of British products, weak management, antagonistic relations on the shop floor, excessive overseas military commitments, etc.) this view carried the implication that Keynesianism was not enough. Further policies were required, to increase productivity and international competitiveness.

As well as the balance of payments, inflation came to be seen as a distinct 'problem' by the end of the '60s. Keynes had argued that excess demand (i.e. above the level sufficient to produce full employment) would cause inflation, and many policymakers had come to assume that *only* excess demand could cause inflation: there was a straightforward trade-off between inflation and unemployment.[4] When in the late '60s inflation and unemployment rose simultaneously this undermined the notion of a simple trade-off, but it did not undermine Keynesianism as a whole. Keynes' macroeconomic theory did not rule out the possibility of 'cost push' inflation deriving from a rise in import prices (such as that produced by the 1967 devaluation) or from wage rises in excess of increases in labour productivity, and many Keynesian economists accepted the existence of such a mechanism. Product and labour markets had become progressively more concentrated, large-scale enterprises were pursuing 'cost plus' pricing and strong trade unions were bargaining on the basis of an expected continuous rise in real wages. The workings of the 'microeconomy' no longer corresponded (if they ever had done) to the conceptions of 'classical theory'.

Under Wilson, the lesson drawn from all this was that the 'microeconomy' could not simply be allowed to get on with allocating resources and determining prices within an overall framework of managed demand. The government had to intervene further with regional, industrial and incomes policies. But although regional and industrial policies were not without real effects they did not achieve the government's aim of abolishing the balance of payments constraint on growth, while *ad hoc* wage restraint only suppressed inflation temporarily. It would be fair to say that at this point Keynesianism was not widely seen as having failed — rather it was the interventionist attempts to alleviate the balance of payments constraint and inflation, in order to permit the full application of Keynesian expansionary policy, which had been less than successful.

Heath, as we saw earlier, began by denouncing such intervention: the unfettered microeconomy could look after itself, given appropriate incentives. Keynesian macroeconomic ideas had not been abandoned by Heath, however, and after the 'U turn' the Chancellor Barber took the view that a big dose of fiscal expansionism and easy credit would solve all problems, provided it was combined with the floating of the exchange rate. A 'dash for growth' would alleviate inflation (since there would be more real income to go around and therefore less conflict over its distribution and less wage inflation) and solve the balance of payments problem (by inducing the investment needed for modernisation and increased competitiveness). Any temporary balance of payments problem could be coped with by allowing the exchange rate to depreciate. This wilfully optimistic doctrine, which had no basis in Keynesian theory or the experience of the 1960s, is of strategic importance, for this is the example which Thatcher commonly cites as evidence for the poverty of Keynesianism (the Barber boom took place, it should be remembered, during her first period in government). The Barber boom certainly raised demand and the GDP (over 5 per cent in a year) but it also took inflation to new heights and the balance of payments current account to new depths, as any Keynesian economist not infected by wishful thinking ought to have been able to predict. Hindsight is perhaps too easy. If Barber's expansionism was reckless, it was exaggerated by the inaccuracy of the data on the GDP available at the time, which under-recorded the pace of the boom until it was too late. And its results might not have been so disastrous were it not for the simultaneous boom in other capitalist economies which drove up world commodity prices and helped to trigger the subsequent oil-price rise. Nonetheless the experience of Maudling's 'dash for growth' should have stood as a warning.

In isolation, the Barber boom might have been written off as another irresponsible Tory 'go' phase, without seriously damaging the credentials of Keynesianism as such. But in the mid-'70s the notion of the 'failure of Keynesianism' began to make more headway among politicians and economists, for a reason which is not hard to see: the simultaneous development of deep recession and accelerating inflation. Even if the Phillips trade-off had broken down before, the scale on which inflation and recession were combined at this time reduced Keynesian pundits to bewilderment and confusion. Harold Wilson (1979) paints a picture of Denis Healey, newly appointed Chancellor in 1974 and trying to formulate a budget, reeling around without any compass and receiving flatly contradictory advice from different academic economists. A fiscal boost would increase inflation and the balance of payments deficit, but deflation would worsen the recession, yet all of these were already off the scale of 1960s experience.

But if Keynesianism was at this time useless as a guide to Chancellors attempting to plan their budgets to achieve stable prices and full employment, that by no means proves that basic Keynesian theory had been invalidated (no more, one might say, than Stalin refutes Marxism). For the inflationary recession of the mid-'70s (and the impossible position of chancellors) is clearly explicable in terms of Keynes' — and Kalecki's — theory. I cannot offer a detailed justification of this claim here, but I shall draw attention to the effects of the oil price rise.

It would hardly be exaggeration to say that over the post-war years the metropolitan capitalist countries had built their economies around cheap oil; certainly the growth sectors of the automobile industry, petrochemicals and electricity generation were very dependent upon oil. But by the early 1970s oil production among the major industrial capitalist economies was declining as reserves became depleted, and these economies were forced into greatly increased reliance on the previously marginal energy supplies from the countries which were to form OPEC. When a changed balance of international forces permitted the formation of the OPEC cartel and the abrupt raising of oil prices, the nature of their dependence meant that the industrial economies were in no position to cut their consumption drastically. The inelastic nature of the demand for oil even in the face of a quadrupling of the price meant a massive increase in OPEC revenues which could not possibly be matched by a commensurate increase in OPEC expenditures on the exports of the main oil-consuming countries, and hence also a massive OPEC financial surplus. This financial surplus produced a severe deflation of demand (by way of a reduction of net exports) for the oil-consuming countries, in accordance with the classic Keynes/Kalecki reasoning. At the same time the substantial increase in costs faced by the consumers of oil (direct and indirect) were transmitted in the form of higher prices; not surprisingly workers demanded pay rises to keep up with price inflation, and so on it went. Because not all prices are adjusted simultaneously to a 'shock' of this nature, and the process of adjustment and counter-adjustment is potentially endless, inflation continued at a rapid pace over the following years. And rapid inflation, which erodes the 'real' value of financial assets, had the further perverse effect of stimulating extra personal savings, deepening the recession. This is only a sketch of the mechanisms of inflationary recession in the mid-'70s, but it shows in outline, on the basis of Keynesian theory, why government economic policy at a national level was powerless to prevent 'stagflation'. A Keynesian policy-solution for the recession could only have operated on a world scale (increase in OPEC's marginal propensity to consume, socially planned investment of the OPEC surplus in the deficit countries) and that was a clear political impossibility. This mode of argument also helps to explain why there should have been a particularly acute crisis of state finances in this period. Recession, as was pointed out in chapter 4, tends automatically to raise the state's budget deficit even if the government does not pursue an active counter-cyclical expansionary policy, since it leads to a simultaneous deterioration in the tax base and increase in mandatory income-maintenance expenditures. The reduction in net export demand and rise in the personal savings ratio in this period could therefore be expected to increase the state's borrowing requirement as a fraction of GDP. If at the same time the 'cost-push' impulse from import prices, and wage claims intended to maintain living standards, were causing inflation of the nominal GDP then the actual amount of money which the state had to borrow would be pushed up sharply. This in fact happened,[5] giving greatly increased leverage over government policy to the financial institutions (domestic and international) operating in the market for government debt and enabling them to impose on the government their principles of financial rectitude.

For the British economy then, the longstanding balance of payments constraint was exacerbated by the new constraint posed for all the non oil-producing economies and the option of fiscal expansionism at a national level was foreclosed. It was under these circumstances that politicians for whom 'Keynesianism' was merely an easy technique for achieving growth and popularity began to lose faith, to listen to the ideologues who were announcing its death, and to subscribe to the instant mythology that fiscal expansion had 'only ever worked by injecting inflation into the economy' despite the record of a long period in which relatively full employment had been combined with only moderate inflation.

To summarise: by the end of the 1960s it was realised by governments that Keynesianism was 'not enough'. The problems of the balance of payments constraint and inflation were in some sense 'structural' and their alleviation demanded additional interventionist measures, but it was not clear precisely how these measures could be made more effective. Under the Tories in the early '70s the view gained ground that the only 'additional measure' required was the floating of the exchange rate, then fiscal expansion would work wonders. The effects of the application of this doctrine helped to discredit Keynesian doctrine by association. Then in the mid-'70s worldwide inflation and recession, associated with the rise in oil prices, severely reduced the scope for fiscal expansionism — most severely for highly open economies with a weak competitive position already, such as Britain's. Even mild expansionism would (a) produce a substantial trade deficit and put the national economy more deeply in debt to the international financial institutions and/or (b) force down the exchange rate and exacerbate inflation. But even then Keynesianism might not have been rejected with such alacrity by the likes of Callaghan, or even the Tories, were it not for the presence of a seemingly coherent and plausible 'alternative' which had growing (if minority) support among academics and which was strongly espoused by both respectable economic commentators and certain important financial institutions.

This leads me to consider the conditions for the rise of 'monetarism' as an alternative to Keynesianism. In the first place it should be noted that the Quantity Theory of money, the core of 'monetarism' in the narrow sense and a longstanding principle of classical political economy, had never really disappeared. In Britain it had been virtually relegated to the status of an eccentricity by the dominance of the Radcliffe view that changes in the money supply had little effect on aggregate demand, but in the USA economists such as Friedman and Patinkin had revived and modified the Quantity Theory, and Friedman in particular had sought to verify it empirically by drawing up correlations between changes in the money supply and subsequent movements in the general price level.[6] So monetarism as an intellectual construction remained a latent force even through the years of Keynesian orthodoxy, awaiting its cue to achieve a wider impact. The inflationary surge of the late '60s and early '70s provided the first cue: during the years when inflation had not been seen as a major problem there had not been much call on a theory which took movements in the general price level as its central object of interest, but once inflation did emerge as a 'problem' demanding the attention of government and economists, the Quantity Theory was at least in the running again.[7]

At first, in Britain at any rate, it did not break the hold of Keynesianism either in academic or governmental circles. The dominant view of inflation among academic economists was the 'cost push' theory: it was widely admitted that expansion of the money supply was a necessary 'permissive' condition for continuing inflation, but the impulse for inflation was seen as deriving from cost pressures (or from excess demand, but the movements of unemployment and job vacancies were taken to show that demand pressure was not excessive, except possibly at the height of the Barber boom (Kennedy, 1978)). And the costs of attempting to prevent cost pressures from generating inflation, by means of restriction of the money supply, were seen as too high. This view was also accepted by the Bank of England and the Treasury in the early 1970s. As O'Brien, the governor of the Bank of England, put it in 1971:

'It cannot be emphasised too strongly or too often that attacking a severe inflation simply by holding down the growth of the money supply means reducing real activity' (quoted in Bonnet, 1981, p. 16).

This view was certainly correct. The inference made was that in order to avoid massive unemployment and stagnation in the 'real economy', inflation had to be tackled by means of prices and incomes policy. The problem with this view, however, was that successful prices and incomes policy depended on a political accommodation between governments and unions, and control by union leaders over their memberships in the matter of wage-bargaining, and this accommodation and control were hard to come by. Keynesian economists could argue the merits of a long-term, rational and equitable incomes policy but governments became enmeshed in *ad hoc* and impermanent dealings. The unions could be corralled for brief periods in the name of the 'national interest', but periods of severe (and uneven) wage restraint eventually undermined their acquiescence and provoked bursts of rapid wage inflation to 'catch up'. The *political* failure of incomes policy under Heath, as under Wilson before him, prepared the ground for the political advance of monetarism. This advance was not uniform however. Much of the Cambridge/Whitehall economic 'establishment' remained firmly wedded to the notion of a rational incomes policy and deeply sceptical of monetary restraint as a mechanism for controlling inflation, but attitudes were changing elsewhere. There are three aspects to this which merit attention: the rise of monetarism in the Tory Party itself; the development of monetarist views in the City and the intrusion of IMF monetarism; and the half-reluctant conversion of the Labour leadership.

For the Tory party, smarting after the politically ruinous consequences of Heath's interventionism and Barber's expansionism, monetarism offered a convenient and comforting doctrine. Convenient, because the Quantity Theory suggested that inflation could be conquered without entering into damaging dealing with the unions. According to Friedman, the unions were not the instigators of inflation — their wage demands merely reflected the inflationary impulse generated by irresponsible expansion of the money supply. This doctrine meshed perfectly with the emerging right-wing Tory view that Heath's U turn was a disastrous mistake and that the 'over-mighty state', the vehicle of 'creeping socialism', was to blame for the relative decline of the British economy. For a party not greatly given to theoretical reflection, it might be added, the Quantity Theory had an appealing intellectual simplicity: inflation is 'too much money chasing too few goods' and where can 'too much money' come from, if the state does not 'print' it? The sophisticated Keith Joseph could easily get this message across to the economically unsophisticated Margaret Thatcher.

The Tory party was in opposition. But meanwhile the acceptance of monetarist views among leading commentators and analysts connected with the City stockbroking firms and the financial press[8] was to invest these views with a respectability and a material force which would greatly increase the plausibility of a 'monetarist' political party contending for office. This acceptance (again it was not uniform) had a number of bases. First, it might be pointed out that monetarist policy to counter inflation brings immediate short term benefits to certain of the financial institutions, since it involves the raising of interest rates in the attempt to restrict the growth of the money stock. But this point should not be overstressed. The Supplementary Special Deposits scheme, also part of the apparatus designed to restrict the money supply, acted to curtail profitable banking activity to some extent, and further, the interests of the financial institutions cannot be divorced from the health of their corporate customers, which is adversely affected by high interest rates. Besides, it is not very convincing to suggest that financiers and their spokesmen adopted monetarist views purely because they thought that the promulgation of those views would line their own pockets.

Two other reasons for acceptance of monetarist views in City circles can be adduced. There is the matter of political judgement which I mentioned above in relation to the Tories; the idea that incomes policy was a dangerous failure and that monetary restraint was the only way to cure inflation in the long run. And the control of inflation has a special importance for financiers since inflation erodes the 'real' value of financial assets and can turn even very high interest rates into negative 'real' rates. On the Keynesian view the costs of monetary restraint would be too high, but what monetarism offered here was a rationalisation of deflation, a theoretical guarantee that any effects of monetary restraint on ouput and employment would be merely temporary since variations in the money supply ultimately affect only monetary variables. Now a rationalisation does not necessarily become convincing merely because it is convenient, and here I come to my second point: the monetary theory of inflation appears to be daily confirmed in the markets for financial assets. Unlike 'real' commodities, financial assets have no cost of production and therefore the 'cost push' theory of inflation cannot apply. Financial markets are very peculiar markets, quite unlike the markets for industrially-produced commodities or for labour power: buying and selling take place continuously; operators have very full information concerning prices; and the *stock* of existing financial assets changing hands is always much greater than any new issues of assets. These features give financial markets the peculiar property that an inflow of new funds to the market will immediately drive up the prices of the assets being traded (and an outflow immediately reduce prices). A sudden increase in the monetary demand for, say, cars will first lead to the running down of stocks, then perhaps to increased output to match the demand. The price may or may not be raised, depending on the policy of the enterprises in question. But an increase in the monetary demand for, say, government bonds, US dollars, or company shares is bound to inflate the prices of those assets, unless the authorities take specific offsetting action. My suggestion is that agents in day-to-day contact with the latter kind of market will tend to find the purely monetary theory of inflation confirmed by their experience in a way in which industrialists and union leaders, for instance, will not.

It must be said, however, that the turn to 'monetarism' within both the Tory party and financial capitalist circles was not wholly dependent on the credibility of the theory which promised that monetary restriction would have no more than a passing effect on real output and employment. That is, it may be possible to interpret the 'monetarist' move as at least in part linked to the calculation that even if monetary restriction were to have a real recessionary 'cost' there was no alternative if inflation was to be reduced substantially and permanently. If this meant confronting the unions rather than conducting deals over incomes policy, then so be it.

Once the analysts and operators on the main financial markets had adopted a monetarist outlook, this put an important constraint on government policy. Any policies which appeared irresponsible from a monetarist viewpoint would lead to speculation against government stock and/or the pound, not necessarily out of political motivation, but on the basis of perceived economic self-interest: if one reckons that a given policy will lead to higher interest rates, then one gets out of gilts; if one reckons that the pound is going to slide as a result of expansionary policy, then one sells sterling. And in this way the monetarist expectations are self-fulfilling.

The IMF intervention of 1976, as noted in the previous chapter, with its conditions of adherence to specified restrictions on public sector borrowing and the growth of the money supply, obviously strengthened the hand of indigenous monetarism. In effect, the ideology and practices prevalent within British financial institutions, the intervention of the IMF and the doubts already present among the Labour leaders concerning the validity of Keynesianism were mutually reinforcing. If monetarism was still a minority position with British universities and even the Treasury, it made great gains as a theoretical ideology imposed upon/employed by government (Healey's monetary targetry from 1976). The field of economic ideology was prepared for the advance of the fully-committed monetarism of Thatcher, Joseph et al.

Monetarism and the 'social market' doctrine

'Monetarism' in the strict sense of the Quantity Theory of money is not *logically* tied to the social market doctrine or to anti-statism generally. It would be possible, for instance, to accept the propositions (a) that inflation is caused by excessive growth of the money supply and (b) that such monetary growth is the result of large scale public sector borrowing, but also to hold that inflation is not a serious problem. Or, if one accepted propositions (a) and (b) and also believed that the control of inflation was of prime importance, it would be possible to argue that public sector borrowing should be reduced by means of increased taxation, that public services and industrial support policies should be expanded even, but should be financed by means of, say, more progressive income tax, taxation of wealth and withdrawal of tax relief on the various forms of personal saving. This hypothetical position would in fact have the advantage over Thatcherist doctrine of economic feasibility, since increased taxation in these forms would be much more effective in reducing public sector borrowing than expenditure cuts.[9] In practice, however, the re-emergence of the Quantity Theory of money has been closely linked with a thorough-going critique of the usurpations of the state within the social democratic 'mixed economy' and the re-affirmation of the virtues of the market as an allocative mechanism. For Friedman and Hayek, for the ideologues of the Institute of Economic Affairs and the Centre for Policy Studies, inflationary growth of the money supply is no accident. It is the classic symptom of an over-mighty state, resorting to the 'printing press' when it can no longer screw any more tax revenue out of the populace. If the post-war expansion of public expenditure has not been undertaken merely for the self-aggrandisement or military adventures of the rulers, as in an earlier era, but partly out of a misguided philanthropic intent, that neither excuses the agents of public-sector profligacy nor mitigates the consequent debauch of the currency. And it is this conception which has inspired Thatcher and her associates more than any technical arguments concerning the 'real balance effect' or debates over the relative generality of Keynesian and neoclassical theory. Let us look more closely at the free market ideology which is tied up with Thatcher's monetarism.

As with the Quantity Theory, the theory which affirms the efficiency of the market is by no means new. It is a revival in new circumstances of the neoclassical economics which developed in Austria in the late nineteenth and early twentieth centuries as an explicit ideological riposte to Social Democracy, a thorough theoretical defence of Capitalism (one can trace it back to Adam Smith, but from the neoclassical point of view Smith was not rigorous enough — a pioneer, but unfortunately encumbered with misleading notions such as a labour theory of value). Neoclassical theory 'proves', on the basis of highly restrictive assumptions, that the competitive market mechanism will lead to an equilibrium in which firms produce the goods which consumers value most highly, using the lowest-cost methods of production. It is admitted that there are certain 'public goods' such as defence, policing and lighthouses which unfortunately cannot be supplied by the market mechanism, but these goods form a strictly circumscribed category: any goods or services which *can* be supplied by the market will be supplied with the greatest possible efficiency.

Now this position, as we have seen, was not attacked by Keynes (Keynes argued merely that market equilibrium was not necessarily achieved at the full-employment level of aggregate demand) but it did come under *de facto* attack by social democrats of left and right over the post-war years. The idea that the state could organise the health service better than the market, that the state should play a greater role in education, that certain industries could be better run as nationalised enterprises not necessarily aiming at maximum profitability, that the state could usefully 'distort' the market by means of regional policy, industrial policy, incomes policy etc. — these ideas which were the common currency of Labour and Tory governments after 1945 (and were, of course, not unique to Britain) all involve the assumption that the market is seriously defective as a mechanism for achieving social ends, even for achieving a healthy and profitable growth of private industry. However, the kind of pragmatism which led to the extension of state intervention, partly to satisfy popular demands and partly to meet the demands of large scale capitalist industry,[10] was by its nature not susceptible to formulation as a rigorous theoretical system at par with neoclassical economics. So when it 'failed' in the British case it was vulnerable to ideological attack from the neoclassical camp.

What does the 'failure' of state intervention, which opened a space for the resurgence of social market ideology, actually amount to? We already have the elements of an answer in the account of political developments in the previous chapter and in the discussion of the 'failure of Keynesianism' given above. The main points here are (a) the failure of state intervention to carry through a restructuring of industry and trade relations sufficient to alleviate the balance of payments constraint on growth (closely connected with the unpopular rise in personal taxation which has been required to finance recession); (b) the political failure of prices and income policy as a means of controlling inflation; and (c) the growing popular dissatisfaction with the bureaucratic form of provision of public services. I shall examine each of these points in turn.

(a) *The balance of payments constraint.* I have already outlined the problem here: the export performance and propensity to import of the UK economy are such that fiscal expansionism designed to promote growth and employment consistently runs into the barrier of an escalating balance of payments deficit. And experience over the 1970s shows that an 'over-valued exchange rate' is definitely not the only obstacle here. In principle there are two ways in which this constraint might be overcome: by becoming *more* competitive on the world market (raising export volumes and reducing the propensity to import), or by *withdrawing* from competition (i.e. setting up import controls which would forcibly reduce the propensity to import). These strategies may be seen in combination — it can be argued that the imposition of import controls would provide a 'breathing space' to restructure industry for greater competitiveness in future — or they may be presented as alternatives. But although successive governments have willingly taken responsibility for breaking the balance of payments constraint they have proved incapable of carrying either strategy to the point of success. As regards the strategy of increasing competitiveness we have seen that neither 'planning' on the Wilsonian model, nor the less grandiose industrial policy of later years, nor devaluation of the currency, have proved equal to the task. The state has simply lacked the material means to carry out the radical restructuring of industry (in terms of sectoral distribution, investment patterns and social relations within enterprises) which would have been necessary to boost productivity, cut unit costs and overcome the fossilisation of Britain's industrial structure. Governments neither desired (with the possible exception of Heath) nor were politically able to impose an outright 'capitalist' solution in the sense of breaking working class resistance to state-backed managerial dictation, and anyway there is no evidence that British management, given a clear run, could have greatly increased industrial competitiveness. On the other side, the organised working class has never been unified around a programme of radical restructuring on its own terms, so that even if Labour governments had wished to impose a 'working class' solution to the declining competitive position of British industry that too would have lacked an adequate material basis. As regards the forcible limitation of imports, while there have been pressures in this direction from sections of industry and the trade unions, and while certain temporary and limited measures have been taken, this option has not to date been adopted as a consistent strategy. Governments, even if inclined in this direction, have had to consider the political difficulties both in terms of the possible reaction of Britain's major trading partners (particularly since joining the EEC) and in terms of the sacrifice of popular consumption standards which would be involved, at least in the short to medium term.

With the balance of payments constraint unbroken, the preservation of the external balance has necessarily involved periodic deflation and foreign loans (generally with deflationary conditions attached). Unemployment has inevitably risen and growth slowed, frustrating the popular expectations of the earlier post-war years and aggravating the struggle over the distribution of national income, with its inflationary consequences. In addition to the profits/wages struggle analysed by Glyn and Sutcliffe (1972), taxation has played an important role here. Quite apart from expenditure on social service programmes, governments have been obliged to spend increasing sums merely to cope with the consequences of slow growth and deflationary policy, in the form of support for both ailing industries and the unemployed. This has pushed up the tax burden on the employed workforce, bringing ever broader strata of the working population into the 'tax net', and further intensified the distributional struggle.[11]

(b) *The political failure of incomes policy.* The failure of incomes policy has two sides. On the one hand governments have been unable to use incomes policy as a unilateral discipline over wage-bargaining in the face of trade union resistance. They have been obliged to find an accommodation with the trade unions over the question, and the problem has been that the acceptability of incomes policy among union members has proved temporary and unstable. On the other hand, the organised working class has proved unable to *exploit* incomes policy as a means of restructuring the distribution of National Income and extending the scope of collective bargaining. Let me try to justify the second, more controversial, part of this claim.

I examined in the previous chapter the conjunctural factors which first sustained the acceptability of incomes policy in the period 1975-78 then led to its breakdown. Now this breakdown arguably lost Labour support in two ways. First, many union members who had seen their real wages falling over previous years resented Callaghan's autocratic insistence on further stringent wage restraint and second, when the union revolt came, people who did *not* support the strikers against the

pay limit lost their faith in Labour as the party which could deal with
the unions, the 'natural party of government'. The Tories were able,
opportunistically, to make political capital on both counts, to say to
the disaffected workers that they would not impose an incomes policy
and to the anti-striker public that they would legislate to control the
'abuse' of union power. This irony has important implications. It suggests strongly that 'free collective bargaining' over wages is not a means
of forging unity among the working class. This in turn suggests that
the trade union movement could have been on much stronger ground
had it *used* incomes policy instead of just resisting it, if instead of
pushing for a return to free collective bargaining it had pushed for a definite *quid pro quo* in terms of industrial policy and workers' control.
This view is, of course, contested on the left. Arthur Scargill expressed
a common view among left-wing union militants when he said, in
criticism of *any* incomes policy, 'You cannot plan one element of a
totally unplanned economy. You can't have a system of free enterprise and then seek to regulate one factor within it' (Scargill, 1981).
But this principled position avoids the question of whether incomes
policy might be used as a means of forcing the introduction of further
elements of planning; the planned economy, it seems, must come all
at once. Equally, it avoids the point that free wage bargaining can
be seriously divisive. Perhaps the main fear of incomes policy on the
left is that although 'in principle' it might have certain attractions,
in practice it would mean the demobilisation of the shop stewards'
movement and the concentration of power in the hands of the centralised union bureaucracies acting in collusion with the state. But here
Hirst's comment is apposite:

> 'there is no reason why the powers of shop stewards need be weak-
> ened by a successful incomes policy. What is needed is the develop-
> ment of new objectives and new forms of struggle at enterprise level.
> The scope of bargaining must be extended from questions of imme-
> diate personal benefits to questions of enterprise policy and opera-
> tion' (Hirst, 1981, p. 56).

This is a challenge for the future: we know that these 'new objectives'
and 'new forms of struggle' were not sufficiently developed over the
1970s and that most union leaders continued to think of incomes policy
as a temporary crisis measure which should give way as soon as possible
to business as usual.

    To conclude on the question of the 'failure of incomes policy', I believe that this failure should be seen at two levels. First there is the specific conjunctural collapse of Callaghan's 5 per cent limit over the winter of 1978-79 which greatly undermined the credibility of the Labour government and helped to hand the 1979 election to the Tories. But then at a deeper level, there is the impasse of the trade union movement — strong enough, in certain sections, to resist successfully government pay restraint measures yet at once unable to achieve a hegemonic appeal on a platform of unrestrained wages struggle and unready to trade off free bargaining in the labour market against the achievement of broader social and economic objectives.

(c) *Bureaucracy and the welfare state.* Popular dissatisfaction with the workings of the 'welfare state' has emerged as a central theme in recent Marxist writing on Thatcherism. It is argued that Thatcher was able to capitalise on a widespread feeling among the working class that state provision means unresponsive bureaucracy, arbitrary authority and in many cases humiliation for those receiving state benefits. It is also argued that this problem goes to the heart of social democracy, that the Labour Party with its faith in *state* ownership and *state* provision has set itself up for the Thatcherist attack, by failing to question the social form in which state services are provided and administered. Corrigan made the point some years ago:

> 'The British working class has struggled hard for the provision of welfare but has done so without any concrete appreciation of the need for specific class policies and administrative forms' (1977, p. 93).

More recently the London Edinburgh Weekend Return Group (1979) said, of the Tory opposition to centralised bureaucracy and state control, 'these policies are attractive to working class people because they speak to their experience of the state' (p. 64). Leonard (1979) has put forward a similar view, noting in particular the basis for the Tory policy of council house sales: 'The ghettoisation and poor quality of council housing together with authoritarian housing management... contributes to the legitimation of the policy of selling council houses' (p. 10). Hall (1980) has elaborated the notion of social democratic 'statism', as an ideology in which the state appears as a 'neutral beneficiary' and a class practice in which the 'dominated classes' are represented as 'passive recipients', as clients of a state run by experts and professionals over which people exercised no real or substantive control' (p. 27).

There is undoubtedly an important point here. The dominant Fabian tradition within British socialism is strongly paternalistic, and 'statist' in the sense which Hall has elaborated. Social progress has been seen as something to be achieved by wise governments rather than by popular struggle. Socialists in the Fabian tradition have in the past praised Stalin's Russia, but have not incorporated in their conception of socialism the kind of comments which Marx made on the Paris Commune, or which Lenin made in 'State and Revolution', on the paramount need to break down the 'state' as a distinct bureaucratic apparatus (or set of apparatuses) and to foster popular participation and accountability in administration. Therefore although one cannot write off state welfare services as merely 'requirements of capital', in the functionalist mode,[12] it is true that these services have generally been administered in a bureaucratic and unaccountable manner. And this has had differential effects on the 'manual' working classes and the 'educated' middle classes. The educated middle classes have been in a much better position to discover and demand their rights, to avoid intimidation by state-employed professionals and have done relatively well out of the welfare services. The manual working classes, the council tenants and the unemployed, generally *dependent* on state benefits and services to a greater extent than other groups, have tended to experience the state as more alien and oppressive — talking a bureaucratic language which is hard to understand, carefully policing their eligibility for benefits, fobbing them off with the mystique of professional expertise. This is perhaps a caricature, but it does help to explain the apparent 'paradox' of the working class turning against the 'socialist' welfare state. It connects with the comments in the previous chapter concerning Hindess' account of the decline of working class influence in the Labour Party, and the resulting tendency for the party to pursue a form of politics which is oblivious to the day-to-day interaction between working class people and the state apparatuses. It also clearly is of considerable importance as regards revitalising the 'popular image' of socialism: to return to the quotation from Corrigan, there is indeed a need to develop 'specific class policies', in the sense of maximising benefits where they are needed most, and new administrative forms which will be as transparent and open to popular participation as possible.

The Thatcherist fusion and the Tory party

As Stephenson (1980, p.17) has pointed out, Thatcher became leader

of the Tory party 'not by emerging as a candidate of the party establishment, but by a bold commando raid whilst that establishment was in
disarray after the second 1974 election defeat'. Heath and his supporters had suffered a double demoralisation, first when the Selsdon
programme was abandoned in the face of 'political realities' and then
again when the nation failed to endorse Heath's stand against the usurpations of the trade unions in February '74. The way was open for
the radical right tendency which was pushing for a clear re-definition
of Conservatism as an anti-state, free market political force, and for
a break with patrician 'crisis avoidance'. For a time Keith Joseph
looked a credible candidate for the leadership of this tendency, and
the party. Joseph staked out his view, that post-war economic policy
and the Heath government's economic policy in particular had been
entirely wrong, in a major speech in Preston in September '74. But
this challenge was then followed by a further speech in which he
alienated much of his support by suggesting that the nation's stock
was degenerating as a result of a high birth rate among the poor. Tories
may think these thoughts but it is bad form to voice them from a
political platform. With Joseph's political judgement in doubt, it was
Thatcher who emerged as the candidate able to win the leadership
for the new right.

Over the years from 1975 to 1979 the Thatcher faction managed
to make the political running in the Tory party. It did not capture
all the key posts in the Opposition, and did not allay the scepticism
of many 'traditional' patrician Tories, but nonetheless became the
dominant tendency, able to define party policy and philosophy. The
Thatcherites were able to exploit, amplify and fuse the ideological currents which I have examined above: the perceived failure of Keynesianism and state intervention in economic policy, the rise of
monetarism in the City, the resurgent neoclassicism of the IEA,
popular dissatisfaction with the welfare state and 'high taxation',
resentment at the disruptive activities of the trade unions. Joseph taught
Thatcher his monetarism, and Thatcher lent to theoretical 'anti-
statism' a petty bourgeois passion and populist mode of expression
which Joseph could not muster. As the ideology cohered, it provided
a pole of attraction for certain Tory 'progressives' of earlier years who
now recognised the error of their ways (Howe, for instance), and for
old stagers like Thorneycroft who had never quite approved of Tory
progressivism since the days of Macmillan. And it was undoubtedly
more in tune with the 'grassroots' Toryism of the constituencies than
Heath's post-Selsdon modernism had ever been. For instance, if

monetarism taught that inflation was the result of an excessive state budget deficit, Thatcher could link this to the 'commonsense' of 'every housewife' and every petty bourgeois — the need for careful budgeting and the dangers of debt.

There were some discreet challenges to the direction the party was taking. Sir Ian Gilmour, the most literate of the traditional Tory rearguard, published in 1977 his 'Inside Right' in which he took a long historical perspective on the Tory party and claimed it as the party of moderation and balance. The essence of true Toryism was the avoidance of grand theoretical systems (such as that of the monetarists) and the painstaking maintenance of a broad 'national' constituency, as seen in the practice of Halifax, Disraeli, Baldwin and Macmillan. To stir up populist antagonism against the Civil Service and even the trade unions was, by implication, to betray Tory principles. But it was precisely the system-less 'moderation' and trimming of the Callaghan government which Thatcher was attacking, to considerable effect. Gilmour was not alone in his doubts, but in the aftermath of Heath's defeat the doubters could not deflect the leadership from its chosen course.

Outside of the Tory party itself, among the electorate, indications were not so clear. On the one hand opinion polls consistently showed Thatcher to be markedly less popular than her party, and there is no evidence that Joseph was ever a popular man. In the latter half of 1978 when Labour's moderation and 'governance' seemed to be paying dividends, Thatcherism did not appear to be the inevitable inheritor of the 'failure of social democracy'. On the other hand, the Institute of Economic Affairs (and other) opinion polls showed a consistent decline in support for high-taxation, high public expenditure policies, particularly among the working class and even among Labour supporters. As I argued in the previous chapter, it was the particular conjuncture of 1978-79 which tipped the electoral balance, with its combination of well-publicised industrial disruption, and blatant parliamentary opportunism on the part of the Callaghan government. Thatcher's radicalism gained an electorally crucial margin of credibility over Callaghan's 'safe' no-change governance. One can trace the extent of this shift in the results of the 1979 election, and of the surveys which accompanied it.[13]

The 1979 election saw a slight recovery in turnout, and in the proportion of the vote cast for the two major parties relative to 1974; to this extent the 'verdict of the polls' was more decisive. But the Tory lead over Labour (some two million votes) owed more to a slump in

Labour support than to a surge of Tory support: the proportion of the electorate voting Tory in 1979 (33 per cent) was lower than in 1970. One can disaggregate the vote, and hence gain a clearer view of the pattern of party allegiance, in three ways: (a) by previous party support; (b) by 'social class' (the data available are based on the market research A to E scale); and (c) by region.

a)   In terms of previous party support, the 1979 result was much affected by a two way traffic in Liberal votes. Almost half of the 1974 Liberal voters defected, splitting in a ratio of around 3 to 1 in favour of the Tories over Labour. It would appear that many marginal Tories disaffected by Heath were willing to throw in their lot with Thatcher five years later. Opinion surveys showed that the issue of taxation was a particularly important influence on these Liberal defectors. On the other hand the Liberals picked up some voters who had supported one or other major party in 1974. Labour lost 10 per cent of its 1974 supporters in this way, as against only 4 per cent for the Tories. Evidently there were many erstwhile Labour supporters disaffected by the experience of the Callaghan government, yet not thinking in terms of the 'failure of social democracy' and unwilling to give their votes to Thatcher.

b)   Looking at the vote in terms of 'social class' (see Table 7.1), it appears that the swing to the Tories (and collapse of Liberal support) since 1974 was greatest among skilled manual workers. In this group the Tories increased their share of the vote by 18 per cent, nearly drawing level with the Labour vote. There was also a substantial swing to the Tories among semi- and unskilled manual workers, although here there was a smaller reservoir of Liberal support to drain back to Toryism and Labour's diminished share of the vote was still well ahead of the Tories'. The pattern at the other end of the social scale is interesting: although the A and B groups together gave far more of their votes to the Tories than to Labour the increase in the Tory share of the vote was only marginal, and *less* than the increase in Labour's share. It is safe to assume that much of the increase in Labour support here came from the public sector salariat who saw their position clearly threatened by Thatcherism.

c)   The geography of party support which emerged from the 1979 election showed a strengthening of the demarcation lines between Labour and Tory territory. To an even greater extent than before Labour's main electoral strength lay north of the Trent and in the inner cities. In Scotland and the north of England the swing to the Tories was very much below the national average and Labour received

Table 7.1   *Electoral Support in 1979 by Social Class*

% of total vote in 1979 and change in that share since October 1974.

	May 1979			Change since 1974		
	Con	Lab	Lib	Con	Lab	Lib
Professional and Managerial						
(AB)	65	17	15	+ 2	+ 5	– 7
Office & Clerical (C1)	57	21	20	+ 6	– 3	– 1
Skilled Manual (C2)	44	45	10	+ 18	– 4	– 10
Semi and unskilled Manual						
(D)	31	53	12	+ 9	– 4	– 4

Source: adapted from 'the Economist' (1980).

substantially more votes than the Tories (the most cheering result for Labour was the unseating of that caricature Thatcherist, Teddy Taylor, in Glasgow). Voters in the north tended to regard inflation and unemployment as the main issues, and to be sceptical about Tory policy with regard to these issues. The Tories, on the other hand, were strongest in suburban and rural areas and in the south of England. Here the issues of strikes, taxes and law and order were given a higher priority than in the North. But perhaps the most crucial marginal shift of allegiance came in the Midlands, the site of the biggest pro-Tory swing among skilled manual workers.

The aggregate result of the vote, which gave the Tories a comfortable parliamentary majority of 44 seats, must therefore be seen as the product of a complex pattern of cross-currents: skilled workers who had seen their pay differentials eroded under incomes policy deserting Labour and the Liberals for the Tories, particularly in the South and the Midlands; working people who had lost faith in the 'welfare state' being attracted by the promise of tax cuts and an attack on bureaucracy; salaried public sector employees shifting to Labour, maybe out of plain self-interest given the menacing Tory talk about 'bureaucracy' and 'unproductive jobs', and maybe out of conviction in the 'caring' intent of social democracy.

These, and other, cross-currents marked a further stage in the breakdown of the 1960's pattern of 'working class'/Labour and 'middle class'/Tory partisanship, a development which becomes clearer in the light of opinion survey results of the time. There are two main points here. First, the surveys show a further weakening of subjective 'class identification' among the electorate, linked with a further dissociation of the elements which had previously combined to form distinct popular images of 'working class' and 'middle class'. As Crewe (1981) puts it,

> 'The British election study found that at the last election less than half of the electorate even thought of themselves as belonging to a social class. The number of electors with uniformly middle class or working class characteristics — in terms of occupation, family origins, house ownership etc. — was only one in five'.

Second, although the two-party *vote* had picked up to some extent since 1974 the substantive commitment of voters to the party of their choice had not. Only 20 per cent of voters were found to have a 'very strong' Conservative or Labour identification (as against 40 per cent in 1964). This weakening was most marked on the Labour side: although Labour still picked up a majority of votes among the manual working classes, from communities in which Tory voting would be virtually unthinkable, the proportion of Labour identifiers supporting the time-hallowed party policies was at its lowest ebb. Only 32 per cent of Labour identifiers supported more nationalisation, 30 per cent favoured increasing expenditure on social services and 36 per cent did not believe that trade unions have too much power. In fact, many Labour supporters actively approved of policies put forward by the Tories, such as council house sales and more spending on law and order. Such approval as there was for Labour's social democratic 'statist' policies tended to be concentrated among the 'professional and managerial' strata.

In interpreting these points, it is important to stress that the weakening of the 'class'/party link was a double process: on the one hand it is true that neither party presented itself in 'class' terms — both appealed to the 'nation'. Neither party, in other words, attempted to make 'class' into the politically pertinent basis of collectivity. But equally there is no evidence that a party offering an explicit 'class' cue could have made much headway at the time. In particular there was no ready-made 'class politics' which could have united industrial workers, and sufficient of the salariat, to form a winning bloc for Labour.

Where Thatcherism came from — reprise

In this section I have stressed the complexity of the conditions which combined to permit a Thatcherism-dominated Tory party to form a government in 1979. Thatcherist ideology does not 'represent' a pre-constituted class interest, but as we have seen it draws upon the concerns of a wide range of social collectivities: the monetarism of financial circles; the neo-classicism of right-wing intellectuals among the 'ideological classes'; the classic anti-tax, anti-debt ideologies of the petty bourgeoisie; the widespread concern over disruptive union power (even among union members); working class objection to wage restraint, rising taxation and state bureaucracy. I have outlined the particular political conditions under which this ideological amalgam could achieve a position of dominance, first within the Tory party and then at the level of national electoral politics, and in this context I have stressed the weakness of the incumbent orthodoxy which Thatcherism opposed: first the demoralisation of the Tory 'left' or statist wing, incapable of offering the party any direction after 1974, then in 1979 the political bankruptcy of Labour. These conditions at the level of party politics must in turn be set against the background of certain broader developments: the world wide inflationary recession of the mid '70's which sapped the confidence in 'Keynesianism' of governments everywhere, and the long-term failure of state interventionist measures to halt the relative decline of the British economy.

The question arises as to whether it is possible to condense all these elements under a generalised claim of the order that the rise of Thatcherism represents an historic response to the crisis of the foregoing 'social democratic consensus', an authentic attempt to break the 'stalemate' in the class struggle referred to in the previous chapter. It is true that Thatcherism does mark a break with the bi-partisan baseline, in Stuart Hall's phrase, from which both Tory and Labour governments have governed since the war. To give two indices: the proposition that the government cannot usefully assume any responsibility for maintaining the level of employment breaks with the thinking which goes back to the National Government's White Paper on employment policy of 1944; the determination to pursue certain economic policies entirely regardless of trade union opposition breaks with the implicit commitment to tripartite discussion and accommodation which can also be traced back to the war. Although there are post-war antecedents to Thatcher's 'free market' ideology (the Selsdon Heath), monetarism (under Healey as Chancellor) and restrictive policy vis-à-vis the unions (In Place of Strife, the Industrial Relations Act), and although the Labour government of 1974-79 presided over levels of unemployment which would have been thought outrageous even in the 1960s, it is clear enough that the rejection of expansionary demand management and tripartite accommodation on the part of Thatcherism is far more thorough-going than ever before. Thatcherism has quite self-consciously undertaken to carry out a counter-revolution against what it sees as the 'creeping socialism' inherent in the post-war consensus. And this counter-revolution certainly cannot be conceived as an arbitrary political choice on the part of the Thatcherite cohort of Tory politicians. I have tried to show that the existence of Thatcherism as a serious political force is grounded in an impasse confronting the foregoing mode of socio-economic development.

What remains to be seen, however, is just how much of an 'historic' turning point the rise of Thatcherism will prove to be. The stakes here are obviously very high: if Thatcherism can 'succeed', if the Thatcher government really has a programme capable of regenerating British capitalism, and of carrying a substantial social bloc along with that course, by anti-socialist means, then clearly the kind of *socialist* transformations of economic class relations discussed earlier, and put forward as potential means of breaking out of the circle of relative economic decline, are off the agenda for a long time to come. If, at the other extreme, Thatcherism proves an historic dead end, an outright 'failure' incapable of regenerating the national economy or sustaining popular support then there may be a more auspicious opportunity than ever before for putting forward a socialist alternative, although in this case there will also be powerful forces working for 'neither Thatcherism nor Socialism', i.e. for a return to a (revamped) social democratic centre politics. There remains, however, a third possibility, which is that although Thatcherism fails in an economic sense, with continuing stagnation of output, weak balance of payments position and very high unemployment in the UK, it nonetheless 'succeeds' politically, at least in the sense that the Tory Party wins a further general election and forms another government. Such a possibility, virtually unthinkable in 1980 or 81, became alarmingly real in 1982.

The next two sections of this chapter are addressed to aspects of this complex of problems. In section 7.2 below I shall concentrate on the 'economic core' of the Thatcherist programme. In opposition, this programme gave an appearance of clarity and coherence but I shall argue that it is fundamentally unrealistic, being based on a radical misapprehension regarding the conditions required for the successful accumulations of capital. In other words, I wish to claim that Thatcherism cannot fulfil the particular 'historic' role which it has set for itself. In the light of this claim I shall examine some of the economic effects of Thatcherism in practice. In section 7.3 I shall return to the politics of support for and opposition to Thatcherism.

7.2   The Economic contradictions of Thatcherism

In general terms, the principal economic commitment of Thatcherism is to 'roll back the state' and create incentives for the famous 'entrepreneurs' of free enterprise. So much was also true of Heath in the Selsdon phase, but the monetarist component of Thatcherism gives a more precise programmatic commitment. The new monetarism places a special emphasis on the achievement of a steady reduction in the level of public sector borrowing (the Public Sector Borrowing Requirement or PSBR), since it is believed that excessive borrowing is the cause of the growth of the money stock which in turn is the root cause of inflation. The full argument is actually more complex, and contains a conditional element: public sector borrowing can be financed in two broad ways, either by sales of financial assets (Treasury stock) to non-bank financial institutions or private individuals — which does not expand the money stock — or by borrowing from the banking system, which creates new money. But to sell extra stock the government has to offer attractive yields, and the greater the bond sales needed the greater the upward pressure on interest rates. So a high level of government borrowing, on this view, has two possible and equally undesirable effects: either it pushes up interest rates or contributes to inflationary growth of the money stock. Either way, it undermines the project of regenerating private enterprise, since high interest rates crowd out private sector investment and inflation weakens the market order generally (in particular, inflation in excess of that in the country's main trading partners weakens national competitiveness). The dual project of ensuring a steady reduction of the PSBR and of the rate of growth of the money stock was therefore given pride of place among the government's economic aims, and was formalised in the Chancellor's 'medium term financial strategy'.

Now, as I remarked earlier, the PSBR, which is the gap between public sector revenue and expenditure, could in principle be reduced by means of higher taxation, but this course obviously flies in the face of the avowed aims of Thatcherism. In order to create incentives, as well as maintain the political support of the many Tory voters who were attracted by the promise of tax cuts without necessarily having any appreciation of the finer points of monetarism, the Tories were clearly obliged to cut rather than raise taxes — or at least to appear to be so doing. This then put public expenditure under a double squeeze: cuts were required both to satisfy the general aim of reducing the role of the over-mighty state, and also to balance the conflicting aims of cutting taxation and cutting the PSBR. This can be seen most starkly in the following presentation, where G stands for public expenditure and T for public sector revenue:

$$PSBR = G - T$$

If the intention is to cut both the PSBR and T then a sharp drop in G is clearly a prime necessity.

Creating prosperity while cutting the PSBR by means of expenditure-reduction, sufficient to make room for substantial tax cuts: it is this project which is impossible, despite Thatcher's personal conviction that it can be done if the government only emulates the thrifty housewife or small businessman and 'lives within its means'. The basis for my argument here has already been laid out in chapter 4, on classes and the financial circulation. There it was shown that the financial surpluses and financial deficits of the various sectors of the economy (public sector, corporate sector, personal sector, and overseas sector) must sum to zero. In other words one sector can reduce its deficit only to the extent that the other sectors' combined surplus is reduced. So, more specifically, the public sector financial deficit can be reduced only to the extent that the personal sector surplus falls and/or the corporate sector deficit rises and/or the overseas sector deficit rises. The financial circulation process is a system of interdependencies, and the massive public sector is simply not able to cut its borrowing unilaterally in the way a housewife or small businessman may.

Let us consider the mechanisms of financial interdependency more closely. Public sector expenditure has both discretionary and mandatory components. The level of expenditure on supply services, capital investment programmes, industrial aid and so on is discretionary in the sense that, formally at any rate, it is a matter for government decision. On the other hand the level of expenditure on supplementary benefit, unemployment benefit, pensions and so on is not under government control — once the government has set the *rate* for these transfer payments the volume of expenditure is determined by the number of eligible applicants claiming their rights. Public sector revenue has a formal similarity with mandatory expenditure in this sense, since once the government has set the rates of income tax, VAT, charges for services, and nationalised industry prices, the actual *volume* of revenue is determined by the level of taxable income and transactions. So the overall impact on public sector finances of a cut in discretionary spending crucially depends upon its repercussions for mandatory expenditures and public sector revenues, and that in turn depends on the reactions of the other economic sectors. In general terms, a reduction in discretionary public expenditure is bound to reduce the incomes of the other sectors of the domestic economy — either the corporate sector (reduced orders for enterprises which supply the public sector) or the personal sector (public sector redundancies). Either way, this reduction will then have the Keynesian 'multiplier' effect on other incomes (as the enterprises supplying the public sector cut their purchases of materials and lay off labour, and/or the redundant public sector employees cut their expenditure). The overall result will be a fall in the level of demand. Now in the short term this may shift some of the public sectors' financial deficit onto the corporate sector, as firms find their revenues reduced and are forced into increased borrowing to cover current costs. But over time firms will react by cutting their expenditure — shelving investment plans and laying off workers — and when this happens unemployment will rise further. This in turn will raise the level of mandatory public sector expenditure on income maintenance and cause public sector revenues to fall (less income tax, VAT, and nationalised industry sales revenue). The PSBR will be driven up. It is a task of considerable complexity to quantify this effect, but the Treasury (1981) has given a conservative estimate of £340 million added directly to the PSBR per 100,000 extra registered unemployed. To summarise, the attempt to cut public sector expenditure will cause a recession, the financial consequences of which will tend to frustrate the objective of reducing the PSBR.

There is, however, one escape route into a recessionary 'equilibrium' of a kind. In the case of domestic economic agents, if the government reduces its (discretionary) payments to those agents this causes a fall in the payments of those agents back to the government, along with a rise in (mandatory) income-maintenance payments on the part of the government. In the 'overseas sector', on the other hand, we have a sector such that a reduction in its income from Britain (i.e. revenue from exports to this country) does not directly cause a significant fall in its payments to Britain. This is mainly for the reason that Britain, as a source of income, is small in relation to the rest of the world. Further, insofar as the income of the rest of the world, or particular parts of it, *is* reduced by British fiscal deflation, the British government has no obligation to make good any of that loss of income through mandatory payments. In other words, the deficit which the government is attempting to reduce can be shifted onto the overseas sector, provided that the deflation is severe enough to drive down imports to a level at which a trade surplus is generated. This situation may become unstable, however, if too many governments emulate the principles of Thatcherism and try to cut their financial deficits at once, bringing competitive deflation and its accompaniment, protectionism, on a broad scale.

So whether the PSBR is reduced following a government policy of cutting expenditure depends on the behaviour of the corporate sector (whether firms cut their expenditure fast enough to shift the financial deficit back onto the state), the personal sector (whether recession reduces this sector's financial surplus) and the overseas sector (whether other countries tolerate a deflation-induced trade surplus on Britain's part, without emulation or retaliation).

Let us examine the economic record of Thatcherism in the light of these propositions. As of 1982 this record could be divided into two phases: a first phase in which *everything* seemed to be going wrong (output and profit rates falling, unemployment soaring, inflation running at a rate of up to twenty per cent, financial targets hopelessly breached), followed by a second phase in which, although the economy remained sunk in recession with unemployment rising, the government was able to claim that inflation was in single figures and falling and that public sector borrowing and money growth were 'under control'.

The first phase first: apart from the severe *political* difficulties of cutting expenditure at all in the first place, given the trimming of plans which had already been going on since 1976, expenditure cuts deepened the recession and pushed the PSBR hopelessly off the course of the medium term financial strategy. The hapless chancellor solemnly explained that the 'unexpected' recession had made it impossible to meet his financial target. The recessionary effects of the attempt to cut the PSBR were compounded by the government's reaction to the continuing high level of borrowing by both itself and the corporate sector. If expenditure cuts were not working then the government tried to get a grip over borrowing (and hence the rapidly expanding money supply) by raising interest rates. Hence the record Minimum Lending Rate (MLR) of 17 per cent from November 1979 till the summer of 1980. Interest rates at such a level were sure to deter *voluntary* borrowing for new investment purposes, but could not deflect the rise in involuntary borrowing as firms struggled to meet current costs, including the increased interest charges on debt already incurred. The effect of high interest rates on the foreign exchanges added another twist, by causing the pound to appreciate against other currencies, hence cutting exporting firms' margins and markets and exposing domestic firms to 'artificially' cheap foreign competition. Deeper recession, more involuntary borrowing, more unemployment, and a further deterioration in public sector finances.

During 1980, when these recessionary effects became increasingly obvious, with registered unemployment rising beyond two millions and manufacturing output and investment slumping, the government's first ploy was to blame the 'world recession'. James Prior, then secretary of state for employment, expressed his 'concern' over the level of unemployment but said that it showed the impact of the world economic downturn on the British economy. Nothing, in other words, to do with the government's economic policies. This is clearly false, and was shown to be false by information published by the Bank of England around the same time. There was a world recession beginning to make itself felt after the rise in world oil prices in 1979, but that could not explain the particular severity of the British recession. As Blake (1980) pointed out, 'the volume of trade in manufactures in the first half of this year in our markets was up 7 per cent on the previous year; the volume of our exports was virtually the same. So our share of world trade has been declining rapidly, no doubt in response to a drop in competitiveness'. That the British recession was largely 'home made' is shown very clearly by the trade figures throughout 1980. Although, as Blake remarks, British export volumes were virtually stagnant between 1979 and 1980, the balance of payments current account began to show large surpluses from early 1980. Partly this can be explained by the rising exchange rate of the pound, which in the short run raised the revenue from a given volume of exports, but the major explanatory factor is the slump in imports of intermediate goods as British industry ran down its production. This effect was so strong that it overwhelmed the 'natural' tendency towards a deficit on the current account with a rising exchange rate, as predicted by the Treasury for 1980.

It is tempting to ascribe the government's failure to unravel the 'paradoxical' effects of its policies to mere stupidity. After all, anyone with a reasonable grasp of Keynesian economics could (and did) predict the severe recessionary effects of public expenditure cuts and high interest rates. But it is important to grasp the image which blinded the Thatcherites to such reasoning. If Britain were Thatcher's ideal world, a world of self-sustaining petty bourgeois convinced of the virtues of the free market, then none of this should have happened. The income returned in the tax cuts of 1979 would have been invested in small enterprises or otherwise stimulated productive effort, economic activity would have increased and the tax base would have widened. By reducing the *rate* of taxation the government would have at once stimulated free enterprise and actually increased total tax *revenue* (this proposition, advanced by the American economist Arthur Laffer, was explicitly endorsed by Thatcher in 1979). Government spending cuts would simply have 'made room' for the expanding claims on resources on the part of the private sector, and the public sector's books would have progressively come into balance. Let us admit some wage-workers into the scene: if they were rational beings, appraised of the Quantity Theory and basing their expectations of future price movements on the government's announced target for growth of the money stock, then they would realise that 'excessive' wage rises could only cause unemployment, and would have adjusted their wage demands accordingly. The inflation rate would have fallen sharply, the international competitive position of the economy would have improved, and net export demand would have risen. National recovery.

Alas, Britain is not this ideal world. Britain's is a capitalist economy (with a large state sector) in which, as I stressed in chapters 3 and 4, the separation of individuals from the means of production has reached an advanced stage. Well-off individuals who receive tax rebates cannot generally put the money 'into the business'. Instead it goes into the bank (or other financial institution), reducing effective demand, so that eventually the government is compelled to borrow it back to pay the costs of recession. The particular form of 'tax cuts' in the 1979 budget is important here. Despite Thatcher's brief flirtation with Laffer the Treasury ministers well realised that a big tax giveaway must conflict with the aim of reducing the PSBR, so the budget was really an exercise in rearranging rather than cutting overall taxation. The form this took was a reduction in income tax (skewed towards the upper income groups) coupled with a sharp rise in indirect taxation (principally VAT). The net effect was to leave the tax burden on lower-paid workers virtually unchanged but to give a large handout to the upper income groups for whom expenditure on consumer goods forms a smaller proportion of income (so that they pay proportionately less VAT). In other words, the big rebates went precisely to those social strata which would be most inclined to add the monies to their stock of savings, increasing the personal sector financial surplus. The other effect of the 1979 tax changes was, of course, to raise retail prices, reinforcing the trend consequent upon the oil-price rise, and since the British trade unions do not base their wage demands on the

Quantity Theory of money but customarily on the prior changes in the cost of living this contributed to a continuing wage-price spiral. Rising labour costs coincided with a rising exchange rate to put industrial enterprises under a double squeeze. Government policy succeeded not only in generating recession, but an inflationary recession at that.

Against this background, the ghost of Heath haunted the Tory party during 1980. As unemployment mounted and recession deepened, and the government's financial plans went by the board, political commentators speculated on the possibility of a 'U turn' back to 'consensus' politics. But such a move was politically and ideologically impossible for Thatcher and her supporters. The Thatcherites had a firmer certitude in their policies than the Selsdon Heath ever had. They maintained, and no doubt believed, that there was 'no alternative' — that fiscal expansionism would drive the PSBR even higher, push up interest rates, expand the money supply faster, and lead to even worse ruination. All the same, although it could not be acknowledged as a radical break, the government was forced into a series of accommodations. The recession was bearing particularly heavily on the nationalised industries, as suppliers of basic commodities to the rest of the economy, and many NEB subsidiaries were in financial trouble as well. The government was forced to recognise that the degree of internal financing envisaged for these enterprises in the 'medium term financial strategy' was (as almost all independent observers had said at the time) out of the question. So along with social security payments, the government was obliged to increase its expenditure in the support of these enterprises. Small profitable sections could be sold off to private financiers but the private sector was hardly interested in taking on British Steel, British Rail, or BL. For Tories who had been expecting the aid to 'lame ducks' to be cut off this was in itself a kind U turn, all the more galling in that Keith Joseph, then at the Department of Industry, was responsible for providing much of the finance.[14] Joseph, unable to impress his civil servants with academic oppositionist pronouncements, had to recognise that his neoclassical ideology was not applicable.

These accommodations had a price, however. If public expenditure could not be cut and the PSBR was out of control then the only course at all compatible with monetarist financial rectitude was to raise taxation. A rise in the actual rate of income tax was considered too much of a blatant contradiction of the Tories' electoral promises, so in the 1980 budget, the mini-budget of late 1980 (the chancellor's 'economic statement') and the budget of 1981 taxation was raised in a number of other less visible ways: increased national insurance contributions; failure to adjust tax thresholds fully in line with inflation; increased duties on alcohol, petrol, tobacco; profits tax on the banks; adjustment of taxation of North Sea oil revenues. All this was in addition to other measures designed to raise public sector revenues such as increased council rents and the raising of nationalised industry prices (those not in direct competition with overseas suppliers) well in excess of the general rate of retail price inflation. One effect of this form of tax increase, bearing as it did upon both industrial costs and retail prices, was to contribute to the maintenance of a double-figure inflation rate into 1981. Also the pattern of taxation was arranged to fall most heavily on lower income groups. Westlake (1981) showed that even if one accounts only income tax and national insurance contributions, the level of taxation on the 'average family' (with two children) rose steadily after the initial hand-out of 1979. For the financial year 1981-82 it was estimated that the proportion of gross earnings taken in tax was 22.8 per cent for a family on two thirds of average earnings, as against 18.7 per cent in the last year of the previous Labour government; 27.5 per cent for a family on average earnings (25.2 per cent under Labour); and 31.3 per cent for a family on twice average earnings (29.9 per cent). To look at it another way, the threshold of income taxation dropped under Howe's chancellorship from 45 per cent of average earnings to 38 per cent. For a family on five times average earnings, however, the proportion taken in tax was estimated at 44.7 per cent for 1981-82, as against 49.8 per cent under Labour.[15]

So no U turn was acknowledged, indeed the idea was firmly quashed on several occasions, but all the same there was a marked discrepancy between the effects of Tory policy and the promises of 1979. This discrepancy was of necessity rationalised by a change of ideological stance. In 1979, Thatcher did not exactly promise a painless adjustment to the new economic order, but the future was certainly painted in rosy colours. She genuinely believed that tax cuts would stimulate enterprises; she claimed that public expenditure cuts would fall only on bureaucracy and waste and would provide an occasion for improving services; the professors told her that any recessionary effects of restrictive monetary policy would be strictly minor and transient. When the recession came it was an unpleasant surprise, caused by difficult world economic conditions and irrational trade unionists. But then as the recession deepened, there came a change in emphasis — a subtle shift towards 'taking credit for the recession'. The most candid expression of the new view was given by relatively junior ministers: Biffen, at the Treasury, with his talk of 'three years of austerity' as the necessary precondition for a return to the realm of 'Gladstonian Freedom'; Nicholas Ridley, at the foreign office, who felt able to vouchsafe to the Conservative ladies of Circencester and Tewkesbury that the unemployed formed a 'useful reserve'. Mr Ridley was reported in the 'Times' as saying:

> 'I have good news for you. Our labour is cheaper to employ than that of our major competitors... We are becoming increasingly competitive internationally. Britain is now a most attractive place for industrial investment'.

At the top levels of the party there was less willingness to admit that the recession was the inevitable result of government policies, but the view was often put that industry would emerge from the recession 'lean and vigorous'. If the new economy could not be born of spontaneous entrepreneurial initiative, perhaps its birth could be forced by the exposure of industry to severe competitive pressures. Trade unions would learn moderation and managers learn to manage and to rationalise their enterprises. Even if the government insisted that it had not caused the recession, it recognised that recession was perhaps no bad thing.

This orientation raised an important question concerning the economic programme of Thatcherism. Was it perhaps the case that all the talk of precise monetary control, stimulation of small businesses, reduction of state bureaucracy and so on, was really beside the point? Did Thatcher have an ulterior programme, the success of which was not be judged against electoral promises or the medium term financial strategy, nor against the petty bourgeois ideology of balancing the books? This is what was suggested by Tony Benn, in his speeches in parliament and elsewhere: it was quite wrong to judge Thatcher, Howe *et al.*, as incompetent or misguided — they knew what they were doing only too well, and that was making a calculated and cynical attempt to break the strength of the organised working class by any available means, in the belief that this alone would permit a profitable regeneration of capitalism. Further, they might be correct in this regard, and the only force that could stop this project from 'succeeding' was the resistance of the organised working class, Thatcherism, in other words, should be seen as the authentic political face of capital itself, behind an increasingly ill-fitting populist mask.

This brings us to the second phase of the economic record of Thatcherism. Over 1982 there was no sustained recovery from recession and unemployment rose inexorably to three and a quarter millions and beyond. Manufacturing output fell to its lowest level for fifteen years. Profits remained depressed. But the Thatcher government could now claim certain 'successes': inflation was, by November, at around seven per cent and falling slowly; the PSBR and growth of the money supply were at last 'on target' (even if the targets had been revised more than once); labour productivity in manufacturing industry had shown quite a sharp increase. A close examination of these 'successes' shows, however, that they were intimately connected with recession. The fall in inflation was entirely explicable in terms of the old-fashioned deflation imposed on the economy, rather than any 'new' monetarist mechanism. The stabilisation of the PSBR depended on reduced personal saving out of reduced personal incomes plus a trade surplus which also depended upon a recession-induced squeeze on imports. The lack of worker militancy clearly reflected the constraint of mass unemployment and the threat of further job-losses: talk of a 'new commonsense on the shopfloor' was mere speculation. The sharp rise in manufacturing productivity reflected in large measure the reduction in industrial capacity (the least productive plant being the first to go).

In this (limited) sense the recession was 'functional' in achieving the 'successes' of Thatcherism, but can one go on to argue that it has laid the basis for a regeneration, that deflationary policy was 'just what capital needed'? I think not, since many of the supposed achievements listed above are unlikely to be maintained outside of the recessionary conditions which produced them. And the idea that, with the working class 'defeated', British capitalism is now in a strong position is quite misleading. The class struggle is not a 'zero-sum game' in which any loss for one side is a gain for the other, and while Thatcherism has undoubtedly inflicted losses on the working class — unemployment, curtailment of union rights, falling living standards and public service provision — it has also inflicted losses on capitalist enterprises. Large and previously successful companies have been forced into profitability crises;[16] large sections of manufacturing capacity have been scrapped; overseas markets have been lost; unemployment and lack of training facilities are building up a potential shortage of skilled labour; resistance to state sector investment plans is weakening the technological capacity of British industry. Of course the effects are not uniform. Some enterprises have doubtless taken advantage of the recession to rationalise and achieve a more competitive adjustment to world market conditions. But the idea that this will happen quite generally, that a good 'shake-out' is the necessary first step on the road to recovery, is belied by the experience of past recessions. The Cambridge Economic Policy Group (1981) have analysed the effects on industry of the recessions of 1967, 1971 and 1975. At an aggregate level, they point out that the '67 and '71 recessions were each followed by two years of rapid growth of output and productivity. After 1975, when the recession was deeper and labour productivity fell, recovery was weaker. In all three cases however, recovery of output and increased productivity depended upon devaluation of the currency and rapid expansion of world trade in manufactured products, leading to a fast growth of exports — a condition which is unlikely to be met after the 1980/81 recession 'because UK cost competitiveness has deteriorated by nearly 50 per cent compared with the situation in the recovery phase of earlier cycles. The level of competitiveness achieved then could not be restored in the early 1980s without a huge and unprecedented devaluation which would have very serious consequences for the rate of inflation' (CEPG, 1981, p. 51). Looking at the trading performance of the different branches of manufacturing industry in more detail, the CEPG conclude that there is no evidence that those branches which undertook shake-outs of labour in the early 1970s 'made any gain in competitiveness relative to those which had expanded their employment. The latter group continued to have a considerably better export performance than those which cut their manpower' (ibid., p.52). The redundancies and closures of earlier recessions, it seems, achieved 'no more and no less than a contraction of the industry in question' (ibid.). And the scale of the contraction achieved makes it probable that in the event of a recovery of domestic demand British industry will be worse placed to respond than before, so that the balance of payments constraint will be tighter than ever.

It might be claimed that this kind of argument misses the point; maybe, given the development of the international division of labour and the changing pattern of competitive advantage, there are branches of industry or particular enterprises which *should*, according to capitalist rationality, simply be wound down, and their resources transferred to more optimal uses. Thre ar two problems here. First, the extremely adverse trading conditions of the current recession have not necessarily hit hardest those industries or enterprises which are 'least efficient'; they have been more arbitrary in their impact. For instance, the over-valued pound bore especially hard on enterprises producing internationally traded commodities with a relatively high price elasticity of demand, such as bulk chemicals, regardless of the efficiency with which those commodities were produced. Or again, the moratorium on council house building hit the building trades hard, regardless of their level of efficiency. Secondly, even if it is true that conditions of generalised recession produce a certain 'weeding out' effect on producers whose market position is most marginal by reason of inefficiency, this is at best only half of a programme for economic regeneration. That is, recession can force the withdrawal of resources (plant, labour power) from certain lines of production but there is no guarantee that market mechanisms will lead to the re-employment of resources in more optimal lines of production. Thatcherist ideology, of course, absolves the government from any responsibility for ensuring this re-deployment and maintains that it will be accomplished by unfettered private initiative. We shall see — the record of the British economy after the return to the gold standard in 1925 is hardly encouraging. And it can be argued that the kinds of transformations of the industrial structure which are called for in the 1980s — development of more 'knowledge-intensive' industries and a broad move 'up market' to reduce the vulnerability of the national economy to competition from the newly-industrialising countries — are transformations which call for a more active role for the state than previous industrial mutations, in terms of developing a skilled, knowledgeable and mobile workforce and funding applicable research and development. In other words, the production of the social surplus product is becoming an increasingly *social* process in the advanced capitalist economies, so that a policy which achieves the object of enforcing labour discipline through the reconstitution of a reserve army of unemployed, at the cost of running down the social preconditions for raising productivity (education cuts for example), appears increasingly myopic.

To summarise the argument of this section: I have maintained that the economic programme of Thatcherism is unrealisable, and that the attempt to put it into effect produced a result which appears highly paradoxical to its supporters: the rapid dwindling of private sector productive capacity. Further, if the Thatcherites have shifted their ground and are inclined to 'take credit for the recession', believing that its purgative effects will lay the basis for a sound economic recovery, it is very doubtful whether even this 'cynical' version of Thatcherism can succeed. Belief in recovery through recession is an act of faith in the adaptive capacities of the market, unsustained by evidence. But if Thatcherism fails in its mission to create a thriving free-market British economy it will clearly not be without real political effects. In the third and final section of this chapter I shall consider the politics of support for, and opposition to, Thatcherism, and try to identify some of the constraints and opportunities for socialism connected with the effects of Thatcherism.

7.3   Political effects of Thatcherism

Over 1980 and 1981 it seemed clear that the specific electoral support bloc which carried Thatcherism to power had already broken up. The manual working class voters who turned to the Tories in large numbers in 1979 had emphatically withdrawn their support, according to the opinion polls.[17] This is hardly surprising, given that much of this support was motivated by the wish to see taxation cut and as we have seen taxation actually increased under the Tories for all but the most highly-paid. Also unemployment rose particularly rapidly in the very industrial areas of England — such as the West Midlands — which provided the biggest pro-Tory swing among working class voters in 1979. Further, any worker voting Tory in expectation of better and less bureaucratic public services would have been sorely disappointed. Polls also indicated that the Tories' electoral lead among the middle classes, which as we have seen was already being eroded by 1979, had declined further: certainly the public sector salariat at all levels had good reason to withdraw support from a party committed to cutting their numbers, privileges and influence, and there must also have been private sector salaried employees who saw Thatcherism in practice as destructive and dangerous for industry.

In this period, that is, the devastating effects of the Thatcher policies on the economy were clearly reflected in a slump in popular support for the Tory government. Aside from the opinion poll data there were plenty of other signs of deep discontent with Thatcherism and its effects, including dissent in the cabinet from the so-called Tory 'wets', trade union arguments against monetarism and demonstrations against unemployment, and a continuing flood of critical declarations emanating from the high-level public sector salariat in the National Enterprise Board and the National Economic Development Council, in the nationalised industries and the Manpower Services Commission, from former top-ranking civil servants, university vice-chancellors, academic economists, education inspectors and even churchmen. The general tenor of most of this criticism was that Thatcher and her associates were carrying out an arbitrary and destructive reversal of the broadly social democratic postulates of post-war British politics; some changes might be necessary but Thatcherism was indulging in dogmatic and dangerous excesses. The social dangers were vividly illustrated by the series of inner city riots during 1981, arguably the spontaneous reaction of those occupying what were already the most disadvantaged loci within the British social formation, to the worsening of their position resulting from deflation and recession.

And if Thatcherism was under fierce attack from left and centre positions in the British political spectrum, there was also vocal criticism from the right. In this case the argument was that the disastrous economic record since 1979 reflected a failure to meet the government's monetarist and 'free market' commitments in a sufficiently rapid and thorough manner. Friedman and Hayek castigated the authorities for failing to control the money supply; Britain's own monetarists, Minford and Peel (1981), thought that the government was in danger of missing its opportunity to carry out the radical reform of the trade unions necessary to cut out the 'inflexibility' of the labour market, which they saw as the cause of unemployment. The CBI too was highly critical of the government's performance, but the criticism forthcoming from this source betrayed political schizophrenia. Most industrialists were committed to the Thatcherist aims of 'sound money' and an end to bureaucratic and socialist waste in the public sector, yet they rebelled against the practical consequences of the pursuit of these aims, such as high interest rates and an overvalued pound. Suffering the consequences of deflation and lack of demand, the CBI still called for deeper cuts in public spending — to match the emasculation of their own businesses, it seemed — although of course industrialists in particular sectors such as building saw little logic in the cutting of the public expenditure which provided their own livelihood. The schizophrenia of British industrialists in this period provides as good an example as any of the problematic nature of class 'interests': while the Thatcher policies were ruining many businesses, the political leaders of corporate capitalism were unable to carry through a political break with the Tory party which so evidently and sincerely *intended* to favour the development of capitalist enterprise.

The scene on the right was, therefore, one of political disarray in 1980 and 81. Yet Thatcher and her close associates, showing political astuteness worthy of Louis Bonaparte, managed to retain their dominance. They made certain tactical concessions — the softening of the original Thatcher line on labour law by James Prior was permitted for a while; confrontation with the miners' union over pit closures was averted by tactical retreat, avoiding Heath's mistake; Thatcher's personal intervention to hold down mortgage interest rates — but such concessions were kept to the minimum necessary for short-term political survival. If public expenditure and monetary controls had failed this was not for want of trying, and if other policies had been toned down this represented a partial accommodation to *realpolitik* rather than a basic change of line. Thatcher and her close associates managed to overrule the cabinet dissenters on what they took to be the crucial issues of fiscal and monetary policy, to pursue deflation even as the recession deepened in 1980, and again in 1981. The Thatcherites were so firmly wedded to the idea that Heath's U turn, his decision to 'cut and run', was a political disaster that they would never willingly concede that their own programme was fundamentally misguided. A decisive break with Thatcherism on the part of the Tory party could occur only if Thatcher herself were displaced from the leadership, and while this possibility was the subject of political speculation in 1981, the challenge from the Tory social democrats proved mainly rhetorical: the ties of loyalty were strong, there was no obvious candidate for leadership of the 'social democratic' tendency within the party and it was not united around any definite alternative programme. The government was deeply unpopular, but Thatcher was still unmistakably in charge.

According to the 'normal' mechanisms of post-war British politics, this apparent failure of the Tories should have led to the expectation of a Labour victory at the next election, but matters were less clear than that. Over 1980 Labour did achieve the greatest support in the polls, but during 1981 political prediction became highly problematic in view of continuing internal conflict in the Labour Party along with the rise of the new Social Democratic Party (SDP) and the moves towards an SDP/Liberal Alliance. Would the Alliance, riding high in the opinion polls and winning by-elections on the basis of very large swings at Croydon, Crosby and Hillhead, form the next government? Would the Labour Party tear itself apart over the contested issues of party constitution and policy? These were the questions which exercised the political commentators. On a different but related plane of discussion the question was whether it was now possible or desirable to envisage a post-Thatcher return to the broadly social democratic 'consensus' politics of post-war Britain, or whether Thatcher's radicalism marked the terminal crisis of that political accommodation, so that the failure of Thatcherism pointed towards the necessity of a counter-radicalism of the left. I have already indicated that although the economic programme of Thatcherism is unrealisable, the problems of the foregoing political accommodation were real enough, and certainly not merely a figment of the new Tory imagination. I shall now

examine the developments among those political forces competing to
define an alternative to Thatcherism in this context.

First the Labour Party. The crisis in the party following the election
defeat of 1979 marked the latest and most aggravated phase of the
dislocation between the objectives and principles of the parliamentary
leadership and those of the unions and of the constituency parties
(allowing that none of these formations are homogeneous). The 1979
party conference showed up very clearly the bitterness on the left,
among MPs, constituency parties and the unions, concerning the
autocratic leadership of Callaghan and Healey, which, it was argued,
was responsible for the election defeat. The alternative interpretation
on Labour's right wing was, of course, that it was the irresponsible
behaviour of the unions that gave the Tories their election victory.
But it was not until 1980 that the lines of division became clarified.
During that year it became increasingly evident that there were two
forces within the party with clear – and clearly incompatible –
political objectives. On the one hand there were the acknowledged
social democrats, led by the so-called 'Gang of Three' (Shirley
Williams, William Rogers, David Owen). This group made it plain
that they stood for a 'mixed economy' with a strong private sector,
for continuing EEC and NATO membership, for incomes policy, and
for the autonomy of the parliamentary party to pursue these aims.
They clearly wished to weaken the 'corporatist' ties between the
parliamentary party and the unions, and emphasised MPs' responsibility to the electorate at large. Their support came mainly from
within the parliamentary party, but also from some right-wing unions
such as the electricians. On the other hand there was the radical left,
headed by Tony Benn and his associates and organised by the Labour
Co-ordinating Committee and the Campaign for Labour Party
Democracy. In policy terms this tendency stood for the 'Alternative
Economic Strategy' including large scale nationalisation, for
withdrawal from the EEC and NATO, against incomes policy, and
for the close accountability of the parliamentary party and its leadership to the party conference and constituency parties. This tendency
had some support in the parliamentary party but was based primarily
on the left in the unions and the constituencies.

But it would be an over-simplification to suggest that the conflicts
within the Labour Party could be read simply as 'socialism' versus
'social democracy'. Apart from these two opposed forces with their
definite programmes and uncompromising stands, there were also large
sections of the party unwilling to commit themselves either way: left

MPs dubious about the workability of 'Bennite' policies and constitutional arrangements; 'social democratic' MPs appreciative of the value
of the party/union link and unwilling to provoke a split in the party;
trade unions taking the view that there should be a clear 'division of
labour' between the parliamentary party and the union movement,
yet not necessarily 'right-wing' on other issues (e.g. The National
Union of Railwaymen).

The 'political indeterminacy' of which Stuart Hall wrote (1981),
must be seen against this background. The radical left made sufficient
gains (in terms of policy on the EEC and disarmament at the 1980
conference, and in terms of constitutional change at the special conference of January 1981) to make the position of the principled and
consistent social democratic right untenable. The latter group felt compelled to break with Labour and found the Social Democratic Party.
But despite this, the 'centre' of the party did not accept defeat, over
policy or the constitution, and the left was soon divided over the means
which should be employed to consolidate its gains. In this regard the
outcome of the leadership election following Callaghan's resignation,
before the electoral college mechanism was set up, was important. The
MPs gave Michael Foot the leadership, and Foot was in the pivotal
position of having a left-wing reputation and left-wing friends, but also
of upholding the right to, and necessity of, 'relative autonomy' of the
parliamentary party. He was also strongly committed to the 'unity'
of the party and for that reason was happy to have Denis Healey as
his deputy, to balance the leadership from the MPs' point of view.
Foot therefore strongly resisted Benn's campaign to contest Healey's
position under the new electoral rules and more broadly to make MPs
into the 'parliamentary delegates' of the extra-parliamentary party.
This left many on the Labour left (primarily but not exclusively in
the parliamentary party) in an awkward position: on the one hand
they did not want to see the party return to the Mandarin style and
centrist line of Wilson and Callaghan, but on the other hand they may
either have felt loyalty to, and trust in, Foot, or were personally
suspicious of Benn's ambitions, or reckoned that the 'mandating' of
MPs by the Party conference was not the way to achieve a coherent
and practicable socialist programme or to win elections.

With the Labour Party in this state of indeterminacy, its capacity
to get across any coherent alternative to Thatcherism was severely
limited. But what of the new SDP? It too suffered from a degree of
indeterminacy. The SDP shared certain principles with the Liberals
and it was clear to them that some sort of alliance was essential: divided,

both parties of the 'centre-left' would be condemned to marginality. But there were still problems in constructing an alliance: was it to be merely a short-term electoral pact or a long-term coalescence? Would the rank-and-file of each party accept alliance? There were indications that many Liberals were uneasy about throwing in their lot with a new and untried party which was attempting to 'usurp' the Liberals' claim to the 'centre ground'. There were also those in the SDP who saw their party as more distinctly left-wing than the Liberals, and feared the consequences of too strong a Liberal identification. Nonetheless, over 1981 the minimal condition of alliance — an agreement not to stand competing candidates in the same constituencies — was achieved, although not without tensions. What then were the prospects of the Alliance? How likely was it that such a political force could win popular support on a scale sufficient, if not to form the next government then at least to produce a 'third bloc' within parliament which could hold the balance between the major parties? Could the failure of Thatcherism be turned to advantage by those social forces pressing for a 'return to the centre', a move which would clearly undercut the left's attempts to gain acceptance for a counter-radicalism premissed upon the idea that there can be no such 'return'? The importance of the putative SDP/Liberal alliance and its electoral prospects must be seen in this context, since I have suggested that with the Labour Party in its then state and the anti-Thatcher Tories paralysed the fate of the 'centre' seemed to rest with this new and untried political force.

As regards the opinion surveys, these produced contradictory findings: some polls showed a high level of support for the Alliance (up to 46 per cent of the vote), but the level of support was highly variable and the hypothetical nature of the questions asked of respondents suggested that these findings should be regarded with some scepticism. The policy of the SDP/Liberal alliance remained very sketchy, and polls discovered a marked discrepancy between the views of 'supporters' of the SDP and the party's leadership especially over the issue of EEC membership. Many people willing to give their hypothetical vote to the centre party remained ignorant of such policy positions as were avowed by the SDP leaders, and they expressed their hopes of the Social Democrats in widely differing terms — from the disaffected Tory businessmen hoping for a boost to business and the resurrection of 'the old values of decency and liberalism', to disaffected Labour workers who expected the SDP to be 'more for the working class than Labour is' (interviews in the 'Times' 18/2/81).

Nonetheless, the near miss for Roy Jenkins at the Warrington by-election and the subsequent by-election successes for Jenkins, Shirley Williams and the Liberal, Pitt, took the Alliance into the headlines and gave an impression of political vitality which contrasted sharply with the travails of both the Tories and the Labour Party. What was open to doubt, however, was the staying-power of this development. As the fortunes of the Alliance rose during 1981 widely differing assessments of its long-term prospects were offered, not all of them, of course, disinterested. On the one side mainstream Labour and Tory politicians tended to discount the SDP as largely a creation of the media, destined to fade as it lost its novelty value, although by mid-1981 they came to admit that the Alliance could pose a threat to majority government. The chance of an Alliance government, however, was discounted outright. On the other side the SDP and Liberal leaders and sympathetic political commentators heralded the emergence of a centre alliance as the first step in a fundamental realignment of British politics, the most important development in party politics since the emergence of the Labour Party around the turn of the century. Political analysts such as Crewe (1981) linked the question of a centre alliance to the changing class structure of British society, arguing that the blurring of the working class/middle class division provided the social conditions for the emergence of a 'non-class' political party appealing to moderate-minded citizens of whatever social background. On this view the emergence of a strong SDP/Liberal force in parliament would bring the party-political realm into correspondence with the already identifiable changes in the social realm.

Arguments over the future of the Alliance had a particular relevance in 1981 when that force was riding high. Even though support for the Alliance, as registered by the opinion polls and local by-elections, fell heavily in 1982, these arguments are still of interest. The Alliance may have an important future even if its rise is not a linear process. So let us examine the issues. It is a useful starting point to compare the views of Crewe with the discussion offered by Stuart Hall (1981), from a Marxist, or more particularly a Gramscian, standpoint. He rejected the notion of the rise of the SDP/Liberals as the necessary accompaniment to a supposed 'drift to the centre' at the level of public opinion, but at the same time did not write off the centre party as a nine days' wonder. In effect Hall advanced two theses, between which there is a certain tension. On the one hand he brought into play Gramsci's concept of 'crisis of representation', a situation in which 'social classes become detached from their traditional parties' and the organisational forms and leaderships 'who constitute, represent and lead them are no longer recognised... as their expression' (Hall, 1981, p.12). One main reason for such a crisis may be that 'the ruling class has failed in some major political undertaking for which it has requested or forcibly extracted the consent of the broad masses' (ibid.). Hall suggested that this may have happened in the British case: both Labour and the Tories had 'requested the consent of the masses' in their attempts to revitalise the British economy and it now looked as if both were discredited. As a result both working class support for Labour and middle class support for the Tories had become increasingly problematic, possibly creating a space which the SDP/Liberal parties could exploit. Hall claimed that 'neither of the main electoral machines now offer themselves as a credible occupant of power at another turn of the electoral wheel' (ibid.), and that the centrist policies of selective reflation plus incomes policy could look credible. Further a centre party 'could secure powerful support "from above", amongst all those forces currently detaching themselves from the Thatcher path to the brink' (ibid.). This then is Hall's first thesis: the centre party could appear as the beneficiary of a 'crisis of representation' affecting the existing major parties and their traditional support blocs. Hall's second thesis, however, tends to undermine the first. This is the argument that we have had the 'centre' in power for years despite the ideological jousting between Labour and the Tories and it was precisely the *failure* of the centre which licensed the rise of Thatcherism: 'the progressive abandonment of "the centre" has taken place for the best of all possible reasons: it failed' (ibid., p.13). As I noted earlier, this is a common view of Thatcherism on the left — Thatcherism as the beneficiary of the failure of the social democratic 'centre' in both Labour and Tory variants — and on this view it is hard to imagine how an avowedly social democratic grouping could make any political gains out of the failure of Thatcherism.

From the arguments mentioned above, three main themes emerge concerning the potential support base for a centre party alliance: first, Crewe's argument that the social conditions for a radical realignment of party support are favourable; second, Hall's thesis of a political 'crisis of representation' affecting the major parties; and third, Hall's thesis — shared by many on the left — that the political 'centre' is basically discredited already. The first and third of these themes give rise to definite, and opposite, views as to the potential long-term success of a centre alliance. I would argue, however, that they are both problematic, and that the future of the Alliance will be determined by the particular mode of development of the 'crisis of representation' of which Hall wrote, over the next few years — a development in which the intervention of socialist political forces will be of great importance. Let me justify this claim. First, consider Crewe's theme. Crewe basically reads off the potential success of a political party or alliance of the 'centre' from the social changes which have been in progress at least over the 1960s and '70s, changes which have blurred the traditional British 'class structure' and loosened the ties between definite social collectivities and the two major parties. I have considered these changes in the previous chapter, and there is no doubt that they are real enough: supporters of the major parties are, in general, less committed now than in the 1960s, and Labour's traditional distinctive proposals of nationalisation and increased social expenditure have been subject to diminishing support even among Labour identifiers, as has been the party's traditional link with the trade unions. But all the same this evidence is not sufficient to support the claim that a fundamental realignment of party politics is at hand. After all, a third political force, in the form of the Liberal Party, has been playing for the centre ground over the whole period without a great deal of success. In February 1974 the Liberals gained rather more than half as many votes as Labour and the Tories, but that result was obtained under rather special circumstances which arguably produced a conjunctural 'flight to the centre' among voters who did not wish to take sides in the battle between a confrontationist Tory government and the trade unions. After February '74 the proportion of the electorate voting Liberal declined, and in May 1979 the Liberals received around a third as many votes as the major parties. Now it may be argued that the formation of the SDP, with the defection from Labour of a number of prominent and experienced politicians, will give the 'centre' a credibility it previously lacked and therefore bring out a massively increased vote. It may happen, but my point here is that one cannot read off the likelihood of such an event by reference to the changing social composition of the electorate: the Tories were quite effective in rallying electoral support in 1979 after the debacle of 1974 and it is quite possible — although by no means certain — that Labour may do the same.

Then consider Hall's theme of the 'failure of the centre', which gives rise to the opposite long-term assessment from Crewe's argument. The problem here is that the view of Labour and Tory politics prior to the Thatcher period as mere variants of social democratic centrism is not very widespread outside of Marxist circles. If one compares the practices of previous Labour and Tory governments against a hypothetical true socialist government then Labour and the Tories can appear essentially similar, but if one does not have such a hypothetical comparison in mind then they can look 'extreme' and 'divisive'. Even if both parties have been pushed into a broadly similar politics of corporatist accommodation and crisis avoidance over their terms of office they have been sufficiently different in their political approaches, particularly in the earlier years of government, to dismantle and undermine each others' policy achievements: think of the nationalisation, de-nationalisation and re-nationalisation of steel; the emphasis and de-emphasis of comprehensive education; the scrapping of the Industrial Reorganisation Corporation; the repeal of the Industrial Relations Act; the scrapping of the Price Commission, and so on. Also the conditions of electoral competition between two major parties with roughly evenly-balanced support blocs may be argued to have contributed to the practice of 'electioneering' fiscal policy, and therefore to have aggravated 'stop-go'. There is therefore a space in which the centre party alliance can propose its arguments along the following lines: better government could be attained by an *avowedly* centre or social democratic alliance unencumbered by right or left wing dogma, and not beholden to the sectional interests of business or the trade unions; and further, such an alliance, once in power, could reorganise the British electoral system along the lines of proportional representation, thus destroying the conditions which have sustained the damaging oscillation between 'extremes'. There is evidence from opinion polls that these arguments are not without popular appeal, although whether they are likely to figure as the major consideration in determining many people's voting pattern is uncertain.

Of course, winning votes and being able to govern effectively are two different things. If a centre alliance can convince enough people of all classes of the virtues of 'moderation' in politics, of 'continuity' in government and of proportional representation to undercut the position of both Labour and the Tories it does not follow that such an alliance would be able to deliver in office the revitalisation of economy and society promised in opposition, any more than the electoral success of the Tories in 1979 guarantees the eventual success of the Thatcherist programme. In attempting to assess the prospects of an hypothetical centre alliance *government* what is important is not so much whether Hall's 'failure of the centre' thesis is broadly accepted within popular ideology, but whether it is *correct*. That is, would a centre alliance government committed to moderate reflation rapidly find itself running up against the same old problems of inflation and balance of payments constraint, without the capacity to transform the underlying social relations which sustain these problems? Certainly there is little evidence so far of hard-headed proposals on the part of the Social Democrats/Liberals for the planning of incomes, the restructuring of industry and trade or the transformation of social relations at the point of production. On the other hand, it would be dangerous to assume that an electoral victory for a centre alliance would be of little consequence on the grounds that centrist politics would be bound to be rapidly discredited in practice, re-opening the way for the left. A new party in government, with a message of conciliation and entrusted with the obviously difficult task of picking up the pieces after Thatcherism, might not lose support so quickly, and one point worth considering is that the trade union movement would find it much more politically difficult to take up a stance of outright opposition than in the case of Thatcherism.

To return to the positions of Crewe and Hall, my argument is that neither Crewe's thesis nor Hall's 'failure of the centre' thesis provide an adequate basis for assessing, either way, the political capacity of the SDP/Liberal alliance. In my view Hall's first thesis is the most useful; this capacity will depend crucially on the playing-out of the 'representation crisis' affecting the major parties, on whether the Tories and Labour can succeed in winning back their supporters and 'crowding out' the new centre or whether, as Hall has it, 'neither of the main electoral machines offer themselves as a credible incumbent of power'. In relation to this question it might be argued that neither of the 'main electoral machines' were really trying wholeheartedly to achieve maximum electoral popularity in 1981. The Tory leaders were concerned to drive through a particular socio-economic programme with scant regard to the polls, and the Labour Party was more concerned with internal issues of policy and the party constitution than with its popularity rating. And even in these circumstances it is noteworthy that although the *voters* appeared highly sceptical of both the Tories and Labour, the *corporate bodies*, which provide their support at a different level from the electoral, maintained their (admittedly tense) loyalties. We have seen how the CBI leadership could not bring itself to any outright dissociation from the Tories; neither did the trade union leadership desert Labour, despite rumblings from some unions about the possible attractions of the SDP.

The starting point for the foregoing discussion of the Labour Party and the Liberal-SDP Alliance was the politics of 1981, and the competition to define an alternative to the evident disaster of Thatcherism.

By mid-1982 the short-term political situation and pattern of alignments had clearly changed radically. Thatcher and her associates, having maintained their dominance over the general line of the Tory government during the lean years of 1980-81, were in a position to reap the political benefits of 1982.

Partly this was a matter of the economic 'successes' discussed earlier, 'successes' very much bound up with recession. But then there was the so-called 'Falklands factor'. One is reminded of Marx's discussion in the 'Eighteenth Brumaire', of the way in which distant military struggles can complicate domestic politics, adding a dimension which is in no way reducible to the representation of class interests within the 'home' social formation. Marx argued that the Montagne foundered on its ill-timed opposition to Bonaparte's military adventurism, alienating an army which saw the Montagne as giving comfort to its enemies. Wherever the blame may lie for permitting the Argentine invasion of the Falkland Islands (and the indications are that the Thatcher government has a lot to answer for), one can argue that the British left suffered from a kind of 'Montagne effect' during 1982. The left resisted Thatcher's militarism, but while it may have been correct to argue that Thatcher's response was motivated in part by the desire for political self-preservation the issue nonetheless appeared, to the majority of British people, as one which justified a military response in the last resort: after all, the inhabitants of the Falklands, who had been farming the islands peaceably for generations and who clearly wished to retain their British status, were suddenly invaded by the agents of a brutal and dictatorial regime. At this point the left's attack on Thatcher's militarism could be presented as a case of spineless pacifism. Aside from any 'Montagne effect', however, even those opposition politicians who supported the British military response in the South Atlantic lost out heavily to the Tories. The undoubted heroism of the campaign and the boost to national self-confidence redounded to the credit of the country's political leadership, whatever the deserts of that leadership.

The political effects of the Falkands crisis were important, but should not be overemphasised. In late 1982, with Tory support falling only slowly from the Falklands peak and no sharp recovery in progress for the opposition forces, it seemed that other factors were perhaps more important. For instance, although high and rising unemployment remained a prime issue of popular concern, surveys showed that the Thatcher government had been highly successful in shifting the blame for unemployment onto 'world conditions', and in fostering the attitude that unemployment was pretty much inevitable (a survey conducted by the Economist Intelligence Unit, 1982, found that only a quarter of the unemployed themselves blamed the government for their predicament). Popular expectations had been successfully depressed, to the point at which, for many people, the sober prospects offered by Thatcherism could appear as mere 'honesty' and the promises of the opposition as wildly optimistic. The 'crisis of representation', as it affected the Tory party, had, it seemed, been quite effectively overcome.

There is, however, little point in trying to predict the result of the general election of 1983 or 84, a result which the reader will doubtless know. Whatever the result may be, it may in retrospect appear inevitable: arguably, in late 1982, it was not. Thatcherism had effectively failed in economic terms yet that did not guarantee success to Labour or the Alliance. These forces still had to convince enough people that they had a valid alternative. Conversely, the Tories' success at this time in establishing their credentials for 'realism' and 'honesty' depended upon an incoherent and subdued performance on the part of the opposition forces. And while this weakness of the opposition had real causes and was not merely an effect of 'accidental' personal squabbles it was nonetheless a specifically *political* phenomenon. It was not inscribed indelibly within the class relations of the British social formation.

In the preceding pages I have given some indication of the changes in the terrain of political competition during almost four years of Thatcherism. In the final section of this chapter I shall focus on the British left, and the ability of the left to advance the socialist project, against this background.

The radical left opposition

I have returned an open verdict on the prospects of the social democratic opposition to Thatcherism. The social democratic forces face severe difficulties in (re)establishing their credibility, but they cannot be written off on the grounds that social democracy is already a proven failure. I now turn to the radical left opposition. Here I propose to concentrate on the left in and around the Labour Party, on the grounds that no other left political force stands a real chance of substantially influencing the course of political development in Britain during the 1980s. I shall organise this account around a series of questions as follows: (1) who is the 'left' in and around the Labour Party?

(2) what does the left propose? (3) how far has it been successful in getting these proposals accepted by the Labour Party, and what are its chances of making further gains? (4) assuming a strong left influence in the Labour Party, what are the party's chances of winning and sustaining popular support? Finally I shall pose the question of how far the developments on the left of the Labour Party provide favourable conditions for the advance of what I have earlier referred to as 'the socialist project' — whether they open up a real prospect of achieving the strategic economic objectives outlined in chapter 5.

(1)

First, the question of who is the 'left'? The Labour left is not a homogeneous force, but one can identify certain centres of left activity. There is the 'traditional' parliamentary left of the Tribune Group of MPs, but the left which has emerged to a position of prominence over the last few years draws its main support from outside the parliamentary party: I refer here to the cluster of organisations grouped together under the banner of 'democratisation' of the party and supportive of Tony Benn — the campaign for Labour Party Democracy (CLPD), the Labour Co-ordinating Committee (LCC) and the Rank and File Mobilising Committee (RFMC).[18] These organisations, and their foremost spokesman Tony Benn, have a support bloc which is concentrated in the constituency parties and certain of the trade unions, primarily among the activists in both of these areas. The social composition of the left activist groups is quite varied. It has been shown (Denver and Bochel, 1980) that the General Management Committee (GMCs) of the constituency parties show a strong 'over-representation' of professional and managerial employees, relative to their share of the Labour vote (the latter group provided 33 per cent of GMC delegates as against 5 per cent of Labour voters). But the constituency parties are not uniform in this respect and there are doubtless many Benn-supporting manual workers active in the constituencies. Further, the tally of trade union conferences which were swung to support Benn for the deputy leadership contest of 1981 shows that the policies and political practice which he proposes are not supported by intellectual 'middle class' socialists alone.[19] The 'Bennite' left (I use this term as a convenient label for the tendency of which Benn is the foremost spokesman, without implying that 'personality' is a dominant consideration for that tendency) is clearly aware of where, within the party as a whole, its strength lies, and has devoted most of its persuasive energy to campaigning in the constituencies and the unions rather than attempting to win over MPs.

(2)

What does this left propose? Its proposals may be grouped under the two heads of policy and party constitution. In terms of policy the Bennite left stands for the 'Alternative Economic Strategy', which is not a fully-elaborated programme but at least involves planned large-scale reflation, import controls, further nationalisation, workers' 'self-government' in industry and expansion of the public services. It also stands for withdrawal from the EEC, for unilateral nuclear disarmament and withdrawal from NATO, and for the unconditional defence of trade union rights. It is hostile to talk of incomes policy under a future Labour government, but inclined to favour price controls. It wishes to see the House of Lords abolished. Finally, although Benn has not campaigned on these issues at the union conferences, it favours withdrawal of British troops from Northern Ireland and tends to be hostile towards civil nuclear power. The Bennite left, in other words, has the makings for a quite comprehensive political programme.

In terms of the party constitution, this left has the objective of ensuring that any gains it can make in the party outside parliament, at the annual conference and in the National Executive Committee, will be translated into definite manifesto commitments and will then be implemented by the parliamentary party, insofar as the PLP is necessary for their implementation. Hence the threefold aims of reselection of MPs by constituency activists, election of the leader and deputy leader by a broad electoral college, and abolition of the leader's 'right of veto' over the contents of the party manifesto, or even a two year 'rolling manifesto' the implementation of which should be supervised by the party conference. These constitutional issues are accorded a crucial importance, since the analysis of the previous performance of Labour governments offered by the Benn tendency is one which stresses the pusillanimity and even treachery of the PLP in failing to implement perfectly good conference policies. In an image which Benn has favoured in several interviews, the party in the country has acted in the past as a mere 'rocket launcher' sending the PLP into government but without any means of controlling its subsequent trajectory. Or as Frank Allaun has put it, writing in 'Labour Activist', the organ of the LCC:

'We have a fine programme which has not been carried out. Our job now is to find a way of so democratising the Labour movement that the parliamentary leaders will implement it' (Allaun, 1979).

If one has a 'fine programme' already, then the emphasis of one's activity must be on ensuring its implementation, rather than on further elaborating the programme.

Aside from questions of policy for a future government and constitutional matters, it should also be stressed that the Bennite left has a conception of politics which places considerable emphasis on extra-parliamentary mobilisation, particularly in the 'labour movement'. Winning a left government is seen as an essential component of political progress, but the need for strong popular pressure both to back up and to push forward such a government is clearly recognised.

(3)

Then there is the question of how far the left has been successful in pressing its case within the Labour Party, and of the prospects for further gains. Here one cannot be so definite. Take the question of party policy as decided by conference. Certainly motions have been passed supporting certain elements of left policy: withdrawal from the EEC, nuclear disarmament, opposition to incomes policy, abolition of the Lords. But on closer inspection it appears that policy as decided by conference is not always consistent, and motions qualifying or undermining the left positions have also been passed. For instance, the 1980 conference passed one motion from a constituency party rejecting incomes policy, as a major factor in the past electoral defeats of the Labour Party, but shortly afterwards it also passed a motion from the Union of Communication Workers which rejected the idea of 'an incomes and prices free-for-all inherent in the nature of free collective bargaining and free price fixing' (quoted in *The Times* 5/6/81). Similarly, while conference called upon a Labour government to pursue nuclear disarmament and rejected British participation in any defence policy based on the 'use or threatened use of nuclear weapons' it also rejected a motion calling for withdrawal from NATO. Considering the broader 'labour movement', as the left is wont to do, one finds other inconsistencies of policy. For instance in 1980 the Labour Party conference called for outright withdrawal from the EEC, while the

TUC favoured a further referendum on the subject. And certain other policies favoured by the Bennite left, such as withdrawal of British troops from Northern Ireland, have been firmly defeated at conferences to date. The general point here is that it is something of a bluff on the part of Benn and his supporters to present themselves as the sole force consistently pressing for the implementation of conference policy. Each tendency within the party stresses those elements of conference policy which fit best with its own conception of politics, and the Bennite left is no exception.

Then there is the constitutional question. On this score, as noted earlier, the left was successful in altering the mechanism of election of the party leaders. An electoral college was established giving 40 per cent representation to the unions, 30 per cent to the constituencies and 30 per cent to the parliamentary party. The left also won the principle of periodic reselection of MPs by their constituency parties, but has not (1982) managed to change the method of arriving at a final draft of the manifesto. The constitutional changes achieved to date will have real political effects. Benn has already demonstrated that the electoral college mechanism permits, even necessitates, a new form of campaigning for leadership positions. Candidates must actively lobby not only their parliamentary colleagues but also the trade union conferences, putting themselves and their policies publicly on the line and at the same time politicising union conferences to a hitherto unprecedented extent. There can be little doubt that Benn's campaign has got across the rudiments of the 'Alternative Economic Strategy' to a much larger public, at least among union activists, than was ever the case in 1973/74. Also the reselection system is going to cost a number of right-wing MPs their seats, and install supporters of the left as candidates if not as MPs. This latter effect should not, however, be exaggerated. The study by Denver and Bochel (1980) suggests that most GMC delegates have a preference for parliamentary candidates towards the 'centre' of Labour's political spectrum, even if personally they see themselves as 'right' or 'left' of centre.

Projecting forward, can one assess the extent to which the left may be successful in getting its policy positions further ratified by conference, and at the same time exploiting the constitutional changes so as to ensure that the parliamentary party is firmly committed to implement left policy? In this regard, the optimism on the left during 1981 gave way to defensiveness and gloom during late 1982, following the election of a right wing NEC at the 1982 conference and the prosecution of a 'witch hunt' directed against the Militant Tendency. Aside from 'conjunctural' setbacks, however, there is a damaging split on the left of the party, broadly defined, between Benn's unequivocal supporters who see him as the champion of 'conference policy' and 'accountability', and indeed a popular socialism, and those others on the left who believe the issues are more complex than Benn allows. When Benn contested the deputy leadership of the party against Denis Healey, we saw Michael Foot attack him in no uncertain terms for questioning the integrity of the party's leadership, for attempting to make MPs into mandated 'marionettes', for posing falsely as the champion of conference policy, and for dividing the party. Foot was supported in this by a section of the left and aside from personal loyalty to him on the part of old friends, his arguments carried some weight. In particular, he was surely correct to insist that conference decisions do not provide an adequate means of deciding the actions to be taken by the PLP in office. Even if Foot has an inflated notion of the role and powers of parliament it is true that the party in government, faced with the definite constraint of maintaining a parliamentary majority, receiving advice and information from informed sources which may take time to filter through to the party at large, and acting under definite pressures from, for instance, trade unions and other governments, must have a certain 'relative autonomy' from the party conference.[20] It is not realistic to imagine that the PLP can be a simple mechanism for 'implementing' pre-given conference policy — even if that policy were self-consistent — and irresponsible to encourage that expectation. For these reasons and for others, such as the alleged intolerance of Benn and his active supporters, there are many on the left who do not see the campaign of the Bennite left, whatever the result, as strengthening the ability of the Labour Party to achieve socialist change in Britain. Even if they see the degree of commitment to socialism of the PLP as problematic and in need of reinforcement they do not see the Benn strategy as the best way of achieving this.

This division makes it particularly hard to assess the chances of 'the left' advancing its position further. Certainly, one can argue that the right-wing counter thrust of 1982 did not have a very stable basis, dependent as it was upon some rather tricky block voting. But then the form of electoral college which pleased the left so much in the previous year was equally dependent upon a block voting pattern of questionable 'representative' value. The issue, it must be said, remains indeterminate.

(4)

The fourth question posed above concerned the degree of popular support for the positions staked out by the Labour left. Take first the issues of party policy as such, rather than the constitution. A National Opinion Polls survey of August 1980 produced an interesting picture of the state of play among Labour supporters. Some of the left's favoured policies had widespread support: 79 per cent favoured import controls; 74 per cent favoured withdrawal from the EEC; 51 per cent were opposed to the siting of cruise missiles in Britain. But on the other hand 66 per cent of Labour supporters favoured incomes policy and only 36 per cent supported more nationalisation (opposed by 53 per cent). Interestingly, Denis Healey included the issues of import controls and 'restoring the sovereignty of Britain from control by the Common Market' in his personal manifesto for the deputy leadership election (*The Times* 16/6/81). Where 'left' policies appear to have clear majority support among Labour voters, it is hard for others to resist them! But equally, the lack of support for nationalisation and for the rejection of incomes policy is important. Nationalisation remains fairly unattractive except to the 'party faithful', and if it is to be a major plank of a left-leaning Labour Party platform then it must be redefined and clearly distinguished from the disappointing performance of the past in order to achieve much popular resonance. The popularity of incomes policy shows that if one moves beyond the circle of union activists then 'free collective bargaining' is regarded with circumspection. This raises the question of the credibility of Labour as a party that can contain inflation, a question to which I shall return below in assessing the potential of the Labour left for advancing the socialist project.

Moving to the constitutional issues, the reaction to these on the part of Labour voters was investigated in a poll published in *The Times* (9/2/81) shortly after the Wembley conference. Only 57 per cent of voters were aware that the conference had taken place, despite the fact that all the papers were full of outraged commentary. Anyway, among those who were aware of the Wembley decisions and were also Labour voters there was generally only minority support for the idea that the constitutional changes mean increased democracy (29 per cent), or enhanced Labour's electoral chances (20 per cent). Regarding the issue of an electoral college with a trade union majority, for selecting the leadership, 78 per cent disapproved and only 15 per cent approved. This finding tallies with the longstanding opinion poll result that trade union 'domination' of the party is highly unpopular among Labour voters. Of course the role of the media on this issue was far from neutral, but one must credit people with some ability to come to their own conclusions. Further, the principle of majority union representation in the electoral college was actually opposed by the majority at the Wembley conference, and it was only because the engineering union was tied to the rejection of any proposal which did not give the PLP a majority that the final result was obtained. On the other hand, the principle of reselecting MPs was found by the 'Times' poll to have substantial majority support among the supporters of all parties. Reselection is after all a 'commonsense' proposition if parliamentary candidates are in the main seen as *party* candidates rather than as individuals campaigning on their own merits, as is generally true in Britain. Since reselection was generally presented by the media as equally sinister as the role of the union vote in selecting the party leader, this finding reinforces the idea that the people whose opinions were assessed in these surveys were not merely parroting a line put across in the papers and on TV.

Summing up, the whole programme of the Bennite left is presently backed by only a minority of Labour voters (*a fortiori*, by a smaller minority of the electorate as a whole). But the party constitutional issues, on which popular support for the Benn tendency is weakest — apart from the issue of reselection — are probably of less importance than the policy issues when it comes to voting in a general election. It is likely that voters will concern themselves with the quality of the party leadership as they see it, and with the credibility of the overall policy stance of the party more than the method of selecting the leadership or of generating party policy. As of late 1982 it appears that Labour had an uphill struggle ahead to win an election convincingly, and that within the party the left had an uphill struggle to establish its policies as the party's operational programme. The result of the first struggle, at least, will be known to the reader, and I have already eschewed prediction. There is, however, the more general issue: would a Labour Party shifted significantly to the left vis-à-vis the Wilson-Callaghan period be able to *sustain* popular support, and would its programme make a substantial contribution to the advance of socialism in Britain? This is the final question which I wish to consider here.

(5)

In the previous sections I have tried to bring out some of the positive aspects of the Labour left's campaign, in relation to the socialist project: the emphasis on the need to do more than elect a 'left government'; the carrying of left policy, and the Alternative Economic Strategy in particular, into the trade union movement. At the same time, however, I have emphasised certain problems in the strategy of the Bennite left. These problems may be grouped under three headings, although the distinction here is analytical and in practice the three sets of problems are closely related: the construction of a workable political 'vehicle' for socialist change; the development of a hegemonic appeal to counter the possible attractions of resurgent Toryism or of social democracy for certain social collectivities; and the development of practical policies which stand a good chance of producing their intended effects, rather than alienating support.

On the question of the political vehicle, I have already indicated the difficulties in the strategy of the Benn tendency. This strategy, with its emphasis on the potential treachery of the parliamentary party and the need for mechanisms to ensure that the PLP follows the conference line, underestimates the necessary autonomy of even the most committed socialist PLP from the extraparliamentary movement, if one takes seriously the need for an effective parliamentary contingent in achieving socialist advance. The PLP cannot merely 'express the will' of the 'labour movement' since the notion of a homogeneous 'will' of the movement is a myth and the PLP has to operate within definite political conditions which may not be immediately apparent to the rest of the party. The notion of political forces 'representing' pre-given class interests, which I have consistently argued is inadequate, may have malign effects on the workability of the Labour Party as a socialist political force.

On the issue of hegemonic appeal, again I have adumbrated some of the difficulties faced by the Labour left. There is a need to build support beyond the trade union movement, and *a fortiori* beyond that subset of trade unionists who are also committed left activists (and who are often misleadingly identified as the 'labour movement'). This means taking seriously the point that 'socialism' does not have a built-in majority in British society, or even among the 'working class', and painstakingly constructing a support bloc among those people who do not have any prior faith in nationalisation as such, who do not necessarily regard public expenditure as an intrinsic good but who are open to persuasion by concrete arguments, and who are worried by the possible inflationary effects of the left's programme to counter unemployment. Non-union workers, women both within and outside of the workforce, members of the salariat who have been putting forward reasoned and considered arguments against Thatcherism — if socialism is to be advanced then these groups should not be allowed to slip away to the SDP and the Liberals in the belief that a 'dogmatic' or 'union-dominated' Labour Party has nothing to offer them. This is not a matter of simple opportunism, of selecting policies on the basis of the opinion polls, but of honestly facing the problems which a left programme entails and encouraging informed and open debate over policy, as well as taking advantage of the positions of strength which Labour has — in the metropolitan local authorities for instance — to promote popular participation and accountability and break the connection between 'socialism' and bureaucratic statism.

The development and popularisation of practical socialist policies clearly has a crucial importance in relation to both of the previous points i.e. the construction of a workable political vehicle and the development of a hegemonic appeal. If the left is seen to be advancing credible policies which provide a workable alternative to both Thatcherism and a 'return to the centre' then this will help both to sway Labour MPs and maintain the cohesion of the Labour Party, and to broaden the party's electoral appeal and continuing support bloc. But here again the strategy of the Benn tendency has serious weaknesses both as regards the substance of policy proposed, and the means of generating party policy. Take the Alternative Economic Strategy (AES): there is no doubt that more critical thought has gone into the elaboration of this strategy over the last few years than at any earlier stage (I have made particular mention of the CSE London Group's contribution in conjunction with the LCC, in chapter 4). But all the same there is a damaging tendency on the Bennite left to minimise the costs and problems associated with the AES and even to present it as a panacea. To substantiate this claim I shall briefly consider two problem areas: inflation and international trade.

The question of inflation has been touched upon previously, but merits more consideration. The particular problem here is that the principal macroeconomic measures connected with the AES, i.e. large scale reflation and import controls, would undoubtedly tend to raise the rate of inflation. Certain policy measures could be proposed which would tend to reduce prices — such as lower interest rates and a reduction of indirect taxes, national insurance contributions, and public sector charges — but the overall impact of import controls, whether by means of a tariff or quotas, and increased monetary demand would be to raise prices. Blake (1981) simulated the effects of a £6,000 million reflationary impulse plus a 30 per cent tariff on manufactured imports, using the Treasury model of the UK economy.[21] While unemployment ends up half a million lower by 1984 than on unchanged Tory policies, and GDP 3 per cent higher, inflation rises to around 20 per cent over a year and the retail prices index stands 17 per cent higher by 1984. Further, because of the import controls the real take-home pay of those in work falls 3½ per cent over a year, and ends up 3½ per cent lower by 1984 than on present policy.

The Treasury model is not, of course, infallible in its predictions but it does represent a sophisticated means of economic projection, assuming the continuing validity of relationships between economic variables constructed on the basis of past data. Either the left must accept the validity of such projections, at least in outline, in which case it is clearly dangerous to pretend that the central policies of an AES can simultaneously reduce unemployment, keep prices steady and improve living standards, or else the projections may be contested. But in the latter case it is incumbent upon the left to show *why* the projections are invalid, and precisely what kind of social and economic changes are envisaged which would render the equations derived from past data irrelevant in judging the future success of the AES. The easiest answer here is to say that price controls would be enforced, so that accelerating inflation would be impossible, but although price controls could have some role this answer is not very convincing. If import prices rose and workers demanded commensurate wage rises then strict price controls would tend to bankrupt firms and lead to increased unemployment. Then if one argues that bankrupt firms would simply be nationalised and run on the basis of state subsidies, one has to explain where the finance will come from (taxation, borrowing or creation of new means of payment) and how it can be ensured that the extra monetary demand will be channelled into higher output and employment rather than just driving up money wages. Besides, the strategy of bankrupting firms in order to nationalise them is unlikely to prove popular.

To produce a more plausible answer to the question of inflation under the AES one would have to raise the issues of (a) incomes policy in some form and (b) policy to improve labour productivity. Increased productivity would help to offset the inflationary impact of higher import prices and permit higher levels of real income than would otherwise be available, while the planning of personal incomes would help to ensure that the reflation of domestic demand was not dissipated in inflation of wages and salaries. I cannot offer a full discussion of these issues here, but I point them out as an area in which informed debate is greatly needed on the left. Unfortunately there is no sign that the Benn tendency is ready to encourage such a debate, partly because it would necessarily raise problems concerning the connection between wage-militancy and socialist advance.

Similar considerations apply in the case of policy towards international trade. I made the point (section 7.1 above) that the easing of the balance of payments constraint on the growth of output and employment basically depends upon becoming more successful in international competition and/or withdrawing from that competition. The strategy of import controls puts the emphasis on the latter course, but while this is a defensible position it must be recognised that the improvement of the competitive position of UK industry is in fact an essential complement of import restrictions. The protection afforded by controls must be exploited to build up a more sustainable long-term trading position, otherwise the maintenance of a reasonable balance of trade will necessitate *escalating* import controls, with malign effects on inflation and popular living standards. Then there is the related question of EEC membership. We have seen that withdrawal from the EEC is currently a popular demand, but is it really necessary in order to pursue radical industrial and trading policies? And what precisely would the UK pattern of trade look like if we withdraw from the trading bloc with which almost half of our trade is currently conducted? Perhaps the answer to the first question is 'yes', and perhaps it is possible to construct a feasible alternative trading pattern, but again I believe that these issues have not been the object of full and informed debate. The Bennite left is too ready to write off the EEC as a 'capitalist club', to invoke the atavistic demand for the 'restoration of national sovereignty' and to minimise the difficulties of developing an alternative pattern of trade.

The general point which emerges from this brief discussion of inflation and trading policy is the need honestly to face the unresolved problems associated with left policy. But this would mean breaking with the influential left view that 'the movement' already has a 'fine programme' and the only problem is ensuring its implementation. Hindess (1980) has argued forcefully that this latter view gives rise to a peculiarly limited conception of the kind of 'debate' needed in the Labour

Party. Debate is required to overcome residual rightist views in the movement but the fundamental conclusions of that debate are known in advance — they are given by the 'fine programme' of conference policy already in existence, which expresses the fundamental interests and objectives of the Labour movement. Little attention need be devoted to 'working out the details of how policy is to be put into effect and what consequential changes might be needed in the organisation of government, unions, and other bodies, to the obstacles that would have to be overcome and the sources of effective resistance, and so on' (Hindess, 1980, p. 50). Sidney Weighell, lately of the Railwaymen's Union, argued that the existing arrangements at the Labour Party conference are not conducive to the kind of detailed debate which is required:

> 'Policy is all too often decided on the basis of composite resolutions which are hastily scrambled together, often self-contradictory and disposed of in ludicrously abbreviated debates. Ministers or Shadow spokesmen have little or no opportunity to contribute to conference's cursory debates ... We believe that the present arrangements for policy debate hamper rather than encourage the detailed and considered evaluation of policy options' (Weighell, 1980).

So long as this situation continues and the left does not mount an effective challenge to the existing means of generating policy — indeed considers those means as working in favour of left policy — the chances of building active support for socialism outside of the ranks of the faithful will remain limited.

Reprise

In this chapter I set out to consider three main questions, those of the 'origins' of Thatcherism, of the economic feasibility of the Thatcher programme, and of the political effects of Thatcherism in practice, including the main forms of opposition which were developing and competing to define the 'alternative' which Thatcher insisted was nonexistent. The underlying interest in these discussions was to advance the analysis of the conditions under which movement in a socialist direction might be possible in Britain. I have argued that the rise of Thatcherism must be seen against the background of a series of 'failures' afflicting the previous mode of social development and the previous politics of both Tory and Labour governments. Some of these failures were narrowly conjunctural, such as the miscalculation of

Callaghan concerning the timing of the last election and the severity of pay restraint acceptable to union members in the winter of 1978, but Thatcherism was only able to capitalise on these conjunctural factors because of the seeming plausibility of its response to a deeper-seated impasse confronting the kind of social democratic politics practised over the post-war years, which had by the late 1970s proved powerless to reverse the relative decline of the British economy.

With regard to the feasibility of the Thatcher programme, however, I have argued that the 'economic core' of that programme flies in the face of the form of capitalist property which is dominant in Britain, and that the theoretical ideology of Thatcherism, with its heavy dependence on petty bourgeois and financier concerns, badly misrecognises the effects of that form of property at the level of the financial circulation process. This explains the deeply paradoxical effects of Thatcherist economic policy in practice. I argued further that the aggravation of recession and increases in taxation which have resulted from the application of 'monetarism' by the Thatcher government cannot be conceived as the 'short-term costs' of a strategy which nonetheless holds out a real prospect of regenerating British capitalism. It is no paradox to say that Thatcherism, while inflicting defeats on the working class and talking an openly pro-capitalist language, was at the same time weakening the prospects for profitable real accumulation in Britain. The key to the apparent paradox (a paradox from the viewpoint of an over-simple Marxism) is the recognition that the accomplishment of the changes in industrial structure and the distribution of social labour required to break out of relative economic decline depend on a positive and constructive intervention by the state, and will not be achieved by the 'unfettered market'.

On the question of the political opposition to Thatcherism and the definition of alternatives I have claimed that a resurgence of social democracy cannot be ruled out, that it is over-simplistic to regard the rise of Thatcherism as marking the terminal crisis of social democracy in Britain, much as certain sections of the left would wish to believe this. Any post-Thatcher social democratic 'centre' government would certainly face serious problems. Indeed the old problems of social democracy would be more acute than in the past, given the run-down of British industry which has been proceeding under Thatcherism. But there is no guarantee that Britain will not slide back to 'moderation', made more acceptable by a change of cast: the crusading 'moderation' of David Steel, Roy Jenkins, Shirley Williams *et al.*, in place of the tired conservatism of Callaghan. The prospects of a radical left alternative emerging within the Labour Party have also been considered and I have maintained that such an alternative has no historic guarantee of success, although Labour may be well placed if the party develops a greater degree of cohesion around the theme of reducing unemployment. I have stressed that winning an election on a manifesto containing left policy commitments would be only the beginning and that Labour left policies remain problematic. There would be a real danger of losing popular support and creating further disillusionment, unless the left questions its own assumptions in good time and takes on board the need for a serious critical evaluation of its programme, in terms of the practicability of left policies, the conditions required for their implementation, and the politics of support among social groups which are not already 'safe' for the left.

Certain aspects of my discussion in this chapter may date rather quickly, given the fluidity of current British politics and the manifest difficulty of predicting developments. I should like to emphasise, therefore, the aspects which I believe will be of continuing importance. These relate back to the conclusions derived in chapter 5, concerning the constraints and opportunities posed for the socialist project by the current forms of capitalist property relations in Britain, and also to the conclusions of chapter 6 concerning the conditions of formation of support blocs for political forces. That is, in Chapter 5 I outlined certain strategic socialist aims regarding the transformation of capitalist property relations, but left open the question of the political means of achieving those aims. Then in chapter 6 I examined some of the conditions governing the division of the economic category of wage and salary earning employees into distinct collectivities, and the alignment of those collectivities with definite political forces. An examination of the record of post-war politics in Britain led me to emphasise the difficulties in constructing a support bloc for the radical transformation of support blocs for political forces. That is, in chapter 5 I outlined ing class' majority for such a transformation which was thwarted by betrayal on the part of Labour leaders. The Labour leadership since the 1950s has indeed shown a paucity of socialist imagination and determination, but more important than this was the fact that for a long period the majority of the British people simply did not experience a pressing and urgent need for a radical shift in the direction of social development. By the end of the 1970s, however, as I have emphasised in the present chapter, more people of all classes were willing to subscribe to a new radicalism — unfortunately a radicalism of the right. The left, which was attempting to offer an alternative radical solution to the impasse of social democracy, was imprisoned within a Labour

Party led from the centre-right (or else marginal to British politics); it was also, however, imprisoned within a circle of left policy commitments which were not credible or convincing to a sufficiently large social bloc, and had failed to dissociate itself sufficiently clearly from the very 'statist' mode of development which was seen by many people as part of the problem. If the left is to capitalise on the failure of Thatcherism it will not be sufficient to overthrow the centre-right leadership of the Labour Party. It will also have to overthrow the presumption that the party conference represents a hotline to the given interests of the working class, which only have to be presented with sufficient force to be recognised as such. Only then will the progressive transformation of economic class relations be on the historical agenda.

In this sense I would argue that the theoretical positions arrived at in Chapters 1 and 2 above, through a critical examination of the problems which arise in the accounts of social class given by both Marx and modern Marxist writers, are of more than academic importance. The conception of economic classes being endowed with inherent political interests which are then merely 'expressed' by political forces is not only conceptually problematic, but also a political practice based upon that conception jeopardises the chances of achieving the advance of the socialist project — in Britain in the 1980s as much as anywhere else — by short-circuiting the need to devise concrete, workable policies and construct a broad support bloc for those policies.

Conclusion

The main conclusions which I am able to draw from the foregoing
investigations have already been indicated (see chapter 5 and the conclusions to chapters 6 and 7). However, in these concluding remarks
I shall draw together some of the main points made earlier and put
them into perspective. I should like to draw attention to the three broad
'movements' of this book, and bring out the relationships between
these. Briefly, these three movements are: (1) a critical reading of Marx
and modern Marxists on social classes and the class/politics relationship; (2) an investigation of economic class relations defined at the
level of forms of property; and (3) an investigation of the realm of social
collectivities and political forces. I shall highlight the main arguments
of these movements in turn.

First movement   (chapters 1 and 2): In my reading of Marx and modern
Marxists I was concerned to bring out certain problems which seem
to me to be endemic to Marxist class analysis as it has been commonly
understood. First I considered Marx's definition of the capitalist class
and working class at the level of economic property relations: the
capitalist class was defined as the class of owners of the means of production and employers of wage-labour, extracting a social surplus product in a specifically 'monetarised' or commodity-form, while the working class was the class of agents separated from the means of production
and therefore obliged to sell their labour power for a wage or salary.
At this level, there was no particular conceptual problem or ambiguity.
But I then examined the problems which arise when Marx attempts
to specify the relationship between these 'basic classes' and the political
forces active in particular capitalist social formations. In the 'Communist Manifesto' Marx put forward a clear and definite proposition:
there would be a tendential convergence between the two basic
economically-defined classes of the capitalist mode of production on
the one hand, and the political forces active in capitalist societies on
the other. In other words, political forces would become progressively
polarised around the contradiction between wage-labour and capital,

with the proletariat becoming organised into a social collectivity by the pressures of capitalist development, and subsequently organising itself into a political party in order to pursue its historic mission of the overthrow of capitalism. The problem was that this proposition was not sustained by the arguments of the 'Manifesto'; the *necessity* of this convergence was simply not demonstrated. Then in the 'Eighteenth Brumaire' we saw that Marx affirmed the principle that political forces 'represent' or 'express' class interests already given at an economic level, but this principle was effectively abandoned, or at least seriously compromised, in Marx's specific analyses. He could not, perforce, ignore the specific effects of politics: the dislocations between 'representatives' and 'represented'; the ambiguity of the 'representation' relation whereby a given political force might draw its ideology from one social stratum, work it up in certain ways and use it to organise the support of others; the role of political forces which were admittedly *not* tied to any definite economic class interest. We also saw that Marx admitted the real effects of interests other than those of bourgeoisie and proletariat. In other words, it appeared that when Marx was analysing in detail a particular historical period he was led to undermine the conception of the class/politics relationship proposed in the 'Manifesto'. And while Marx himself might have argued that the validity of the propositions of the 'Manifesto' would be proved in the long run, this no longer seems tenable. Well over a century has passed since the Eighteenth Brumaire and historical circumstances are still as 'complex' as ever; nowhere have political forces become reduced to the 'pure' representatives of labour and capital.

It might be said that this would not really have surprised Marx, and certainly would not have surprised Lenin, yet if that is true I believe it only goes to show that their political judgement was not in practice constricted by the general theory which Marx affirmed — that they were able, as we all are, to live with inconsistencies. It does not, in other words, contradict the proposition that the general theory announced in the 'Manifesto' has serious problems. My conclusion from this discussion of Marx was that class analysis, if it is to be adequate as a guide for socialist politics, must respect the specificity of politics. Analysis of economic class relations is important, but it cannot provide a basis for 'reading off' the political forces active in the social formation.

The second chapter was concerned with modern Marxist writing on social classes. I examined the arguments of Poulantzas, Olin Wright, Carchedi and others, who were all concerned in one way or another to draw lines of class demarcation within the ranks of wage and salary earning employees. I argued that none provided a satisfactory solution to this 'demarcation problem', and suggested that this was because the *object* of the 'demarcation' was not specified clearly enough. The kind of demarcation which one carries out must depend on the aims of one's analysis, and the demarcation will be valuable only to the extent that these aims are adequately thought out. For instance, if one is attempting to give an account of the dominant system of economic property relations in order to develop a strategy for its transformation, then one's conceptual 'demarcation' should be squarely based on the criterion of possession/separation from the means of production. If, on the other hand, one is attempting to assess which social collectivities can be won to support a certain socialist political force, then one's 'demarcation' must take into account specific social and political factors other than property relations. Knowledge of an agent's position with respect to property relations will not enable one to 'derive' that agent's political affiliations.

In effect, Poulantzas was searching for a conceptual line of division which would both (a) respect the supposedly determinant role of economic relations in defining classes and (b) at the same time grasp the 'political and ideological' aspects of class. In my view this project was bound to fail, since one concept cannot fulfil both functions simultaneously. As I argued in relation to Marx's own work, there must be two movements in 'class analysis': one which identifies economic class relations and one which traces the specific connections between classes, social collectivities and politics. To approach the problem from a different angle: Poulantzas, Olin Wright and Carchedi all draw attention to the point that capitalist enterprises have in general (and not by chance) developed a division of labour characterised by hierarchy, bureaucracy and authoritarianism, a structure in which access to information, 'knowledge' and decision-making is distributed highly unequally. Clearly it is an important task of socialism to attack this division. But the writers I have considered make this hierarchical structure into a principle of class division, claiming that the employees occupying the higher, or even intermediate, reaches of this structure cannot really be 'workers'; they are either 'new petty bourgeois' (Poulantzas), 'new middle class' (Carchedi), or in 'contradictory locations' (Olin Wright). The problem is that the 'class' demarcation operated here is not at par with the definition of classes in 'classical' Marxism, since it is not based on property relations (all wage and salary earning employees including those in the 'higher' positions are separated from the means of production), yet neither is it of direct relevance to the analysis of political forces, since there can be no presumption that all 'true' proletarians will support socialism (think of Tory-voting, anti-union manual workers), nor that all those in 'new petty bourgeois' class places or occupying 'contradictory locations' will be opposed to socialism (think of Mike Cooley and his colleagues in the design staff at Lucas Aerospace).

The debate over the class determination of the middle strata conducted by Poulantzas and his critics — the search for a synthetic totalising definition of social classes — has a peculiar interminable quality. There can be no one position within that debate which is finally and authoritatively 'Marxist', since Marx's various writings on the subject are highly 'open' and there is always room for argument over the nature, applicability and relative importance of the various criteria which have been brought to bear (productive/unproductive labour, mental/manual labour, function of labour/function of capital). And at the same time the lack of specification of the precise objectives of the theoretical demarcation of classes means that no contributor can show definitively that his or her contribution meets those objectives better than others.

My reading of modern Marxists on social classes therefore reinforced the critical conclusions arrived at earlier, and gave me my programme for the remaining two 'movements' of the thesis: first to analyse the structure of economic property relations, then to consider the pattern of social collectivities and the line-up of political forces attempting to organise those collectivities in certain ways in support of their political projects.

Second movement (chapters 3, 4 and 5): These chapters were concerned with the dominant form of economic property relations in contemporary capitalism, and British capitalism in particular. In chapter 3 I examined the rise of the 'impersonal capital' and argued that this form of possession of the means of production has become dominant in Britain over the post-war years, although this dominance is not even across all branches of production and sectors of the economy. The evidence I considered suggested that the major form of impersonal capital was the multidivisional joint-stock company, employing salaried managerial staff to direct its operations. Such enterprises were not, however, 'autonomous' centres of economic decision-making since they were obliged to enter into relations with financial enterprises which gave the latter some leverage over them. I examined two main forms of relationship between financial and other enterprises: shareholding by financial institutions and the provision of loan finance. In the British case these relations were relatively distinct, with the long-term savings institutions such as life assurance companies and pension funds appearing as the major shareholders but the banks appearing as the main providers of external finance. Neither of these forms of relationship, however, amounted to the kind of 'dominance' of financial over industrial capital specified in Hilferding's conception (taken up by Lenin) of 'finance capital'. The contractual savings institutions rarely carry out active intervention in the affairs of the enterprises whose shares they hold, and the British banking policy of relatively short-term lending has not encouraged close relations between the banks and industry (although I suggested that the effects of the current recession might modify somewhat the latter situation). Nonetheless, to say that financial enterprises in Britain do not 'dominate' industrial enterprises is not to say that the financial system is without important effects upon industry. The cautious but speculative mode of calculation of the financial enterprises which deploy the financial surplus of the personal sector has arguably tended to produce a degree of industrial concentration higher than in other national economies, and in excess of the level required to take full advantage of economies of scale, while at the same time 'retarding' the development of new 'growth industries', relative to the situation in other advanced capitalist economies.

   The other side of the coin from the development of the impersonal capital was the expansion of the category of wage and salary-earning employees, i.e. the 'working class' in the economic sense. These latter, whatever their position within the division of labour in capitalist enterprises (or state apparatuses), were unable personally to carry out real accumulation, in the way that the owner-manager of early capitalism might, on account of their separation from the means of production. This point, which is effectively obscured by the theories of Poulantzian inspiration which exclude managers, professional workers and others from the working class, I regard as one of the most important aspects of my own investigations. I pointed out that the high level of personal saving in Britain was an index of the payment of 'surplus income' over and above employees' regular consumption requirements (particularly in the case of the better-paid salaried employees), which nonetheless could not be channelled directly into real investment. Instead the funds poured into the financial institutions and eventually tended either to inflate house prices (the building society financial circuit) or to pass through the hands of the contractual savings institutions into the purchase of shares, property or government debt — a debt increasingly bound up with the financing of recession and unemployment rather than real investment.

This analysis of the dominant form of capitalist property and its effects led me to offer an account of the possible ways in which it might be transformed in a socialist direction, i.e. towards the goal of a democratically-controlled social appropriation. In this account I envisaged a 'pincer movement' requiring both governmental action 'from above' and popular struggle 'from below'. The former was necessary to gain state control over investment funds and to ensure that the 'people's savings' (the surplus income referred to above) were channelled into productive and employment-creating investment, and could also play an 'enabling' role in relation to the latter, by providing appropriate legal forms and incentives to help workers gain control over the operation of the impersonal enterprises which employ them. In effect, by challenging the prerogatives of the financial institutions the state could gain an important measure of leverage over the composition of the social product and in particular over the disposition of the social surplus product. And there is a great opportunity here: an opportunity to make a broad popular appeal by arguing that the only way to ensure a reasonable standard of living in the future for today's savers is to channel the savers' financial surplus into productive investment now, and that the private capitalist deployment of the surplus militates against such investment on a sufficient scale. Nonetheless, there was an urgent need to develop socialist thinking on the criteria for resource allocation which would be employed in such an exercise, and to drop the damaging formula of 'nationalisation as panacea': the 'people' remain to be convinced that the state could manage their surplus income to better social effect than private financial capitalist enterprises. I also pointed out that the two 'pincers' referred to were not at par and could not be expected to develop with perfect synchronisation, and that the relationship between them was more problematic than many on the left would like to admit. There are virtually bound to be conflicts between the interests of workers generated 'from below' at enterprise or industry level, and the 'general interest' constructed at the level of national politics and national planning. Yet these are conflicts which socialism will have to live with since both aspects (central planning and 'grassroots' enterprise democracy) are indispensable if the socialist project is to be advanced. Central planning alone would not of itself alleviate the hierarchy and oppression built into the division of labour in most enterprises, while enterprise democracy alone

would lead to the maintenance of competitive market relations between 'worker-controlled' enterprises.

The analysis of economic property relations, therefore, made it possible to identify certain problems and opportunities for socialism. Such
an analysis however, had to be complemented by an examination of
the political forces which might actually take advantage of those
opportunities, and of the social collectivities which might support or
oppose the socialist project. My intention in the remaining chapters
was to make a start on this examination.

Third movement (chapters 6 and 7): In chapter 6 I explored some of
the various divisions which can form the basis for the formation of
social collectivities. In view of the emphasis placed upon the division
of labour in both the Marxist and the sociological traditions, I began
by examining this division, and came to the conclusion that the term
'division of labour' refers to a complex interlocking set of divisions
(by branch, sector, enterprise and stratum) which cannot yield any
unique determination of social collectivities. Rather, collectivities with
common interests and political orientations can be formed in a variety
of ways within or against the 'division of labour grid', depending upon
further social and political factors.

There was therefore a need to be more specific in giving an account
of collectivities, and I undertook an outline account of the post-war
development of politics in Britain, showing the various ways in which
certain principles of collectivity could be made politically pertinent,
and collectivities drawn into support blocs for definite political forces.
This meant considering the 'middle class'/'working class' distinction
within popular ideology in Britain. This is another point which has
received little comment in Marxist discussions of class: there has been
a tendency to discount 'subjective' class identification on the grounds
that Marxist theory deals not merely with what people think of
themselves, but with their 'objective' class place. Now while it is quite
reasonable to say that the self-estimation of people (or for that matter
parties, governments, etc.) should not be taken at face value, and that
one cannot take notions from popular ideology and treat them as if
they were rigorous concepts, it is nonetheless important to analyse the
phenomenon of 'class' division as it exists within popular ideology in
particular social formations. Just because the lines of 'class' division
of the latter kind do not at all coincide with the lines of economic class
division within Marxist theory is no reason to ignore them, for they
have an undoubted political pertinence.

So I examined the 'working class'/Labour and 'middle class'/Tory links within British politics, and also the weakening of this polarisation and so on — with the changing divisions of social labour, large scale social mobility and the spread of owner-occupation. Nonetheless, two views of this partial breakdown of the 'working class'/'middle class' popular image of 'class' in Britain — character of occupation, family background, level of income, form of housing tenure, style of consumption and so on—with the changing divisions of social labour, large scale social mobility and the spread of owner-occupation. Nonetheless, two views of this partial breakdown of the 'working class'/'middle class' dichotomy have to be resisted: the result is neither an 'embourgeoisement' in which the traditional working class is ultimately dissolved into an affluent 'middle class' society, nor a 'proletarianisation' in which the whole working population is progressively homogenised and turned into an overwhelming support bloc for socialism. The traditional 'manual' industrial working class has been shrinking, and losing leverage within the Labour Party, but it has not disappeared and upward social mobility for some has not dissolved its (uneven) collectivist propensities. On the other hand the expansion of the salariat, and in particular the public sector salariat, and the spread of union organisation within the salarian ranks, has rendered problematic the old 'middle class' ideological complex. But although the salariat is a part of the working class, defined at the level of property relations (i.e. sellers of labour power separated from the means of production), it is far from becoming socially and politically homogeneous with the 'working class' of British popular ideology (which is itself not homogeneous either). Consider for instance the contrast between a salaried public sector employee who supports Labour as the party more committed to expanding opportunities within the public sector, and the manual worker in private industry who supports Labour out of a 'class' reflex but who is suspicious of 'bureaucracy and waste' and wants to see taxation cut.

My discussion of post-war politics also showed up the problematic relationship between the corporate bodies in which many workers are organised, and the political. For Marx in the 'Communist Manifesto' the corporate organisation of the working class was just a step on the way to its formation as a socialist political party. We have seen, however, in 1974 and again in 1978-79, that while the corporate struggles of certain unions achieved 'success' in the sense of breaking government pay policies, in neither case could this success be translated into political gains for socialism — indeed although in 1974 a Labour government was narrowly elected, largely by supporters uncommitted to left policies, in 1979 popular reaction against the activities of the unions provided part of the grounds for a swing to Toryism. On these occasions the trade unions were strong enough to resist government policies but were not in a position to translate that defensive strength into a positive programme capable of playing a hegemonic role. And I argued that this was not just a matter of isolated incidents, but was an index of a more general and serious incapacity. Of course Marx, and more particularly Lenin, long ago made the point that trade union organisation and action were 'inadequate' from a socialist point of view, and that the working class needed a specifically political arm — a Party — to give its aspirations a consistent socialist direction. But the point I wish to make here is in a sense stronger than that: there is a severe dislocation between the defensive industrial strength of certain sections of the working class and its political capacities; bluntly, the trade unions are not popular as a national political force, and their activities have on more than one occasion undermined popular support for the Labour Party. Naturally, it takes two to generate union/party conflict and the Parliamentary Labour Party has, to say the least, often shown itself insensitive to demands emanating from the unions, but the fact remains that, in their conflicts with the Labour Party, the trade unions have not been capable of carrying the mass of the working class, of laying claim to a popular 'legitimacy'. In post-war Britain at any rate, trade union politics are not merely the 'bourgeois politics of the working class' (Lenin), but rather exist in unstable tension with social democratic politics, without pointing in any clear way to a radical yet potentially hegemonic alternative.

In view of the real social and political divisions within the broad working class, economically defined, and the dislocation between the industrial strength and political weakness of the 'organised working class' in industry, I argued that it was quite misleading to suppose that socialism in Britain has an essential majority which has been held back by the 'betrayals' of the Labour leadership or the blandishments of the media. A hegemonic socialist force still remains to be *constructed*, and if it is ever to be constructed this will require building support beyond those social collectivities which are already 'safe' for the left, which in turn can happen only if those on the left take seriously the reasons for many people's resistance to what they see as 'socialism': suspicion of 'free collective bargaining'; suspicion of state 'bureaucracy'; fears of arbitrary allocation of resources in the public sector; fears of inflation and so on.

Following up my general account of post-war politics, in chapter 7 I attempted what can really only be the beginnings of an analysis of Thatcherism. My intention here was (1) to discover why it was that a 'Thatcherist' Tory party could win the election in 1979 and dominate British politics, (2) to examine the chances of 'success' for the Thatcherist programme (for the success of such a programme would clearly put socialism off the agenda for a long time) and (3) to assess the forms of opposition to Thatcherism, and in particular the prospects for advancing the socialist project. My conclusions were (1) that Thatcherism was able to make a broad, and opportunistic, appeal to the concerns of a wide variety of social collectivities on the basis of the 'failure' of previous political forces: failure to alleviate the balance of payments constraint (with all the consequences in terms of slow growth, unemployment and high taxation); failure to develop a workable long term incomes policy (with its consequences for inflation and disruption in industrial relations); failure to develop forms of state provision open to popular participation and accountability (which gave popular resonance to the 'anti-bureaucracy' populist streak in Thatcherism). But (2) I argued that the economic core of Thatcherism did not provide a feasible project — here I drew upon the arguments of earlier chapters concerning classes and the financial circulation. Thatcherism did not have the means to produce economic regeneration in the private sector, and neither could it provide the cheap yet efficient government promised in 1979. Then (3) I argued that it could not, however, be assumed that the economic failures of Thatcherism will lead Britain to socialism. Socialists will have to convince enough people (not only at the Labour conference) that their policies offer a credible and superior alternative. And this cannot just be a matter of propaganda and persuasion, but must involve re-examining, debating and developing left policies and aims. Contrary to the apparent belief of many on the Labour left, the 'movement' does not already have a 'fine programme', an unproblematic set of objectives which merely await the political will to realise them. A genuine debate over policy is needed, without the debilitating presumption that the conclusions of that debate are known in advance, that the programme of the Labour left has a privileged 'expressive' link with the given 'interests of the working class'.

These then were the three movements of the book. The second and third have a double status. First, they are intended to show that the critical conclusions of the first movement can have a fruitful effect, that they do not merely lead to the rejection of certain aspects of Marxism (a negative function) but can open the way to useful kinds of investigation. Second, they may be regarded as a contribution to the debate over the future of socialism in Britain. As I pointed out in the Introduction, the basic object of the theoretical and empirical investigation of class relations from a Marxist standpoint is to help to orient socialist politics, to 'change the world'. I hope that the investigations in the preceding pages may aid in that task, first by identifying some of the problems and opportunities associated with the dominant form of modern capitalist property relations in Britain, and second by identifying some of the problems and opportunities for a popular political force which might accomplish a measure of socialist advance in the particular conditions of British politics. Of course, neither of these investigations is complete; in many contentious areas I have only been able to suggest an approach to the problems rather than to offer solutions. And even those questions which have been discussed more fully are far from resolved. In this context I should like to draw attention to two areas in which the foregoing analyses might usefully be extended:

1. I have laid stress on the importance of the surplus income saved by wage and salary-earning employees, and on the strategic opportunity to subordinate the disposition of this surplus to social control. If this argument is to be advanced it would be useful to have a more detailed analysis of personal savings, of which strata carry out what proportion of saving, of the forms which saving takes and of the particular ways in which these flows of funds might be socially appropriated. This would help to take the left beyond the simple call for 'nationalisation of the banks', and to develop an adequate conception of how the financial institutions might be reorganised and used to achieve socialist objectives.

2. I also emphasised the importance of 'enterprise democracy' as an element of an overall strategy to break down the capitalist separation of the working class from the means of production. Here it would be useful to investigate in more detail (a) the decision-making structures of modern capitalist enterprises, so as to know how practicable alternative forms might be developed, retaining any advantages of efficiency or flexibility while breaking down hierarchy and bureaucracy so far as possible, and (b) the kinds of aid which a government might be able to provide for workers struggling for control over the enterprises which employ them (e.g. changes in company law, taxation and industrial policy). This would help the left to get beyond the paralysing dichotomy between 'workers' con-

trol' (mechanisms unspecified, but an essential part of socialism
some time in the future) and 'Industrial Democracy' (despised as
a mere trick to incorporate the workers in their own exploitation).
These two points concern strategic objectives. There is also, of course,
the whole question of the currently developing alignment of social
collectivities and political forces and the approaches which might be
made to different groups to win their support for the socialist project.
If I have offered only the beginnings of an analysis here, it is important to emphasise a point of *approach* which has, I hope, been well
established: the building of support for socialism among the classes
of society should not be represented as simply one of 'class alliances',
in the sense in which this project has commonly been understood by
Marxists, i.e. where one takes the basic allegiance of the 'proletariat'
to socialism for granted and then poses the question of the terms on
which it can recruit 'allies'. Since common membership of an
economically-defined class does not carry a necessary implication of
political unity, the building of a 'socialist alliance' means constructing forms of political unity between the workers of different industries
and regions, unionised and non-union, men and women, homeowners
and tenants, public sector and private sector, as much as between the
'proletariat' and the supposedly 'non-proletarian' strata of employees
(however conceived). Needless to say the elaboration of the objectives
referred to above, concerning the socialisation of investment and enterprise democracy, will be only one part, if an important one, of the
political enterprise which might achieve such forms of alliance.

Notes

Introduction

1 In particular, I cannot deal specifically with the question of ownership of land, although this is clearly not unimportant. An interesting recent Marxist discussion of landed property in Britain is given by Massey and Catalano (1978).

2 It may not be out of place to mention in addition one of the *political* consequences of the 'orthodoxy' expressed by Stalin. The thesis that if only the productive forces were developed then 'corresponding' socialist relations of production would spring into being was the licence for the introduction of 'one-man management' and dictatorial methods in Soviet industry.

3 The complexity of the problem of the relationship between relations of production and productive forces is also revealed in the debates over the 'transition to socialism' (see, for instance, Bettelheim, 1976). Here the problem lies in determining the transformations in the relations of production which will mesh most closely with the productive forces inherited from capitalism, and push the development of the productive forces in a socialist direction. In this sense the importance of the productive forces as a constraint on the possible forms of relations of production must be recognised: the former cannot be transformed by fiat.

4 The *locus classicus* of this conception is 'Reading Capital' (Althusser and Balibar, 1970). It is also taken up by Poulantzas (1973).

5 The most developed form of this argument that Marx had to reject all forms of 'theoretical humanism' before he could develop his own revolutionary theory is found in Althusser (1973). The first formulation was given in Althusser (1969). It seems clear that in proposing the case against 'theoretical humanism' Althusser was being faithful to the conceptions of the 'mature' Marx, particularly his claim that, for the purposes of materialist analysis, individuals should be conceived as 'personifications of economic categories, the bearers (Trager) of particular class-relations and interests' (Marx, 1976, p. 92).

6 Hindess and Hirst (1975) have argued that there are problems even in the account of feudal exploitation given by Marx and taken up by Poulantzas, particularly the idea that the peasant households were perfectly capable of producing on their own account, and therefore that exploitation by the feudal lords was, in a sense, 'external' to the actual production

345

process and so had to be enforced by direct coercion or religious blackmail. They maintain that feudal lords and land-owning religious orders played a more active and necessary part than Marx and Poulantzas allow in organising the general conditions of production, such as, for instance, irrigation and drainage schemes. Nonetheless, the contrast with the capitalist economy in which workers cannot even begin to produce their own means of subsistence outside of the wage-contract with a capitalist enterprise is reasonable enough.

7   I use the term 'historical analysis' in what I take to be Marx's sense, i.e. to refer to the analysis of the development of social formations. In this sense 'historical analysis' need not refer to the study of the past.

8   Lenin emphasised that the 'dictatorship of the proletariat' could be realised in a wide variety of particular political arrangements (electoral systems, forms of administration, military systems and so on), just as the political dominance of the bourgeoisie is not restricted to any one particular form of state.

9   Marx and Engels (1968, pp. 311-331).

10   The Marxist discussion of the conditions for the 'withering away' of the state constitutes a partial exception to this claim, and is given consideration later.

11   I shall return to this question in Chapter 1, so my remarks here are purposely brief.

12   The position I have sketched here, involving the critique of neoclassical economics and 'consumerism', is of course a relatively modern Marxist development. Marx had relatively little to say about 'abundance' and 'scarcity'.

13   Balibar's answer would doubtless be that communism exists in the form of *tendencies towards communism* even in capitalist society. But this begs the question of where precisely these 'tendencies' are leading — the very question I have attempted to probe above.

14   And although I have not developed the point earlier, there may be a continuing need to offer higher material rewards to encourage the supply of labour for particularly demanding or arduous tasks, if 'moral incentives' are not sufficient and if a coercive direction of labour is to be avoided as far as possible.

Chapter 1

1   It is not necessary that this 'equivalence', defined in exchange, is conceived as an *equation* of the labour-times embodied in the products. The latter view may be criticised (although I shall not pursue the point here) without undermining the present argument. For a fuller discussion of this point see Cottrell (1981).

2   See for example, Brus (1972 and 1975).

3   Unqualified page references in this section are to the one-volume selected

works of Marx and Engels, otherwise referred to below as Marx and Engels (1968).

4 Again, unqualified page references here are to Marx and Engels (1968).

5 This point is argued by Fernbach in his introduction to Marx (1973).

6 Marx (1969, part two, p. 573).

Chapter 2

1 See for instance the quotation from Marx in the conclusion to the previous chapter, concerning the 'intermediates' between bourgeois and proletarian. Other, similarly brief, acknowledgements that there is some sort of problem here may be found elsewhere in Marx's writings, but no systematic discussion of the issue.

2 These dates refer to the original publications. English editions were published in 1973, 1974 and 1975 respectively. References henceforth will be to the English editions.

3 The principal sources for the following account are 'Capital' Volume Two (Marx, 1970), the so-called 'unpublished chapter of Capital' entitled 'Results of the Immediate Process of Production' (Marx, 1976, pp. 948-1084), and 'Theories of Surplus Value' (Marx 1969). I have also drawn on the account of Marx's theory given by Berthoud (1974).

4 Of course commercial capital does employ workers. In Marx's argument this is because of the pressure to reduce the time of circulation so that capital may remain in the sphere of production for as long as possible during its cycle of reproduction, and thus produce a greater mass of surplus value in a given time.

5 This critique was first put forward in New Left Review (Olin Wright, 1976) and it is this article that I refer to here. It has subsequently been developed in Olin Wright (1978).

6 There is also the rather different case in which workers grudgingly accept the interests of the enterprise as tied to their own, in a situation of mass unemployment where the failure of the enterprise might mean a long period of unemployment for the workers involved.

7 It is interesting in this context to note the representations made by the professional managers of ASSET to the Labour Party Conference in 1948. H.G. Knight of ASSET talked of the 'thousands of managers who are socialists' and described professional management as a 'section of the working class' wishing to offer their organisational ability for the 'benefit of the country as a whole and not for that of a few individuals at the top'. Knight and Tom Sargent made a plea for the representation of professional management on economic planning bodies, but ASSET was effectively frozen out by the rules of tripartism. Herbert Morrison explained that the National Economic Planning Board had TUC, employer and government representatives only. If ASSET wished to be represented then

they should ask the TUC to 'remember' them when selecting Board members. Some chance. (This exchange can be found in the Labour conference report of 1948, pp. 165-7.) Of course one can question just how representative Knight and Sargent were, of management in general, yet it is possible that an opportunity was missed here, that the exclusion of managers by the left helped to drive them into the arms of the 'employers'.

8 Admittedly this argument begs the question of a Marxist conceptualisation of the Soviet-type economies. Some writers have claimed that these economies should be analysed as 'state capitalist'. I shall not get involved in this debate here, but the point remains that the kinds of differentiation among employees referred to above are found in economies with widely differing forms of property relations.

Chapter 3

1 Pavitt (1980) has shown that while the overall level of research and development spending in the British economy compares favourably with other economies, this expenditure has been excessively concentrated in government-sponsored 'big technology' such as aerospace, defence and nuclear power. The principal exception is in the chemicals industry, not accidentally the domain of one of Britain's longest-established large integrated enterprises, ICI.

2 The information below is taken from 'Financial Statistics', February 1980 (CSO).

3 'Secondary banks' include the British merchant banks, foreign banks operating in Britain, and Consortium banks.

4 Figures taken from Bank of England Quarterly Bulletin vol. 20, no. 3, September 1980.

5 Poulantzas also offers a reminder that the phenomenon of interlocking personnel at top level cannot be 'read' in any simple manner. He notes that '... the presence of representatives of the big banks on the board of directors of large enterprises is found both in France and in Germany, but it does not have the same significance in each case. In Germany in particular, banking monopoly capital has always had a direct policy of intervention and investment in industry, while banking capital in France has even today an extremely speculative character (stock-exchange operations or massive investments in landed property)' (Poulantzas, 1975, pp. 182-3).

Chapter 4

1 Office of Population Censuses and Surveys (1975).

2 Figures calculated from Economic Trends Annual Supplement, 1980 edition (CSO).

3 In other words, saving is calculated as a residual — which means that

the figures for personal sector saving are subject to quite a wide margin of error. Nonetheless the trend increase in personal saving noted above is well-established even if the absolute figures may be inaccurate.

4 The Economist, January 17 1981.

5 Social Trends 10, 1980, Table 6.19 (CSO).

6 Social Trends 10, 1980, Chart 6.5 (CSO).

7 Social Trends 10, 1980, p. 156 (CSO).

8 The Family Expenditure Survey includes an estimate of the distribution of owner-occupation among 'social classes' in 1978. Among households where the head of household was in a 'professional or technical' occupation, 77.8 per cent were owner-occupiers; among 'administrative and managerial' householders, 79.0 per cent; skilled manual workers, 50.1 per cent; semi-skilled manual workers 39.9 per cent; and unskilled manual workers 28.9 per cent (Department of Employment, 1979, table 24).

9 The building society financial circuit may, however, have redistributive effects within the personal sector. If, as seems likely, the distribution of building society *deposits* is more unequal than the distribution of mortgage *loans*, then the result will be a net transfer of funds, through the mechanism of the collection and payment of interest, in favour of the larger depositors.

10 Marx also conceptualised the rate of interest in this way. For a critical discussion of this point see Cutler *et al.* (1978, Chapter 6).

11 It can also frustrate 'monetarist' attempts to return towards 'sound finance'. If governments cut discretionary expenditure, e.g. on health and education, and the resulting fall in demand increases unemployment, then tax revenues will tend to fall and statutory 'income maintenance' spending will rise. This point, which has been quantified by the Treasury (1981), is dealt with more fully in Chapter 7.

12 This point is developed by Hirschmeier and Yui (1975).

13 Kalecki (1968, Ch.3).

14 Figures taken from the National Incomes and Expenditure 'Blue Book', 1979 edition, table 4.6.

Chapter 5

1 Questions of sex and race, for instance, are not mentioned. This is not at all because I consider these unimportant for socialists. Rather, I believe they are 'relative autonomous' issues and the foregoing investigation of property relations does not provide a basis for saying anything new or important concerning them.

2 See for instance, Poulantzas (1975, pp. 62-65) and Cutler *et al.* (1977, pp. 149-152).

3 See for instance the collections edited by Kindleberger (1970) and Radice (1975).

4 This is despite the fact that the left has often been very critical of existing

nationalised industries while generally being unable to specify the definite forms of organisation and criteria of operation appropriate to 'socialist' nationalised industries. Lack of clarity on these issues has apparently not detracted from the socialist appeal of nationalisation as such.

5   It is relevant here to note the argument put forward by Lavigne (1974) concerning the obstacles placed in the way of growth of trade between the member countries of Comecon by the practice of *national* economic planning. She points out that 'within the framework of Comecon the tendency of each country towards autarky is counter-balanced by policies of plan coordination, cooperation and specialisation, policies which are proving very difficult to implement' (p. 342).

6   The 'Campaign for a Socialist Europe' has been a rather lonely voice arguing for serious consideration of the EEC along these lines.

7   This has been argued by Bourdieu (1971).

8   The present argument works on the assumption that the principal target of such a policy would be the contractual savings institutions which collect the greater part of personal savings. It could be argued, however, that such measures should also be extended to cover the banks, which, as we have seen above, provide the greater part of external finance for companies at present. An interesting discussion of possible measures to control the banking system which goes beyond the simple call for nationalisation is contained in Thompson (1981).

9   Nove (1973) has developed an interesting discussion of cost-benefit analysis along these lines, providing a counter to both the technocracy with which this form of analysis is often invested and the dismissiveness of many on the left.

10 Kalecki's suggestion was that returns should be discounted at a rate equal to the projected real growth rate of the economy.

11 The difference between this case and competition from 'cheap labour' on an international scale should be evident. In the latter case although socialists may express solidarity with the wage struggles of foreign workers there is not a great deal that can be done from outside to advance that struggle, while in the matter of *internal* 'cheap labour' there is much that can be done.

12 This raises a rather important issue: the need for socialists to have something to say about the 'nuts and bolts' of running enterprises in an efficient but non-oppressive manner. The lack of interest in such questions on the left has been noted by the CSE Money Group (e.g. Fishman, 1980, p. 175).

13 One must be careful here. It would be quite utopian to imagine that any socialist government could put its programme into effect without reference to 'ad hoc political pressure' — any more than a 'monetarist' government can. All governments run into particular forms of opposition, and compromises are necessary where the opposing social forces cannot be tackled head-on. The point being made here is that the better rationalised

the criteria for investment planning, the better the chance of retaining the overall coherence of the policy in face of ad hoc pressures. If the criteria for planning remain at the level of pious generalisation, which provides little guidance for dealing with concrete cases, then ad hoc decisions will become the rule rather than the exception.

14 A qualification here: one component of the argument above involves creating conditions under which certain 'socially desirable' investment projects become sufficiently profitable to induce capitalist enterprises to undertake them. As a complement to this it would be necessary, to retain any socialist credentials for such a scheme, to ensure that the profit generated does not simply line the pockets of the privileged (this points to an incomes policy) but is in turn re-appropriated for further useful investment.

15 The CSE London Working Group (1980) cannot really be accused of dodging these issues. Nonetheless they are weaker on the 'conditions of implementation' than on the proposals for policy.

16 Marx (1974, p. 89).

17 To be somewhat speculative, one could say that the possibility of increasing automation of large-scale industry permits a future in which a substantial fraction of the 'working day' is available for the pursuit of creative projects on the part of individual workers or small-scale collectives, including 'craft' production. On this point see for instance Gershuny (1978).

18 In particular I have in mind Engels' formulations in his 'Anti-Duhring' (Engels, 1962). But the idea is also found in Marx's writings.

19 See for instance the argument in the 'Economist' of 19/4/80 concerning the implications of flexible programmable automation in the car industry.

Chapter 6

1 See Chapter 2.

2 Babbage (1832, pp. 34-35), quoted in Braverman (1974, pp. 79-80).

3 In this calculation 'skilled' manual work was defined as manual work requiring an apprenticeship or other lengthy period of training. The 'administrative and technical' category explicitly excluded clerical work. Gershuny is aware of the problems in defining 'skilled work' but concludes that, on the best available evidence, his general point holds.

4 It is this feature of hierarchy, with its implications for the 'market position' of the employee, which Weber (1970) takes as definitive of *classes*.

5 This 'mobility' is powerfully portrayed by Dos Passos (1938).

6 It is clear that some people use 'working class' simply to mean 'employees', or 'those who work for a living'.

7 The study of 'affluent' car-workers by Goldthorpe et al. (1969) showed, however, that high income is not a *sufficient* condition for 'middle class' self-identification.

8 In Poulantzian terms (See Chapter 2) the British 'working class' would

include elements of the proletariat, new petty bourgeoisie, traditional petty bourgeoisie and possibly even bourgeoisie (i.e. 'working class' managers). The British 'middle class' would also include elements of Poulantzas' proletariat, new and traditional petty bourgeoisie, and bourgeoisie. In other words the British 'classes' cut right across his demarcations.

9 Data from Economic Trends Annual Supplement, 1980.

10 The British share of this investment in Europe as a whole rose from around 25% in 1943 to around half in 1950 (Overbeek, 1980).

11 The Gallup poll in March 1954 found more people critical of Bevan as 'too anti-American' than approved of him as 'likely to stand up to the Americans' (Gallup, 1976).

12 The context was a criticism of those pressing for unilateral disarmament in 1957 (quoted in Foot, 1973).

13 It is interesting to note that both the 'Economist' and the 'New Left Review' supported Wilson in 1964.

14 The conditions of existence of the 'strike problem' in the car industry are graphically described by Beynon (1975).

15 Gershuny (1978) has described this as a trend towards the 'self-service economy': the increasing displacement of personal services by the use of consumer durable goods, which results in part from the relative cheapening of the latter as labour productivity in industry moves steadily ahead of the 'service' sector (particularly in the 'face to face' personal services, productivity is intrinsically limited).

16 For a detailed account of this constraint see Thirlwall (1978 and 1980). This point will also be taken up again in the following chapter.

17 Unfortunately it also has a different, and restricted, time scale. This is because the only commensurable statistics in this regard are from the sample Census of 1966 and the 10% sample of the 1971 Census.

18 The term 'salariat' has been used by Kumar (1976) and Jenkins and Sherman (1979) to refer to the salaried employees of both capitalist enterprises and the state.

19 Nonetheless, Poulantzas (1975, Part III Ch.9) is quite right to point out that this transformation remains very uneven.

20 The 'closure' thesis states that the higher reaches of the occupational hierarchy will be virtually inaccessible to the 'socially mobile', while the closely-related 'buffer zone' thesis states that large-scale social mobility will be restricted to the interface between 'higher manual' and 'lower non-manual' categories of employees. Arguments to this effect may be found in Bottomore (1965), Miliband (1969), Giddens (1973), Parkin (1972) and Westergaard and Resler (1975). Using a schema of occupational classes roughly similar to those of Townsend and Butler and Stokes, Goldthorpe found that in 1972, about quarter of the (male) members of his 'highest' class were sons of fathers from the same class, while over a quarter were sons of manual wage-workers.

21 Marx (1970, p. 103) and Feuer (1969, pp. 494-5).

22   It may be noted that the substantial proportion of recruits from 'lower' occupational backgrounds also renders problematic the conception of 'proletarianisation' through the 'degradation of work'. If it is true that many salaried non-manual jobs have been becoming more routine, and more closely monitored than previously, it does not follow that the individuals working in those jobs experience this as 'degradation', since many of them come from families which have known considerably worse degradation in manual wage-labour.

23   'Heath's rule' must not be interpreted too literally. Basically it refers to the period during which the Tory party was in government and Edward Heath was Prime Minister: one is not subscribing to the 'Great Men' school of history. Nonetheless the emphasis on Heath is not without justification, given the notoriously autocratic manner in which he led his party through the twists and turns of 1970-74.

24   Data from McLean (1978), citing Crewe, Sarlvik and Alt.

25   The preponderance of council housing in Scotland is relevant here, both as cause and effect.

26   The expectations of the 'social contract' on the part of both Wilson and the left are discussed more fully below.

27   This can perhaps be partly explained by a kind of 'demonstration effect'. A minor party vote in the British electoral system is often considered a wasted vote since it stands little chance of affecting the pattern of parliamentary representation. But the sevenfold increase in the number of SNP MPs in February showed that an SNP vote did count for something, making it easier to mobilise latent electoral support.

28   In this conjuncture, when trade deficits were being enforced quite generally as an effect of the OPEC surplus, circumstances were very inauspicious for making these acceptable to Britain's trading partners.

29   Warren (1977) argued this strongly.

30   According to Keegan and Pennant-Rea (1979) the proximate cause of this was a deliberate attempt by the Bank of England to push the exchange rate downward in order to ease the pressure on the corporate sector. Since sterling's strength had been founded on the unstable base of renewed foreign holdings of short-term sterling balances this move was enough to undermine speculative confidence, and the pound could not be stabilised anywhere near the $1.95 level which the Bank had been aiming for.

31   For an argument to this effect, see Bosanquet (1980).

32   Roy Jenkins' pronouncement, that once public expenditure had reached 60 per cent of the Gross Domestic Product democracy was under threat, is, however, noteworthy in this context. The 60 per cent figure is highly debatable, resting on the widest possible measure of public spending and the narrowest possible measure of GDP, but its political use indicates the mood among some of the right wing of the Labour Party. The notion that such and such a level of public expenditure is incompatible with democracy rests implicitly on the conception, propagated by the IEA,

of economic democracy operating through market forces.

33 Bacon and Eltis' categories, which have shifted over time, are not equivalent to the Marxist concepts of productive and unproductive labour. Nonetheless, an analysis based upon the latter would yield similar economic conclusions: any expansion of unproductive labour must be supported out of surplus value, hence reducing the fraction of surplus value appearing as profit. A disproportionate growth of unproductive labour could therefore cause a profitability crisis and lead to reduced investment. Cockshott (1978) has argued along these lines. It is, of course, open to Marxists to argue that there is a 'deeper cause' at work here, if the expansion of unproductive labour is seen as a contradictory effect of the attempt to mobilise 'counter-tendencies' to the 'tendency of the rate of profit to fall' due to rising organic composition of capital (Gillman, 1957). See, however, my critical comments on the view that state expenditure squeezes profits in Chapter 4 above.

34 The failure to convince the parliamentary party is demonstrated by the election of Callaghan to replace Wilson as leader. Callaghan had the political credentials of a man who could get along with the unions, having been the principal opponent of 'In Place of Strife' in Cabinet, but no MP voting for him can have imagined that he would lead the party leftwards.

Chapter 7

1 This is the term which Gamble (1979) had used to label the resurgent belief in the beneficent effects of the free market.

2 This view has been advanced by Mandel (1975) among others.

3 Kellner (1980) was therefore quite right to attack the philistinism of Callaghan's famous 1976 speech, which implicitly represented Keynesianism as coterminous with a shallow post-war Treasury orthodoxy.

4 This was a widespread interpretation of the famous 'Phillips Curve' correlation between wage rises and employment levels.

5 Between 1973 and 1975 the Public Sector Borrowing Requirement rose from 6.5 per cent of GDP (at factor cost) to 11.2 per cent, and in money terms from £4.2 billion to £10.5 billion. I am not arguing that the recessionary impulse deriving from the reduction of net export demand and increased personal saving is a complete explanation for this drastic deterioration of the state's finances, but it was certainly a major factor. For a further discussion of the determinants of Public Sector borrowing over this period see Tomlinson (1980b).

6 Both the 'money supply' and the 'general price level' are awkward concepts to define operationally, and such correlations as the Quantity Theorists were able to draw up remain open to a variety of interpretations. This empirical work did not, therefore, lead to a mass conversion of academic economists.

7 In Britain the monetarist researches of Laidler and Parkin at Manchester University began to attract some attention.

8 The journalistic support for monetarism is charted by McDonell (1977) and Bonnett (1981).

9 Arguably, however, such a course would not be politically feasible, given the clamour against 'excessive taxation' which was developing strongly by the mid 1970s. This clamour had two apparent bases: the high marginal rates of taxation on high income groups, and the progressive lowering of income tax thresholds in real terms as a result of inflation, drawing more of the working class into the income tax net. The combined effect of these two factors was to create the basis for a broad anti-tax bloc spanning managers, professionals and manual workers. Whether the tax system could have been restructured so as to split this bloc and overcome the apparent 'limit to taxation' is an open question. Certainly there could be no easy and painless recourse to corporation tax, given the low level of profitability, or to indirect expenditure taxes, for indexing these taxes fully would have contributed to inflation.

10 These 'demands' were not always made by industrialists themselves. It is partly a matter of what governments took to be the requirements for a strong national economy.

11 For a detailed argument to this effect see the Cambridge Economic Policy Group (1981).

12 This kind of Marxist-functionalism can be found in Muller and Neusus (1978).

13 The survey data below are taken from the Economist (1980) and Crewe (1981).

14 A vitriolic attack on Joseph was launched by the Tory Bow Group in May 1981. But Thatcher had enough realism to stand by her 'renegade' mentor.

15 It is ironic to note the behaviour of the new 'Tax and Prices Index' (TPI). This index was constructed in 1979 in the attempt to demonstrate that the overall effect of the 1979 budget, while it pushed up prices, did not warrant commensurate wage claims since increases in expenditure taxes were compensated by income tax reductions. The government wished to deflect wage negotiators' attention from the Retail Price Index (RPI), the normal guideline for assessing movements in the cost of living. Embarrassingly for the government, since 1979 the TPI has recorded larger increase than the RPI.

16 Over 1980, the only major area of high profitability among industrial and commercial companies' activities in the UK was the North Sea sector. The real profitability of companies' non-North Sea activities as measured by the real rate of return on trading assets (gross trading profits net of stock appreciation and depreciation as a percentage of capital employed, valued at replacement cost) fell to a record low of 3 per cent. This compares with an average figure of 5.5 per cent over 1974-79 and

10 per cent from 1963 to 1973. Financial companies and institutions, by contrast, did very well out of a regime of high interest rates (Treasury, 1981a).

17 A summary of poll findings, by social class, for early 1980 is presented by Kellner and Worcester (1980).

18 There is also of course the infamous 'Militant Tendency' and a scatter of smaller avowedly Marxist groups, but the role of such groups has been greatly overestimated by the media.

19 For instance Benn secured the support of the train drivers (ASLEF), the bakers union, the furniture workers, and the print workers of SOGAT, as well as the 'white collar' groups of ASTMS and TASS.

20 This point is argued fully by Hindess (1980).

21 Blake's assumptions are quite generous to this strategy. In particular he assumes that retaliation, in the form of import controls imposed by other countries on British goods, would be minor.

Bibliography

AARONOVITCH, S. (1961), *The Ruling Class*, London, Lawrence and Wishart.
AARONOVITCH, S. and SAWYER, M. (1975), *Big Business*, London, Penguin.
ABRAMS, M. and ROSE, R. (1960), *Must Labour Lose?*, Harmondsworth, Penguin.
ALLAUN, F. (1979), article in *Labour Activist* No. 5, July.
ALTHUSSER, L. (1969), *For Marx*, Harmondsworth, Penguin.
ALTHUSSER, L. (1973), 'The Conditions of Marx's scientific discovery', *Theoretical Practice*, No. 7/8.
ALTHUSSER, L. (1977), 'The historical significance of the 22nd congress', in *Balibar* (1977).
ALTHUSSER, L. and BALIBAR, E. (1979), *Reading Capital*, London, New Left Books.
BABBAGE, C. (1832), *On The Economy of Machinery and Manufacturers*, London.
BACHELARD, G. (1972), *La Formation de l'Esprit Scientifique*, Paris, J. Vrin.
BACON, R. and ELTIS, W. (1976), *Britain's Economic Problem: Too Few Producers*, London, Macmillan.
BAIN, A. (1980), 'Is public sector borrowing too high?' *Quarterly Economic Commentary*, vol. 5, no. 3, January.
BALIBAR, E. (1970), 'The basic concepts of historical materialism', in *Althusser and Balibar* (1970).
BALIBAR, E. (1977), *On the Dictatorship of the Proletariat*, London, New Left Books.
Bank of England (1980), *Quarterly Bulletin*, vol. 20, no. 3, September.
BARRAT BROWN, M. (1968), 'The controllers of British industry', in *Coates* (1968).
BEAN, C. (1978), *The Determination of Consumer Expenditure in the UK*, HM Treasury Working Paper No. 4, July.
BEED, C. (1966), 'The separation of ownership from control', *Journal of Economic Studies*, vol. 1, no. 2, Summer.
BEGG, H. and LYTHE, C. (1977), 'Regional policy 1960-1971 and the performance of the Scottish economy', *Regional Studies*, vol. II.
BERLE, A. and MEANS, G. (1932), *The Modern Corporation and Private Property*, New York, Macmillan.
BERTHOUD, A. (1974), *Travail Productif et Productivite du Travail chez Marx*, Paris, Maspero.
BETTELHEIM, C. (1974), *Les Luttes de Classes en URSS, Première Periode 1917-1923*, Paris, Maspero/Seuil.

357

BETTELHEIM, C. (1976), *Economic Calculation and Forms of Property,* London, Routledge and Kegan Paul.

BEYNON, H. (1975), *Working for Ford,* Wakefield, EP Publishing.

BLACKABY, F. (ed.) (1979), *De-industrialisation,* London, Heinemann.

BLAKE, D. (1980), 'No use blaming the rest of the world', *The Times,* 18 September.

BLAKE, D. (1981), 'The case for a touch on the accelerator', *The Times,* 3 June.

BOLOGNA, S. (1976), 'Class composition and the theory of the party at the origin of the workers' councils movement', in *CSE* (1976).

BOLTON, J. (chairman) (1971), *Report of the Committee of Inquiry on Small Firms,* London, HMSO.

BONHAM, J. (1954), *The Middle Class Vote,* London, Faber and Faber.

BONNETT, K. (1981), 'Classes, class fractions and monetarism', paper presented to the British Sociological Association conference.

BOSANQUET, N. (1980), 'Labour and public expenditure: an overall view', in *Bosanquet and Townsend* (1980).

BOSANQUET, N. and TOWNSEND, P. (eds.) (1980), *Labour and Equality,* London, Heinemann.

BOTTOMORE, T. (1965), *Classes in Modern Society,* London, Allen and Unwin.

BOURDIEU, P. (1971), 'Reproduction culturelle et reproduction sociale', in *Informations sur les Sciences Sociales,* UNESCO.

BRAVERMAN, H. (1974), *Labour and Monopoly Capital,* New York, Monthly Review Press.

BRUS, W. (1972), *The Market in a Socialist Economy,* London, Routledge and Kegan Paul.

BUDD, A. (1978), *The Politics of Economic Planning,* Glasgow, Fontana/Collins.

BULLOCK, SIR A. (Chairman) (1977), *Report of the Committee of Inquiry on Industrial Democracy,* London, HMSO.

BUTLER, D. and STOKES, D. (1974), *Political Change in Britain,* second edition, London, Macmillan.

CALDER, A. (1969), *The People's War: Britain 1939-1945,* London, Cape.

CAMPBELL, A. (1980), *Mondragon 1980,* Industrial Common Ownership Movement Pamphlet No. 9.

Cambridge Economic Policy Group (1980), *Cambridge Economic Policy Review,* vol. 6, no. 1, April.

Cambridge Economic Policy Group (1981), *Cambridge Economic Policy Review,* vol. 7, no. 1, April.

CARCHEDI, G. (1977), *On the Economic Identification of Social Classes,* London, Routledge and Kegan Paul.

CHANDLER, A. (1980), 'The United States, seedbed of managerial capitalism', in *Chandler and Daems* (1980).

CHANDLER, A. (1980a), 'The growth of the transnational industrial firm in the United States and the United Kingdom: a comparative analysis', *Economic History Review* vol. XXXIII, no. 3, August.

CHANDLER, A. and DAEMS, H. (eds.) (1980), *Managerial Hierarchies*, Cambridge, Mass., Harvard University Press.

CHANNON, D. (1973), *The Strategy and Structure of British Enterprise*, London, Macmillan.

CLARKE, T. (1977), 'Industrial Democracy: the institutionalised suppression of industrial conflict', in *Clarke and Clements* (1977).

CLARKE, T. and CLEMENTS, L. (eds.) (1977), *Trade Unions under Capitalism*, Glasgow, Fontana/Collins.

COATES, K. (1968), *Can the Workers Run Industry?*, London, Sphere.

COATES, K. and TOPHAM, A. (1975), *Industrial Democracy and Nationalisation*, Nottingham, Spokesman Books.

COCKSHOTT, W.P. (1978), 'The recession and socialist strategy', mimeo produced for the CSE conference.

COLE, G.D.H. (1917), *Self Government in Industry*, London, Bell and Sons.

COLLIOT-THÉLÈNE, C. (1975), 'Contribution a une analyse des classes sociales', *Critiques de l'Economie Politique*, no. 21, July.

COOK, C. and RAMSDEN, J. (eds.) (1978), *Trends in British Politics since 1945*, London, Macmillan.

CORRIGAN, P. (1977), 'The welfare state as an arena for class struggle', *Marxism Today*, March.

COTTRELL, A. (1981), 'Value theory and the critique of essentialism', *Economy and Society*, vol. 10, no. 2, May.

CRESSEY, P. and MACINNES, J. (1980), 'Voting for Ford: industrial democracy and the control of labour', *Capital and Class*, no. 11, summer.

CREWE, I. (1981), 'Why the going is now so favourable for a centre party alliance' *The Times*, 23 March.

CREWE, I., SARLVIK, B. and ALT, J. (1974), 'The election of February 1974', mimeo, Essex University.

CREWE, I., SARLVIK, B. and ALT, J. (1977), 'Partisan de-alignment in Britain 1964-1974', *British Journal of Political Science*, vol. 7, pt. 2.

CROMPTON, R. (1979), 'Trade unionism and the insurance clerk', *Sociology*, V, 13.

CSE (1976), *The Labour Process and Class Strategies*, CSE Pamphlet No. 1.

CSE London Working Group (1980), *The Alternative Economic Strategy*, London, CSE Books.

CSO (1978), 'Personal Sector Balance Sheets', *Economic Trends*, January.

CUTLER, A. (1978), 'The romance of "labour" ' , *Economy and Society*, vol. 7, no. 1, February.

CUTLER, A., HINDESS, B., HIRST, P. and HUSSAIN, A. (1977 and 1978), *Marx's 'Capital' and Capitalism Today*, Vols. 1 and 2, London, Routledge and Kegan Paul.

DENVER. D. and BOCHEL, J. (1980), 'Left come to aid of Party', *The Scotsman*, 7 November.

Department of Employment (1979), *Family Expenditure Survey for 1978*, London, HMSO.

Department of Industry (1976), 'The importance of the "top 100" manufacturing companies', *Economic Trends*, August.

DEVINE, P., LEE, N., JONES, R. and TYSON, W. (1979), *An Introduction to Industrial Economics*, 3rd edition, London, George Allen and Unwin.

DOS PASSOS, J. (1938), *USA*, London, Constable.

DOW, J. (1965), *The Management of the British Economy 1945-1960*, Cambridge University Press.

The Economist (1980), *Political Britain*, London.

The Economist Intelligence Unit (1982), *Coping with Unemployment*, London.

ENGELS, F. (1962), *Anti-Duhring*, Moscow, Progress Publishers.

ERRIT, M. and ALEXANDER, I. (1977), 'Ownership of company shares: a new survey', *Economy Trends*, September.

FALUSH, P. (1978), 'The changing pattern of savings', *National Westminister Bank Quarterly Review*, August.

FEUER, L. (ed.) (1969), *Karl Marx and Frederick Engels: Basic Writings on Politics and Philosophy*, London, Fontana.

FISHMAN, D. (1980), 'A radical view of the European Monetary System', *Politics and Power* No. 2.

FISHMAN, N. (1980), 'The Labour governments 1945-51', *Politics and Power* No. 2.

FLORENCE, P.S. (1961), *Ownership, Control and Success of Large Companies*, London, Sweet and Maxwell.

FOOT, M. (1973), *Aneurin Bevan 1945-1960*, London, Davis-Poynter.

FRASER, W.H. (1978), 'Trades councils in the labour movement in nineteenth century Scotland', in *MacDougall* (1978).

FREEMAN, C. (1974), *The Economics of Industrial Innovation*, Harmondsworth, Penguin.

FRIEDMAN, M. (1952), *A Theory of the Consumption Function*, Princeton University Press.

GALLUP, G.H. (ed.) (1976), *The Gallup International Public Opinion Polls, Vol. 1, Great Britain 1937-1964*, New York, Random House.

GAMBLE, A. (1979), 'The Free Economy and the Strong State: the rise of the Social Market Economy', *Socialist Register*, London, Merlin.

General Register Office (1960), *Classification of Occupations*, London, HMSO.

GEORGE, K. and WARD, T. (1978), *The Structure of Industry in the EEC*, Cambridge University Press.

GERSHUNY, J. (1978), *After Industrial Society?*, London, Macmillan.

GIDDENS, A. (1973), *The Class Structures of the Advanced Societies*, London, Hutchinson.

GILLMAN, J. (1957), *The Falling Rate of Profit: Marx's Law and its Significance to Twentieth Century Capitalism*, London, Dennis Dobson.

GILMOUR, L. (1977), *Inside Right*, London, Hutchinson.

GLYN, A. and SUTCLIFFE, B. (1972), *British Capitalism, Workers and the Profits Squeeze*, Harmondsworth, Penguin.

GOLDTHORPE, J., LOCKWOOD, D., BECHOFER, F. and PLATT, J. (1969), *The*

Affluent Worker in the Class Structure, Cambridge University Press.

GOLDTHORPE, J. (with LLEWELLYN, C. and PAYNE, C.) (1980), *Social Mobility and Class Structure in Modern Britain,* Oxford, Clarendon Press.

HALL, S. (1980), 'Thatcherism – a new stage?', *Marxism Today,* February.

HALL, S. (1981), 'The "little caesars" of Social Democracy', *Marxism Today,* April.

HALL, J. and JONES, D.C. (1950), 'Social grading of occupations', *British Journal of Sociology,* March.

HALSEY, A., HEATH, A. and RIDGE, J. (1980), *Origins and Destinations,* Oxford, Clarendon Press.

HANNAH, L. (1976), *The Rise of the Corporate Economy,* London, Methuen.

HANNAH, L. (1980), 'Visible and invisible hands in Great Britain', in *Chandler and Daems* (1980).

HINDESS, B. (1971), *The Decline of Working Class Politics,* London, Paladin.

HINDESS, B. (1977), 'Classes and politics in Marxist theory', paper presented to the British Sociological Association conference.

HINDESS, B. (1980), 'A "left" Labour government', *Politics and Power* No. 2.

HINDESS, B. (1981), 'Parliamentary democracy and socialist politics', in *Prior* (1981).

HINDESS, B. and HIRST, P. (1977), *Mode of Production and Social Formation,* Lon- Routledge and Kegan Paul.

HINDESS, B and HIRST, P. (1977), *Mode of Production and Social Formation,* London, Macmillan.

HIRSCHMEIER, J. and YUI, T. (1975), *The Development of Japanese Business 1600-1973,* London, George Allen and Unwin.

HIRST, P. (1981), 'On struggle in the enterprise', in *Prior* (1981).

HOBSBAWM, E.J. (1969), *Industry and Empire,* Harmondsworth, Penguin.

HOLESOVSKY, V. (1977), *Economic Systems, Analysis and Comparison,* Tokyo, McGraw-Hill Kogakusha.

HOLLAND, S. (ed.) (1972), *The State as Entrepreneur,* London, Weidenfeld and Nicolson.

HOLLAND, S. (1980), Interview in *Politics and Power* No. 2.

HOLLOWAY, J. and PICIOTTO, S. (eds.) (1978), *State and Capital: A Marxist Debate,* London, Edward Arnold.

HOWELL, D. (1981), *Freedom and Capital,* Oxford, Basil Blackwell.

HUGHES, J. (1960), *Nationalised Industries in the Mixed Economy,* Fabian Tract No. 328.

HULL, F.M., FRIEDMAN, N.S. and ROGERS, T.F. (1982), 'The effects of technology on alienation from work', *Work and Occupations,* vol. 9, no. 2.

HUNT, A. (ed.) (1977), *Class and Class Structure,* London, Lawrence and Wishart.

HUSSAIN, A. (1976), 'Hilferding's Finance Capital', *Bulletin of the CSE,* vol. VI, no. 13.

HYSLOP, A. (1979), 'The disappearance of Scottish nationalism?', paper presented at CSE Scotland conference.

Inland Revenue (1975), *Estimated Wealth of Individuals in Great Britain 1973*, London, HMSO.

JENKINS, C. and SHERMAN, B. (1979), *White Collar Unionism: The Rebellious Salariat*, London, Routledge and Kegan Paul.

JESSOP, B. (1980), 'The transformation of the State in post war Britain', in *Scase* (1980).

KALECKI, M. (1968), *Theory of Economic Dynamics*, New York, Monthly Review Press.

KALECKI, M. (1971), *Selected Essays on the Dynamics of the Capitalist Economy*, Cambridge University Press.

KALECKI, M. (1972), *Selected Essays on the Economic Growth of the Socialist and the Mixed Economy*, Cambridge University Press.

KAY, J. and KING, M. (1978), *The British Tax System*, Oxford University Press.

KEEGAN, W., and PENNANT-REA, R. (1979), *Who Runs the Economy?*, London, Maurice Temple Smith.

KELLNER, P. (1980), 'The economic consequences of Jim', *New Statesman*, 17 October.

KELLNER, P. and WORCESTER, R. (1980), 'Thatcher loses the working-class vote', *New Statesman*, 2 May.

KENNEDY, M.C. (1978), 'Inflation', in *Prest and Coppock* (1978).

KEYNES, J.M. (1930), *A Treatise on Money*, London, Macmillan.

KEYNES, J.M. (1936), *The General Theory of Employment Interest and Money*, London, Macmillan.

KILROY, B. (1979), 'Housing Finance – why so privileged?', *Lloyds Bank Review*, no. 133, July.

KINDLEBERGER, C. (ed.) (1979), *The International Corporation*, Cambridge Mass., MIT Press.

KUMAR, K. (1976), 'The Salariat', *New Society*, 21 October.

Labour Coordinating Committee (1980), *There is an Alternative*, LCC Pamphlet.

LANDES, D.S. (1969), *The Unbound Prometheus*, Cambridge University Press.

LARNER, R.J. (1966), 'Ownership and control in the 200 largest non-financial corporations, 1929 to 1963', *American Economic Review*, vol. 56, September.

LAVIGNE, M. (1974), *The Socialist Economies of the Soviet Union and Europe*, London, Martin Robertson.

LAZONICK, W. (1979), 'Industrial relations and technical change: the case of the Self-Acting Mule', *Cambridge Journal of Economics*, vol. 3, no. 3.

LENIN, V.I. (1964), 'Imperialism, the Highest Stage of Capitalism', *Collected Works*, vol. 22, London, Lawrence and Wishart.

LENIN, V.I. (1969), *The State and Revolution*, Moscow, Progress Publishers.

LEONARD, P. (1979), 'Restructuring the welfare state', *Marxism Today*, December.

LERUEZ, J. (1975), *Economic Planning and Politics in Britain*, London, Martin Robertson.

London-Edinburgh Weekend Return Group (1979), *In and Against the State*,

London.
LUKACS, G. (1971), *History and Class Consciousness,* London, Merlin.
MACDOUGALL, I. (ed.) (1978), *Essays in Scottish Labour History,* Edinburgh, John Donald.
MCLEAN, I. (1978), 'Labour since 1945', in *Cook and Ramsden* (1978).
MANDEL, E. (1975), *Late Capitalism,* London, New Left Books.
MARX, K. (1963), *The Poverty of Philosophy,* New York, International Publishers.
MARX, K. (1969), *Theories of Surplus Value,* London, Lawrence and Wishart.
MARX, K. (1970), *Capital,* Vol. 2, London, Lawrence and Wishart.
MARX, K. (1972), *Capital,* Vol. 3, London, Lawrence and Wishart.
MARX, K. (1973), *Surveys from Exile* (political writing edited and introduced by D. Fernbach), Harmondsworth, Penguin.
MARX, K. (1973a), *Grundrisse,* Harmondsworth, Penguin.
MARX, K. (1974), *The First International and After* (political writings edited and introduced by D. Fernbach), Harmondsworth, Penguin.
MARX, K. (1976), *Capital,* Vol. 1, Harmondsworth, Penguin.
MARX, K. and ENGELS, F. (1968), *Selected Works in One Volume,* London, Lawrence and Wishart.
MASSEY, D. and CATALANO, A. (1978), *Capital and Land,* London, Edward Arnold.
MEACHER, M. (1980), interview in *Politics and Power* No. 2.
MIDDLEMASS, K. (1979), *Politics in Industrial Society,* London, Andre Deutsch.
MILIBAND, R. (1969), *The State in Capitalist Society,* London, Weidenfeld and Nicolson.
MINFORD, P. and PEEL, D. (1981), 'Is the government's economic stategy on course?', *Lloyds Bank Review,* April.
MINNS, R. (1980), *Pension Funds and British Capitalism: the ownership and control of shareholdings,* London, Heinemann.
MORE, C. (1980), *Skill and the English Working Class, 1870-1914,* London, Croom Helm.
MOYLE, J. (1971), *The Pattern of Ordinary Share Ownership, 1957-1970,* Cambridge University Press.
MULLER, W. and NEUSUSS, C. (1978), 'The "welfare-state illusion" and the contradiction between wage labour and capital', in *Holloway and Piciotto* (1978).
NOVE, A. (1973), *Efficiency Criteria for the Nationalised Industries,* London, George Allen and Unwin.
OECD (1975), *Economic Outlook,* December.
Office of Population Censuses and Surveys (1975), *Census 1971 Great Britain, Economic Activity Part II (10% sample),* London, HMSO.
OLIN WRIGHT, E. (1976), 'Class boundaries in advanced capitalist societies', *New Left Review* no. 98, July-August.
OLIN WRIGHT, E. (1978), *Class, Crisis and the State,* London, New Left Books.
OPPENHEIMER, M. (1975), 'The proletarianisation of the professional',

Sociological Review Monography, no. 20.

OVERBEEK, H. (1980), 'Finance capital and the crisis in Britain', *Capital and Class*, no. 11, Summer.

PARKIN, F. (1972), *Class, Inequality and Political Order*, St. Albans, Paladin.

PAVITT, K. (ed.) (1980), *Technical Innovation and British Economic Performance*, London, Macmillan.

POLLARD, S. (1969), *The Development of the British Economy 1914-1967*, second edition, London, Edward Arnold.

POULANTZAS, N. (1973), *Political Power and Social Classes*, London, New Left Books/Sheed and Ward.

POULANTZAS, N. (1974), *Fascism and Dictatorship*, London, New Left Books.

POULANTZAS, N. (1975), *Classes in Contemporary Capitalism*, London, New Left Books.

PRAIS, S.J. (1976), *The Evolution of Giant Firms in Britain*, Cambridge University Press.

PREST, A.R. and COPPOCK, D.J. (1978), *The UK Economy: A Manual of Applied Economics*, seventh edition, London, Weidenfeld and Nicolson.

PRIOR, M. (1980), 'Problems in Labour politics', *Politics and Power* No. 2.

PRIOR, M. (ed.) (1981), *The Popular and the Political*, London, Routledge and Kegan Paul.

RADICE, H. (ed.) (1975), *International Firms and Modern Imperialism*, Harmondsworth, Penguin.

RAMSDEN, J. (1978), 'The changing base of British Conservatism', in *Cook and Ramsden* (1978).

RAYNOR, J. (1969), *The Middle Class*, London, Longman.

REVELL, J. (1973), *The British Financial System*, London, Macmillan.

REVELL, J. and MOYLE, J. (1966), 'The ownership of quoted ordinary shares', *University of Cambridge Department of Applied Economics: A Programme for Growth*, no. 7, London, Chapman and Hall.

ROWBOTHAM, S., SEGAL, L. and WAINWRIGHT, H. (1979), *Beyond the Fragments*, London, Merlin.

ROWTHORN, B. (1980), *Capitalism, Conflict and Inflation*, London, Lawrence and Wishart.

SCARGILL, A. (1981), Interview in *Marxism Today*, April.

SCASE, R. (ed.) (1980), *The State in Western Europe*, London, Croom Helm.

SCOTT, J. (1979), *Corporations, Classes and Capitalism*, London, Hutchinson.

SHONFIELD, A. (1958), *British Economic Policy since the War*, Harmondsworth, Penguin.

SINGH, A.J. (1975), 'Takeovers, economic natural selection and the theory of the firm', *Economic Journal*, 85, September.

SKED, A. and COOK, C. (1979), *Post war Britain, a Political History*, Harmondsworth, Penguin.

STANWORTH, R. and GIDDENS, A. (1975), 'The modern corporate economy', *Sociological Review*, vol. 23, no. 1.

STEPHENSON, H. (1980), *Mrs Thatcher's First Year*, London, Jill Norman.

SWEEZY, P. and BETTELHEIM, C. (1971), *On the Transition to Socialism,* New York, Monthly Review Press.

THIRLWALL, A.P. (1978), 'The UK's economic problem: a balance of payments constraint?', *National Westminster Bank Quarterly Review,* February.

THIRLWALL, A.P. (1980), *Balance of Payments Theory and the UK Experience,* London, Macmillan.

THOMPSON, G. (1981), 'Monetarism and economic ideology', *Economy and Society,* vol. 10, no. 1, February.

TOMLINSON, J. (1980), 'Socialist politics and the small business', *Politics and Power* No. 1.

TOMLINSON, J. (1980a), 'British politics and cooperatives', *Capital and Class,* no. 12.

TOMLINSON, J. (1980b), The 'economics of politics' and public expenditure: a critique, paper presented to the CSE Conference.

TOWNSEND, P. (1979), *Poverty in the United Kingdom,* Harmondsworth, Penguin.

Treasury (1981), 'The impact of recession on the PSBR', *Economic Progress Report,* no. 130, February.

Treasury (1981a), *Economic Progress Report,* no. 136, August.

WARREN, B. (1977), 'Working-class power: Britain's crisis', *Problems of Communism,* Winter.

WEBER, M. (1970), 'Class, status, party', in *From Max Weber* (ed. H.H. Gerth and C. Wright Mills), London, Routledge and Kegan Paul.

WEIGHELL, S. (1980), 'The railmen's way to reform the Labour Party', *The Times,* 12 May.

WESTERGAARD, J. and RESLER, H. (1975), *Class in a Capitalist Society,* London, Heinemann.

WESTLAKE, M. (1981), 'How Robin Hood in reverse is pushing the poorest worker into the poverty trap', *The Times,* 30 April.

WILLIAMSON, O.E. (1981), 'The modern corporation: origins, evolution, attributes', *Journal of Economic Literature,* vol. 19, no. 4.

WILSON, SIR H. (chairman) (1978), *Committee to Review the Functioning of Financial Institutions, Evidence on the Financing of Industry and Trade,* vol. 3, London, HMSO.

WILSON, SIR H. (1979), *Final Term: The Labour Government 1974-1976,* London, Weidenfeld and Nicolson.

WITTGENSTEIN, L. (1968), *Philosophical Investigations,* Oxford, Basil Blackwell.

Index